Poetics of the Literary Self-Portrait

Michel Beaujour

Translated from the French
by Yara Milos

NEW YORK UNIVERSITY PRESS
NEW YORK AND LONDON

Published in French by Editions du Seuil © Editions du Seuil, 1980
Copyright © 1991 by New York University
Manufactured in the United States of America

Library of Congress Cataloging-in-Publication Data
Beaujour, Michel.
    [Miroirs d'encre. English]
    Poetics of the literary self-portrait / Michel Beaujour.
        p.   cm. — (New York University studies in French culture and
    civilization)
    Translation of: Miroirs d'encre.
    Includes bibliographical references and index.
    ISBN 0-8147-1154-5 (cloth)
    1. Self in literature.   2. Literature, Modern—20th century—
History and criticism.   3. Autobiography.   4. Autobiographical
fiction.   I. Title.   II. Series.
PN56.S46M513   1991
809'.93592—dc20   90-28149
                                                          CIP

New York University Press books are printed on acid-free paper,
and their binding materials are chosen for strength and durability.

To the memory of Jacques Ehrmann and Dominique de Roux.
They are always with me.

Contents

Introduction: Self-Portrait
and Autobiography

I'm not satisfied with the word *self-portrait*. It evokes Rembrandt, Van Gogh, and Francis Bacon rather than Montaigne or Michel Leiris. In a literary context, *self-portrait* remains obstinately metaphorical; and, while self-portraitists often write that they "paint themselves," this metaphor cannot be spun out indefinitely into a description of their texts. It merely allows the definition—and distortion—of some intentions, certain definite limits. Montaigne's portrayal of himself with the self-portraits of Dürer and Rembrandt; Michel Leiris's features with Francis Bacon's likenesses of himself: the comparison might in some respects be enlightening, even fruitful. But one sees that it would prejudice the specificity of both the arts and the works.

Any other term would be even more inadequate, for it would either have to be an ugly neologism (autography? self-writing? autoscription? autospecularization?) or require a broadening of the sense of terms the writers in question have ventured in order to designate their "genre": essay, meditation, promenade, antimemoirs, biography, autoabstraction. The meaning of some of these words is overly specific. In other cases, it is too vague or too closely associated with the work of one particular writer: my terminological hesitation here merely repeats that of the authors themselves. A distinctive feature of the texts in question is precisely that they do not know how to designate themselves. Thus, *self-portrait* it is, and I accept willingly the negative definition proffered by Philippe Lejeune, apropos of Montaigne's *Essays:*

> One sees that the text of the *Essays* has no connection with, as we define it, autobiography; there is no continuous narrative nor any systematic history of the personality. Self-portrait rather than autobiography. (*L'Autobiographie en France,* 57)

And of Cardano's *De Vita Propria Liber* (*The Book of My Life*):

> whence (Cardano's) desire to do his self-portrait—but how? He failed because he lacked a usable type of narrative. His book is not a continuous narrative but a sort of bungled patchwork, the incoherent collation of some fifty heteroclite short essays. (56)[1]

The *absence* of a continuous narrative in the self-portrait distinguishes it from autobiography. So does its subordination of narration to a *logical* deployment, a collation or patching together, of elements under heads that, for the time being, we shall call "thematic." Thus, our self-portrait realizes from the outset what Lejeune calls "the secret project of every autobiography," belatedly achieved by Leiris, for whom "thematic order ranks first and chronology second, thus diminishing chronology's traditional explanatory function" (*Lire Leiris,* 16).

But Leiris's works, which are not chrono-logical, do not belong to the lineage of Rousseau's *Confessions,* and they differ radically from the innumerable autobiographies that "will inevitably begin by relating the event of birth and proceed thereafter in chronological order" (*Le Pacte autobiographique,* 197). Instead of wanting, like Lejeune, to realign the whole history of autobiography according to Leiris's telos, it seems more economical to postulate the existence of another genre—or at least of another type of discourse—which might include Montaigne's *Essays* and Cardano's *Book of My Life* as well as certain nonchronological personal texts, such as Rousseau's *Rêveries* or Nietzsche's *Ecce Homo.* These texts, then, are arranged *logically* or *dialectically* (in a sense that will have to be carefully analyzed) and *thematically* (at least in an initial approach). But while the question of what autobiography is has long been a topic for debate, as evidenced by the abundant theoretical and critical work dealing with this genre, there has been no continuous theoretical reflection concerning the self-portrait, except in the texts themselves. Self-portraitists make self-portraits without knowing what they are doing. This "genre" proffers no "horizon of expectation." Each self-portrait is written as though it were the only text of its kind.

Thus, the self-portrait remains an outsider that historians and theoreticians still tend to designate restrictively or negatively: a text that is not quite an autobiography. Without waiving the restrictive mode ("It is almost a literary genre by itself"), Michel Riffaterre proposed a paradoxical and startling definition of self-portrayal in an essay on Malraux's *Anti-Memoirs*, provided that this text is part of a self-portrait that goes under the general title of *Le Miroir des limbes:*

Memoirs can follow the chronology, or the logic, of events; then they are narrative. The *Anti-Memoirs* rest on analogy (the superimposition method is identical with metaphor); therefore they are poetry. (*Essais de stylistique structurale*, 296)[2]

Such an opposition between the *narrative* and the *analogical*, the *metaphorical*, or the *poetic* text sheds some light on a salient trait of the self-portrait. This genre attempts to create coherence through a system of cross-references, anaphoras, superimpositions, or correspondences among homologous and substitutable elements, in such a way as to give the appearance of discontinuity, of anachronistic juxtaposition, or montage, as opposed to the syntagmatics of a narration, no matter how scrambled, since the scrambling of a narrative always tempts the reader to "reconstruct" its chronology. The totalization of the self-portrait is not *given* beforehand; new homologous elements can be added to the paradigm, whereas the temporal closure of autobiography already is implicit in the initial choice of a curriculum vitae.

The operational formula for the self-portrait therefore is: "I won't tell you what I've done, but I shall tell you *who I am*." One recognizes here a variant of the end of chapter 3, Book X, of Saint Augustine's *Confessions*, where the author contrasts the confession of what he has perpetrated to the disclosure of "what I am at the very time that I am writing these *Confessions*" (204). Now, Book X is a meditation on memory and forgetting, and on the memory of forgetting, but in it, Augustine says nothing about "himself." Probably because the self-portraitist's inaugural experience is one of emptiness, of absence unto himself: there lies the cause of the sterilizing panic which Artaud, for example, records in his letters to Jacques Rivière.[3] Artaud thinks only in terms of ownership: *my* mind, *my* thought. As might be expected, those steal away when he tries to hypostasize them on paper, like an actor observing his own motionless body in a mirror.[4] But, even if the "self-portraitist" has only started to write—if he has written anything at all—he sees what at first was *nothing* becoming a plethora. From beneath his pen gush forth stupidities, vagaries, fantasies, without any warranty that any of this has pertinence or value and without any foreseeable limits, except those of the religious law (hence, Augustine's abstention) or those imposed by the moral code of his time and social class, accepted proprieties, current psychological and cultural conventions. These rich and constraining codes, however, readily generate the discourse they channel: the aphasia and subsequent embarrassment of riches of the one who originally wanted to "paint himself" or "show his mind" easily find their match in cultural commonplaces, unless, like Artaud, the would-be self-portraitist impugns a priori any and all discursive conventions and stubbornly insists on grappling directly with "his mind." Or unless, renouncing all concern for structure and reflective consciousness, he merely lets his writing stream forth.

The plethora of fragmented discourse, of "stupidities"[5] that pour out, is such that alphabetic writing, in its relative linearity, imperfectly represents its criss-crossings, its pentimentos, its overlays. The text that results does not correspond to the idea one has of the self-portrait if one relies on the pictorial metaphor or the rules of the parlor game with which La Rochefoucauld amused himself in the seventeenth century. The self-portraitist does not "describe himself" in the way the painter "represents" the face and body he perceives in his mirror: he is forced into a detour that seemingly thwarts the intention of "painting oneself," should we assume that the self-portrait is ever born of such a naive "project": X *by himself*. That's improbable.[6] The self-portrait is in the first place a *found object* to which the writer imparts the purpose of self-portrayal in the course of its elaboration. A kind of misprision or compromise, a shuttling

back and forth between generality and particularity: the self-portraitist never has a clear notion of where he is going, of what he is
doing. But his cultural tradition is well aware of it for him: his
culture provides him with the ready-made categories that enable
him to classify the fragments of his discourse, his memories and
fantasies. Categories of sins and merits, of virtues and vices, of lik-
ings and loathings; the five senses; humors and temperaments; the
faculties; the local psychological vulgate with its "passions" and
"sincerity," its bits and pieces of characterology or psychoanalysis,
its astrology, its beliefs in the influence of the race, the milieu and
the moment . . . all that, and more, gets mixed up, crossed out,
ironized, euphemized, recycled. For the self-portraitist reworks these
unprocessed givens; he arranges them under headings only to con-
nect them haphazardly according to the imperatives of a personal
taxonomy whose configuration and reasons often elude him, for he
is as blind as Oedipus when he keeps on equating his writing with
his freedom, his self, his unique utterance. At best, the self-portraitist sees in those headings a referential virtuality bound up with
the "mimesis of the self." That's more or less what Lejeune concludes from his perspicacious analyses of Michel Leiris's *L'Age
d'homme* (*Manhood*):

Thus, the associative method will allow the production of a vast corpus
that will combine not just the narratives of dreams and fantasies but all
childhood memories and all recent experience, likewise invested with the
same *sign* function and brought together in the same autobiographical
space. It will also allow utilization of analogical links in order to weave
together the inventoried material. Association is utilized to open the mental network and to shut it again. (*Le Pacte autobiographique*, 263)

And of *La Règle du jeu*:

The woven writing of *La Règle du jeu*, on the contrary, will assemble a
mechanism capable of dealing with no matter what and, conceivably, even
with nothing. This language machine is capable of producing its own
material, of milling or weaving facts, memories, fantasies, and, also, lines
of argument or abstract analyses, always according to the same dream logic
. . . The further *La Règle du jeu* advances, the more it resembles the
dizzying discourse of a Beckett or a Laporte, where the uttering ends up
becoming the only subject of the utterance. (272)

But the opposition between those two modes of textual production may depend on the illusion of someone who as yet has no

clear grasp of the ramifications of either the "language machine" or the "writing machine." As for the "dream logic," a somewhat vague notion alluding to Freudian theory, it only opens up the boundlessness of language under the protection of an expected closure (256), because that "logic" functions, to some extent, like a *dialectic of invention.* If one steps back somewhat from Leiris's undertaking, one may see that its method is a variant of the procedures of traditional rhetoric, diverted towards a goal other than the persuasion of others.

It may seem surprising that texts in principle so personal and individual as self-portraits where the writer, making do with whatever means he believes to be at his disposal, attempts to say what he is, right then, while writing, can be described as being variants of procedures so collective and so precisely coded as rhetorical invention and rhetorical memory were at one time.

In order to justify this paradox, the first step is to admit that constraint can be experienced as freedom and, even, as mental confusion. The self-portrait's text-producing machine is not perceived more distinctly by the writer than are the rules of grammar by most speakers or the processes of persuasive rhetoric by those who naively make constant use of them. Which does not mean that those "rules" and "processes" cannot be formulated, or constructed, as an *art.* Attempts at theorization that are found in self-portraits—and that, in diverse degrees, constitute one of their distinctive traits—seem to be insufficient, fragmentary, and short-sighted, inasmuch as they all fail to recognize the rhetorical matrix that, if they were more clearly aware of it, would paralyze and trivialize the writing of a self-portrait. Certain recent texts (Laporte, Thibaudeau),[7] where practice is reduced, so to speak, to its theorization, or to the attempted description of a textual production machine, arise from a context ideologically favorable to the notion of "production" and hyperconscious of the "unconscious" constraints that burden all writing: they still maintain that denial of rhetoric. Only at the price of a naive or cultivated unawareness can the writer indulge in the pleasure of describing the pangs of his pararhetorical patchwork while nurturing the illusion that his innocence and torment allow him to dodge narcissism. Thus, Jacques Borel, author of a vast corpus of self-portrayal, still is able to ask himself: "Does Narcissus write?"[8] The answer ought to be that he always manages to believe he is the first one to do so: the self-portrait always, and with good reason, goes beyond primary narcissism.

While "genres" have been evolving in the course of the modern period (through the unveiling and foregrounding of devices—with that evolution going so far as self-destruction), the self-portrait stagnates: one would be hard put to say what *formally, fundamentally* differentiates Montaigne's *Essays* from Leiris's *La Règle du jeu* or *Roland Barthes by Roland Barthes*, or even what separates all those from the ancient text of which modern self-portraits appear to be variants, if we take into account the Renaissance's ideological break concerning the subject and the sequels thereof during the modern and contemporary periods. Indeed, a careful examination of Saint Augustine's *Confessions*, especially Book X, does enable one to grasp certain essential traits of the self-portrait in a perspective that may seem paradoxical, since Book X constitutes a template for self-portrayal, a self-portrait without a Self, without epithets or predicates, with nothing but the lineaments of the machine that produces any self-portrait once God keeps aloof from man, and His death incites the individual to set himself up in His place, in the tomb of writing, between Invention and Memory.

Because of its very marginality, the self-portrait is a dump for our culture's refuse. Nothing is more archaic or transhistorical than those texts claiming to disclose "what I am now, while I'm writing this book." Nothing is on worse terms with time than that discourse in the present. The fact is that the writer, having withdrawn from the world only a touch, having barely attempted to say who he is, rather than avow what, in his past dealings with others, he committed, quickly finds himself caught between two limits: that of his own death and that of the *impersonal* as constituted by the most general and anonymous of categories, the latter being mediated by a language that belongs to everyone. Thus stuck between absence and Man, the self-portrait must tack about so as to produce what, essentially, turns out to be the interlocking of an anthropology and a thanatography. The presence of a Self, unto oneself, which one could naively think of as constituting the illusory subject of the self-portrait, is but its lure, or its reverse side.

No writing is less innocent, more harrowed and harrowing than that of the self-portrait through which the material presence of writing itself is foregrounded. The self-portrait's tragedy lies in that it has nothing to hide, nor to confess (counting in advance on mercy and forgiveness), except that it is produced by rhetoric and that it is a purely idle, bookish discourse. A book among books.

Our culture, which nonetheless produces self-portraits, recognizes our unforgivable faults as, precisely, retirement, idleness, retreat: we know the last word used to denote a privy in several languages. Montaigne does not hesitate to designate the *Essays* as "excrements of an old mind, now hard, now loose, and always undigested," at the very moment when he realizes at once that the writing of his "fantasies" allows of no last word and that the idlers of his century partake of crime as much as do its warlike men of action: "Scribbling seems to be a sort of symptom of an unruly age" ("Of Vanity,", III, 9, 721). Those who find in the *Essays* a degree of smugness do not see the *guilty writer* who, in his meditations on the social context of his excremental and unruly writing, foreshadows Blanchot, Bataille, and a few other literary culprits. Thus, from Montaigne to Barthes, the self-portrait finds itself *guilty:* not because it confesses or conceals a crime, but because it is mere scribbling. On the other hand, the confession that is slipped into the self-portrait, as in Leiris for example, has the effect of adding a touch of piquancy (the reader, in turn, being transformed into a bull or bloodhound) or virtue to a writing that remains without any useful public purpose. For the purposelessness and pointlessness of the self-portrait brutally disclose a fundamental trait of our culture that is masked by the ideological scramblings of post-Romantic modernity. Ancient rhetoric and the various classical poetics never stopped averring that writing must be of some use, for somebody's use; writing is a modality of action, of public service, and it must be efficacious and transitive—it must persuade, blame, dissuade, or praise. In this perspective the avowal does partake of a purpose, since it becomes *exemplary*. Therefore confession is the self-portraitist's alibi. What other types of discourse (especially novelistic fiction) can comfortably ignore to the extent that they are remote from the mode of rhetorical production, cannot be eluded by the self-portrait which is a direct transgression, and transformation, of the procedures of rhetoric.[9] Uneasiness with respect to commitment is the other way in which the self-portrait pays paradoxical homage to civic virtue and to rhetoric as it betrays them.

Thus, the self-portrait's original sin is that it perverts exchange, communication and persuasion itself, while denouncing this perversion. Its discourse addresses the putative reader only insofar as he is placed in the position of an overhearing third person. The self-portrait speaks to itself, for want of being able to address God. Whence the unease of a Barthes, who, wishing to preserve an "I-You" relation, despite the resistance of the discourse adopted, and to reserve in his text a fictional place for the reader, is sometimes forced to refer to himself as "he." This disclaimer gives the show away, as did Augustine's soliloquy destined for God, or the brutal dismissal of the reader in the foreword to Montaigne's *Essays*. There remains one extreme solution, which Nietzsche inscribed in his *Ecce Homo*: as the author puts himself in the place of Christ, or his divinity exculpates him from the charge of addressing only himself.[10]

Self-portraits that assume this solipsism as their original fault paradoxically manage—better than those which attempt to compensate for it by their play on verbal registers—to captivate the reader. For the reader, if he has not closed the book again soon after the first page, cannot remain in a third-party position; he has no choice but to place himself in the position of the *addresser*. It is a commonly noted phenomenon: each reader *knows* himself in the *Essays* or in *La Règle du jeu*, if he enters at all into the spirit of the game, and adopts a relation analogous to that of the self-portraitist to books, writing, language, and rhetoric. This means that each reader of those books can become, in turn, the one who writes them, as Lejeune demonstrated in his reading/writing of Leiris's self-portrait. This emphasizes the difficulty of "critical" discourse, of a hermeneutic process, always in jeopardy of becoming a self-portrayal of the commentator.[11]

In a paradoxical reversal, the self-portrait reveals itself to be a modeling system, never ceasing, for all that, to be guilty excrement. Certainly it does not model the human condition in general, but only that of the intellectual or, more precisely, that of the writer in the modern Western world. There is no self-portrait that is not of a writer *qua* writer, of one whose guilt results from his writing at the hub of a culture where things are not running smoothly for rhetoric, where utilitarian or intransitive writing grants in turns power and impotence, where the subject looks for fellow-creatures while asserting his absolute difference. That is why the only true readers of the self-portrait are writers yearning for self-portrayal. This is another trait handed down to the self-portrait from ancient rhetoric, whose treatises were addressed only to those who themselves desired to become eloquent—a trait it shares with the meditative texts and religious exercises that only address potential contemplatives: it is evident that the class of virtual addressees has appreciably dwindled. Nevertheless, a whole sector of contemporary literature aspires to that eccentric status and is addressed to (potential) writers alone: the self-portrait, in turn, has become the text matrix through which rhetoric, betrayed but not abolished, makes a comeback and demands our attention. This is what Tzvetan Todorov seemed to suggest when he wrote:

Today, literature is oriented toward narratives of a spatial and temporal type, to the detriment of causality. A book like Philippe Sollers's *Drame* combines these two orders in a complex interrelation, while accentuating the time of writing and alternating two types of discourse, respectively led by an "I" and by a "he." Other works are organized around an arrangement of verbal registers or grammatical categories, of semantic networks, etc. (*Poétique*, 77)[12]

If that is the case, then the literary margins are beginning to get crowded around the self-portrait: the traits detected in *Drame* and in other spatial kinds of narratives, according to Todorov's oxymoron, were present from the start in the self-portrait, although more discretely so, than in the texts of the "avant-garde" of the 1960s. In fact, the self-portrait is a type of discourse that *prematures* its text while laying bare—or deliberately dramatizing—the dialectic processes and the semantic and linguistic operations that engender it. The self-portrait lays its cards on the table: its secret lies in that obviousness which draws it readily toward the fantastic. Whence the uneasiness expressed by Roger Laporte, grappling with the imperious writing machine he thinks he is inventing, and from which Augustine alone was able to free himself by surrendering himself up to God:

Writing protects, but how might I be reassured! Since writing is the only shelter, then I'll be secure only if I continue to write: then I ought never to stop writing! I'm incapable of getting through my work in one go, and yet if I stop writing, if I again slackly attempt to take shelter in the world of everyday commonplaceness, where by good fortune, sad fortune, *it* cannot penetrate, I know from experience that I'm not sure to succeed. (*La Veille*, 45)

Laporte, through his cliches, perspicuously points out the stakes of the dilemma: either retirement, a shelter in whose womb lurks the threat of an *it*, the "writing machine," along with its commonplaces, its public encyclopedia, its topics, its psychoanalytic or other "structure," its encroaching fantasies; or the everyday banality that only a conqueror's project might turn into a universe of action. It is not enough for the self-portraitist to write the noble word *work* for his condemned man's writing to stop being a *solitary vice*.

Thus, one can wonder whether the fantastic register in which is formulated here a possession or dispossession by *it*, that Other (Montaigne also inscribes *it* as early as "Of idleness," chapter 8 of the *Essays*, evoking "chimeras and fantastic monsters,"[13] "ineptitude" and "strangeness"), inheres in the anxiety that is immediately aroused in the self-portraitist by his own transgression of rhetorical finalities. Is the incontinent scribbling (for which one metaphor by Laporte—"I am the dam and the dam's guardian at the same time" [*La Veille*, 43]—proposes a precarious variant) a cause or an effect of that dislocation, that dismembering, that anxiety whose stigmata we encounter as often in Montaigne as in certain texts of Michaux, of Blanchot, or in *The Unnamable* by Beckett? Surely, unease and guilt overflow the self-portrait, but is it not precisely because the outside of our literature, whose inside is defined by theoreticians as narrative and fiction, an outside to which the self-portrait was relegated because of its ties to rhetoric, might stop being outside, yet without actually becoming the inside, still occupied in principle by the mimesis of action? In other terms, has not the "outside" of literature, for which the self-portrait is a *model*, already dispossessed the "inside" without placing itself, for all that, in a position of mastery, inasmuch as that displacement has had the effect of generalizing exteriority, impotence, and anxiety? This is what Roger Laporte suggests in a commentary on the works of Maurice Blanchot, where he ascribes to the latter the invention of a type of discourse that he himself practices in his odd "biogra-phy:"

> he has "freed art from the bondage of naturalism and psychology" by instituting a new mode that is neither novel, narrative, nor essay, a "genre" that bears no name but that leads to seeking, to writing in a new dimen-sion: that of the neutral, a dimension which, although Heraclitus formerly explored it, is still little known and will someday introduce an entirely new way of answering the question: "What is thinking?" ("Le Oui, le non, le neutre," 590)

And, while one can doubt the absolute novelty of this mode of writing, the reference to Blanchot allows us to glimpse why the self-portrait and meditation tend to encroach upon French literary space to assert themselves as the book-to-come, under the aegis of the Mallarméan Book.

Philippe Sollers also mused about Mallarmé's Book (and about his own books, no doubt) in terms that recall those of Laporte:

> *Igitur*, which means therefore in Latin, has in effect replaced another *therefore*, that which is present in Descartes' *cogito* . . . With Mallarmé, the "I think, therefore I am" becomes so to speak: "I write, therefore I think of the question: who am I?" or even: "*who* is that *therefore* of the phrase 'I think, therefore I am?' " ("Littérature et totalité," 70) [14]

And, further on in that same essay, Sollers indicates that the Book implies "a suppression of the author (the book is often compared by Mallarmé to the *tomb*) who gives up speaking for the sake of writing and also contributes to the transformation of time into space . . .; and also, a creation of the reader that confirms the victory thus achieved over chance and silence" (78).

We have picked out along our way a cliché of modernity, a cliché whose variants proliferate in blissful ignorance of their genealogy. But the opposition between "I think" and "I speak" (or, rather, "I write"—for the "work" in question is writing, as Sollers aptly ob-serves) results from two variants of one and the same structure descended from the rhetorical matrix: religious *meditation*, those of Descartes being a laicized version, and the *self-portrait-essay* as created by Montaigne. Nowadays, meditation is held in disrepute on account of its leading to interiority, to the certitude of the "I," or of the Barrèsian Ego, whereas the self-portrait introduces a dislocation of the subject through "the naked experience of language" (Foucault). Does this opposition bear up under analysis?

All self-portraits teach us through their topical dispersion, their restless metadiscourse, the splitting among the dislocated agencies of enunciation, that there is, in Foucault's words, "an incompatibility, perhaps without recourse, between the appearance of language in its being and the self's consciousness in its identity" ("La Pensée du dehors," 525). But it ought to be emphasized that Montaigne's *Essays* revealed that incompatibility (as did in their own way Saint Augustine's *Confessions* and the whole of Bacon's works) well before the formulation of the Cartesian *cogito*, that is, previous to the birth of the *subject* whose disappearance is sought or diagnosed by French modernism. Foucault seems to realize this when he writes that the reciprocal exclusion of "I speak" and "I think" engenders "a form of thought whose still uncertain possibility Western culture has adumbrated in its margins" (525). Aren't exclusion and marginality in question within the rhetorical *cogito*, which, from the *Confessions* to the *Essays* and to their modern avatars, presents itself as a *cogito* of dislocated instances, the interminable uttering of which constitutes self-portrayal? Ignoring the "margin" where the being of language and the "void in which it plots its space" were being thought out would entail a radical oversimplification of the history of Western culture. A very wide margin indeed, since rhetoric is incribed in it: one may recall the old dispute opposing it to philosophy, which always accused it of playing fast and loose with the truth.[15]

But it would be equally simple-minded to maintain a dichotomy between the inside (philosophy descended from the "I think") and the outside (the transformation of rhetoric, the variants of the "I speak" and "I write"). The self-portrait stages and dialecticizes the tension between "I speak" and "I write," for the Cartesian *cogito* does not answer the question: "Who am I?" "What do I know?" etc. It fills up an absence, and it censures (at least for a century, during which the ego will be hateful and the self-portrait disappears as a genre if not as a parlor game) that endless writing activity which was the oblique and veiled acknowledgement of the death and transfiguration of rhetoric.[16] Guilty scribbling stretched over the void left by the demise of the oral culture whose survival was to some degree assured by rhetoric, a culture where the question of the "subject," of language and communication, was posed in completely different terms from those that emerged during the Renaissance, with typography and its solitary *cogito*. The role of the self-portrait will always be to make up for those deficiencies—of community, of dialogue, of communication—and to contest that excess of ego and interiority, which becomes the norm of the modern period. All ego manifests itself by a particular implementation of discourses, of modes of meaning and such archaic arts as rhetoric, mythology, allegory: a heteroclite and ageless encyclopedia. For the self-portrayer, the "Cartesian break" invented by modern philosophy is always somehow null and void.

Let us take an example. In March 1975, Roland Barthes published in *La Quinzaine Littéraire* a review of *Roland Barthes by Roland Barthes:* from then on, that review became a part of the corpus of Barthes's self-portrait, the end of which could come only with the writer's death, since it is characteristic of the self-portrait to integrate its own commentary in an ever foiled and deferred attempt "to give meaning" to that endless undertaking. Barthes's commentary shows much lucidity, and also blindness, as regards the "meaning" of his own undertaking.

"What," he writes, "is the sense of a book? Not what it discusses, but what it grapples with." As a corporeal individual subject, Barthes is obviously wrestling with two Figures (two Allegories, in the medieval sense): *Value* (that on which, in taste and distaste, everything is founded) and *Stupidity;* as historical subject, he does so with two period notions: the *Imaginary* and the *Ideological.*

By presenting the "sense" of his book to be not so much "what it discusses" as what "it grapples with," Barthes designated the dual movement that consists first in laying as his foundation a series of *places* (*loci, topoi,* in this case, Value, Stupidity, the Imaginary, the Ideological, etc.) that can be treated by the dialectical method known to all Renaissance schoolboys, the set of which constitutes an encyclopedia or, at least, a *liber locorum.* In the second movement, one dislocates, exorcises, strikes out, and scrambles those *places.* In this connection, Barthes can write with insight: "—certain fragments of 'R.B.' are short;. . . in a way, that entire little book plays deviously and naively with stupidity—not with the stupidity of others (that would be too easy), but that of the subject *who is about to write:* what comes to mind is stupid *to begin with* (all tangled up with the Other, who prompts my initial discourse)." Thus, the generic term *Stupidity* designates an encyclopedia of the trivial, cant, the commonplace, a farcical encyclopedia of the products of memory, education, the vulgate: yet, that passage through Stupidity is a necessary stage in the process whose second, negative, palinodic movement consists in unwriting or in crossing out the descriptive encyclopedia. The third stage questions the dialectic relations of the first and second movement of the writing. This third movement can be inscribed right on the same page within the same sentence, through retouching strokes, additions, commentaries, as happens frequently with Montaigne, or through resumptions, obliterations, palinode in the extension of the text, as in the works of Leiris, Laporte, or Jacques Borel.

As regards allegory, which takes Barthes by surprise, it is, as a *figure,* indissociable from the encyclopedia of "Virtues" and "Vices" (Desire, Pleasure, the Lacanian "symbolic", the Body) which Barthes borrows from the *doxa* (or Stupidity) of (Parisian) intellectuals and whose *places* or headings he takes up successively. Allegory is inherent in the *speculum* (in the medieval sense) and inseparable from the metaphor of the mirror, an indispensable allegorical accessory. Roland Barthes's self-portrait is therefore typical in that it combines an understanding of the moral and ontological stakes with a very marked ignorance of the rhetorical machine that produces it. Barthes's torment concerning Stupidity echoes Montaigne's concerning pedantry and memory, school rhetoric. That revulsion reveals to Barthes the structural and semantic necessity of images, of myths, of allegorical figures; but it also hides it from him. There is no self-portrait that is not at grips with the *thing* or *res:* the commonplace. The self-portrait ineluctably sets itself up as topography or description, a scanning and destruction of *places,* which implies a rhetorical, mythological, and encyclopedic horizon.

This amounts to saying that the self-portrait is always absolutely modern. The places, the stupidities, which the subject can utilize as his foils, as his dialectical raw material show him at grips with

the Other who haunts him and from whom he tries to escape—
that encyclopedia is constantly modified even if only superficially,
according to fashionable ideologies and local traditions. Barthes's
doxa is no longer Leiris's *Koinè* nor Barrès's "barbarousness." But
the self-portrait proves to be transhistorical, if not anachronistic:
the utilization of the commonplaces, whose deep structure is as-
toundingly stable, operates like a time machine that lures the subject towards the prehistory of modern literature and plunges him
again into the depths of a very ancient culture, where more recent
notions about the person, the individual, and, a fortiori, the subjectivity or the Self, are abolished.

No one writes a self-portrait to repeat, or imitate, Montaigne.
On the contrary, the writing of the self-portrait is always an attempt, bound to fail so long as it is necessary, to efface the *Essays*.[17] For the past four hundred years, the *Essays* have displayed
the opacity and impossibility, the solitude and retirement, and also
the vacuity of the modern individual. He may think that his misfortune comes from his being too much (of an egotist, a skeptic, a
hedonist) or lacking (in his commitment, his frenzy, his intelligence, his altruism . . .). This is his predicative and medieval illusion. But the curse on him was simply the result of his *birth:* ex-
pelled from the maternal womb, branded with the sign of *ego*,
pledged to quest and conquer (to transform the world), or to the
reverse of all that: interminable writing. Cain, Melmoth, Zarathustra, Maldoror, Bouvard, and Pécuchet—the Damned, condemned
to a "naked experience of language" and doomed to find the *commonplaces* "stupid." Misunderstood, because he is no longer included within the cave and the tribe, in the polyphony of anonymous discourses; because he has been excluded from intemporal copresence in the network of the exchanged and uncentered
world.

One sees why the self-portrait is so closely related to utopias.
They share a mythic fantasy of a community alien to history: the
"neolithic dream" that haunts Montaigne's "Of Cannibals" and
Rousseau's works also marks the anthropology of contemporary self-
portraitists. Therefore the conjuring up of traditional societies, a
nostalgia for which (or the model of which) motivates utopian dis-

course, can also define that which haunts by its very absence the self-portrait's fragments and palinodes:

> The man of traditional civilizations, no matter to which civilization he belongs, believes that, as Saint Paul says, sin introduced evil into creation (Romans, VIII, 20–22). The city, the whole of society, was then conceived of as being like a magic circle consecrated by the founding ancestor, renewed through the blood of sacrifices, destined to protect the individual from all evil and the consequences of his own sin. The individual, as an integral part of a vindicated collective being, fears nothing but exclusion or separation from his group, which would not merely expose him to suffering but also to his causing evil around him—at once "evil of sorrow" and "evil of being." (Jules Servier, *Histoire de l'utopie*, 13)

The self-portrait is haunted by the fantasy of a blissful city, of a stable cultural community whose maternal symbolics no one has intimated better than Roland Barthes: he placed at the beginning of his book a fuzzy, sunlit, summery snapshot of his own mother, followed by pictures of the town, the house, the garden of his childhood, images on the basis of which he develops his meditation (his "sideration"). This small book of man, the self-portrait, emerges from the backgrounds of the maternal places of memory, of the imaginary, and, also, against the backgrounds furnished to it by the great book of the City, of culture, with its ethical *topoi* that evoke the lost harmony of an intemporal order. But, unlike Utopia, the self-portrait is not a closed and stable system standing against a violent, anarchic outside. It is internally prey to violence, rupture, the incontinences of writing, and, also, to the upheavals of society and history.

Utopia and the self-portrait are constructed around an absent structure—vanished places, disrupted harmonies—whether it is, as for Montaigne, the steadiness of a seat, lacking ever since the death of the "Other-Self" who was the repository of his likeness; or, for Barthes, the consistency of an *imaginary*; or, for Leiris, a magically efficacious and motivated language; or, again, the City, that must be "dead," as Venice is for Vuillemin and Roudaut,[18] Paris for Baudelaire, Du Bellay's emblematic Rome in *Les Regrets*, the island paradise in Rousseau's Fifth Reverie or Jacques Borel's House.

It is characteristic of the self-portrait's places to be as *retired* as those of Utopia since they are cut off from every *real* or accessible referent.[19] The only real place to which Utopia and the self-portrait refer is the text, the book in its own materiality, and language itself: the book is their sole body (and their tomb). Therefore, ideological certitudes, wisdom, reassuring adages, assured culture are always unavailable to the self-portraitist: if he builds on places, it is because he is unhoused from the start, condemned to exteriority, exile, the impersonal, the antihistorical.[20]

But the self-portrait's exile is an internal exile. Not so much distant from people or outside the city, as slightly withdrawn, out of the way. Every self-portraitist might say, as did Descartes:

Living here, amidst this great mass of busy people who are more concerned with their own affairs than curious about those of others, I have been able to lead a life as solitary and withdrawn as if I were in the most remote desert, while lacking none of the comforts found in the most populous cities. (*Discourse on the Method*, in *Philosophical Writings*, Part III, 126)

And in *Lazare*, a mimesis of death and resurrection where, supposedly, the subject is already laid down in his tomb, Malraux writes:

We call meditation a thought the aim of which is not action, and that word is not far away from orison. Thus, "to philosophize is to learn to die." A high-flown phrase at La Salpêtrière. Its grave resonance is not a reply to "Who am I?" but to "What is life?" (129–30)

The self-portraitist retreats, not to the desert, but to where all the bustle is, a place where others are busiest, or located near his own business, for the species to which he belongs is no different from that of the producer, the citizen, the man of action. But his text foregrounds idleness, retirement (the *Essays* elide Montaigne's political office; *La Règle du jeu* merely alludes to Leiris's profession; *Le Miroir des limbes* says nothing about Malraux's Gaullist politics . . .): if it is a text for self-entertainment, it is written in the stillness of a room and that self-entertainment is hardly distinguishable from the apprenticeship of death. Writing punctuates, structures, redeems a *solitary debauch*, without ever seeking, not even by means of imagination, a real elsewhere.[21] This is why the self-portrait, born of idleness, mother of all vices and digressions, exhibits such concern for order and its own organization: it must turn itself into a practice, an art and an ethics of language. At the end of *Fibrilles* (243), for example, Michel Leiris formulates the code he has devised for himself—and hastens to debunk those rules of the game which, once stated, immediately reveal their futility and stupidity. These pages of *Fibrilles* are typical in that they clarify simultaneously the self-portrait's mode of writing (to set as "articles of catechism" some "bubbles of thought released by desire" [243]) and the ethics governing that writing, along with the anxiety that impels the self-portraitist to demolish by an overflow of writing what had seemed for a while to be an orderly series, a *cosmos* and a *taxis*.

The ethics of the self-portrait depends upon *art*, which imposes an arrangement on the parts of the text and the faculties of the "soul" and, also, a tempering of desires. Without all this the text would be unable to constitute its places. But that ethics likewise imparts a reverse movement which jostles virtues, art, the controlled writing. Against everything in the self-portrait that is governed by Sophrosyne, Temperance, and that tends to close up the text into a harmonious microcosm, there rises a violence of writing that is incontinent, intemperate, libidinous, and open to death.[22]

As opportunely confirmed in an allegory reinvented by Leiris in *Manhood*, that of Judith (we know her to have been a figure of Temperance in the Middle Ages) and Holophernes (who, together with Lucrecius's Tarquin, represents intemperance, lust, pride, the libido), the self-portrait combines the irreconcilable, the vices and virtues opposed in combat—*psychomachy* or *tauromachy*, if one understands this to mean the chance taken in the encounter with the Brute or with Brutishness (Stupidity).

While the works of Leiris resist classification within the limits assigned to the autobiographical corpus by Lejeune, nevertheless they cannot be regarded as a *hapax*. The recent proliferation of texts, where a bared rhetorical machine produces a sort of discourse already encountered in the works of Saint Augustine, Loyola, Montaigne, Rousseau (the *Rêveries*), Nietzsche (*Ecce Homo*) or Barrès, rather than in the *Confessions* or Chateaubriand's *Mémoires d'outre tombe*, prompts us to propose the model for a type of discourse that is governed by a logic, a dialectic, and, also, an encyclopedic system of places descended from rhetorical invention and memory. This model will provide a better understanding, for example, of the Lullism of Leiris, who derived his procedures of invention from that ancient method as well as from Raymond Roussel's, or his use of index cards and of an analogical system. It will also enable one to obtain a better grasp of the indirect and complex relations that linked this practice with the procedures implemented by Montaigne or Bacon, who attempted to wrench rhetorical Invention away from a repetition of what was already known, and Memory from its mechanical use as a "treasure of invention." Moreover, within the context of the upheavals in rhetoric that occurred during the Renaissance, one will have to examine the links between these practices and other procedures, especially the uses of memory in the context of religious meditations and spiritual exercises which sought to de-center the exercitant, in order to recast him *in figura Christi*. These assertions must rest on analyses, especially of such notions as the *commonplaces* and the encyclopedia and, also, on an examination of the *backgrounds* (house, palace, town) and *images* used by rhetorical mnemonics. It would seem that these systems, with their striking homology, are intrinsically connected to the use of *exempla*, allegorical figures, and stereotyped emblematic images, a vast cultural and transhistorical treasurehouse. The subject who undertakes to say what he is by resorting to these procedures and structures, will immediately be obliged to go beyond his individual memory and horizon and to become a kind of microcosm of the culture, dooming himself simultaneously to displacement, absence and death.

Thus, every self-portrait (unlike autobiography which even when it resorts to a myth such as that of the four ages, is limited to an individual's memory and to the places where he lived) ceases to be essentially individual except, of course, in a purely anecdotal sense. The writing machine, the system of places, the figures used— everything in it tends towards generalization, whereas the intratextual memory, that is, the system of cross-references, amplifications, and palinodes that supplants a memory turned towards "remembrance," produces the mimesis of another type of anamnesis, which might be called *metempsychosis*: it is, at any rate, a type of archaic and also very modern memory through which the events of an individual life are eclipsed by the recollection of an entire culture, thus causing a paradoxical self-forgetfulness. It is, then, not by accident that, along with allegories of the Vices and Virtues, Christ and Socrates in the hour of their death are the most frequent *figures* of the self-portrait—which is haunted by the Passion and the *Phaedo*.

PART ONE

Confessions and Meditation

CHAPTER I

Self-Portrait and Encyclopedia

The Speculum and the Mirror

The self-portrait, then, is a polymorphous formation, a much more heterogeneous and complex literary type than is autobiographical narration. It is easy to see similarities and differences between biography and autobiography. On the other hand, the self-portrait does not appear, at first sight, to be integrated into a vaster discursive ensemble. It is impossible to oppose self-portrayal to the literary portrait in any simple terms. The latter—whether it occurs in a novelistic, biographical, and historiographic context, or whether it becomes, as in the seventeenth century courtly game, a relatively autonomous practice governed by rules—is, nothing more than the development of an *energeia*, the autonomous blow-up of a figure such as *characterismus* or *effictio*, which engenders a precious, playful microgenre with detective or clinical variants,[1] in any case a much more restricted venture than such instances of literary self-portrayal as Montaigne's *Essays* and Leiris's *La Règle du jeu*. Even if it presents itself as a genre with a descriptive dominant, the self-portrait is not a mere "self-description." The heuristic limits of the pictorial metaphor ("to paint oneself") are soon reached. Montaigne and Leiris "paint themselves" according to (non-narrative) strategies that go far beyond those used by the literary portrait. Must one infer, then, that the self-portrait is isolated in our culture's discursive economy? Not being a version of autobiography, nor a variant of the portrait, does the self-portrait have no generic counterpart? This odd asymmetry would threaten a structural and typological conception of literature, since, in the eyes of theoretical poetics, discourses take their meaning from being opposed to other types of discourse. But perhaps one should look farther afield.

In *Aurora* (1927–1928), his first "autobiographical" fiction, Michel Leiris, anticipatorily catching sight of a solution, prompts his anagrammatic hero, Damoclès Siriel, to say:

I always have greater difficulty, compared to others, in expressing myself without uttering the pronoun "I"; not that this must be seen as any particular sign of pride on my part, but because the word "I" sums up for me the structure of the world. It is only in terms of myself and because I deign to pay some attention to their existence, that things are. (39)[2]

This is a rough formulation of a basic rule of the self-portraitist's game: "I" sums up the structure of the world, as the microcosm does that of the macrocosm. In consequence, the discourse of "I" and about "I" becomes a microcosm of the collective discourse on the universe of things—*things* being taken here in the sense of *res:* a subject to be treated, a commonplace, a *topos.* The self-portrait thinks of itself as the microcosm, written in the first person, of an encyclopedia and, further, as the self-awareness of the attention "I" pay to the *things* encountered in the process of scanning the encyclopedia. Not a solipsistic—or narcissistic—portrait of an "I" cut off from things, nor an objective description of things in themselves, independently of the attention that "I" turns to them, the self-portrait, rather, is a sustained textual awareness of the interferences and homologies obtaining between the microcosmic "I" and the macrocosmic encyclopedia. It is in this sense that one should see in the self-portrait a mirror image of the "I" reflecting *en abyme* the encyclopedic mirrors of the "great world."[3]

The Middle Ages called an encyclopedic assembly of knowledge a *speculum.*[4] When Vincent of Beauvais wrote the *Speculum Maius* in the mid-thirteenth century, he intended it to be a circle or complete classificatory system of the diverse branches of learning.

A mirror of the subject and a mirror of the world, a mirror of the "I" that seeks itself through the mirror of the universe—what first might have seemed a simple *rapprochement* or convenient analogy proves, when examined, to be an isotopy sanctioned by rhetorical tradition and the history of letters. It is in the light of this history that one can demonstrate that the literary self-portrait is a transformational variant of a structure that also includes the encyclopedic *speculum* of the Middle Ages. The distinctive trait of this structure, which one might call a *mirror*, is that it has a *topical* dominant: it is entirely opposed to the narrative structure that comprises historiography, the novel, biography, and autobiography. Thus the topical *speculum* is opposed, in the literary economy of the Middle Ages, to allegorical narrative, just as in the modern period the self-portrait is opposed to (auto)biographical narration.[5]

Allegorical narrative (as, for example, *The Divine Comedy, The Romance of the Rose, Pilgrim's Progress,* or *The Faerie Queene*) presents itself as an itinerary punctuated by encounters where the temporal process is dominant, where space, description, and learning are subordinated to a narrative arrangement that progresses towards an end.[6] The mirror, however, is governed by a spatial metaphor that sets the reader on a course, not necessarily determined by the subdivision of a book, through the compartments of a "space" or a sequence of topics. The *specula* are groups of *places* arranged according to a topical metaphor (tree, macrocosm, house, garden, itinerary, and so forth); they furnish (are furnished by) a taxonomy; and each of these *places* contains, in a virtual sense, the dialectic development of a descriptive or conceptual discourse accessorily susceptible to illustration with exemplary micronarratives. The Mirror, then, does not purport to narrate but, rather, to deploy intelligibly a representation of things or of the self to whom these things are known, all the while preserving the possibility of cross-references from place to place, of amplification in the places already seen along the way. So, to all intents and purposes, the mirror is a spatial form—open to subsequent invention. Or, to put it differently, the topical mirror, as it mimics the acquisition and growth of learning, remains in principle an open-ended, scholarly (philosophic) form, whereas the (allegorical or biographical) narrative is a closed, mainly vernacular, didactic, form. Although the latter may (but need not) be naive, the former never is.

In medieval literature, then, the mirror is the dialectical (or rhetorical) presentation of encyclopedic learning (this is certainly true of such a work as the *Speculum Maius*) or else a kind of fiction where the conceptual tenor appears thinly disguised by concrete vehicular images or by exemplary scenes displaying stereotyped characters (which may be allegorical personifications) who engage in typical actions (for example, those typical of a virtue or of a vice). This type of mirror, which was written by scholars and, customarily, in the vernacular of laymen for whom it was intended, can be compared to the structure and iconography of Gothic cathedrals. It would survive in the emblematic works of the Renaissance, most often destined for the moral edification of relatively unsophisticated readers.

The encyclopedic *specula* are organized according to topical divisions, embracing the whole field of the known and knowable during the Middle Ages, *inter alia:* heaven's nine spheres; the nine orders of angels; the four elements; the four humors of the body and soul; the world's four, and man's seven, ages; the seven virtues and the seven capital sins. Vincent of Beauvais's *Speculum Maius,* for example, is divided into four major parts (the fourth was added in the fourteenth century, after Vincent's death): *Speculum Naturale, Speculum Historiale, Speculum Doctrinale,* and *Speculum Morale.*[7]

For the most part, and often in their entirety, the *specula* treat of man and his place in Nature and in the divine Plan. It is understandable that their main divisions—as is notably the case with Raoul Ardent—should correspond with the virtues and sins. These theological, ethical, and "psychological" *summae* describe some exemplary ideal entities—the Virtues—or, conversely, some corrupt entities—Vices, sins, madness—the depiction of which serves, *a contrario,* as an example and, hence, a warning.[8] Therefore, the confessor's handbooks, so numerous in the thirteenth century, need only be a lightened and pragmatic version of such major encyclopedic works as the *Speculum Universale.* A textual nudge is all it takes to transform a speculum of vices into a portrait gallery of typical sinners: in fact, the exposition of doctrine, which follows dialectic rules, likewise engenders, according to rhetorical invention's principles (inartificial arguments), illustrations of concrete examples of virtuous or vicious conduct. There is no solution of continuity at all between the conceptual discourse and *exempla*, between didacticism and fable. This is why we often say pejoratively, inverting the terms, that medieval fictions are "didactic." If the clercs reserve for themselves in their Latin works the use of dialectic, of the concept, of the scholarly example, their works in the vernacular, intended for laymen, always seek the concept through the allegorical fable. Whence it follows that the opposition between *speculum* and allegory is not as absolute as has been indicated above: there exists the possibility of an interference, reinforced by the medieval symbolic universe's relative homogeneity, which underlies the homogeneity of its discursive system.

As a pertinent example, let us take a work that is surely, in doctrine, if not in form, somewhat eccentric: the *Confessio Amantis*, written in Latin by Chaucer's friend John Gower.[9] Rather than a Christian confessor, in this text it is the well-known Genius, priest of Venus, who helps the lover-narrator to conduct a systematic examination of conscience on all points (*places*) of amorous doctrine.[10] Genius refers implicitly to a "Handbook of Sins Against Love," a courtly counterpart to a work such as the *Manuel des péchés*, in Anglo-Norman, by William of Waddinton: the short tales told by Venus's priest to focus the lover's examination illustrate the sequence, transposed onto the erotic register, of the seven deadly sins. This systematic account of amorous doctrine, though eclipsed by the stories, is nevertheless copied from Christian doctrine and provides the structure of *Confessio Amantis*, of which it can be said that it is a courtly (and fictitious) variant of both the *speculum* of sins and the confessor's handbook.[11]

Thus, from the Middle Ages on, the encyclopedia can engender a *confessional variant*, not so much in the form of an autobiographical and chronological narrative as in that of a systematic examination (of conscience) which is conducted as a survey of the *places* constituted by the sins and their subdivisions (*genus* and *species*). That course produces, in accordance with rhetorical invention, developments articulated along "artificial" dialectic arguments and such "inartificial" arguments as testimonials, examples, anecdotes, and so on. Consequently, the relation established between "discourse" and "narrative" is the converse of that which is supposed to prevail in forms with a narrative dominant, whether or not these forms are allegorical. Although such a text has no *post hoc, propter hoc* logic at all, it is logically arranged, first under a taxonomy that distributes the encyclopedic parts and the branches of a tree of knowledge and, secondly, according to a dialectic of rhetorical invention that governs the passage from one place to another. One can, therefore, speak of a *topo-logy,* or spatial logic, as opposed to the *chronology* of the texts with a narrative dominant. This spatialization confirms Emile Mâle's well-known hypothesis according to which the Gothic cathedral is the architectural isotope of the medieval *speculum.*[12] The cathedral is not essentially a "stone Bible" nor is it, more vaguely, a "picture book" designed for the illiterate, but primarily it is an encyclopedia embracing a system of *places* concretized in architecture and iconography, a system that programs a multitude of cross-references among the images and backgrounds that evoke and point one another out in their symbolic context.

The symbolic itineraries that the *specula* encode, just like those the Gothic cathedrals impose, do not shut themselves up in a closed and immanent system. They symbolize *something else:* they always refer to God's two Books, Creation and Revelation, and, beyond that, to divine transcendence. Places and images always designate, manifestly or obscurely, the episodes of Genesis, the Fall, the Incarnation, and the Redemption. Everything in them evokes (negatively, when it is a question of Evil) the stages of Christ's mission and the episodes of his terrestrial life upon which the Christian is presumed to model his own existence. [13]

Thus, the encyclopedic mirror reflects what leads the individual to model himself on Christ; and what draws him away from his model when he, a sinner, allows himself to be inveigled into imitating the Devil. The medieval mirror encodes an ambivalence, and the need for choice—it evokes the risk inherent in every human destiny oriented towards salvation.

For this reason, the mirror can become, by turns, an attribute of the Virgin Mary, sometimes called the *speculum sine macula,* and of the diabolical sin *par excellence, Superbia*. The mirror appears in the allegory of ancient Prudence, the one who "knows herself," but also in that of *Vanitas;* in which anyone happening imprudently to contemplate himself in it sees the impending fleshlessness of his own skeleton.[14]

Roland Barthes, still struggling in his self-portrait, with the ambivalence of the mirror, transposes its Marian and diabolical connotations into the profane and psychoanalytic register: the "maternal" mirror is where the cursed *imaginary* appears, that imaginary which he, following Sartre and Lacan, mistrusts and opposes to good *symbolic* and healthy *reality*. But, while Barthes in principle chooses the Good, he still shifts onto the *Other*, reader or God, the responsibility for judging what eludes his own self-portrayer's awareness. And he leaves the rest to the intercession of the Mother, who, as guardian of the mirror, will manage to clear it of its equivocality:

The title of this series of books (*X by Himself*) has an analytic bearing: *myself by myself?* But that is the very program of the imaginary! How is it that the rays of the mirror reverberate on me? Beyond that zone of diffraction—the only one upon which I can cast a glance, though without ever being able to exclude from it the very one who will speak about it—there is reality, and there is also the symbolic. For the latter, I have no responsibility (I have quite enough to do, dealing with my own imaginary!): I leave it to the Other, to the transference, and hence *to the reader*.

And all this happens, as is obvious here, through the Mother, present next to the Mirror. (*Roland Barthes by Roland Barthes,* 153)

So, the master metaphor of the modern self-portrait as, formerly, of the medieval encyclopedia, will be the mirror whose reflecting function is mimicked in the symmetrical statement: *me by me.* But the Other (Unconscious, dead friend, reader, or God) remains as judge and security for what the writer gathers and distributes in his self-portrait, which is, after all, a kind of encyclopedia. The antithetical and complementary signifieds of *speculum* are still co-present in the modern encyclopedic self-portrait: "Like the encyclopedia, the work exhausts a list of heterogeneous objects, and this list is the work's antistructure, its obscure and irrational polygraphy," writes Barthes (148). Barthes's obscure *speculum* is an encyclopedia with a scrambled taxonomy. The encyclopedia is not the self-portrait's manifest structure but rather its nontotalizing anti-structure, the "last word" of which eludes the self-portrayer. Where transcendent order reigned, *That* now reigns, an infinite, lackadaisically labeled chaos. But the book *qua* book must comport a first (and last) word, or at least a first, and last, signifier. With Barthes, for example, the first "word" is an icon, a photograph of the Mother, who, being "present next to the Mirror," safeguards through her presence the lost, or deliberately misplaced, unity of this double autobiographical and encyclopedic mirror.[15]

Let us not fool ourselves. The stake in this present-absent mirror is nothing less than Western and Christian culture and its reflection in all self-portraits. With Barthes, it is the vanity of the West, and the desire to exorcise it. This is clearly legible elsewhere: in a passage from *The Empire of Signs*, Barthes's apology for that far-off Japan where he though he had discovered an entirely different conception of the mirror, of the subject, and of salvation. Supposedly, the Orient has managed to preserve a *speculum sine macula* (which the West locates in transcendence and the next world), a mirror that neither captures nor retains anything and is, therefore, opposed to the superb mirrors of the West, thoroughly maculated by the imaginary, by depth, by vanity, and even by "psychology"; a fallen specularity in which an "origin" can always be glimpsed, a *fall* from which the modern writer, having in principle broken with the past and its mythologies, impatiently turns aside to aspire at last, like Zarathustra, to a pure, joyous and originless repetition:

The collective body of all haikus is a network of jewels in which each jewel reflects all the others and so on, to infinity, without there ever being a center to grasp, a primary core of irradiation (for us, the clearest image of this ricochet effect without motor and without check, of this play of reflections without origin, would be that of the dictionary, in which a word can only be defined by other words). In the West, the mirror is an essentially narcissistic object: man conceives a mirror only in order to look at himself in it; but in the Orient, apparently, the mirror is empty; it is the symbol of the very emptiness of symbols ("*The mind of the perfect man*," says one Tao master, "*is like a mirror. It grasps nothing but repulses nothing. It receives but does not retain*"): the mirror intercepts only other mirrors, and this infinite reflection is emptiness itself (which, as we know, is form). Hence the haiku reminds us of what has never happened to us; in it we *recognize* a repetition without origin, an event without cause, a memory without person, a language without moorings. (*Empire of Signs*, 78–79)

The Japanese mirror turns out, then, to be the Oriental homologue of the "wild polygraphy" of the shattered Western encyclopedia that forms the self-portrait's antistructure; and Roland Barthes, hollowing out, reducing to form, the two principal meanings of the medieval *speculum*, strives to combine them. Thus, the self-portrait's antinarcissistic mirror is made to represent a "personless memory." *A memory without a person*—do not all self-portraits tend towards the paradoxical status that clearly opposes them to autobiographies?[16] Perhaps the self-portrait is a kind of modulation of the terms of this paradox, as posed by Barthes with exceptional lucidity in the two passages quoted above. What Barthes seeks to decipher in the haiku and the Japanese idea of the mirror is the very mirage that constantly leads the self-portrayer beyond narcissistic or delphic self-knowledge, towards the places of a personless encyclopedia through which his own death would no longer rise to taunt his vanity. The self-portrait is therefore situated in a certain relationship to this *speculum;* without attaining the mirror's pure transitivity sought by the Taoist, it would set up a formal reference system in which, without designating anybody, there would be answers for everybody. It is not only, nor is it primarily, a question of the dictionary of a given language but rather of the encyclopedic taxonomy of a culture, of our culture, with its headings and divisions, always being demolished and reconstructed by ideologies and sciences, in the course of our history; the successive maps of this culture, as imposed upon us by our mythologies, our imagination, our religious and secular education, our milieu; in short, everything on which our writing still depends, despite whatever trouble we may have taken to "deconstruct" them, to acquire a conception of reality and the symbolic less clouded by fantasies. Everything that flouts our attempts to escape from Western awareness, learning, and destiny.

"A consciousness without memory" (Malraux, *Le Miroir des limbes—Lazare*, 128)[17] An awareness without a *self*, without a person. No sooner does a *person* appear than he is replaced by another mask among a host of possible masks: ancestors, contemporaries, fictitious characters whom I or others have created, and, of course, the masks of the readers who "will recognize themselves" in the deployment—or in the *invention*—of the masked places of their own culture. The empirical individual—Montaigne, Nietzsche, Leiris, or Malraux—matters much less, we realize this at once, than the unstable *places* of an impersonal memory always exceeding with its "wild poligraphy" the memories of an individual. Because of this, each reader can put himself in the place of the self-portrayer, and yet never find his resting place there.

A memory without a person: we come upon a first version of this paradox as we read Saint Augustine, since in Book X of the *Confessions*, which already journeys through a memory, *memoria sui*, there is no one. At any rate, there is no encounter with Augustine as the individual whose confessional narration has filled the first nine books of the *Confessions*. Just when Augustine sets up the lineaments for what can be taken as a *model*, if not a *source*, for the self-portrait, the *memoria sui* that he invokes and scans takes him in pursuit of God, in quest of the *All* that excludes what is negative in the particular, transitory, and imaginary. The *memoria* of Book X, which is like the reverse of a profane encyclopedia, points directly, with an extreme economy of resources, towards what is indirectly designated in all places, developments, and examples of a medieval *speculum:* the divine Logos whom the modern self-portrayer attempts to escape or from whom he no longer obtains any response.

Memoria sui: this is another memory, very different from the autobiographical memory on which the unity and continuity of an empirical, historical, and contingent person are founded.

Roland Barthes expresses his fear of being caught in the mirror's "zone of diffraction": this fear finds greater justification in a modern ideological prejudice, or in traces of a Christianity hostile to the vanity of painting oneself, than in the practice without reservations of the self-portrait. For the *memoria sui*, which is implicitly identified with the encyclopedia through the mirror's mediation, does not deliver a sticky packet of predicates that paints a constant "self," but, on the contrary, a series of discrete places—an immemorial and impersonal *Grund*, where an infinite regression begins—no being, but passage: the fragmented encyclopedia that is appropriated and rejected by writing cannot surrender its last word; it cannot snap shut, like a trap, since the self-portrayer has decided that the last word will no longer refer to a transcendent signified, such as God.[18]

The self-portrait, as an encyclopedic *speculum*, is a memory that mediates between the individual and his culture. This memory is especially *attached* to the place where there is a clash in the problematically enunciated relations between the microcosmic monad and the linguistic and cultural macrocosm. Because of this, it prefers to recall the surprises, the misapprehensions, and the failures of an apprenticeship, the resistance to commonplaces, to "stupidity," to rhetoric, and also the passage from the autonomous to the systematic, and vice versa. The self-portrait tends as much to hollow out and contest the empirical individual's memory, by dispersing it amid the contested *topoi* of its culture, as it does to fill it artificially by recentering it on the Other, as always happens in Christian meditative practice: this explains the fact that the self-portrait is haunted—if only to exorcise its haunters—by the exemplary figures of Socrates and Christ Crucified. In some measure, the self-portrayer always paints himself *in figura*.[19]

As a metamorphosis of the encyclopedic mirror, the self-portrait obliquely and obstinately questions itself about the writing subject's own identity with himself. The subject tells himself only through what surpasses, goes through, and denies him. As a result, the diverse self-portraits set up a network of mirrors of our culture, of this ill-centered macrocosm that expropriates the writer and delivers him to all that he is not, a plural, polymorphous and polygraphic *we*, where one reads the destiny of Western culture undermined by its Other: savagery, exoticism, strangeness, what contests but yet fails to elude its sway or to set up at its center in a position of mastery. This expropriating Other is, in the first place, God: he knows all about me; his sovereign gaze awesomely asserts the vanity of my attempt to say who I am, even when I do so to meet the express demand of fellow men who are not blest with divine lucidity. There remains confession. Its aim is not to inform God, but only to humble the sinner by his avowal of what God knows better than the sinner himself. The divine Other—in Saint Augustine's work at any rate —entrenches himself so firmly at the center of the confession that it ends up being but a gloss on the biblical text.

Our study of the self-portrait should nevertheless open with an analysis of the *Confessions*, at least of the portion of them, Book X, that presents in intaglio, so to speak, the lineaments of the meditative and topical self-portrait. This deliberately abortive attempt to explore the human conscience implements and transgresses, with unprecedented discursive and ontological designs, the procedures of rhetoric.

CHAPTER 2

The Evolution of
Meditation

Saint Augustine's Confessions: Book X

Saint Augustine foreshadows the "man of introspection," the one
who, according to Georges Gusdorf, always slips out of his own
grasp so that he always ends up somewhere other than in the inner
being that he claims he wants to explore. But he is an inverted
prefiguration:

the man of introspection is solely responsible for the curse hanging over
him. He has untied the knot of his own personality. He has willingly
deprived himself of every normal means of achieving self-awareness; he
seems struck by the insufficiency of all the usual forms of intelligibility.
Carried to extremes, this deliberate course of refusal and avoidance leads
to disincarnation. When, by backing up into oneself, qualifications and
differences are abolished, there is a loss of all structure in personal life. The
end result of this analysis is a kind of pantheism, or return to the great All,
that seems to resolve itself in a pure and simple surrender to daydreaming
inclinations. (*La Découverte de soi*, 61)[1]

Little do the ideological, metaphysical, religious or political options matter: the curse (or the blessing) in question results from a
refusal or an unawareness of rhetoric. What Gusdorf calls "normal
means of achieving self-awareness" or "usual forms of intelligibil-

37

ity" are the rhetorical procedures available to Western man so that he can form the effigy he calls his self.

Gusdorf's "man of introspection," who resorts to this boundless regression, would be more like the Oriental meditator's brother in search of emptiness and silence. Still, it is difficult to understand Gusdorf's description: by what discursive process does "one back up into oneself?" How are "qualifications" and "differences" abolished? By what logical steps? What is a "pure and simple surrender to daydreaming inclinations?" For the introspection in question to become inscribed in a text, it has to be the product of an invention (or of an "imagination"). Saint Augustine eludes this verbal deception by arranging Book X of his *Confessions* as an empty allocutory and memorial structure which he knows constitutes the hollow mold for a rhetoric.

"The man of introspection," when he wants—or believes that he manages—to strike out rhetoric (the dialectic "differences" and "qualifications," the forms of intelligibility known as *places*), resembles the man of Salesian spirituality who, in his opposition to Loyola's method and all *methods* of meditation, wanted to establish "true prayer" and "acts of pure love."

In the *Confessions*, the autobiographical narrative is interrupted after Augustine's conversion and the death of his mother, Monica. A meditation on memory takes up Book X, followed by an exegesis, spread over three books, of the initial verses of Genesis. A strange structure, if one takes the *Confessions* to be an autobiography, or even a "confession" in the modern and profane sense that has come to prevail since Rousseau. And, if the first nine books of the *Confessions* form a "religious autobiography," the last four appear as incongruous appendices that take the place of the autobiographical narrative's continuation and obliterate it—or censure it—by replacing it with the nonnarrative of Book X and with a commentary on a narrative that concerns humanity and the universe in general since it relates Genesis and the Fall; at the end of his *Confessions*, Augustine turns out to be only one fallen and redeemed creature amid the host of humans.

This structural oddity serves to foreground the relations between the discourse of the "I" in the *Confessions* and that of the divine Other. It suggests—and mimics—the incommensurability between the human word, caught in temporality, and the Word that, although divine, eternal, and simultaneous, is inscribed in Genesis and, taking fallen man as its addressee, reveals itself in Holy Scripture. "The aim of the *Confessions*," writes Eugene Vance, "is to replace what is mortal in the Self's language by the immutable and saving discourse of our divine interlocutor. Obviously, however, the ultimate phase of such an experience cannot be represented in the language of autobiography: for the true 'history' (historia) of the *Confessions* implies precisely a surpassing of the language of 'history' " ("Le Moi comme langage," 171). Because of this, in the last Books of the *Confessions* "God's text moves in to become the center of Augustine's text" (171). The speaking subject attempts to efface himself while he continues to speak: the mortal and fragmented discourse through which, according to Vance, "one experiences not one's expression but, rather, the *loss* of the self" (170), becomes filled with fragments (scriptural citations) of the divine discourse, whose gloss it finally turns into.

"Loss of the self": this is open to diverse interpretations. First: the more I speak of myself, if it is not to confess my faults and thank God for the graces he has granted me, the more I endanger my own salvation. But he who uses human language to praise God and write commentaries upon His Scripture loses himself, or at any rate he loses the empirical and temporal self that the moderns will try to "express." This loss is clearly not one in the eyes of the Christian, who finds himself by losing himself. A trite and essential paradox. But things are not so simple in the *Confessions*, where the loss in question is effected, inscribed, according to the method that will be followed by profane self-portraits to invent (or "express") the self. Augustine the rhetorician, at the very moment when he scuttles pagan rhetoric to found a Christian rhetoric centered on the divine word and the allocution to God, is prompted to employ one of rhetoric's parts, memory, in order to discover God in the depths of the evacuated, lost or, at least, sacrificed Self: "The individual must sacrifice his will to the Other's will for the Word to become actualized in memory, the 'dwelling place' (*tabernaculum*) of the soul. Memory can reform the Word when we give ourselves up to acts of inner regression. The written word is but a sign of the spoken word; the spoken word, in turn, is the sign of the internal Word, which is incorporeal and has been deposited in our intellects by the Other" ("Le Moi comme langage," 170). This is indeed the work carried out in Book X: regression in memory towards the innate trace of the Word. But Augustine's first experience (a sinner's experience to be surpassed as soon as grace intervenes) belongs to an individual full of vanity; it is coextensive with his memory, in the ordinary autobiographical sense. The first nine books of the *Confessions* testify to the existence of this sinner and to his relation to language, focused on fallen man and, in the city of men, on persuasion.

Book X accomplishes—by passing systematically through Memory, previously purged by the narrative confession—the surpassing movement towards the Word that is inscribed there. Book X retraces the process by which one manages to forget oneself while emptying memory of all temporal residues.

But divine intervention alone, the grace of a divine allocution (or what is so interpreted, the well-known *Tolle, Lege*) confirmed by reading Saint Paul, moves the subject off-center, together with the allocutory system in which he was situated: *Tolle, Lege:*

"Take it and read, take it and read." At this I looked up, thinking hard whether there was any kind of game in which children used to chant words like these, but I could not remember ever hearing them before. I stemmed my flood of tears and stood up, telling myself that this could only be a divine command to open my book of Scripture and read the first passage on which my eyes should fall. (VIII, XII, 177)

Natural memory, which enables one to recollect and rediscover one's childhood, must be silent for the epiphanic interpretation to prevail, for *Tolle, Lege* to appear as a divine summons leading Augustine towards the Word, or at least to the inspired apostle's written word. The joy bursting forth through Augustine's contrite tears has a different cause from the delight that seizes the Proustian narrator during the madeleine experience: it does not herald the return to childhood arranged in the places of Combray (or Tagaste): the child's voice that chants and repeats *Tolle, Lege*, not having evoked Augustine's childhood games, must therefore be angelic, the Other's message, rather than an invitation to return to the places and images of childhood, which are canceled out as fast as they appear in the remembrance process by which he attempted to place the child's

song. No, *Tolle, Lege* is not a "memory." And from now on memory will play a paradoxical role: it will serve to "confess, not what
I was, but what I am" (X, IV, 205), that is, as a speaker placed in
a certain relation of allocution and comprehension with the Word.
Henceforth, language and communication are recentered on the divine word, a recentering that is made manifest by innumerable citations from Scripture—the Augustinian text being but a gloss and
an interstice—and by the mode of address to God, which is another
way of letting him speak.[2]

"I go on to confess, not what I was, but what I am" (X, IV,
210), and "so to such as you command me to serve I will reveal,
not what I have been, but what I have become and what I am"
(X, IV, 210): Augustine turns towards the present and no longer,
as he did in the nine preceding books, to the errors and conversions
that marked his history. He will henceforth prefer spatial metaphors to narration. Whence the importance of the oppositions between the without and the within, between interiority and exteriority.[3] Clearly, this opposition arises and is resolved, according to
mystical logic, in a paradoxical hollowing out of the text. For, thinks
the Christian, there is no interiority closed to God. And, consequently, one cannot write a self-portrait where God would be the
addressee: if, to beseech God's mercy, it is indeed necessary to *confess* to him the faults that he, however, knows better than does the
sinner himself, it would be redundant to *describe* to him what I
am. So the reader, being the secondary and very effaced addressee,
will learn nothing about the "speaker."

In Book X, confession assumes two very distinct, though not
contradictory, functions. Augustine holds up to God's judgment not
just what he knows about himself but, again, what is unknown to
him (X, V, 206);[4] and he aims to make himself known to those
whom God commands him to serve (X, IV). So he addresses simultaneously two distinct addressees, one of whom always already
possesses all the information, while the human addressees "wish to
listen as I confess what I am in my heart, into which they cannot
pry by eye or ear or mind" (X, III, 209). Yet, the otherness and
exteriority of Augustine's readers are not absolute, for human addressees are linked to the penitent by charity, which vouches within
them for the veracity of confession. But, since charity itself is di-

vine grace, it is God who safeguards the communication between the within and the without, between myself and others: Augustine desires to reveal himself only to those "fraternal souls" (X, IV, 205) to whom he would be linked by prayer, hope, and repentance.

The Augustinian undertaking makes demands upon divine and human charity, as a conducting medium that creates the conditions under which it is possible to speak through indirections. Augustine still has recourse to language and can constitute a discourse of interiority: neither narration nor the self-serving enumeration of particularities, since either would be tantamount to a conceited display of individual sins. As a result, Augustine's self-portrait is both most disappointing—because it lacks those specific traits, those predicates in which we might, as readers, invest our own narcissism—and, literally, most captivating, for it is reduced to a blueprint, a model to which every Western self-portrait must conform, whether it likes it or not—unless it resolves to transgress it knowingly.[5]

What passes a priori for being *static* (namely, the description of an "inner space") is transformed into an itinerary that reintroduces a duration different from that of an autobiographical narration. This itinerary foregrounds the telescoping of space and time produced in the description's imaginary space by the primacy of the spatial over the temporal; it corresponds to a conception of rhetorical invention as the metaphorical pursuit of a notion through the hunting ground provided by every *place* of invention.

What separates Augustine from his successors is as much the nature of the object pursued as the mode of pursuit. In fact, he harries neither himself nor any metaphoric surrogate, where the concreteness of a "self" would become agglutinated; instead, through the macrocosm and within the microcosmic "recesses" of his own memory, he hunts down God. Augustine's self-portrait is therefore the narrative of a pursuit of God; or, rather, it is the itinerary along which a man seeks God outside, and then inside, himself, destroying as he goes along all the "idols" that come in his way: the perceptions, sensory images, and memory contents that might engender the anecdotes of individuality.

While the within-without opposition cannot be reduced to a dichotomy between memory and perception of the outside world, interiority is in fact conceived according to the pattern of memory, which contains not only the representations or images born of perception and experience, but also a knowledge that is not derived from the senses and is not effaced when whatever had induced the images stored in memory vanishes. This is intellectual knowledge, with its order and its parts, a set of notions produced by the activity of thought—with, in short, its *method*, as Renaissance terminology would have it. Memory, for Augustine, is the "place" where notions and sentiments, memory's memory, and the memory of forgetfulness are collated: it is also the place where thought, which is an act of bringing together, operates (X, XI).

I cannot undertake here an exhaustive analysis of the Augustinian memory and its Platonic or Neoplatonic sources, but at least it ought to be shown that, with Augustine the notion of *memory* (*memoria sui*) occupies the place of what writers after the Renaissance would call the *Self*, a vague and global notion allowing one to designate "interiority" schematically: "But the mind and the memory are one and the same" (X, XIV, 220); "Yet it is my mind: it is my self" (X, XVII, 223–24). When Augustine meditates on memory and its paradoxes, what is most disquieting about them is the fact that the memory of forgetfulness implies a knowledge of the unknown or an awareness of the unconscious. He resorts to a theoretical discourse that enables him to link the multitude of ephemeral experiences and sensations to the deity's eternal transcendence.[6] By designating memory first as a *place* and then as a *nonplace*, he first invents and then strikes out metaphorical discourse for which his rhetorician's education furnished him the lineaments.

In fact, when he designates memory as "a spacious palace," "a storehouse for countless images of all kinds which are conveyed to it by the senses" (X, VIII, 214), Saint Augustine is implicitly referring to the rhetorical, and ultimately Aristotelian, conception of memory.[7] Saint Augustine's terminology derives from the terminology the rhetoricians used to describe artificial memory, which was at once the "treasure-house of invention" and the technique by which the orator recalled the points of his argument.[8]

But the use of his memory that Augustine makes here goes beyond rhetoric—since he conflates his own identity with his memory—and memory itself is exceeded by a quest for God, in the course of which the rhetorical conception of *places* opens onto a mystical vision which abolishes both exterior and imaginary spaces, which cannot encompass divine transcendence.

Augustinian anthropology, at least in Book X of the *Confessions*, is founded on the opposition and conjunction of the within and the without:

Then I turned to myself and asked, "Who are you?" "A man," I replied. But it is clear that I have both body and soul, the one the outer, the other the inner part of me. (X, VI, 212)

Augustine thinks that the body belongs doubly to the outside world: it is perceived as external and as a means of apprehending objects through the senses, as well as the full compass of heaven and earth, which, although they speak of God to men, are *not* God.

The opposition of the within and the without goes along with high appreciation of the within: "But my inner self is the better of the two." Yet, this superiority of the within, a corollary of divine presence in consciousness, is not so absolute as to be an obstacle to communication between the within and the without, since the within contains the image of things external. The within/without opposition is mediated by memory, which is at once container and collating activity. Container: Augustine summons up an anatomical comparison to evoke the memory's capacity for absorbing and storing what comes to it from outside: "We might say that the memory is a sort of stomach for the mind" (X, XIV, 220).[9] Thus we see the emergence of another metaphor, according to which the soul would resemble a body containing a stomach such that the latter itself might contain all the images that the senses have collected in the world without.

But memory is not only a receptacle, a stomach, a palace or even a huge plain: its dual relation to the within and the without enables it to mediate the opposition between them, because it is also a faculty, an activity that transcends their opposition. It is both the *place* and the *agent* of the Augustinian *cogito* in Book X of the *Confessions*:

My memory holds a great number of facts of this sort, things which I have already discovered and, as I have said, placed ready to hand. This is what is meant by saying that we have learnt them and know them. If, for a short space of time, I cease to give them my attention, they sink back and recede again into the remote cells of my memory, so that I have to think them out again, like a fresh set of facts, if I am to know them. I have to shepherd them out again from their old lairs, because there is no other place where they can have gone. In other words, once they have been dispersed, I have to collect them again, and this is the derivation of the word *cogitare*, which means *to think* or *to collect one's thoughts*. For in Latin the word *cogo*, meaning *I assemble* or *I collect*, is related to *cogito*, which means *I think*, in the same way as *ago* is related to *agito* or *facio* to *facito*. (X, XI, 219)

It is difficult to establish whether it is "thought" or "memory" per se that gathers the notions in the *thinking* act, for in Book X memory is presented alternately as the whole and as a part of the mind, or of "myself." Be that as it may, classical rhetoric speaks through the Augustinian text, and there will be numerous occasions for us to recognize the echo of its discourse in other self-portraits. In fact, for rhetoric (at which Bacon leveled this essential criticism, just when he was paradoxically helping to loosen the rhetorical model's hold on Western thought by pushing it to the limit), to *invent* is never to *discover something new*. To invent is to reorder, according to a configuration likewise governed by the codes of invention, a number of innate or acquired notions. To think is to recollect in an orderly way and to combine the data provided by anamnesis.[10]

This is why Augustine's reflection on memory, which results in a rhetorician's *cogito* and the construction of a model of presence as a space where the without is absorbed by the within, may be considered the first occurrence of an intellectual procedure that attempts to grasp the *ego* in the *hic et nunc*. In another context, Paul Ricoeur defines this approach as follows:

reflection is not intuition; or, in positive terms, reflection is the effort to recapture the Ego of the Ego Cogito in the mirror of its objects, its works, its acts. But why must the positing of the Ego be recaptured through its acts? Precisely because it is given neither in a psychological evidence, nor in an intellectual intuition, nor in a mystical vision. (*Freud and Philosophy*, 43)[11]

In the *Confessions*, Saint Augustine managed to fragment the task faced by all those who attempt to "grasp the ego": indeed, because of the nine books that he devoted to his memories of acts, works, and objects, he does not have to burden himself with specific memory contents in Book X and can write it as a pure reflection on memory.

The last three books of the *Confessions*, which are a meditation on the first verses of Genesis, pose the ontological problem separately, as the question of the Creator's relations with his creation, his presence to the world, and to the writer: the problem, that is, of the presence of the Word and the justification of the writing act.

No doubt because he was not a self-portraitist in the strict sense, even in Book X, Augustine was able to outline so clearly and analytically the problematics of self-portrayal: for confessionally addressing God who already knows everything, he could avoid the technical difficulties faced by those who, as opaque to themselves as they are to the readers they are addressing, are nonetheless eager to make themselves known.

Book X, then, completely disregards Augustine's former promise to make himself known as he is now. All that matters henceforth, after his conversion (and the death of Monica, his mother), is the quest for God and the imitation of Jesus Christ, as signified *in figura* at the end of chapter XI, Book IX: "And so on the ninth day of her illness, when she was fifty-six and I was thirty-three, her pious and devoted soul was set free from the body." The carnal being, in the guise of his mother, has vanished: Augustine has been resurrected in the spirit by maternal intercession. Only the most general urgings of pride can still be an obstacle to his identification with the Savior. Augustine's temporal being, previously guaranteed by Monica's maternal intercession, is now but memory—a memory that has exhausted its discursive role by producing an *autobiographical* narrative.

Is Book X of the *Confessions*, then, a self-portrait? Posed in these terms, the question is anachronistic and out of place. While the first nine books of the *Confessions* form a "spiritual autobiography," their continuation, especially in Book X, belongs to another type of discourse, one that props itself up on rhetoric in order to transcend it and one that resorts to spatial metaphors in order to leave space behind on its way to a *nonplace* (or *utopia*).

The *Confessions* belong to a long autobiographical tradition linking them at one end to Neoplatonism and, by way of the Isiac mysteries, to Apuleus's *Metamorphosis* and, at the other end, to an immense Christian and profane progeny.[12] However, the course followed by Book X did not encourage any direct imitation: perhaps because, unlike narrative topoi (for example, *conversion* or the *quest for truth*, which have a history and are situated in history as the variants of related sacred narratives), neither meditation on memory as a mental faculty and as a technique nor the use and transformation of rhetorical memory have any other history than that of rhetoric's vicissitudes.

Rhetoric is in fact the—transhistoric and atemporal—treasure of "eloquence," alternately the light and the shadow of our culture, its keenest awareness of its unconscious. As a permanent resource, a reserve of discursive models, it is susceptible to numerous transformations, according to the functions assigned to it and the ideological contexts in which its avatars are realized.

Our sole concern here will be with those realizations, such as the medieval *speculum*, which have a direct transformational relation to the self-portrait, either because they furnish it a textual model or because they can be contemplated as the variants of memory and invention to which self-portraits resort for their own purposes.

The Renaissance can be defined as the dual restoration of rhetoric and Antiquity; one was but a modality of the other. Reinstated against Scholastic philosophy, exalted, rhetoric becomes the subject of (and the means for) an intense theoretical reflection which will moreover, by metamorphosis, produce original functions in new ideological contexts. Exploding at its modern apogee, rhetoric falls back to earth in diverse variants that shed light on one another: they command a new distribution of "genres," assure the language arts and the speaking subject of a new epistemological foundation, and found new religious practices.

The Spiritual Exercises of Saint Ignatius of Loyola

Methods of meditation, of which the Renaissance was so prodigal, adapt and transform old dialectical and rhetorical procedures.[13] In this rhetorical context, Loyola's *Spiritual Exercises* resort mainly to the *imagination* and the *passions*. *Imagination*, understood here in the Aristotelian and Thomist sense as a faculty made up of experience and of knowledge drawn from sensory experience, places Ignatian meditation in a transformational relation to the rhetorical memory whose theoretical foundation is Aristotelian associationism.[14]

Meditation's rhetorical matrix may be more visible in some of Loyola's predecessors, as in the *Scala Meditationis*, for example, or the *Zardino de Oration*, a pious work, published in Venice in 1494, for the use of young girls. Meditation and religious painting here seem closely linked, since painting will often be charged with furnishing images for the faithful's visual "imagination." But matters are not that simple: in fact, in fifteenth-century Italy, according to M. Baxandall, "the public mind was not a blank tablet on which the painter's representation of a story or person could impress itself; it was an active institution of interior visualization with which every painter had to get along" (*Painting and Experience in Fifteenth Century Italy*, 45). This public was accustomed to meditating on pictorial representations and, in the quiet of the oratory, to directing its mind to scan absent images. Here is what the *Zardino* prescribes for young Venetian ladies:

The better to impress the story of the Passion on your mind, and to memorise each action of it more easily, it is helpful and necessary to fix the places and people in your mind: a city, for example, which will be the city of Jerusalem—taking for this purpose a city that is well known to you. In this city find the principal places in which all the episodes of the Passion would have taken place—for instance, a palace with the supper-room where Christ had the Last Supper with the Disciples . . . And then too you must shape in your mind some people, people well-known to you, to represent for you the people involved in the Passion—the person of Jesus Himself, of the Virgin . . ., Judas and others, every one of whom you will fashion in your mind.

When you have done all this, putting all your imagination into it, then go into your chamber. Alone and solitary, excluding every external thought from your mind, start thinking of the beginning of the Passion, starting with how Jesus entered Jerusalem on the ass. Moving slowly from episode to episode, meditate on each one, dwelling on each single stage and step of the story. And if at any point you feel a sensation of piety, stop: do not pass on as long as that sweet and devout sentiment lasts.[15]

The devout imagination uses a person's own memory (the known town and people) to fashion a system of allegorical places where the meditator *will see* the drama of the Passion unfold. There is a substitution, for a person's own memory, of a collective memory in which the known places and personages one has introduced produce an affect: there is no question of transferring a conventional Little Jesus to a vaguely Oriental landscape, but rather of creating scenes as moving as an automobile accident befalling a near relation under our eyes: thus functioned the *imagines agentes* of ancient mnemonics.[16]

Loyola, in turn, prescribes *compositions of places*. These constitute the preamble of each exercise. Each preamble is supposed to summon up, in the mind of the exercitant, a setting peopled with personages, a scene at once rich in the metaphors of what he is supposed to experience at each stage of the exercises and pregnant enough to eliminate any other imaginary solicitation. Let us take, as an example, the preambles of the fifth exercise:

FIRST PRELUDE. This is a representation of the place. Here it will be to see in imagination the length, breadth, and depth of hell. (*The Spiritual Exercises*, 32)

Regardless of how this composition is articulated (recourse to iconographic memories, remembrance of verbal "topographies" made by preachers), the exercitant has to be brought before a *place* situated in an imaginary three-dimensional space.[17] It is easy to recognize a technique borrowed from mnemotechnics. But whereas within the bounds of ancient rhetoric each orator had chosen at his convenience specific referential places to help him compose his permanent mnemonic system, and those had been most often real places well known to him,[18] Ignatius conversely aimed to furnish the exercitant with an adventitious memory forming a set of coded places foreign to his individual biography and each individual's place of origin: this pseudomemory is the normative local system where the episodes of the mystery of redemption will unfold.

Thus, each exercitant is led to rid himself of the places and images that stock his individual memory, so as to adopt a uniform system of conventional biblical places and images, analogous to those presumed to structure and stock the memory of the Redeemer himself.

In *La Mémoire collective*, Maurice Halbwachs has made a special study of real or "imaginary" holy places (particularly those imagined on site by the Crusaders) as well as the role that the worship attaching to them has played in the history of Christianity. He draws the conclusion that they have had a conservative and normative function:

For the places partake of the stability of things material and it is by electing them, by enclosing itself within their limits and by adapting its attitude to their arrangement, that the collective thought of the group of believers is most likely to become fixed and to last: such is the condition of memory. (165)[19]

Likewise, the successive "points" following Loyola's preamble and articulating the unfolding meditation, serve, against a previously imagined background, to replace individual memories by a sequence of imaginary sensations or *images* through which the exercitant is provisionally turned into one of the damned or the blessed, that is, into a Christian centered not so much upon the contingency of his own life (in principle already put aside in the course of the examination of conscience and general confession preceding the exercises) as upon the essence of his destiny as a sinful creature redeemed by Christ. Barthes speaks of a "christomorphic theme" and a "deiform existence" (*Sade, Fourier, Loyola*, 68) in connection with the "fantasies" proposed to the "I" and their strange status in the *Exercises*. And in fact this "I," namely, the exercitant mimicking the fictitious situations proposed to him while he actively practices the exercises, achieves what Barthes calls an absolute plasticity: "This *I* takes advantage of all the situations the Gospel canvas provides in order to fulfill the symbolic motions of desire: humiliation, jubilation, fear, effusion, etc." As a result, Barthes is able to see the *Exercises* as a "theater" where the exercitant assumes several roles in succession—by turns Christ and spectator of the crucifixion, and so on. The exercitant's I "is nothing more than the word that sustains and justifies the scene" proposed by the theatrical unfolding of the exercise. Having first cited a maxim attributed to Saint Ignatius—*Non coerceri maximo, contineri tamen a minimo, divinum est* (Not to be encompassed by the greatest, but to be contained by the smallest, is a divine thing)— Barthes eventually resorts to psychoanalytic phraseology and is able to diagnose an "evasive presence of the subject within the image which marks both fantasy and Ignatian contemplation" (*Sade, Fourier, Loyola*, 64–65).

But, properly speaking, there is no room for fantasies in the *Exercises* (fantasy, no matter now precisely coded in a specific culture and a given neurosis, is defined by its individuality, by how the subject relates to his own representation of himself)[20] since the individual desires of the flesh and spirit (sins) are supposed to be replaced by the desire for salvation and the courage (virtues) of the Christian imitator of Jesus Christ. This is the aim of the evangelical backgrounds and images proposed systematically to the exercitant's imagination: the vivid images of the collective myth come to take the place of individual fancy.

Barthes is nevertheless right in underscoring the marked antinomy between the Ignatian *Exercises* and the Oriental mystical practices that seek the evacuation of all images. With Loyola, there is no question at all of abolishing the meditator in a wordless illumination.

Consequently, we can look upon the *Exercises* as being a variant of the self-portrait likewise produced by a mutation of the rhetorical matrix. In fact, if fantasies (or personal images) are substituted for the imposed evangelical images that serve to strengthen the subject in a spiritual position where his contingency is abolished, and if the disindividualizing effort is transformed into a contemplation of fantasy and into a cultivation of individual desire, the practice of the *Exercise*, thus fundamentally perverted, will produce the imaginary, a Self, and thus, to a certain degree, a self-portrait.

Loyola's text turns readily into a matrix for the self-portrait because, like technical manuals or guidebooks, it is composed of a sequence of operational prescriptions. In itself, it is neither meditation nor exercise but a machine to produce exercises and meditations and, therefore, to fashion a type of man, the militant Christian. This rhetoric is specialized rather than restricted to one rhetorical "office": a new rhetoric, oriented towards the exercitant's self-persuasion through a sequence of operations during which he plays simultaneously the roles of the addresser and addressee (telling himself the history of Christ, picturing images in his mind, setting his imagination on a journey through a succession of places), a persuasion where the apostrophe to God (prayer) and the interlocution with him preserve a position that, although preeminent in principle, is limited in practice. This internalized rhetoric is a complete one in that it retains, more or less developed and transformed, all the parts of classical rhetoric: invention, disposition, elocution, memory, and delivery. The court and audience of the tribunal are placed inside the human conscience so that the theatrical mimicry, the gesticulation, the body positions are addressed to none other than the very one who practices them. Memory serves to artificially encode in the individual an exemplary sequence that replaces his own memories, while rhetoric's first three parts furnish a content, an order, and a style to the exercitant's soliloquy. Rhetoric even intervenes at the center of the *Exercises*, if one so designates the point at the end of the second week, when the resolve to be reformed takes place since the choices proposed in paragraph 189—"To Amend and Reform One's Own Life and State"—are directly descended from the topics of invention: [21]

If he is really to attain this end [by setting before him the purpose of his creation and of his life and position, namely, the glory and praise of God our Lord and the salvation of his soul], he will have to examine and weigh in all its details how large a household he should maintain, how he ought to rule and govern it, how he ought to teach its members by word and example. (P. 78)

If the *Exercises* are indeed a rhetorical art that furnishes a method of self-persuasion and self-transformation, some of Barthes's remarks, contrasting the almost nonexistent *imaginary* and "strong (tirelessly cultivated)" *imagination* (55–56) of Ignatius, appear somewhat misleading: in fact, from Aristotle to Perelman no writer of a treatise on rhetoric ever proposes to disclose anything about the "imaginary" of the author, but they all prescribe means by which to stimulate and fill the orator's "imagination" with a specific purpose of persuasion. Certainly, as Barthes thinks,

the imaginary can be conceived as a set of internal representations (its usual sense), as the defection of an image (as encountered in Bachelard and thematic criticism) or, also, as the subject's misprision of himself when he assumes the task of telling and filling his *I* (sense of the word in J. Lacan). (*Sade, Fourier, Loyola*, 55)

But this is precisely what Ignatius aims to eliminate in the exercitant and to replace, according to a coded procedure, by an *imagination*, which Barthes defines as "the energy available to manufacture a language, whose units will of course be 'imitations,' but not of the images which a person forms and stores somewhere in himself" (56–57). The *Exercises*, therefore, resemble a machine for manufacturing self-portraits: in principle they always produce them *in figura Christi*. But, by tinkering with the machine, it can also be made to produce what it was designed to eliminate. The poison (the imaginary) to be purged becomes the intended end product: the *Exercises* are thus transformed into a machine to produce a *self*. Whatever may be the case with Loyola's imaginary (surely, no intention of revealing it appears in the *Exercises*), we know that the *imagination*, or imaging faculty, did not enjoy great prestige during the Renaissance and that piety was not about to give it a free rein.[22]

During the Renaissance the good imagination must always, at least with Christian militants, whether Romans or Reformers, lead to the imitation of Jesus Christ. Thus it is in terms borrowed from Christ's Passion that Luther tells of his being summoned before the Diet of Worms. The first Lutherans transformed their life into a Passion play where everyone imagined himself in the role of Jesus: as a result Luther had to reprimand those of his disciples who, in their desire to make their life a Way of the Cross, imposed excessive mortifications on themselves.[23]

But these very "excesses" of piety reveal how easy it is to slip towards less "edifying" fantasies which perhaps occur in the erotic equivocalness of baroque devotion. Exercises and meditation, to the extent that they try to sublimate the imagination and persuasion of rhetoric, are dangerous games. Between the worship of Christ Crucified and the cult of the Ego, between *memoria Christi* and *memoria sui*, grace and a watchful will are the protective barriers: the rhetorical discursive model, which uses passions, images, persuasive allocution and the insinuating charm of tropes, easily allows itself to be invested by the various kinds of libido. And, as we are going to see, the meditative soliloquy lends itself to a variety of uses.

Rhetoric and Meditation: The Seventeenth Century

Some historians of English literature, being struck by the decline of rhetorical theorization in the seventeenth century, after its Elizabethan flowering, have noted a displacement, indeed a transformation, of rhetoric's functions in that period: rhetoric, having been, so to speak, internalized, is made to regulate an allocution the subject addresses to himself in a meditative soliloquy. The reader of the soliloquy is placed in the marginal position of a third party. The meditative posture enables the solitary speaker, if need be, to prompt acts and arouse feelings in an "overhearing audience": this peculiar allocutionary situation is encoded in a multitude of verse and prose texts of a religious character.[24] Jean Rousset confirmed this hypothesis, despite his avowedly antirhetorical point of view: "The writer's paths have not been traced out beforehand, no more in the 17th century than nowadays" ("Monologue et soliloque [1650–1700]," 203).

According to Rousset, then, questions concerning the "expression of the inner way" are transhistorical and pertain more to philosophy than to rhetoric. These questions are of the type "Is it possible to know oneself? What are the means of expression of the private inner self? How does one speak to oneself? One can speak of oneself to oneself and for oneself: self-portrait, *Essays*, meditation, private diary . . . or, one can speak of this circuitously—supposing an absence of fiction and creation in the direct forms of autobiography—through fiction and other persons speaking on one's behalf" (203). Let us put aside, at least as far as their strictly theatrical and fictional context is concerned, the dramatic monologue and novelistic soliloquy (which are of primary interest to Rousset), except to note that Rousset is quickly led to clarify the soliloquy technique in *La Princesse de Clèves* by referring to the "currents, above all Augustinian, that then become backdrops for many literary works" (209).

But it would also be appropriate to cite the excellent passage where Rousset surveys a series of meditative texts—from Saint Francis de Sale's *Traité de l'amour de Dieu*, VI, I, to Pierre Nicole, touching along the way upon Malebranche's *Méditations chré-*

tiennes, Pascal, La Rochefoucauld, and Duguet—where he concludes:

To look into oneself is to disappear into the half light, or into illusion, to enter the labyrinth. Introspection which is both necessary and impossible, has a tragic side that God alone can unravel, since He is the only One who sees the depth of being in its transparency. (211)

These remarks help to explain why the seventeenth century offers no autonomous self-portrait situated between the *self-portrait* (as a salon game) and the religious or metaphysical meditation where the empirical self is transcended. But Rousset's perspicacity here shows all the more conspicuously the limits of another remark: "Introspection demanded the dramatic monologue: such are the soliloquies of *La Princesse de Clèves*" (211). In fact, the monologue-soliloquy relation (the second term implying a split of the subject who says "I") remains lame so long as one is unaware of the rhetorical context and, consequently, of the traits peculiar to meditative discourse, which was equally important in France as it was in England during the seventeenth century. Theological *Augustinianism* is in fact the ideological content of a specific rhetorical form, and each testifies, in its sphere, to a cultural mutation for which the notion of *introspection*, being vague and anachronistic, is inadequate. The collaboration between a "character" in a novel or play and his "creator" appears to us rather as a variant of the "interior dialogue" with the Word, where the reader, placed in an overhearing position, is nonetheless the secondary addressee of persuasion. This is why the seventeenth century did not give rise to the modern novel's "interior monologue," which, according to Rousset, "implies the disappearance of every witness: both author and reader are presumed absent" (212) On the other hand that century did produce a reverse variant of the self-portrait which serves as a relay between Augustinian confessions and the modern split subject's endless self-analysis.

This relay is meditation—for which the soliloquy of the *Confessions*, addressed to God, remains the allocutory model. But meditation is likewise self-persuasion and follows a coded itinerary marked by places and images analogous to those already discussed in reference to Loyola's *Spiritual Exercises* and may in fact be directly derived from them, as is the case for all meditators with Jesuit training.

Commenting on a work by an English Jesuit, Thomas Wright, *The Passions of the Minde in Generall* (this is one of several books anticipating Descartes' *Traité des passions*), Sloan underscores the allocutory situation peculiar to the meditative soliloquy:

The applications of this stance are very profound as they reveal a striking shift in rhetorical theory—from that "looking outward" of the classical tradition to a new "inward dialogue." The communicator, especially one faced with no tangible or easily visualized audience, such as might be the situation when he is preparing his arguments for publication in print, was in effect being shown through the art of meditation how to speak in this solitude, how to address an audience by placing them in a third-person, overhearing relationship while he himself addresses now God, now the divisiveness within his own soul. ("Rhetoric and Meditation: Three Case Studies," 51)

Sloan's comments here bear on a passage from Wright that is a direct echo of chapter IV, Book X, of the *Confessions*, where Saint Augustine discusses the usefulness to his readers of his self-portrait:

Wright: Give me leave O God, to vent out and evaporat the affects of the heart, and see if I can incense my soule to love thee intirely and [incessantly], and that alle those motives which stirre up mine affections to love thee, may be means to inflame all their hearts which read this treatise penned by me.[25]

If Augustine's *Confessions* foreshadow the meditative soliloquy which, it is often overlooked, invaded literary space in the seventeenth century, Loyola's *Spiritual Exercises* attempt "the technical elaboration of an interlocution, i.e., a new language that can circulate between the Divinity and the exercitant" (*Sade, Fourier, Loyola*, 44). It does seem that the emergence of the spiritual—as well as profane—soliloquy accompanies and reveals radical upheavals at the core of the rhetorical system, such as, for example, function shifts comparable to the foregrounding and emptying out of *memory* in Book X of the *Confessions*. In meditation, the placing of the reader in a third-person position as well as internal dialogue have, among other effects, that of *foregrounding* both text and book, which no longer are, as in the "normal" rhetorical regime, intransitive and allegedly nonexistent, that is, copied, without anyone being the wiser, from the situation prevailing in an oral culture. The "communication" between encoder and decoder gets confused or, at any rate, complicated, since the typographical medium and rhetoric itself become part of the message. A new discursive, typographical, and bookish economy is set up under the cloak of a subjective practice, and of a "psychologization" of literature.

Certain consequences of this transformation of discursive economy have been described, many times, from the psychological or ontological point of view: critics see there the birth of the "interior dialogue" or, more generally, of the speaker's "self-awareness," the birth of the modern psychological subject. But the rhetorical approach allows the consideration of those scattered phenomena as variants of a structure, and therefore permits the comprehension of facts that used to seem aberrant or idiosyncratic, since the analysis remained captive to interiority's primacy and indebted to psychological discourses on introspection and sincerity. By expanding Sloan's remarks on religious meditation during the seventeenth century, one is better able to grasp how the self-portrait sets itself up as a transformational variant of ancient rhetoric. This is owing to a series of systematic transgressions made possible by the disruption of interlocution and persuasion that belatedly resulted from the generalization of typography during the Renaissance. Persuasive rhetoric can now pivot on its own axis, as it were, and reverse itself, as Sloan indicates:

Although it has borrowed numerous procedures from traditional rhetoric, including the doctrine of logical arguments, of similitudes and disposition, and above all the use of the passions, meditation is just the opposite of rhetoric insofar as it fosters self-awareness, rather than an awareness of the audience. ("Rhetoric and Meditation: Three Case Studies," 49)

"Just the opposite"—in principle, then, the difference is reduced to an inversion of signs: if one takes into consideration the fact that meditation's speaker, while not having any manifest persuasive design regarding his reader (since his addressee is God or himself), nevertheless manages to stir an addressee undesignated by the soliloquy and in third person (the type of audience that could not exist for classical rhetoric, which supposes the face-to-face encounter of addressor and addressee), one understands how the whole rhetorical edifice of persuasion comes undone and is then rebuilt according to an unprecedented configuration.[26]

Meditation (like the hollowed out Augustinian self-portrait) does not emerge *ex nihilo:* it is built upon the parts of rhetoric which, having been turned away from their civic, political, and collective purposes, undergo a metamorphosis—from now on, the topics of invention and memory serve as a matrix for a discourse that is oriented toward knowing the speaker's "interiority." As for the *passions:* whereas in classical rhetoric the passions were targets at which were aimed the arrows of persuasion, in meditation and self-portrayal the passions become the places to visit according to a coded procedure in order to strike them out or exalt them, as comes about in certain self-portraits, or quite simply in order to *describe* them, if the self-portrait, moving still further away from rhetorical persuasion and the imitation of Christ, relinquishes any self-persuasive design, and thus becomes the description of the "private interior" of an individual, an "imaginary self," a "memory," or a "character." The meditative soliloquy sets out on yet another course: it becomes a dialogue between the layers of a complex writing, the questioning and erasure of a primary, imaged discourse by a dialectical metadiscourse, which in turn becomes the object of another discourse . . . since God and Holy Writ no longer provide it with either an abutment, or a guideline, or a hermeneutic crib.

By turning away from the anguish inherent in the Augustinian and christocentric model—the anguish of incommensurability, of grace, of interpretation—the meditative soliloquy does not, for all that, quite elude anxiety. Since visiting the places and describing them is not enough, enunciation becomes split between several agents, and is caught in a game of doubles. A dialectic is set in motion about the very meditative process. Writing questions itself about its own legitimacy from the moment that self-persuasion for salvation's sake no longer motivates it.

Between a primary, object discourse and the metadiscourse that feels its way and seeks to persuade itself of the validity of undertaking to write about the self, with no other purpose than to know the self in the process of writing, profane meditation sets out once more in quest of a transcendence (the certitude of the Cartesian *ego,* for example) or of a sacred sphere that keeps concealing itself beneath memory's hieroglyphs.

Even when secular meditation attempts to forget its rhetorical and spiritual filiation by giving itself referential justification, even when, seeking in the topography of the external world places likely to arouse or soothe sentiments and passions, it turns into a *reverie* and (rural or urban) promenade, meditation's topical structure and regime of self-persuasion bring back to the fore the discursive constraints and spiritual exigencies encoded in the matrix of Renaissance religious meditation.

Meditation and Reverie: Rousseau

The affinities between Rousseau's "reverie" and religious meditation have not escaped notice. Marcel Raymond, for example, mentions the Ignatian *composition of the place* with respect to the *Confessions* and *Rêveries,* but he does so only to emphasize Rousseau's antirhetorical liberty:

Out of an exceptionally particularized "local memory" there springs forth poetry . . . Beyond all rhetoric or form that one has learned, things are to all intents drawn from the ephemeral to the eternal. And Rousseau *needs* to fix them in detail, to "compose places," to apply his mind entirely to the recreation of this closed world, which has the homogeneity of some dream visions. (*J-J Rousseau: La Quête de soi et la rêverie,* 54–55)

This is a commentary on a passage from the *Confessions.* But Raymond also writes: "The 5th promenade first presents us with a composition of place" ("J-J Rousseau et le problème de la connaissance de soi"). Thus, the critic seems equally aware of a genetic relation among the *Rêveries,* Loyola's *Spiritual Exercises,* and local memory, although he is determined to preserve Rousseau's originality and liberty.

In his excellent introduction to the *Rêveries,* Jean Grenier in turn detects a significant contradiction in Rousseau's terminological hesitation:

One is struck by Rousseau's loose use of words: promenade seems the same as solitude, solitude as reverie, reverie as meditation. It is particularly surprising that he should liken the latter two. A "meditation" has always been an exercise that was regulated, sometimes by conventional rules (as in every religion), sometimes by an author's self-imposed rules (as in philosophy). Saint Augustine meditates. Descartes meditates. So does Malebranche. They direct their thoughts, in an orderly fashion, around a mystery or problem. In Manresa, Saint Ignatius composed a spiritual exercise manual that includes meditations as far removed as possible from personal caprice. (18–19)

In principle, then, Rousseau's meditation-reverie would be opposed to spiritual as well as metaphysical meditation. But Rousseau also asserts that his and Montaigne's aims are opposed to each other: "He wrote his essays solely for others; and I write my reveries for myself alone" (37). Jean Grenier has little difficulty in exposing Rousseau's error or in showing that the opposition, if any, is not on the plane of the allocutive relation to others. On the basis of "De l'oisiveté ("Of Idleness"; *Essays*, I, VIII), Grenier notes that Montaigne "lets himself go, not along the thread of his reveries, but of his thoughts" (18). And, while Montaigne always remains in the human universe, Rousseau consigns us "to nature's magic." This amounts to saying that, while Montaigne's topical system is made up of moral places, Rousseau's constitutes a series of topographies, of compositions of places, in a word, of country walks or promenades.

Rousseau's loose use of words is not without precedent: in Montaigne before him the word *essay*, adopted for want of something better, belongs on the formal level to a paradigm of desultoriness: fantasy, grotesque, piecemeal, medley, timber, fricassee, rhapsody, hodge-podge, and so on. And Bacon will not hesitate to suggest that *essay* and *meditation* are synonymous in the title of his own collection, the essays of which, it is generally agreed, are deployed in a somewhat disturbing "disorder." But meditation follows neither the order of logical reasoning nor that of persuasive dialectic: its order is fundamentally that of "place composition."

Certainly, one can distinguish meditation from reverie as Marcel Raymond does in his essay entitled "Rêver à la Suisse," by resorting to etymology, psychology and metaphysics.[27] But Raymond fails to formulate a formal opposition between these two genres and, therefore, to circumscribe the rhetorical specificity of the *Rêveries* as texts that "compose places."

The paradigm—solitude, promenade, reverie, meditation—can also be receptive, if one takes each of these terms in a broad and figurative sense, to the term *essay*. But, in a strict and technical sense elaborated during the Renaissance and the seventeenth century, meditation is opposed, because of its epistemological and ideological function, to the promenade, the reverie, the essay: the aim of the *religious meditation* is to make the meditator conform to the incarnate divine model, whereas *metaphysical meditation* seeks a *method* that ensures access to universal and permanent truths. In both cases, the imaged and individual approach is aimed at a transcendent, unique and normative truth. On the other hand, the essay, the promenade, and the like, mimic a mind's vagabondage in individual *opinion* and are valuable only for their fidelity to the impulses of a soul, a mind and a body *en situation:* the impulses of *this* stroller, of *that* essayist, each with his idiosyncrasy. In this connection, Jean Grenier mentions secularization: "It is probably with Rousseau that the first secularization of meditation occurs. It had already, with the Cartesians, passed from the religious to the metaphysical plane." At any rate, *secular* should be understood in the sense of "nontheological," "nondogmatic," or, even, "nonnormative." If the *Rêveries* speak of God, he is neither the God of Abraham, nor Christ, nor even the philosophers' divine clockmaker, but a deity who is responsive to Jean-Jacques' feelings and gives itself to him in the impulse through which Rousseau attempts to answer the question "Who am I?": I know what my God is in the measure that I know myself. Christian meditation, on the contrary, is a search for christomophism by the ways of self-denial and imitation of the Other: and metaphysical meditation, striving to surpass subjective error and doubt, reaches for the certitudes of reason which faith guarantees.

In the *Rêveries*, Rousseau claims to be a recluse who "in this world no longer [has] fellow-beings, nor fellow-creatures, nor brothers" (34). This is a way of saying that he no longer has to search for universality, or for conformity to the model of anyone else, even the God-Man. Rousseau addresses himself to no one: an extreme position where rhetoric no longer has any function, since, having attained the perfection of his being, he seeks neither to confess, nor to exhort, nor to convert himself. It remains for him only to describe himself, to tell of his conformity to himself, and to assert his nondifference from this model.

For this reason, Rousseau's meditation does not differ from reverie or from the essay—which, with Montaigne, presents itself from the start as an approach toward the entelechy of the subject and as an anti-imitation of others. Rousseau's promenade-meditations will wander not towards the places of collective memory (the Stations of the Cross, for example), but towards those of his past happiness—which, nevertheless, are scarcely distinguishable from the *stations* of his own passion. *Rêveries*, as text, *imitates* the delirium of an actual daydream: it is a reminiscence, rather than the actuality of reverie. Imagination has become *anamnesis* rather than creation—that is, immediate and mute pleasure. Rousseau realizes that from now on he is a prisoner of the cave; but he is somewhat the richer for this fall, since the Lethean waters have not washed out all his memories. From their depths he has acquired the possibility of writing his *Rêveries*, which we understand to be *The Imitation of Jean-Jacques by Rousseau*, or the worship of an ancient self, of a self from before the Fall and the Resurrection.

Having once been too vivid and clouded by "the contemplation of the object that animated it" (39), imagination prevented writing about reverie, for "remembering this state brings it back, and not feeling it any more, one would soon forget it" (40). But imagination having grown cold, an interruption of pure and silent repetition results. Reverie must in some sense die, so as to be reborn in writing: its resurrection incorporates into it a *nothingness*, without which consciousness and description cannot arise.

This birth of nothingness—where, in the *Rêveries*, the *art* of local meditation will be exercised—is told in parable form in the Second Promenade, which is in fact the first *walk*. Thus, the *Rêveries* open upon a euphemistic death and upon an awakening, where the virtuality of all local meditation is inscribed already.[28] For this awakening's ecstasy will be described and localized: it in fact establishes the possibility of *recognition*. If, at the outset, the "What am I?" and the "Where am I?" are not uttered for obvious reasons, the text's continuation modulates these questions and attempts to answer them. But, perhaps this well-known passage from the Second Reverie should be cited once again:

I came to life at that instant: it seemed to me that every object I perceived was filled with my light existence. All absorbed in the present moment, I recalled nothing; I had no distinct notion of myself, not the slightest idea of what had just happened to me; I did not know who nor where I was; I felt no pain, no fear, no unease. (43)

One usually stresses the pure "feelings of existence" evoked. But one should read on. Before long, this amnesic, bodiless, placeless newborn without identity, this pure selfless existence, will utter the ritual "Where am I?" and, orienting itself, acquire both an identity and a suffering body. It is also going to recover a memory of a particular type—linked to death and metempsychosis. No longer merely the memory that enabled the narration of a story, the writing of a confessional autobiography, but precisely the memory of euphoric reverie and, to begin with, the memory of pure existence without self-reflexive consciousness. Resurrection at last permits the mimesis of those privileged moments when one enjoys "Nothing outside oneself, nothing but oneself and one's own existence; as long as this state lasts one is, like God, sufficient onto oneself" (Fifth Reverie, 98).

Thus Rousseau, in this little death, gained the nothingness he lacked, the necessary negativity with which to describe the divine state. If he has stopped being God, or "like God," now at least the *Rêveries* can be written. From now on, Rousseau will meditate on the places of his own divinization and Passion. Like every self-portraitist, he has become a meditator composing his own sacred places and identifying himself discursively, through invention, with a hero who is, of course, none other than himself, but who appears to him *in figura: ECCE HOMO.*

More resilient than Jean Grenier supposed it to be, meditation still does comport a generic memory where, even when it is metamorphosed into reverie and the subject's quest for himself, its religious origin remains visible. A meditation can be atheistic, atheological, and anti-Christian, still the place of God and Christ is always there, as in the hollow of a mold. The man of meditation is never "free," if one understands freedom as a kind of ontological and cultural tabula rasa. Faithful or a renegade, no matter, he will always be a disciple of Augustine, Loyola, and the Christian tradition. Each in his own way, such modern self-portraitists as Nietzsche, Leiris, Laporte, or Barthes will confirm this paradox inherent in the genetic link of the self-portrait to meditation. These relations will be disclosed and foregrounded in what Maurice Barrès significantly called "the cult of the ego."

Barresian Meditation: A Free Man

When Loyola's *Exercises* are transformed into a method to generate, examine, and cultivate a Self, the result is *Un Homme libre*, a book that, however, poses a problem when it is being considered in the perspective of the self-portrait. For, manifestly, it claims to be a novel, a fiction whose anonymous hero (later named Philippe, in a prefatory note to its sequel, *Le Jardin de Bérénice*) does not explicitly identify with the author in the actual text.[29] Yet, in all that is *essential* (the "restoration" of Loyola's method, the meditation in chapters on Lorraine and Venice), one is led to believe that the author speaks for himself. And the last lines of the *Examination*, where *I* refers to Maurice Barrès, confirm this identification:

Reflecting sometimes on what I had most loved in the world, I thought that it was not really some man flattering me, nor even a woman in tears, but Venice; and there, though I find its canals unwholesome, I became very fond of the fever that overcame me, for it expanded clairvoyance until my deepest unconscious life and my psychic life were so intermingled as to give me an immense store of pleasure. (485)

In *Le Culte du moi* (and especially in *Un Homme libre*) we find a set of places that, after having cross-checked them, we can affirm to be indeed the privileged places Barrès's fantasies and memory so favor that he deploys them throughout his oeuvre. But can a *novel* be a self-portrait? For want of a "self-portrayal pact," the question will have to remain moot.[30] And yet, in a sociocultural perspective, the question implicates the problem of genres, as the sole means of clarifying why the label *novel* is pasted on every work that publishers find "unclassifiable."

Un Homme libre raises further questions that, while they concern the self-portrait in general, are most often brought up in connection with Montaigne's *Essays*. The reader identifies with the subject who is describing himself: a secondary narcissism is invested in the portrait, which, in turn, serves as a mirror in which the reader, not content with re-cognizing himself, *knows* himself through what the self-portrait reveals. While it is difficult to explain this very general phenomenon by a simple "coincidence" or the empirical fact that, across the centuries, many readers have "resembled" Montaigne, on the other hand the fortune of *Le Culte du moi* among the "youth" of the 1890s can be ascribed essentially to the fact that Barrès had found in himself, and projected in his "novels," a composite picture of the introverted young bourgeois of the period.[31]

Likewise, in Leiris, one might see the typical traits of the twentieth-century French intellectual, which coincide with many of his readers' characteristics. While it is difficult to refute empirically this sociopsychological hypothesis in the case of recent self-portraits because we lack social and historical detachment, it no longer seems applicable to Montaigne's oeuvre, nor, a fortiori, to Saint Augustine's. One can then but suppose that this identification, or this revelatory function, has been so permanently encoded in the self-portrait that it prompts the reader (regardless of his historical situation, social position, and psychological makeup) to repeat (at least partially and tentatively) the course and efforts of the self-portrayer. Paradoxically, Barrès seems to have deliberately implemented this constraining code in a context where freedom and individualism are extolled.[32]

When he adopts Loyola's *Spiritual Exercises* as a model, Barrès takes possession of a machine that loses little of its productive power by being diverted form its primary function. *Un Homme libre* reveals the procedure that turns meditation away from its religious aims and, enlisting it in the service of the secularized individual, engenders what Barrès calls "self-cultivation."[33] This was the second major attack against the arts of discourse during the modern epoch: the first was launched by those Renaissance religious thinkers (with Loyola as their foremost representative) who transformed rhetorical devices, which had been designed to persuade others within a given political and cultural context, into spiritual meditation. Barrès gives the game away: his genius (since *Un Homme libre* can pass as a important milestone in the revelation of the codes governing the modern West's discursive practices) consists precisely in having brought to light the deep structures of introspective discourses since the Renaissance. The two attacks evoked above should, however, be considered synchronically, rather than successively, as the two sides, one religious, the other secular, of a rhetoric that, although subjectivized (transposed into the innermost conscience), was initially worked out and designed for exchanges in the public forum. The awareness inscribed in Barrès's text is not limited to the functional role of the meditative method in the production of the Self. Barrès is led by his discovery to perceive the role of the commonplace in Western man's self-representation: he will not stop until he is on the verge of discovering the individualized subject at *homo rhetoricus*. This last realization was reserved to Freud, who, after he had wrapped it once more in neurological, economic, and energetistic metaphor, finally buried it in his topics of the unconscious.

Un Homme libre, which is brutally opposed to the dominant positivist philosophy and introspective psychology of the period, brings to light *discursive* determinations as far removed from racial, environmental, and circumstantial determinism as they are from Bergsonian idealism's vaporous and evasive freedom.

Whence the paradox of freedom in Barrès: no sooner is it proclaimed in *Le Culte du moi* than it annihilates itself in favor of geographical roots, nationalism's collective clichés and the passionate cultivation of the commonplaces of a historical community. In the years of the Third Republic, the cult of the *self* can easily be turned into the cult of France: for example, in Ernest Lavisse's standard elementary textbook *L'Histoire de France*, we are presented with a popularized, childlike and, therefore, more easily perceptible model for repressing an aristocratic and cosmopolitan individualism.[34] *L'Histoire de France* and Loyola's *Exercises* have an analogous function: in both cases the images of *savage* and centrifugal individualism are replaced by a series of good images articulated throughout an exemplary destiny: Christ's Passion or France's mission. The mutation that takes place in Barrès's oeuvre after *Le*

Culte du moi is a *normalization*, for the epithet "rootless" then comes to designate anyone whose imaginary system of *places* deviates from the norm and whose identity is defined in terms of shortcomings or excesses.

Philippe, in *Un Homme libre*, makes up for these shortcomings through *play*, refinement and excess: he is well aware of the constraints imposed by the norm: they produce "barbarians." It is characteristic of the self-portrait to displace barbarism (savagery) from the periphery to the center: savagery and culture, these two symmetrical, alternate temptations to return to one's position and escape from it articulate the reveries about the within and the without. Both these tendencies soon appear to the self-portraitist as antithetical utterances produced by a single cultural grammar, which is so constraining that only the strenuous work of writing can warp it, even if this would only force it to produce playful hyperboles. Such is the perspective in which one can understand this paragraph by Barrès:

> Why would this mechanicalness of Loyola arouse the indignation of philosophers? Is it not thanks to such associations of ideas as have become instinctive in most men that one can at will spring human mechanisms? Utter this or that name before those who are most ignorant, you will see every one of them experiencing identical sensations. To everything scattered in the world, public opinion has attached a determined manner of feeling, which it does not allow anyone to change very much. . . This is the mechanism that all cultures impose on a humanity almost always unaware of the fact that it is being taken in. And you would blame me when, by an analogous and, at least I am aware of it, equally artificial method, I exercise my wits to acquire perfected emotions! (189)

Barrès, then, asserts that his method is a *game*, one that he can stop playing before destroying himself. The deliberate perversion of Loyola's *Exercises* for hedonistic purposes, the writing of a series of witty meditations on Benjamin Constant and Sainte-Beuve (on Baudelaire, also, in an earlier version of the text in question), and the ironically tinted transposition of a Jesuit retreat (with an almost burlesque flavor echoing the antics of Flaubert's Bouvard and Pécuchet), this comes under the heading of play or of an introspective adolescent's game. But isn't it also—as implied by subsequent stages in Barrès's career—the kind of game that plays with the player? Isn't this game the kind of play that is bound to subsist between the elements of a vast cultural machinery, a play that allows one to move parts about, but not to get rid of them at will? When Barrès invokes a state of nature, a nonplace that, with complete freedom and in full awareness, he would transcend to play at meditation and cultivating the Self, isn't he, in turn, like the philosophers whom he denounces, the victim of a delusion? Like all other self-portraits, Barrès's text reveals a high degree of misprision with regard to its rhetorical matrix.

Un Homme libre, then, develops the virtualities that play has to offer. Barrès even presents his book as the rules of a game: if the reader wishes, he may, in turn, play according to these rules. Every reader of *Un Homme libre* is urged to work out his own freedom, to produce his own text according to the artificial and impersonal method derived from Loyola's *Exercises*. The "play" resides in this paradox.

The playfulness of *Un Homme libre* is first visible in the unusual choice of themes for meditation and composed places (the nondescript Lorraine village where Philippe and Simon settle down for their retreat, Philippe's "fin de siècle" predilections for the Riviera, Milan, and "off-season" Venice); there is further play in the humorous hyperbole that occurs in the meditations; play results, finally, from the suggestion inserted in the "dedication" that the course of events described in the book is only one "hand" (as this is called in the game of bridge) among others that would give rise to a multitude of variants: the cultivation of the self passes itself off as a refined game, an idle pastime, rather than the consequence of a moral imperative or psychological necessity.[35]

Because of its playful enlargement and hyperbolic indifference, *Le Culte du moi* implies a radical critique of the quest for the self, which, for the self-portrait, always becomes a lure and a mirage. It transgresses the imperatives of a God-centered contemplative life as well as those of an active life oriented towards other people and the world. But, instead of opening onto freedom, this transgression merely discloses the existence of a machine: the player who knows that he is playing is the only one who is not taken in. The written self is revealed to be a cultural artifice rather than the transcendence of a free subject.

In *Un Homme libre*, the self is defined by the Other. Negatively, at first, by the barbarians—to distinguish oneself from them is an infinite game with multiple hazards—and then, positively, by one's ancestors, by those whose race and places render an instant—the span of an individual life—limitless. Whence the recourse to metempsychosis:

This I say: an instant of things, no matter how beautiful one might imagine it, could hardly interest me. It is my pride, my plenitude, to conceive them in the form of eternity. My being enraptures me when I see it spreading over the centuries, developing itself through a long train of bodies. (274)

Here, then, clearly stated by Barrès, is the paradox that haunts, more or less distinctly, all self-portraits. To fill the irreparable gulf opened in the self-portrait by the death of the individual, there is only the survival of the places, things, and works of art visited by the writer as he threads his way through his invention. Contrary to what one might have naively supposed, it is the pictures, the towns, the museums that confer on the spectator their immortality as works of art:

I am but an instant in the long development of my Being, just as the Venice of this epoch is but an instant in the Venetian soul. My Being and the Being of Venice are limitless. (274–75)

It should, therefore, come as no surprise that *Un Homme libre* proves to be a kind of Baedeker whose two main sections, Lorraine and Venice, follow each other according to a progression borrowed from theology, Lorraine being the Church Militant while Venice is the Church Triumphant. In both cases, it is a question of opening the describer as far as the limit of being that these two places can bestow. So, Lorraine, after it has provided a gloomy exaltation, will be left behind:

Lorraine, you were for me a more powerful mirror than any of the analysts in whom I used to contemplate myself. But, I have touched your limit, Lorraine; you have not come to fruition, you have gone dry. (236)

To which Lorraine replies in a prosopopoeia:

set before you your presentiment of the better, and may this dream be a universe, a refuge, for you. This beauty is imaginative, you can inhabit it.

You will be my embellished *Self:* the Spirit Triumphant after having been, for so long, the Spirit Militant. (237)

Thus, Venice turns out to be a transfiguration of Lorraine or, rather, its superlative within a paradigm of cultural places that serve the self as "powerful" revelatory mirrors: "in the soul of Venice I contemplated my Being, enlarged and nearer to God" (275).

Rather than analyze in detail the extended metaphor through which the Being of Venice, a composite of sites, monuments, and works of art,[36] reveals the Being of "Philippe," one should perhaps consider the question of the death masks which Venice places at the disposal of the modern self-portraitist when his undertaking seems to him to be empty and impossible:

Venice, after Tiepolo, had only to put its catalogue together. Nowadays it is totally absorbed in self-excavation, in exploiting each of its epochs: these are provisions for one's death. (283)

This follows the previously cited passage. The sequence clarifies the metaphorical function of the Venetian place, overdetermined as it is by the cliché of the mirror of Venice, with its stereotyped semantic components—death throes, the archaeological catalogue, the testament, the monument: "These are provisions taken for one's death." Venice, precisely because it is a dead, or dying, city, plunges the individual who contemplates himself in its mirror into the immensity of a collective memory. Consequently, by providing the writer's invention with a host of cultural commonplaces inscribed in a reality that has already become a legend, it can also provoke in him a kind of fleeting euphoria, and grant him a flash of lucidity analogous to a drowning man's anamnesis. If, as in Jean Roudaut's *Trois villes orientées* and Jules Vuillemin's *Miroir de Venise*, the writer takes Venice as a global metaphor for his self-portrait, then he contemplates himself in death: he conjures up a double that is his death.[37] In this manner does the self-portrait of Western man frozen in the monumental mirror of his culture culminate; here ends the testamentary gesture that was inscribed by Montaigne from the moment he opened his *Essays* and addressed himself to the reader. When, through the Being of Venice, one attempts to expand, totalize, grasp one's proper Being, when one brings forth "all the virtualities tormenting themselves within me" (277), spreading them out in the space of Venice in order to achieve self-divinization while in full possession of oneself, then one reaches the end of humanist anamnesis and the invention of its end. By acting as though theological notions, or religious practices, could be diverted to secular aims, by playing the game of imitating Jesus Christ, by dreaming on behalf of man and the individual of a totality previously vested in the divinity—no doubt this humanistic writing has used up all its illusions and Barrès's book becomes a game on the edge of the abyss. Barrès emerges from it no more divinized than was Nietzsche when he played at being Antichrist or when he mimicked the *Ecce Homo*. Of course, later on, Barrès did come down to earth in order to manipulate those who did not share his superior irony, though, indeed, not in order to transvalue all values: this normalization, however, in no way affects the exemplarity of *Un Homme libre*, where modern literature, pushing to the limit the destinies that link rhetoric to Christian meditation, becomes the tomb of both and their monument, which it ironically calls a *self*.

But the vestiges of this self, or of this humanist literature, still had to be broken up; and writing can only achieve this by becoming a paradoxical poetics, by reaching the limits of its forgetfulness of the rhetorical and meditative machine. Having *exhausted* cultural memory, literature can mumblingly attempt to go back to square one, or it can toll the knell of the subject, of philosophy, of learning. It then becomes an unsettled nostalgia, an uneasy oblivion within the very memory to which literature clings despite its misgivings.

PART TWO

From Memory to Antimemory

Salomon saith. *There is no new thing upon the earth.* So that as Plato had an imagination, that *all knowledge was but remembrance;* so Salomon giveth his sentence, that *all novelty is but oblivion.* —Francis Bacon, *Essays*, LVIII, cited by Jorge Luis Borges, as the epigraph to "El Inmortal," *El Aleph*, 7.

CHAPTER 3

Rhetorical Memory

The Aristotelian Theory

Rhetorical mnemonics is an art in ruins: the very memory of it has been blotted out of the consciousness of contemporary man. Rhetoric's adversaries, those modern "terrorists" whose antirhetorical ideology Jean Paulhan exposed, do not even attack rhetorical mnemonics, for they are unaware of its very existence;[1] no doubt this is also the last part of rhetoric that neorhetoricians from Valéry to Paulhan, from Chaim Perelman to Kenneth Burke would have deemed worthy of reinstating. And rightly so, for it is of no further practical use. Information storage and retrieval now probably are in the domain of computer science and biological theories, of electronic techniques far removed from the common practices of literature and rhetoric.[2] Collective memory is inscribed in archives, libraries or the "memories" with which we have equipped computers. But individual memory, now no longer, as in former oral cultures, the guardian of collective knowledge, has become the subject matter of irreconcilable discourses among experimental psychologists, poets, psychoanalysts, philosophers and anthropologists. Thus there appears, in André Leroi-Gourhan's *Le Geste et la Parole*, a hypothesis about the "freeing of memory" process (2:1–34) and "man's unique capacity to place his memory outside himself, in the social organism" (2:63–76). This hypothesis comes within the scope of a theory on:

the evolution of man, a living fossil in relation to his present situation, [who] resorts to pathways other than those of neurons to prolong himself. One notes, more positively, that man, to take maximum advantage of his freedom while avoiding the risk of overspecializing his organs, is led towards a progressive externalization of increasingly higher faculties. (2:75–76)

The invention of printing was, for Leroi-Gourhan, a decisive stage in this process.[3] Previously, "it is difficult to separate oral from written communication" (69). For us, his most significant remark concerns the use and material organization of ancient manuscripts as compared to that of printed texts, which was definitely fixed by the seventeenth century. "Ancient or medieval manuscripts contained texts designed to be impressed for life on the minds of the readers, at least firmly enough for their memory to find its way through them upon perusal." To evoke the manner of this orientation, Leroi-Gourhan makes fresh use of one of rhetoric's traditional metaphors designating the path followed through the places of invention:

During the many centuries that separated Homer or Yu the Great from the first Western or Oriental printed texts, the notion of reference did develop with the growing mass of recorded facts, but each particular writing is a compact series cadenced by signals and marginal notes, *where the reader orients himself along a track, like a primitive hunter, rather than according to a plan*. No one had yet found the way to convert the unwinding of the word into a system of orientation tables. (69, italics mine)

Leroi-Gourhan then studies the alphabetization of subject-matter, the development of indexes and tables of contents and finally alludes to the use of punched cards and electronic machines. Amazingly, in this study so rich in comparisons between memory's externalization and some general aspects of the invention of the machine, "artificial memory" is not mentioned at all, at least in any rhetorical sense, nor is there any consideration of how its decline was articulated with the externalization of memory after the spread of printing.[4] But this historical articulation is of the utmost importance, since the self-portrait appears as an always renewed attempt at reinternalizing memory and arresting man, as a writing subject, at a henceforth archaic stage in the evolution attributed to him by Leroi-Gourhan, that is, at the Renaissance, a stage marked by the production of dictionaries, thesauri, indexed compilations, and encyclopedias.[5]

In the area of pedagogy, for which rhetorical memory long served as a theoretical foundation and technique (being finally reduced to a mnemonics forgetful of its theoretical basis), the role of memory has continually decreased as pedagogic "terrorists" (Montaigne, though not their first, remains their most celebrated, spokesman) stressed the individual's capacity to reinvent knowledge and the wholesome benefits of both personal (re)discovery and "judgment."

A clear distinction was made in ancient treatises on rhetoric between natural memory, which varied with each individual, and artificial memory, and they dealt only with the latter as an art or *technè* reinforcing the natural faculty by a procedure (*ratio praeceptionis*) and training (*inductio*).[6] This art was indispensable for all orators—or for all who were literate, since during the centuries when rhetoric, and later on the trivium, dominated elementary and intermediate schooling, these terms were virtually synonymous. Jacques Derrida's analyses in *Of Grammatology* on writing's status at the core of Western civilization also seem to imply a reflection on memory as an artifice, natural memory being a mode of the "word that is full and fully present (present unto itself, its signified and other people, that is, fulfilling the conditions for the theme of presence in general)" (17), for which mode mnemonics would be a sort of *translation* and ancillary technique. Derrida's examination of the notion of technics in relation to writing seems to imply this:

Technics in the service of language: I am not invoking a general essence of technics which would be already familiar to us and would help us in *understanding* the narrow and historically determined concept of writing as an example. I believe on the contrary that a certain sort of question about the meaning and origin of writing precedes, or at least merges with, a certain type of question about the meaning and origin of technics. That is why the notion of technics can never simply clarify the notion of writing. (8)

But *Ad Herennium*, which is, of course, a much later source than Plato, establishes no explicit hierarchy between nature and art, though it implicitly reasserts that nature precedes art:

We shall discuss at greater length whether memory has some artificial quality entirely in nature [a promise that was never kept]. For the time being, I shall consider as proven that this is a realm where art and method are particularly important and shall treat the topic accordingly. (III, XVI, 28)

If mnemonics is a "supplement to memory," one should not interpret *supplement*, with respect to antiquity at least, in a pejorative or restrictive sense. Artificial memory is mental practice, and its recourse to exteriority ("inscription" of "images" against "background") differs from writing (despite the very widespread metaphor comparing artificial memory to a writing where backgrounds serve as tablets and images as characters) in that these backgrounds and places are never hypostatized or materialized, in ordinary usage, during the classical period. Such place and images "borrowed" from the outside world must be "present in the mind" of the orator to be efficacious. There is absolutely no material support to which, by right or in fact, they can be entrusted. Classical artificial memory is functionally integrated in a culture where orality is dominant.

But artificial memory undergoes certain vicissitudes which, although they are not parallel to those of writing, nonetheless pertain to the history of the sign. Derrida is right to underscore the fact that writing is alternately humbled and exalted within our tradition. What has been disdained is "writing in the 'proper' and ordinary sense, . . . 'sensible' writing, 'in space,' " as opposed to "the writing of truth in the soul . . . the book of nature and God's writ, particularly during the Middle Ages" (27). Then Derrida adds:

The paradox to which attention must be paid is this: natural and universal writing, intelligible and nontemporal writing, is thus named by metaphor. A writing that is sensible, finite, and so on, is designated as writing in the literal sense; it is thus thought on the side of culture, technique, and artifice; a human procedure, the ruse of a being accidentally incarnated or of a finite creature. (15).

One might perhaps write a history wherein there would be some play of analogous ambiguities, where artificial memory would be humbled—as a mnemonic technique[7]—or exalted when, taken in a metaphorical sense, it becomes a *clavis universalis*, an esoteric access to total knowledge—never more exalted than when mnemonic artifice is censured, as happens in literature from the Renaissance on—or when "natural" memory becomes an instrument not only "of the presence which, as presence unto oneself, as subjectivity, is absolute" (*Of Grammatology*, 29), but also of our culture's presence unto itself, of its interiority in history (the narrative of our past) and archaeology (the uncovering of buried, obliterated, strata). Humanism understood both as a historical anamnesis and as the construction of the subjective subject. One should, in short, inquire into the opposition that, following the collapse of artificial memory and coinciding with the voluntary forgetting of rhetoric, arises between voluntary and affective memory and, redistributing connotations, contrasts the former's dead letter to the latter's living spirit and breath. Thus, according to Jules Vuillemin, "I do not call memories the traces that objects leave in us, without moving us, the image of a bridge, of a square, of a picture, which does not awaken even an echo of what we were when it was imprinted upon us" (*Le Miroir de Venise*, II).[8]

While one leaves Derrida responsible for the proper sense/metaphorical sense opposition that tends to immobilize a distinction drawn for purposes of demonstration and, furthermore, that fails here to take into account the notion of the hieroglyph, and whereas his reference to an "accidentally incarnate Being" (Holy Writ) remains highly disputable, one has to agree that our culture's discourses on natural and artificial memory are trapped in ambiguities and that these are analogous to those provoked by writing. Nonetheless, there is no perfect overlap of relations between memory and mnemonics and those supposed to exist between the spoken and the written word. For, if writing's status as a technique is controversial, memory (to the extent that it is not reduced to writing) does seem to belong among the psychosomatic "techniques": *essentially* there is no difference between mnemonics and the natural memory it reinforces but does not translate or betray.

This is not the place for a fresh survey of the history and theory of mnemonic art, with its numerous and often strange detours. Several recent and accessible studies have accomplished this task: the reader can refer to them as well as to the textbooks of classical rhetoric that have been copied, paraphrased, and misunderstood thousands of times over the centuries.[9] A reminder of such traits of *Memoria* as can help us to understand the form and procedures of self-portrayal should suffice here.

The scientific bases of this imaged mnemonics are in Aristotle's psychology of memory, as set forth in *De Memoria et Recollectione* and *De Anima*.[10] Let us summarize:

1. Images are indispensable to thought: voluntary memory must therefore resort to images.
2. Remembrance proceeds along a course of sequentially inter-linked *places* that involve relations of similitude, opposition, and contiguity.
3. The order and regularity of the sequences facilitates recall;
4. Finally, memory and imagination are linked, both are grounded in the common sense, and they proceed according to the same dialectical development, by steps analogous to those of *invention*.

Backgrounds and Images

We must now examine the nature of the places and images, as conceived and codified by classical theoreticians of the art of memory.[11]

While theoreticians differ greatly in what they think about images, the way these are constructed, their function, and their meaning, they all agree on the principle that images become lodged in *places* and *backgrounds*. One metaphor returns constantly: the wax tablets, the papyrus, the parchment, or, finally, the paper on which characters are inscribed. But the places are a *permanent* support that lends itself to indefinite reutilization; the imaged "writing" can be effaced and replaced by another inscription. The backgrounds are fixed, whereas the images are temporary.

These *backgrounds* are almost always borrowed from a real, physically visitable building, of sufficiently vast proportions to furnish a large number of regularly spaced architectural elements suitable as frames or niches for images. Anyone wishing to acquire a series of mnemonic backgrounds with which to form an artificial memory has to start by a habitual and frequent ambulation among the detours of an edifice, a house, palace, basilica, cathedral, theater, even of a town. He must follow a fixed, round-trip itinerary in the course of which these *places*, with the intervals between them and their respective positions, are impressed in his natural memory. The mnemotechnician carries with him permanently, "in his head," an architectural or urban ensemble, to which he can constantly refer to store or retrieve the images that he has consigned to it. He is an edifice-man, a house-man, in short, a town-man.[12] And he is a stroller.

While these backgrounds are in themselves devoid of contents, while it is sufficient that they be varied, well lighted, and numerous, one cannot disregard the amalgam resulting ever since Antiquity from the use of the same words—*topoi* and *loci*—to designate both the "real" places of memory and the (metaphorical) places of invention and dialectic.[13] Whence a confusion—baffling, fruitful, and finally abolished by the triumph of the Romantic *imagination*, when a merger occurred between invention and memory, between the dialectical places indicating logical operations and the "cumulative" places disposed according to an order derived from the architectural model of memory. One notes a homogeneity, disconcerting to the modern reader, between the *thesaurus*, an edifice containing treasures, the *theatrum* that deploys encyclopedic knowledge, and the *compendia* which were sometimes called *encyclopedia* during the Middle Ages and Renaissance, or, more often, *speculum, tabula, synopsis*, and *methodus*. There is no solution of continuity between what pertains to collective knowledge, or encyclopedia, and individual memory; remembrance of ancient contents consigned to the collective or individual memory becomes confused with the discovery and use of new information, although the moderns have reserved the name *invention* to the latter operations. Furthermore, this lack of distinction between invention and memory in the rhetorical regime is such that it assigns no specific function to that tinkering with old and new that we call *imagination*. This refusal of difference, a tendency common to medieval thought and to certain aspects of the Renaissance (the hermetic or "Neoplatonic" Renaissance) causes feelings of claustrophobia in modern readers: it is a closed, harmonious, and tautological building riddled with analogy.

An analogical tautology also informs some anamnesic modern texts that present, locally or in their structure, certain traits of the self-portrait, yet give it the slip in other ways.

Butor: The Portrait of the Artist

Michel Butor's *Portrait de l'artiste en jeune singe*, for example, draws on the resources of *analogy*, in the esoteric sense. One would say that it is an entirely "bookish" analogy, combining fragments of alchemistic texts and "fabulous" narratives, the *Thousand and One Nights* or Jules Verne's Carpathian novels, with an evocation, in the fantastic register, of the liberal arts in a huge museum-library, except that it also includes the iconography of Renaissance chateaus adorned with mythological, allegorical, cosmographic, and astrological paintings.

A precious bric-a-brac of geological samples, of old alchemical and astronomical instruments is matched, according to astrological and numerological correspondences, with playing cards for solitaire and emblematics, in order to constitute the *images* of an artificial memory. The textual elements set forth during the narrative exploration of a library-chateau-museum and strange adjoining manors are repeated and transformed, as dreams, in seven interpolated stories. Everything fits together.

This itinerary is a prelude to the departure of the young artist or monkey scribe for an Egypt towards which he is ineluctably drawn by Father Athanasius Kircher's speculations on hieroglyphs.

This book can therefore be considered an archaeology of the writer's psyche:[14] the evocations of a moment of discovery as he emerges from a childhood already dazzled by an esoteric hodgepodge, a moment just before the break (metempsychosis) that will be effected by the voyage to Egypt. That it what the book's epigraph suggests: "It was before I left for Egypt, a very long time ago in my life, since Egypt was like my second birthplace, where I lived a second childhood so to speak." A coherent and secret, but far from undecipherable world of signs that answer one another and confirm in every domain, from nature, reduced to a lapidary museum, to musical harmony: here Butor constitutes his own oeuvre's myth of origin, always marked in both content and composition by a preoccupation with correspondences, numerology, analogy, and myth—a complex, meticulous, and closed tinker-toy.

But this is also an archaeological dive towards the esoteric Renaissance, which, from Paracelsus to emblematics, from Ficinian and Mirandolan magic to the architectural[15] and pictorial use of mystical and astrological allegory, and in its determination to find the *universal key* to immediate and absolute power, is a dream that still haunts the rationalist and scientific sequels of humanism and stocks with its images the twilight zones of the modern consciousness. Last of the great unitary constructions where a series of harmoniously distributed and tiered places correspond with one another to infinity, like the shelves of the famous library of Babel, this is the utopia of every writer seeking a transparent relation to the world, through signs and language, within an infinitely reversible duration.[16] This book of Butor's, which professes to be a *capriccio* and a modern version of the German Romantic tale, offers, then, the *prima materia* for a self-portrait: it is a "treasure-house" from which the author might draw images and the technique of *mise en abyme* (where, for example, the text reproduces itself in the pseudodream narrative) to invent a self-portrait. Yet, this is not a work torn by a conflict, since it comes from before (the second) birth and swims too happily in the amniotic fluid of universal analogy for *loss*, the fall into multiplicity, dereliction, and nonsense, to be inscribed in it. As a fairy tale, it evokes anxieties easily exorcised on awakening, old violence now mellowed and picturesque because distances: neither the poignant desire nor the torment of writing are decipherable here. The writer yet has to be born in his book, where he appears only in intaglio, like an expectation or a promise.

This book is then an embryonic self-portrait that does not pose the problems of writing as invention, of interiority as a lure and a cause of anguish, of the writer's solitude, or of the text as *memoria sui:* in this universe of the analogical imaginary everyone thinks he is Adam Cadmon, an inheritor of totality and immortal demiurge.

Michel Butor disperses and somewhat distances these problematics in the form of fiction and "critical" essays (*Essais sur les Essais*, among others). But Butor refuses to write an "I am alone here now" where the referent of the *I* would indisputably be Michel Butor: therefore, in the strict sense, he is not a *self-portraitist*. Yet, throughout his novels, essays, and other works, Butor uses techniques borrowed from the self-portrait. (So it is tit for tat when Michel Leiris writes a postface for *La Modification* in the "10/18" series.) On the whole, Butor's oeuvre can be read as an attempt to utilize the self-portrait's materials and techniques while avoiding being imprisoned by it; for he wants to make this *without*, which the self-portrait still was, the matrix of a new literature. It is easy to trace the genealogy of such new genres as Butor invents, beyond the self-portrait, back to the Renaissance's rhetorical and encyclopedic matrix, which is so often thematically evoked in what Georges Raillard calls the Book-Temple (postface to *L'Emploi du temps*). Thus, one is tempted to see in Butor's works a euphoric variant of the self-portrait, which, substituting itself for the former literature based on mimesis and plot, renounces the guilt, exile, and torment of self-portrayal; in short, Butor's oeuvre prefers the cultural and collective macrocosm to the individual subject's tormented microcosm. In this respect, it converges with Jung's psychoanalysis, also steeped in Renaissance esotericism and euphorically structured by the correspondence between the microcosm and macrocosm. It may therefore be worth our while to examine points of similarity between Butor's *Portrait* and chapter 8, (entitled "The Tower") of C. G. Jung's strange autobiography, which, like Book X of Augustine's *Confessions*, inserts elements of a self-portrait within an autobiographical narrative.

The Autobiography of C. G. Jung

The tale of the construction of the tower, the description of the circular central building with its annexes, the transcription of the epigraphs Jung himself had engraved on the stone, the narration of dreams (which are the pseudoanamnesis of an ancient historical past), and, in the course of some digging work, the discovery of the grave of a French soldier from 1799—all this serves to weave a network of necessary analogical relations. The site chosen, the structure of the buildings, and the writer's narcissistic image reflect the relationship of the psychologist with his ancestors, as well as the main themes (duality/unity, psychologization of alchemy, recourse to myth, to ritual, and the sacred, return to primitive ontogeny, etc.) of Jung's psychoanalysis. This preestablished harmony is clearly placed under the protection of a maternal presence:

> From the beginning I felt the Tower as in some way a place of maturation —a maternal womb or a maternal figure in which I could become what I was, what I am and will be. It gave me a feeling as if I were being reborn in stone. It is thus a concretization of the individual process, a memorial *aere perennius*. (*Memories, Dreams, Reflections*, 225)

The tower becomes "a symbol of psychic unity." The same movement that constitutes it as a cenotaph and analogon for the maternal womb makes it also a symbol of his own body and a body of Greco-Latin inscriptions.[17] As an intemporal or transhistorical "maternal womb," the tower, from which running water and electricity are banished, is a feudal castle as well as a primitive cabin. The epigraphs are fragments borrowed from the Presocratics, Homer, and medieval alchemists. Associations are established, along the narrative thread, among Wotan, Merlin, Paracelsus, Michael Maier, and Gerard Dorn, the Rosicrucians and the Freemasons, Goethe's Faust and familial Karma. Jung's chapter concisely gathers many elements which, from Montaigne to Leiris, are scattered through the self-portraits as the description exhausts the traditional tower sememes that form the metaphorical center and circumference of the Jungian psyche. Moreover, the metaphorical Tower extends well beyond all the limits of the conscious individual:

> At Bollingen I am in the midst of my true life. I am most deeply myself. Here I am, as it were, the "age-old son of the mother." That is how alchemy puts it, very wisely, for the "old man," the "ancient," whom I already experienced as a child, is personality No. 2, who has always been and always will be. He exists outside time and is the son of the maternal unconscious. (225)

But while this unity, won in the course of a contemplative return to the "old man," is capable of richly imaged developments (true, this richness is tautological and results from a purely rhetorical amplification), it can also turn into a cosmic solipsism:

> At times I feel as if I am spread out over the landscape and inside things, and am myself living in every tree, in the splashing of the waves, in the

clouds and the animals that come and go in the procession of the seasons. (225)

The Romantic symbiosis with nature, which recalls Rousseau's Fifth Reverie, is preserved here from any gap, from death, reabsorbed in intemporality, or from the splitting of the subject. There is no anguish here: the signifier adheres to the signified, the mode of utterance to what is uttered. Nothing in this maternal bosom comes to disturb the Swiss-style reverie of the "old man," like the biblical patriarch blessed in his ancestors, his herds, his house, and his descendants.

Euphoric texts such as those of Jung and Butor thus seem ineluctably regressive, involuted: they attempt to mimic poetically the historically, culturally, and ontologically outdated conditions under which the individual subject dissolves itself in a rhetorical network of which the analogical system seems to be a kind of ideological doublet. It engenders the "old man," immemorial son of the mother," and the brother of the neolithic man about whom Lévi-Strauss dreams, taking his cue from Rousseau. This is the utopia of the uncentered word, the Word whose circumference is everywhere and whose center is nowhere, which is reabsorbed into myth and the collectivity. Rhetoric, encoding the ideal conditions of linguistic exchange in a prescribal culture, offers an ambiguous mediation towards this vanished universe; it bears witness to our fall, which the self-portrait hopelessly attempts to redeem by its infinite darning of a very ancient topic.

Rhetorical memory's architectural places or backgrounds, which we first found to be empty, varied, and suitably spaced, have already been metamorphosed into an encyclopedia crammed with symbolic icons. We must now retrace our steps in order to examine how rhetorical mnemonics conceives of the distribution of places and the formation of the images used to store a discourse or to assemble an encyclopedia that will serve as a "treasure-house" for every possible invention.

Backgrounds and Images (Continuation)

We should recall the fundamental mnemonic metaphor: places are tablets, and images are a kind of writing. To deposit images in the places is to "write"; to retrieve them is to "read." According to Aristotelian psychology, iconic and visual images are the strongest and are durably imprinted in memory.

Rhetorica ad Herennium prescribes the use of *tableaux vivants* to stimulate the memory of both *words* and *things*. A less theatrical method, suggested by Quintilian, calls into play such iconic signs as an anchor to designate the *thing* navigation or a weapon for the martial arts. Since these texts are very obscure, perhaps A. R. Luria, the Soviet psychologist, can shed some light on them through the book he wrote on Shereshevsky, a contemporary mnemonist. Shereshevsky seems to have reinvented for his personal use the techniques of the ancient *Ars Memoriae*. Luria presents Shereshevsky as a case, a misfit, almost a monster.[18] Perhaps, born in the twentieth century by mistake, he is but an avatar of the ancient rhetorician. Like Luria himself, Shereshevsky is completely ignorant of the classical *Ars Memoriae* and its transformations during the Middle Ages and Renaissance. But his practice suggests— as do, for that matter, modern self-portraits—that ancient mnemonics can be spontaneously reinvented. It imposes itself, in all its details, upon certain exceptional individuals, so much so that eidetic memory and synesthetic correspondences tyrannize their psyche and their relations to the world, marginalizing them in contemporary typographic and electronic society.

Whence the hypothesis that the essential processes of artificial memory (and, consequently, of the self-portrait), to wit, the utilization of *backgrounds* and of *images* placed in these backgrounds, correspond to a transhistorical mental function. But the ideology and the practical imperatives of our culture, at a given historical moment, favor, repress, or channel this imaging memory for diverse purposes. It is transferred or forgotten, sprouts pragmatic or esoteric variants, reappears more or less distorted in the Renaissance's magical encyclopedism and the modern self-portrait in response to specific cultural needs. In the contemporary period, the first effect of the gift of *Memoria* is to isolate certain individuals in a marginality that is both alleviated and reinforced by the practice of literary self-portrayal. One may wonder whether this function (like, in other instances, the trance, glossolalia, possession) was not often highly developed among adults in antiquity, given the fact that the dominantly oral culture provided a favorable ground for it to flourish; on the other hand, *Memoria* seems to suffer from true functional repression during the modern period. This would help to explain the playful (parlor games, music hall numbers) or esoteric (mystic analogy, "correspondences") character of its sporadic reappearances during the Romantic and contemporary periods. One should note besides, that this repression is accompanied by a dissociation, for as a rule the ludic use of artificial memory retains only the backgrounds and images, whereas esotericism stresses synesthesia and the notion that images "are like a writing," to the detriment of the local system.

Images, Analogy, Synesthesia

Since the Renaissance, the notions of *correspondences* and *analogy* have been indissociable from belief in a natural divine "writing." Schelling still echoes Renaissance esotericism (Paracelsus and Cardano, for example) when he claims that "what we call nature is a poem in secret and mysterious signs." To this cliché Baudelaire's friend, Esquiros, proposes a variant: the forest is "a vast church" where the tree "speaks to the soul of poets" (*Les Chants*, 1841). And l'abbé Constant (alias Eliphas Lévi), a grand master of esotericism during the nineteenth century, published a poem entitled "Correspondances" (*Les Trois harmonies*) in 1845, where the world is conceived as God's dream "formed with visible words."[19] But the belief in a divine writing, supposed to be Nature or inscribed in nature, a writing that anyone possessing its code could decipher and that man could imitate—either by a poem or by any other mimological process, such as the "hieroglyph" as it was imagined to signify before Champollion—is linked to the desire, very widespread during the seventeenth and eighteenth centuries, to set up universal languages, "real" tongues, presumed to facilitate communication among all men and to vest magic power in those who were fluent in them.[20]

According to James Knowlson (who refers to Rossi, Yates, and De Mott),[21] the question of a universal or philosophic language is closely connected with artificial memory, not only because the mnemonic value of the "universal" or "real" "character," *per se,* would be such that it could improve or replace ancient mnemonics, but especially because of the elaboration of a universal idiom with tables and classification systems that facilitate lexical taxonomy and distribution according to logical and semantic categories, like genus, species, and so on. This "real character," through the coding of its distinctive features, was supposed to allow classification of a given character (and its signified) in its proper category. Such a taxonomic disposition was also supposed to facilitate grouping of characters according to semantic affinities and to permit rapid progress from the general to the particular, and vice versa, during logical operations. But the system adopted by certain creators of universal languages to distribute their lexicon was directly copied from artificial memory's system of places (city, street, house, etc). This is the case in Sir Thomas Urquhart's *Ekskubalouron* (1652), where the words of the lexicon are distributed

into so many cities, which are subdivided into streets, they againe into lanes, those into houses, these into stories; whereof each room standeth for a word; and all these so methodically, that who observeth my precepts thereanent, shall at the first hearing of a word, know to what City it belongeth, and consequently not be ignorant of some general signification thereof, till after a most exact prying into all its letters, finding the street, lane, house, story and room thereby denotated, he punctually hit upon the very proper thing it represents in its most special signification.[22]

If artificial memory furnishes creators of "real language" with a classification system (or "method" in Ramus's sense), which, at this level at least, shows no esoteric or magical traits, the ambition of these mimologists may also bring them closer to the Lullian tradition and, according to a frequent Renaissance amalgamation, to the Cabala. Lully had attempted to constitute a "universal art," a key with which to understand the Universe and the Creator, founded on a combination of letters representing the divine attributes, to which all reality could be reduced. And Rossi and Knowlson also show that all the authors interested in universal languages and real characters were familiar with Lullian logic, even when, like Bacon and Descartes, they pretended to disdain it.

From Lullism to Renaissance hermeticism (whether expressed through alchemistic and astrological emblematics or by a passion for "hieroglyphs," as in John Dee's *The Hieroglyphic Monad*) and even up to (especially Jungian) psychoanalysis and (particularly Breton's and Leiris's) surrealism, one observes, if not a true "tradition," at least a partial transmission of a semiotic and analogical system utilized in some self-portraits, such as, for example, Cardano's *De Vita propria* or Leiris's *Manhood*.

We are therefore dealing with two distinct branches of a single semiotic current: artificial memory subdivided into the system of places and images, and hermetic analogy. These two branches overlap sometimes in text and iconography: this happened during the Renaissance and, more recently, in psychoanalysis and surrealism. Regardless of the ideology that appropriates them and their assigned function in each context (encyclopedia, scientific discovery, psychology and therapeutics, magic, poetry), eidetic memory and synesthesia are the two psychic faculties on which these semiotics are based. Without any ideological reinforcement or apprenticeship whatsoever, they can sometimes impose themselves on someone. Shereshevsky's spontaneous mnemonic exploits, which provide us with a clearer understanding of obscure points in the ancient rhetorical manuals, would seem to offer proof of this hypothesis.

Shereshevsky and Ad Herennium

We will therefore attempt, with the help of Shereshevsky and Luria, to understand the most difficult aspects of artificial memory, as set forth in the *Rhetorica ad Herennium* and in Quintilian's *Institutio Oratoria*, without losing sight of our purpose, which is to clarify the relations between mnemonic semiotics and the literary self-portrait.

We find very strange some of the ancient manuals' prescriptions concerning the dispositions and especially the *lighting* of *backgrounds*. Contrary to modern beliefs, they seem to postulate that imaginary vision and perception are governed in every detail by the same optic laws and "consciousness." While it is easy to grasp that the backgrounds must be *varied* in order to avoid confusions, still it seems aberrant to insist that their dimensions should remain fixed: it matters little to us whether the eidetic imagination presents us with "lifesize" images or scaled-down models. Yet the ancient author writes:

And these backgrounds ought to be of moderate size and medium extent, for when excessively large they render the images vague, and when too small often seem incapable of receiving an arrangement of images. (*Ad Herennium*, III, XIX, 213)

Eidetic images lend themselves only to certain imaginary manipulations: their resistance is analogous to that of "real things," and they likewise suffer insurmountable spatial constraints. Although we are dealing with images here, they are definitely not those of an imagination or imaginary in the modern sense. This is confirmed by the following sentence: "Then the backgrounds ought to be neither too bright nor too dim, so that the shadows may not obscure the images nor the lustre make them glitter" (213). If the backgrounds are permanent and, as a rule, borrowed from real places whose disposition and details have been recorded *in situ*, the images, on the other hand, when they derive from specific perceptions rather than an "imaginary" synthesis or abstract process producing iconic signs, are "deposited" in these backgrounds at another time according to the orator's specific and ephemeral needs. How then could these images be swallowed up in light or penumbra? Are the mnemic traces so vivid that the lighting operates in memory as it does in the world of the senses? *Ad Herennium* does not treat distortions or interferences, errors or pseudorecollections produced by memory's elaboration, but rather voluntary eidetic configurations subject to optic hazards similar to those that deform perception, precisely as if memory did not distort images.

As for active images (*imagines agentes*), supposed clear and distinct, their baroque grotesque and melodramatic character strikes us as uselessly excessive, and the profusion of eye-catching and picturesque details that they require seems quite mad. The two examples given in *Ad Herennium* offer an extraordinary excess of imagery, more apt to confuse a modern mind than to facilitate recollection. The orator should make these images of "exceptional beauty or singular ugliness; if we dress some of them with crowns or purple cloaks, for example, so that the likeness may be more distinct to us; or if we somehow disfigure them, as by introducing one stained with blood or soiled with mud or smeared with red paint . . . or by assigning certain comic effects to our images" (III, XXII, 221). All this in order to encode simple enough contents (or *res*), or utterances that would seem easy to learn by heart. This plethora of personages, accessories, rebuses, synesthetic approximations (even if a modern mind could manage to pile them all up in an imaginary scene), this transitive and ephemeral masquerade, seems a waste of psychic energy, especially since the examples cited in the manuals are minuscule compared to the imaged material that the orator must utilize to remember a single discourse, let alone all the speeches of his career. Mnemonics seems on the whole just as uneconomical as the disguises achieved, according to Freud, by the "dream work." The recommended method for retaining the words of a single line of a tragedy is the strangest example of recourse to a muddle of heteroclite and proliferating visual images. Take, for instance, the verse: "Iam domum itionem reges Atridae parant" ("The Atridae kings are preparing to return home now"):

If we wish to remember this verse, in our first background we should put Domitius, raising hands to heaven while he is lashed by the Marcii Reges— that will represent "Iam domum itionem reges" ("And now their homecoming the kings,"); in the second background, Aesopus and Cimber, being dressed as for the roles of Agamemnon and Menelaus in *Iphigenia*—that this will represent "Atridae parant" ("the sons of Atreus, are making ready"). By this method all the words will be represented. But such an arrangement of images succeeds only if we use our notation to stimulate the natural memory, so that we first go over a given verse twice or three times to ourselves and then represent the words by means of images. In this way art will supplement nature. (III, XXI, 217)

Although we learn in Caplan's notes to the Loeb edition that Domitius stands for a plebeian *gens* while the Rex are a family of the aristocratic Marcian *gens*, which explains the power relations pictured here, and although we know that Aesop was a famous tragedian, with whom Cimber probably acted on stage, still the process remains mysterious, for the theatrical representation is but contingently related to the sense of the verse in question, and the phonetic encoding is only very approximate. We are willing to admit that Roman orators proceeded in this manner but would be hard put to reproduce their practice on the basis of these incomplete indications.

In the memory of things (*res*), the transposition seems less arbitrary, for it rests on an incipient conceptualization or abstraction, and phonetics do not intervene. One can judge from the following example, where the object is to recall the circumstances of a criminal poisoning. The alleged victim, against a background, is represented by someone well known to the orator lying on a sickbed: "and we shall place the defendant at the bedside, holding in his right hand a cup, and in his left tablets, and on the fourth finger a ram's testicles. In this way we can record the man who was poisoned, the inheritance, and the witnesses" (III, XX, 216). Even if we know that *testiculi* suggests *testes* (witnesses), this does not seem particularly helpful. Did the prosecution and defense at Rome really resort to such complex procedures to encode such simple circumstances? Or was the example hastily contrived for this manual? Did orators spawn multitudes of *Grand Guignol* playlets and picturesque accessories? It seems unlikely, and yet Shereshevsky's method, which he worked out independently of classical mnemonics, is surprisingly similar to the procedure recommended by *Ad Herennium*, so much so that his interviews with Luria enable us to fill in hypothetically of the lacunae of the ancient manual.[23]

Shereshevsky's technique is, in principle, very simple: it consists in transforming any utterance—whether or not it is intelligible to the mnemonist (apparently this does not matter)—into a series of images with an eidetic dominant; these images are then distributed over a sequence of places or backgrounds. The most striking example, in the context of a comparison with *Ad Herennium*, concerns the subject's memorization of a text in a language unknown and, therefore, unintellible to him: the first stanzas of *The Divine Comedy*. According to Luria, the reproduction was perfectly faithful, even in its pronunciation and the placing of tonic accents.

The text was read aloud to Shereshevsky, who only asked that the words should be pronounced distinctly, with a brief pause between them. Here are the poem's first lines:

Nel mezzo del cammin di nostra vita
Mi ritrovai per una selva oscura
Che la diritta via era smarrita
Ah quando a dir qual era e cosa dura . . .

Fifteen years later, Shereshevsky recited the text to Luria, and described his technique as follows:

(*Nel*)—I was paying my membership dues when there, in the corridor, I caught sight of the ballerina Nel'skaya.

(*mezzo*)—I myself am a violinist; what I do is to set an image of a man, together with (Russian: *vmeste*) Nel'skaya, who is playing the violin.

(*del*)—There's a pack of Delhi cigarettes near them.

(*cammin*)—I set up an image of a fireplace (Russian: *kamin*] close by.

(*di*)—Then I see a hand pointing toward a door (Russian: *dver*).

(*nostra*)—I see a nose (Russian: *nos*); a man has tripped and, in falling, gotten his nose pinched in the doorway (*tra*).

(*vita*)—He lifts his leg over the threshold, for a child is lying there, that is, a sign of life-vitalism. (46)[24]

Shereshevsky's technique seems analogous to the method recommended in *Ad Herennium* for the memorization of a line from a tragedy in Latin (the Roman orator's mother tongue). In both cases, the mnemonist practices a *semanticization of the signifier* that brackets both the *signified* of each word and the meaning of the syntagm as a whole. By a procedure resembling a *rebus*, the signifier is transformed into a succession of eidetic elements combined to form *pictures* (Nel'skaya and the violinist; the man with the squeezed nose lifting his foot to step over the child). Yet, one notices that the transformations may be more or less elaborate. On the first level: *cammin—kamin*: fireplace. But, why, and how, does Shereshevsky retain only the first syllable of the name *Nel'skaya?* All that remains of the pack of cigarettes is the brand name (*Delhi*), reduced to its first syllable. And the figuration of the child lying across the threshold introduces, in this context, an altogether unexpected degree of abstraction or allegorization (*vitality*). One also notes approximations: *vmeste* for *mezzo*, *dver* for *di*. What compensates for these approximations, and how are the excess phonemes eliminated? Luria's protocol and Shereshevsky's report are as mute on these matters as is *Ad Herennium*. But, according to reliable testimony of the Soviet psychologist, the system allowed a perfect recitation of the Italian text after a fifteen-year interval.

One must distinguish between two kinds of *places* pertaining to the process of recall used by Shereshevsky. First are the *real* places, which, as elements of the pragmatic context of encoding, allow the pertinent sequence to be selected from among analogous sequences. In this sense, *place* means a complex sensorial and synesthetic context, which includes the interlocutor, his voice and clothes, as well as the respective position of the persons present, the setting, the atmosphere, the tonality of surrounding sounds, odors, lighting, and so on. *Place* designates here something analogous to the contextual ensemble that provides the stimulus in the Proustian type of involuntary memory, except that with Shereshevsky the process is triggered at will, and there is nothing epiphanic about it. On the contrary, he seems condemned to experience a plethora of little *madeleines* and uneven paving stones.

But *place* also means *background* (in the rhetorical sense). *Place* is then opposed to *image*. The images are distributed throughout a sequence of places borrowed from referential space, independently of the specific context in which the sequence has been encoded. Luria describes as follows the encoding process for a long list of disparate lexemes:

When S. read through a long series of words, each word would elicit a graphic image. And since the series was long, he had to find some way of distributing these images of his in a mental row or sequence. Most often (and this habit persisted throughout life), he would "distribute" them along some roadway or street he visualized in his mind. Sometimes this was a street in his home town, which would also include the yard attached to the house he had lived in as a child and which he recalled vividly. On the other hand, he might also select a street in Moscow. Frequently he would take a mental walk along that street—Gorky Street in Moscow—beginning at Mayakovsky Square, and slowly make his way down, "distributing" his images at houses, gates, and store windows. At times, without realizing how it had happened, he would suddenly find himself back in his home town (Torzhok), where he would wind up his trip in the house he had lived in as a child. The setting he chose for his "mental walks" approximates that of dreams, the difference being that the setting in his walks would immediately vanish once his attention was distracted but would reappear just as suddenly when he was obliged to recall a series he had "recorded" this way. (31–32)

Shereshevsky's systems of backgrounds, which can be read in either direction, are therefore analogous to those used and recommended in the ancient rhetorical manuals. But a striking difference should be noted: while the orator's backgrounds are permanent, stabilized once and for all, protected from all surprises, Shereshevsky may jump unexpectedly from Gorky Street (belonging to his adulthood space) to the town and house where he spent his childhood. He thus dizzily spans the distance separating the place systems of *ars memoriae* (in principle devoid of affect, alien to desire and individual nostalgia) from those often deployed and considered in the works of modern self-portraitists. Shereshevsky thus leaps without warning from Cicero's practical world, where the backgrounds system is a simple and arbitrary mnemonic tool, to the imaginary universe of Leiris and Borel. But, unlike the latter, he deposits in these backgrounds and retrieves from them images that are indifferent, transitive, and effaceable at will. Suspended between the *dwelling* (that which, according to Jacques Borel, *dwells*), the town of his adulthood (curiously marked by literature in its toponymics: Gorky Street, Mayakovsky Square, Pushkin Square), and his lists of heteroclite and syntaxless words, Shereshevsky never achieves the status of a self-portraitist. He is not a *writer*, and his inexhaustible supply of building material for a self-portrait remains there, as it were, waiting for someone to put it to some use.

But the very richness of Shereshevsky's sensorial impressions, which produced the synesthesias peculiar to each background and image, sometimes provoked interferences within a plethora of sensations that slowed down his recording and complicated his professional mnemonist's task. This overabundance also complicated Shereshevsky's daily life, especially his readings, for he was unable to eliminate at will the extraordinary proliferation of synesthetic associations provoked by the polysemy of poetic language.

Within the scope of his professional practice, Shereshevsky therefore perfected a system of iconic abbreviations relatively devoid of affect. Instead of forming detailed and "realistic" *imagines agentes*, he managed to constitute iconic and conventional images. "Say I'm given the word *horseman*. All it takes now is an image of a foot in a spur . . . I try just to single out one detail I'll need in order to remember a word" (42). The procedure is close to what Quintilian recommends: "Let us suppose a sign derived from navigation as, for example, an anchor: or from warfare as, for example, a weapon" (*Institutio Oratoria*, XI, II, 17–22). This is likewise close to the "pictographic" procedures employed by certain American Indian or African tribesmen to record songs, proverbs, and events, according to iconic images more or less strictly coded and, sometimes, undecipherable except by the one who formed them for his own use or for the use of such of his acquaintances as were apprized of the encoded meanings.[25]

Besides, one should draw an important distinction between Shereshevsky's iconic images and those to which they have just been compared: the professional mnemonist concentrates all his efforts on remembering the *words*, not the *things* (*topoi*, *loci*), whereas Quintilian's icons and "pictographs" encode generic notions or complex events.

But outside his professional practice—for example, in his recollections of childhood—Shereshevsky's memory can also play with the complex polysemic evocations attached to images and words. Certain remarks on the synesthetic images induced by *words* in the context of a child's world reveal rich associations which, though they do not amount to an entry in a synesthetic encyclopedia, manifest nonetheless striking affinities with the practice of self-portraitists—and with that of modern lyric poets. Shereshevsky evokes, for example, the network of recollections and associations, both semantic and synesthetic, suggested to him by the Russian word *zhuk*, which means *bug:*

A *zhuk*—that's a dented place in the potty . . . It's a piece of rye bread . . . And in the evening when you turn on the light, that's also a *zhuk*, for the entire room isn't lit up, just a small area, while everything else remains dark—a *zhuk*. Warts are also a *zhuk* . . . Now I see them sitting me before a mirror. There's noise, laughter. There are my eyes staring at me from the mirror—dark—they're also a *zhuk* . . . Now I'm lying in my crib . . . I hear a shout, noise, threats. Then someone's boiling something in the enamel teakettle. It's my grandmother making coffee. First she drops something red into the kettle, then takes it out—a *zhuk*. A piece of coal—that's also a *zhuk* . . . I see them lighting candles on the Sabbath. A candle is burning in the holder, but some of the tallow hasn't melted yet. The wick flickers and goes out. Then everything turns black. I'm scared, I cry—this is also a *zhuk* . . . And when people are sloppy pouring tea, and the drops miss the pot and land on the plates, that's also a *zhuk*. (Record from September 1934)

Luria is correct in noting that these memories, through which the signified of a word is extended by association (in the paradigm of harmfulness and darkness), are typical of childhood and ordinary experience. Other connotative networks are more allusive and overdetermined:

Take the word *mama*, or *ma-me*, as we used to say when I was a child. It's a bright haze. *Ma-me* and all women—they're something bright . . . So is milk in a glass, and a white milk jug, and a white cup. They're all like a white cloud.

But, then, take the word *gis* [Yiddish: pour]. That came up later. What it meant to me was a sleeve, something trailing down, long, the stream that flows when people are pouring tea . . . And the reflection of a face in the polished surface of a samovar—that's also *gis*. It glistens like the sound *s* . . . But an oval face is like a hand in a sleeve slowly lowering to pour tea. (Record of September 1934)

Shereshevsky thus resorts to synesthetic associations that evoke fragments of familial scenes. The first descriptive system covers the paradigm of anguish provoked by a gap or a foreign body; the second bathes in a fostering and maternal plenitude. The mother's presence or absence is articulated with the—euphoric or painful—specularity. Shereshevsky differs little from Barthes, who states less concretely that the "imaginary" is constituted "through the Mother, present next to the Mirror" (*Roland Barthes by Roland Barthes*, 153). These "memories" are analogous to those already taken into account by Leiris, when he wrote *Manhood*—for example, in the meditation on the word *suicide* (7). But Shereshevsky's memories are documents in the rough, devoid of the artistic elaboration that amplifies, interprets, and links memories together, as with Leiris, Barthes or Borel, when they integrate them within the typical structure of the self-portrait.

Shereshevsky's example, therefore, provides us with a counter-proof: the self-portrait is neither memory nor mnemonics (even if certain traits of both appear in its structure and the details of its *invention*); it is a book, the present of writing. It elaborates upon the local or fragmentary structure and upon the encyclopedia that totalizes it: the system of cross-references, the text's internal memory and coherence, as well as its faults through which the *simulacrum* of a self can be shaped (and above all, undone). It also refers constantly to cultural memory, to mythologies, to literature; it is a relationship to history and language. There is no Shereshevskian universe—or self—for *other people*. In Luria's book, we are dealing with a clinical protocol, just as rich—just as poor—just as foreign to literature as are other cases reported by psychologists. Such cases can bring further scientific glory to those who have set them down and analyzed them, but they cannot guarantee the immortality of those whom they discuss. Shereshevsky's case reminds us of the writer's exorbitant privilege: the self-portrait is not a memory, with which everyone is endowed in some measure, but a machine to perpetuate the present of writing after death of the one who remembers. And Shereshevsky's memory could not die in writing, and thus survive death. For him, *the middle of the journey, the dark forest*, remain a dead letter: he did not succeed in grasping the symbolic hint that Luria, no doubt unwittingly, offered him in an unknown language. A memory among so many others, not the opening of a *vita nuova*. He remains stuck in his house, and his mind is but a vast warehouse, a file cabinet that no project puts to work.

Global Metaphors: The Drawer, the House

"Let us not stop at the labels on drawers, even if many people confuse them with the fruit of science" (Lacan, *Ecrits*, 620). And yet, without drawers or labels, that is, without an encyclopedic topical system, there is no self-portrait, for this metaphor is as central to self-portrayal as it is to rhetoric: it links memory to invention.

The "drawer" metaphor, as applied to rhetoric, is a late stereotype. It reduces rhetoric to a bag of tricks and signifies the disdain of the one who uses it. When it resurfaces, in a variant, as a *card file*—for example, in Leiris, who knows nothing of rhetoric—this metaphor signals the return of the repressed through the contemporary ideology of spontaneity and fortuitous order.

As a result, Roland Barthes may even present himself in his self-portrait as an index-file man. Under the heading "Daily Schedule" (84–85), he narrates a typical day in the country, with alternate moments of writing and reading, *farniente* and tinkering about. A twofold tinkering: "I make myself a reading stand, a file, a paper rack," and "I listen to music and take notes" (82). But this euphoric activity characterizes him as "belonging to a class." Whence the wish for an *atopia*, the antithesis of the file:

Pigeonholed: I am pigeonholed, assigned to an (intellectual) site, to residence in a caste (if not in a class). Against which there is only one internal doctrine: that of *atopia* (of a drifting habitation). Atopia is superior to utopia (utopia is reactive, tactical, literary, it proceeds from meaning and governs it. (49)

Indexed-indexer: the dual status of the self-portraitist and intellectual is sketched in these exemplary fragments, where the classified-classifier produces a text while pacing his cage: rhetorical invention.

Gaston Bachelard, in *The Poetics of Space* (19), reactivated the drawer metaphor; but, in this study, he contrasts the *drawer*, as well as furniture with drawers—commodes, wardrobes, and filing cabinets—to the house. Drawers are miniature houses.

It is in "Du Bellay: Poète du retour" that Jacques Borel first formulates the function of the *house* as a system of memory places, and as a global metaphor capable of structuring a self-portrait. Reading the *Regrets*, which is itself a rewriting of Ovid's *Tristia*, Borel manages to articulate loss with the desire for a *return*, unwriting with writing. It is clear to any reader of *Le Retour* that the *Regrets* foreshadowed Borel's undertaking. As with all the self-portraitists who regret their childhood, efforts to recapture lost time often are a thwarted and depreciated motive for writing, ashamed as the writer may be, of his attempt to return to the maternal bosom. Barthes will succeed in deflecting this motive by making it part of his book's iconography. But the regressive sentimentality exculpates itself by producing the excuse that it appears only in the pictures, in the interstices of the text.

Yet, Barthes does *write* about his childhood house:

That house was something of an ecological wonder: anything but large, set on one side of a considerable garden, it looked like a toy model (the faded gray of its shutters merely reinforced this impression). With the modesty of a chalet, yet there was one door after another, and French windows, and outside staircases, like a castle in a story. (8)

This paradoxical house, vast and minuscule, simple and bizarre, is the very model of the place where one may imagine oneself a happy child. The description of the three gardens modulates this variety in unity, which should be understood as a metaphor for the nostalgic self-portrait: "The worldly, the domestic, the wild: is this not the very tripartition of social desire?" (10). This statement is both underscored and euphemized by the parenthetical remark: "The house is gone now . . ." One suspected as much: henceforth, the childhood house belongs to the imaginary, to the book's memory and its semiotic system. The house enters the self-portrait (this applies to the town, too) when it has disappeared or is about to disappear, its disappearance already as good as accomplished. Thus it is with Venice, a dead but still dying city, a ghost town. Similarly, the late house of the self-portrait haunts a writer exiled in his writing and who is losing any hope of returning.

Jacques Borel already suggests this apropos of Du Bellay's *Regrets:*

The *house,* such is the deep, whether expressed or implicit, theme which organizes the whole architecture of the *Regrets.* Both the hearth and the thin smoke exhaled by it—revealing it and, one would say, dispersing, ravishing it at the same time—the homeland, the land of birth, the secret and deep origin, childhood, the air one breathes, the language of the living and humus of the dead, the living heart of memory: absent and everywhere present at the core of the work, it is the fundamental image towards which the wrenched and orphan soul feels itself invincibly drawn back. (625)[26]

But Borel is well aware that this "living heart of memory," situated at the "core of the *work,*" is a system of backgrounds, a support, or a scene that induces images. Moral and "psychological" places join with it to constitute an encyclopedia of the topics of invention, precisely what a self-portrait would resort to:

Around it, as though summoned, induced, by it, is established and radiates all the imagery, the entire thematics of the *Regrets,* the voyage and return, the long wait, the sorrowful experience, age, lost time, absence, the feeling of being a foreigner, exile and the shore, the sea, the port . . .

An always incomplete enumeration: one sees how other places or images might easily be added to or be substituted for the above, provided that the sememes of break, absence, aging, and return are included.[27]

The mnemonic system of the childhood house and the sort of invention it induces are not as euphoric as they first seem: abundance is eaten away and neutralized by an irreparable loss. For example, Borel's *copia,* like the one recommended by Renaissance humanists, is not so much a triumph of eloquence as the sign of the impossibility of *return.* Nor does Barthes, cutting it short by falling back on photographic images, elude the snares of what he pejoratively calls the *imaginary:* he only spares himself from modulating to infinity the poignancy of the impossible return. By evoking castration and the symbolic, Barthes refuses to transform the tomb of writing into a long regret. When, in *Roland Barthes by Roland Barthes*, he opposes the house (which classifies him and assigns him a place) to the desire for an *atopia* ("the habitation adrift" [53]) where a sememe of maritime vagabondage is opposed to a rooted terrestrial sememe, Barthes inverts the values informing Du Bellay's *Regrets* or Borel's *Retour;* but he does not go beyond them. For they are indelibly inscribed in the chosen places.

House and card file are homologues as *containers* (each also containing the other) but they differ in contents: the house is "the house of men," the receptacle for hidden things: "To anticipate on the phenomenology of things hidden," writes Bachelard, "a preliminary remark will suffice: an empty drawer is *unimaginable*. One can only *think* it. And for those who, like myself, must first describe what they imagine, before what they know, what they dream before what they verify, all wardrobes are full." The "phenomenology of imagination" links up spontaneously with the metaphorics elaborated throughout the centuries by rhetoric. If rhetoric was a learned discourse on communication, eloquence, and "psychology," it was also, in its metaphorics, a vast reverie on houses and towns, the hearth and civilization. Bachelard sees in the house "a *tool for analysis*" of the human soul" (xxxiii), and he asserts that "the things we have forgotten are 'housed' " (xxxiii), that "the unconscious abides" (9); one understands more readily why rhetoric resorts to the domestic topical system. The places of memory and rhetorical invention are isotopically related to those of Bachelardian "topo-analysis." Rhetoric seems to rest on the tritest of metaphors: "our soul is a dwelling place," "the house of things." Yet, rhetorical places do not only metaphorize the intimacy of the house in the narrow sense of a private dwelling place and an inviolable domicile; they also designate the collective space of the city, the forum and the basilica: the within and the without are imagined there in terms of a *political* community. Whence the necessity of contesting Bachelard's overly intimist choice. Of course, for the purposes of analysis, one is justified in privileging metaphors of integration, retreat, solitude: the image of the house as "topography of our intimate being" (18), as a matrix of "snugness." This is the metaphor of a rhetoric deprived of its vocation to persuade other people—in short, a rhetoric of meditation. In Bachelard, the without and the within are opposed, as the privacy of the house is opposed to all that is not in it; he neglects the opposition between the city and the barbarians, between the *polis* and what is external to it, which is the basis of classical rhetoric. If rhetoric proposes the image of a "human soul," this is first and foremost the image of a collective soul, a network of exchanges, forces and powers, the macrocosm of a historical society rather than the microcosm of an individual subjectivity. Leiris's self-portrait, for example, will repeatedly treat this shift thematically by using places that belong alternately to his own imaginary topography and to the community's imagination: myth, the history of France, and the biblical stories children are taught, the common denominators of a culture.

One recalls that Flaubert's Bouvard and Pécuchet, attempting to recall historical "facts" and "dates," resort to mnemonics. They elaborate a method (derived from early nineteenth-century mnemonics) that is burlesque to the extent that it combines several disparate systems that are all, however, rooted in the classical tradition. They prescribe the setting up of a system of backgrounds in which images will be "deposited":

For greater clarity, they took their own house, their domicile, as their mnemonic basis, attaching to each of its parts a distinct fact, and the only meaning retained by the courtyard, the garden, the surroundings, the whole countryside, was that of facilitating memory. The stone field boundaries limited certain epochs, the apple tree were genealogical trees, bushes were battles, the world became symbol. They searched on the walls for loads of absent things, ended up seeing them, but did not remember the dates that they represented. (*Bouvard et Pécuchet*, 149–50)

As familiar places can serve to support historical knowledge, history itself or, at any rate, an elementary textbook of French history, can in turn become the system of places that sketches the space of a "home" or, rather, of a *homeland*, where it is demanded of each child that he leave behind him the particularities of his own home, in order to reach the topical system of his national culture, which erases local and individual differences. All these devices find their way into the self-portrait, and contribute to its ambiguity between self and selflessness.

Thus, if there is any discourse where artificial memory has left a trace, it is in self-portrayal, where the subject of writing is foregrounded. Moreover, the self-portrait often takes memory as its theme, and, while it may ignore or challenge its own rhetorical origins, the reader is reminded of them despite the self-portrayer's intentions. Before the house, the palace, the town, or even a sequence of engravings, pictures, and so on, become metaphors of "interiority," they are treasure houses of invention and supports for memory. One therefore often notes a coincidence between the deployment of spatial backgrounds and the order of presentation of themes (topoi), between the remembered "things" or words and the dialectic of the reflection in progress. The *intro-spection* or *circum-spection* effect results from this superimposition: the self-portrait is first of all an imaginary perambulation through a system of places, around a depository for memory-images.

This homology between a system of places and memory, long ago postulated by rhetoric, was independently confirmed by the sociologist Maurice Halbwachs. In his essay entitled *La Mémoire collective*, he rediscovered, perhaps unwittingly, the theoretical foundation of local memory.[28] Halbwachs's analysis of the role played by "the stones of the city" in forming and preserving a culture's "collective memory"—which he opposed to written history —leads him to a meditative conclusion that sums up his thought on the spatialization of individual and collective memory:

Let us now meditate, close our eyes, go back in time as far as possible, concentrate our thought as much as we can on the scenes or persons still in our memories. We never get out of space. Nor, furthermore, are we in some undetermined space, but in regions known to us or which we know full well that we could locate, since they are always part of the material environment where we are today. . . . So it is not true that in order to remember one's thoughts must carry one out of space; on the contrary, only the image of space, because of its stability, creates for us the illusion that we never change as time passes and that we recapture the past in the present; but this is indeed how one can define memory; and space alone is stable enough to endure without aging or losing any part of itself. (167).

This primacy of space over duration in memory encounters strong resistance from the modern writer and reader, for whom the "spatialization" seems to violate "life" or transcendence, so that there is an attempt to deny or blur as soon as possible the mnemonic and inventive topical system which models the self-portrait. Thus, in a recent study on Montaigne, Frederick Rider notes:

> But even if we accept that Montaigne's essays are essentially his composite self-image, it is no simple matter to unfold that image for study. For one thing, it is an image of change, and we must translate its spatial arrangement back into temporal terms. (*The Dialectic of Selfhood in Montaigne,* 29)

The urgency of our desire for temporality, diachronic intelligibility, and evolution is perhaps, in the final analysis, the major obstacle to the study of the self-portrait, whereas autobiography, with its reassuring narrative thread, offers a credible mimesis of life envisaged as progress transcending spatial contingencies. But contemporary poetics facilitates the understanding of rhetorical spatialization and spares us the wasted effort of *translating* the spatial into narrative terms, which in any case would yield only a tissue of misconceptions. The topical system of the self-portrait, its mnemonic and encyclopedic structure, the procedures of its invention can be expressed only in terms of space, and this may well be the grounds of their paradoxical modernity, as Gérard Genette suggests:

> Nowadays literature—thought—can speak of itself only in terms of distance, horizon, universe, landscape, place, site, paths and dwellings: naive but characteristic figures, quintessential figures, where language spaces itself out so that the space in it, having become language, may be spoken and written. (*Figures,* 108)

Of course, this linguistic "space" is both the space of writing and the one that, since antiquity, has been expressed through the stereotyped comparison between local memory and wax tablets. But his space is above all that of the book, particularly of the printed book, which allows either a permanent stability of the text, or its deliberate modification, throughout successive editions, by addition, deletion, and self-reference: no doubt, at the dawn of typography, Erasmus's *Adages*, with their multiple printings and expansions, offered a model for the staging of becoming within the space of a book. Montaigne's *Essays* present us with a more familiar and more relevant example. The *Essays* manifestly thematize an *amnesia*, as well as a rejection of rote knowledge and mnemonics, which typography in fact rendered obsolete. In the *Essays* this rejection is offset by the elaboration of a "memory of the book" which is inherent in this (non-narrative) topical disposition, in its malleability and singleness, since Montaigne opted for the obstinate revision of a single book rather than the production of multiple opuscules, as was the ordinary practice during the scribal epoch.[29] The writing of the *Essays* engenders its own memory by foregrounding, in the course of successive editions, its corrections, pentimenti, and additions, so much so that it can be said, without punning, that Montaigne's book introduces a bookish and typographical variant of the Augustinian *memoria sui*.

CHAPTER 4

Intratextual Memory

Montaigne's Essays

When reading Montaigne's *Essays*, one cannot fail to be struck by
the abundance of remarks relative to memory. At first these statements seem divisible into two categories: some deplore, or at least
affirm, the self-portraitist's exceptional amnesia, whereas the others brutally oppose two faculties that were habitually conceived of
during the Renaissance as having a complementary relation: *judgment* and *memory*. This opposition is summed up, in the standard
schoolroom reading of the *Essays*, in the value judgment according
to which "a well-made mind" is preferable to a "well-filled mind."[1]

What then is the function in the *Essays* (rather than in Montaigne's "life" or in his pedagogical reflection) of a disavowal of
memory which one is tempted to call systematic, or at least symp-
tomatic? In his splendid book, Hugo Friedrich goes straight to the
point: "If he asserts so often that he has no memory, it is not only
a jab at the pedants and their materialistic science. It is also a way
of repudiating rhetoric" (*Montaigne*, 351). Friedrich makes this remark on memory in the context of his analysis of the composition
and style of the *Essays*, which he links to the "open form" of the
ordo neglectus.

Thus, the *Essays* would transgress, simultaneously, and correlatively, three parts (or "offices") of rhetoric: *inventio, dispositio,*

107

and *memoria*. Which, as a result, would liberate *elocutio*, that is, style. After this *coup*, there is not much left of traditional rhetoric in the *Essays*. Yet can one simply affirm this opposition between rhetoric and liberty, between premeditation and spontaneity? Let us examine Friedrich's commentary:

[Artificial] memory reproduces discourse in the order of its outline, and thus is under constraint. It follows that Montaigne, loving freedom, finds still another argument in favor of the open form in his refusal of a premeditated order which would be obliged to lean on memory: it would have deprived him of the fecundity of the instant, the first impulse for his writings. (351)

Friedrich bases his line of reasoning on a psychological motivation outside the text: ". . . Montaigne, loving freedom . . ." But there is more to it than that: to the extent that he opposed memory's constraints (which fix invention and composition) to the open form's fecund spontaneity, Friedrich remains caught in an antihistorical *terrorism* (in Jean Paulhan's sense) that is somewhat anachronistic in relation to Montaigne. This "terrorism," founded on an ideology of spontaneity and expressiveness, is all the more inadequate in that it projects onto the *Essays* an ontology of the subject formulated later, or foreign to them.

It is true that artificial memory, which implies an effort of remembrance, seems somewhat alien to a *subject* who makes spontaneous utterance his specialty. Memory, as the storehouse of invention, does not belong to him *in his own right*, is not part of his property, of his predicates, whereas judgment is a personal activity which never is lacking, unless the subject should lapse into unconsciousness. Montaigne particularizes this opposition:

Memory is the receptacle and container of knowledge; mine being so defective, I can hardly complain if I do not know much. I know in general the names of the arts and what they treat, but nothing beyond that. I leaf through books, I do not study them. What I retain of them is something I no longer recognize as anyone else's. It is only the material from which my judgment has profited, and the thoughts and ideas with which it has become imbued, the author, the place, the words, and other circumstances, I immediately forget. (II, XVII, a 494)

An aristocratic disdain for whatever in the liberal arts still remains laborious and servile and scorn for the outward signs of erudition: sources, references, quotations, and so on. More interesting is the clearly marked distinction between the *foreign* (for example, bookish knowledge), what others have done and remains their property, and what my judgment is imbued with. Here, as elsewhere in the *Essays*, the efforts and artifices of voluntary memory are banned because they generate "inner distance" and a difference between one's own invention and the borrowed quotation, between the text and the intertext whose acceptance hinges on naturalization and on forgetting its foreign origin. In short, striving to remember, and that which preserves the trace of this effort in the text, deprives the subject and his utterance of their presence unto themselves in the very act of uttering. In voluntary remembrance (a fortiori, in the recourse to artificial memory and methodical invention), my past, the discourses I have made and retained, even my own previous writings, become as foreign to me as the texts of other people: in the *Essays*, in the last cited passage anyway, what is *one's own* or, which is the same, what one *appropriates* (what has been taken in and embodied into the text)—only this and the *present* of the utterance are appreciated. Not that Montaigne denies the possible sudden and constraining *return* of the past and the foreign: but this—uncontrolled, tyrannical—return snatches from the present subject his presence unto himself and the world, intercalating between the conscious agencies and one's awareness of oneself in the world (for example, in writing) the rise of a nonconscious biological or psychic agency whose manifestations assume the hysterical consistency of what Montaigne calls, always pejoratively, the *imagination*. Effort, especially the effort of remembering, also dissipates the euphoria of self-presence in writing, it breaks the charm and dries up writing. Albert Thibaudet has aptly formulated the status of this effort in Montaigne: "Everything that is an effort for him bears the stamp of a downfall, it is unwelcome"[2] (*Montaigne*, 200), and in support of this he cites: "I flee from command, obligation and constraint. What I do easily and naturally, I can no longer do if I order myself to do it by strict and express command" (II, XVII, a, 493).

One sees then what separates the *Essays* from *A la recherche du temps perdu*. With Proust, "the memory of intelligence" is capable of laboriously exhuming "dead" information stripped of affect and unsuitable for satisfying the desire that triggered and sustained the effort. Chance alone, provoking a repetition of sensation, can stimulate affective memory and induce a feeling of existence, pure presence unto oneself in the present:

A delicious pleasure had come over me, isolated, with no notion of its cause. It had at once made life's vicissitudes indifferent to me, its disasters inoffensive, its brevity illusory, in the same way as love operates, by filling me with a precious essence: or rather, this essence was not in me, it was me. I had ceased to feel mediocre, contingent, mortal. (1:45)

But the unexpected bounties of chance and the involuntary yield nothing more. This Proustian pleasure is not certain to trigger the process of remembrance; in the case of failure, it becomes in turn an object-memory, like the instants of pure existence reported by Montaigne in "Of Practice" and Rousseau in the Second Reverie, blissful and empty moments that come about after a faint. For plenitude to disclose its cause and the recaptured presence of the past, there must be a search, an *invention*, subject to the reemergence of a connected spatial system, such as Combray or Venice. If enjoyment of the present is a free and fortuitous gift, then the rise of the past, the recognition of the little *madeleine*, of the paving stones in the Venetian baptistry, of the blossoming out of Combray reward a concentrated effort that would sweep away Montaigne's enjoyment of the present in the *Essays*.

Consequently, the *Essays*, arranged so as to capture the presence unto itself of present discourse, cannot be the anamnesis of a past prior to the actual writing of the book. The *Essays* are deployed in the fictional present of description and the mimesis of invention— that is, in the textual duration of an utterance that comments on itself to capture its own presence in the act of writing, which is a kind of speaking.

Thibaudet has aptly stated the primacy of presence, prohibiting a return to the past as it does a premeditation: "Montaigne's thought is a kind of musical suite. It bears at each moment the fresh imprint of the present, and yet it takes its place in a series. However, this series excludes what is *preformed, determined*. It is free at each one of its moments" (200). Yet, the musical suite and improvisation leave the composer with a limited freedom, for he must yield to the constraints inherent in the chosen form, even if it as supple as a "rhapsody." Similarly, in Montaigne's *Essays* neither plan nor (topical) memory can be eliminated from the self-regulating dialectic process of invention. But even though the text may ideologically claim an absence of memory and refuse to encode voluntary anamnesis, a memory nevertheless controls its production. In no text is this constraint more manifest than in the *Essays*.[3] Let us then examine the paradox of a text that refuses memory and yet keeps talking about it.

One may well wonder why the *Essays* so often deal with bad and pernicious memory. By their obstinate disparagement of memory, the *Essays* try to indicate what sets them apart from *memoirs* and *autobiography;* in so doing the *Essays* also draw attention to what distinguishes them from such kinds as the *miscellanea*, compilations, and treasures, the Renaissance mnemonic contraptions that served as auxiliaries or substitutes for artificial memory. The criticism of memory at the core of the *Essays* does indeed seek to bury rhetoric, or go beyond it, as Hugo Friederich has suggested.

But one must go much further than Friedrich and Holyoake, who see in this transgression an aristocratic revolt against the constraints of an outline, against a premeditated order, and an attempt to eliminate the nonbeing that separates projects from their realization: this is exactly what an ideology of writing as a presence-unto-itself would attempt to discard. The swerve of the *Essays* does not merely serve to free a gentlemanly writer from the servile constraints of composition and stylistic decorum. Dismissing the imperative of textual elaboration and completion, the *Essays* foreground the procedure that produces them, especially the mechanisms of a new memory and invention immanent in the text. By drawing attention to the code rather than the message, the *Essays* engender the figure of the subject who manipulates the code to produce a new sort of message: this message is precisely *the foregrounding of the code by the addresser*—an innovative variant of what Aristotle called *ethos*.

Warranting special attention among the typical texts of the sixteenth century are those that, not classified under any recognized genre, overflow the bounds of literary art: the *miscellanea* and diverse and motley compilations share at least one feature: they gather fragments under more or less traditional headings.[4] All these texts are *premature* products: they give the public raw or barely processed materials. Their role is to mediate between a producer—classical antiquity—and a user—the modern poet, the orator. The semiprocessed state is the result of a set of activities: reading/writing (copying), grouping together (collecting or collating), and sometimes commentary (intercalated text, moralization, philology). These works, though not designed to persuade, praise, or blame, still serve to instruct and also to please and surprise by the variety and strangeness of the examples they assemble. They are not intended for aesthetic, hedonistic, or consecutive reading, since they are readymade commonplace books whose function is transitive and instrumental. Constituting a pseudomemory, or an exomemory, like a reference library, they furnish the raw material for a second-degree invention, for a secondary elaboration aimed at producing literary works of art, which, in principle, *would* usually be subject to rhetorical, stylistic, and generic imperatives, as well as to criteria such as the verisimilitude of mimesis.[5] According to Quintilian's metaphor designating rhetorical memory, these centos form "treasure houses of eloquence." They are not themselves eloquent, nor do they contain writing as presence unto itself, but they are easily accessible, and as they handily substitute for individual memory and its vagaries, they are emblematic of the new typographic age. Individual memory stopped serving a crucial function in the production of discourses when two cultural conditions were met:

1. When the solitary writer had within arm's reach a reference library complete enough to form, virtually at least, an encyclopedia. Montaigne's library combines the metaphorical circularity of the encyclopedia with the circular bookshelves along the walls of his round tower. One need only be adept at looking up data, but as every user of the dictionary, encyclopedia, compilation, index, bibliography, and library knows (as opposed to the user of much more specifically programmed *electronic* memories), there occurs a dispersion, whether because his attention is deflected by something for which he was not looking, or because he finds, next to what he was searching for, more pertinent data. From the end of the sixteenth century on, the writer becomes accustomed to leafing through printed books, to consulting indexes and tables of contents; even if Montaigne does not use a *card index*, at least he is already in the

position of a modern researcher prior to the introduction of electronic memories. With this exception however: Montaigne claims
to find what he needs without looking for it.

2. Memory becomes less important when texts, not being designed to praise or blame, to persuade, exhort, or preach, no longer
has to obey rhetorical codes of composition and style, one of whose
functions in scribal culture was to make it easier for the listener-
reader to understand and remember data by introducing a coded
redundance, or *copia*, which was moreover the object of an aesthetic appreciation. So great is the disdain of Montaigne's task for
these obsolete imperatives that the reader has difficulty in remembering the order and tenor of the *Essays'* long chapters. The *Essays*
are indeed, in this sense, antimemoirs.

Thus, the *Essays* constitute a purely bookish book whose writing
is almost entirely divorced from the tenacious fiction, derived from
a former oral and scribal culture, of a writing that reproduced
a public and oratorical utterance, linearly and consecutively carried by voice and that vanished as fast as it was uttered or read.
The new typographical writings are no longer, as were so many
medieval books, the kinds of memory aids that always suppose the
reader's prior knowledge of the text inscribed in them (a knowledge previously acquired by listening to oral readings, magisterial
lectures, declamations, and so on). Montaigne insists that nobody
can know beforehand the substance of what he will read in the
Essays.

What the *Essays* foreground is the presence of the present—to
wit, the ephemeral. It is not only a matter of the subject's full
presence unto himself in the act of writing, even if this presence is
conceived as a victory over the ineptitude, *strangeness*, and alienation that are provoked by the chimeras born of imagination (I,
VIII, a, 21), but also of the ephemeral presence of a knowledge
manifested only in the reading/writing process of which the *Essays*
are so often a trace:

I go about cadging from books here and there the sayings that please me,
not to keep them, for I have no storehouses, but to transport them into this
one, in which, to tell the truth, they are no more mine than in their
original place. We are, I believe, learned only with present knowledge, not
with past, any more than future. (I, XXV, 135c, 100)

Yet, this passage from "Of Pedantry" testifies (at any rate in an edition where the chronological layers of the text are indicated) to the labile status of that "present." Written in "c" (Bordeaux copy), it comments on the immediately preceding "a" passage, accusing itself of a practice as blameworthy as that of the pedants who "go pillaging knowledge in books and lodge it only on the end of their lips, in order merely to disgorge it and scatter it to the winds" (100). There is, however, a major difference between the pedants' futile practice (memorizing for immediate pedagogical and ostentatious oral use) and that of the *Essays:* the transfer of sentences serves to create this book, the so-called Bordeaux copy, in whose margin the handwritten commentary added to the printed text opens up a space in which is inscribed the duration inherent in the copresence on the page of the printed text and of the holograph commentary: this copresence is further underscored by the fact that there are no extraneous citations in this place, where the text of the *Essays* folds back onto itself and becomes its own interlocutor, its own marginal gloss and the foregrounding (on the very page of the Bordeaux copy) of its own mode of production.

In his *Montaigne paradoxal,* Alfred Glauser comments on the above-cited passage (I, XXV) and notes that "the book is augmented by its negative avowals . . . Montaigne confesses to a weak memory so that it will impregnate his work all the more." Further on, he adds "Montaigne performs memory exercises. He asks himself 'What do I know?', which is not a skeptical 'What do I know?' but, rather, a query to himself regarding his essential acquisitions. The *Essays* create a container for knowledge and wisdom. Montaigne realizes that he is filling his artificial memory, his book, while leaving 'understanding (c) and the conscience (a) empty' " (100). If one may take exception to his (perhaps) paradoxical interpretation of the "What do I know?" one has to agree with Glauser that the *Essays* become an "artificial memory," even if this notion assumes here a sense rather remote from that ascribed to it by rhetorical tradition descended from oral culture. The sense proposed is that of "memory turned into a book by an artist," the function of this artifice (this crutch) being to liberate the present, to confer upon it a unity that would be shattered by the effort of voluntary remembrance, rather than turning the book into a "storehouse." But indeed the *Essays* are also a "storehouse" (*gardoir*): whether a tomb or a cenotaph bearing Montaigne's effigy, the book preserves a *corpus* continuously exercising its posthumous prestige, like those kings' corpses dealt with in I, III, "Our Failings Reach Out Beyond Us."

The *Essays* are the trace of thinking in the presence of texts by others and in its presence unto those texts that were inscribed by a former self in the book that is the *analogon* of the writer's own body. An earlier "a" passage from "Of Pedantry" is sufficiently clear, even if not entirely free of illusions:

We take the opinions and the knowledge of others into our keeping, and that is all. We must make them our own. . . . What good does it do us to have our belly full of meat if it is not digested, if it is not transformed into us, if it does not make us bigger and stronger? (I, XXV, a, 101)

The illusion still harbored here (and denounced by the *Essays* in their relative entirety) concerns the possibility of amassing a fund of experience, of appropriating a consubstantial *knowledge* without resorting to the artifices of memory, and of increasing Michel de Montaigne's wisdom rather than the volume of his book. But the only "body" that irreversibly increases and grows stronger, that produces its "own" substance out of a foreign one, that assimilates, and that can be legitimately used as a metaphor for the "ideal self" with its properties, is the *Essays*, the book in which "the opinions and knowledge of other people" are inscribed. Thus, the condemnation, or at least disparagement, of a constant and capricious recourse to reference books, which is an essential theme of the chapter on pedantry, should be reexamined in the light of the entire *Essays*, particularly II, XVII, "Of Presumption," and III, III, "Of Three Kinds of Association," where Montaigne's library is described and the impulsive use of it is foregrounded in the text. Let us consider the end of this *topography*, which is unique in the *Essays*:

There I leaf through now one book, now another, without order and without plan, by disconnected fragments. One moment I muse, another moment I set down or dictate, walking back and forth, these fancies of mine that you see here. (III, III, b, 629)

And, a little further on, this assertion: "There is my seat" (c, 629), an odd seat indeed (where one "settles down in oneself"), is this

place devoted to perambulation, foraging, random readings, dicta-
tion on the spur of the moment, the rapid jotting down of "dreams";
but here the library seems to be a spatial and domestic metaphor
for the *Essays*, and vice versa. The presence unto oneself (implied
in the notion of a seat or resting place, so often modulated
throughout the book) is (paradoxically) evident only in the alter-
nation of reading and writing; the plenitude of self-possession is
manifest only in discontinuity, in improvisation, and in the mode
of a mimesis of purposeless activity without past or order. Yet, this
activity does leave a written trace; it produces (but as by-products)
an order, a past and, eventually, a purpose: to represent oneself in
one's own presence in motion, which rules out premeditation, or
at least *dispositio*, in the rhetorical sense:

It is many years now that I have had only myself as object of my thoughts,
that I have been examining and studying only myself; and if I study
anything else, it is in order promptly to apply it to myself, or rather within
myself. . . . There is no description equal in difficulty, or certainly in
usefulness, to the description of oneself. Even so one must spruce up, even
so one must present oneself in an orderly arrangement, if I would go out in
public. Now, I am constantly adorning myself, for I am constantly describing myself. (II, IV, b, 273)

And again:

What I chiefly portray is my cogitations, a shapeless subject that does not
lend itself to expression in actions. (274)

This whole reflection *on* the self-portrayal (in II, VI, "Of Practice," which, with the reflection *on* infinite invention and interminable commentary in "Of Experience" [III, XIII, 817–18] is the
most sustained metadiscourse is the book) is situated after the narrative of the pseudodeath-and-resurrection provoked by falling from
a horse during a skirmish. There is probably nothing fortuitous about
this encounter, for the experience of (even an illusory) death is a
typical example of nontransferable *practice*, and the account is not
designed to instruct or persuade others but, rather, to examine oneself passing from unconsciousness to pure enjoyment of one's own
being.

Hence, the role reserved for memory, in the ordinary sense, in
the self-description of the *Essays* is to place once again the subject

making a present statement in the context of a crucial event or of a typical action related to the diverse modes of being and having, of possessing or losing oneself; this always amounts to an examination of experience of losing and regaining consciousness. But memory is excluded, if not censored, as soon as it presents itself as the "treasure-house of invention," the encyclopedic source of *copia*, or as a simple return to humanist commonplaces dissociated from presence unto oneself. Memory, in the *Essays*, is not supposed to play any of the disindividualizing roles assigned to it by traditional rhetoric.

To the extent that, under the pretext of arriving at the authentic meaning, the gloss and commentary only widen the gap and strangeness separating the second text (the commentary) from the first (the commented text) and encourage a futile effort to remember meanings, they are subject to the same condemnation as memory; glosses proliferate without a center, fallen from self-presence: "The world is swarming with commentaries; of authors there is a great scarcity" (III, XIII, c, 818); and above all: "It is more of a job to interpret the interpretations than to interpret the things, and there are more books about books than about any other subject: we do nothing but write glosses about each other" (b, 818). A disillusioned remark (and perhaps even the founder) of an ideology of creative originality. But the repentance that follows soon afterwards again challenges everything, especially the *Essays* themselves: "How often and perhaps stupidly have I extended my book to make it speak of itself?" (b, 818).

Thus, the newest and most antirhetorical procedure used to produce the *Essays* seems condemned in its turn, because of its affinity with the procedures of recalling. But in the Bordeaux copy a reversal occurs in the process of justifying, against outside criticism, a text that folds back on itself through its own commentaries and intercalated self-glossing, a procedure that manages to mimic textually the discourse's presence unto itself and its ontological permanence through the duration of a writing henceforth coterminous with the life of the writer: "For as for my excuse, that I ought to have more liberty in this than in others, precisely because I write of myself and my writings as of my other actions, because my theme turns in upon itself—I do not know whether everyone will accept it" (818). My theme turns in upon itself: this is indeed the effect of specular reduplication that produces the intratextual-memory effect in all self-portraits, since all of these develop either by commenting upon themselves or by taking on additions or by intercalating glosses or, even more often, by deploying themselves in a spiral. Each revolution (for example, each new volume) brings its corrections, second thoughts, additions, new points of view, in the form of a philological or archaeological commentary on the chunks of text previously delivered to the reading public. By dialecticizing it, the *Essays* push to the limit the confusion, deeply anchored during the Middle Ages (when civil eloquence had disappeared), between the two rhetorical offices apparently the least likely to be confused: invention and memory.

Instead of exhuming contents, things (*res*, in the rhetorical sense) or past events (in short, history and knowledge), memory functions in the *Essays* by passing repeatedly over the same trace, as a series of inscriptions inserted where the textual web is pulled apart. Memory usually turns towards the steps and procedures of invention that produce this ever premature and incomplete text. Invention and memory become one in the above-cited "rhetorical" question: "How often and perhaps stupidly have I extended my book to make it talk of itself?" Taking the discourse back over the procedures that produced it is not purely and simply a matter of authorial vanity or narcissism; it would be easier to invest such a narcissism elsewhere, and it is jeopardized by this indiscreet baring of devices. On the contrary, the folding back results from a structural constraint of the self-portrait: "My theme turns in upon itself" does not mean that the writer drowns in his mirror. But this remark is itself somewhat performative, since it realizes a turning in upon itself of the commentary, which becomes both an internal self-commentary and a metaphor, on a metadiscursive plane, of the specular theme that haunts all self-portraits. This, then, accomplishes a mimetic reduplication, which is emblematic of the textual layering of the *Essays* and of self-portrayal in general.[6]

This *memory of invention* (these two terms are taken in their strictly rhetorical sense) introduces an infinite, inexhaustible, and labyrinthine quest, which has prompted Merleau-Ponty to say, in his "Reading Montaigne:"

So there cannot in all good conscience be any question of solving the human problem; there can only be a question of describing man as problematic. Hence this idea of an inquiry without discovery, a hunt without a kill, which is not the vice of a dilettante but the only appropriate method for describing a man. (*Signs*, 202)[7]

This "method" breaks with the traditional rhetorical practice in which any hunt, if it is carried out according to dialectic rules, must necessarily lead to a catch. The completed poetic text records the capture, not the steps of invention whose trace it blots out, for the chase is but a temporary and transitive stage whose mistakes are deliberately expunged.

The *memory of invention* then, is a contradictory notion and practice during the Renaissance, which clearly distinguished between the preliminary work and the goal to be achieved, between the scaffolding and the structure it helps erect, and, although it was keenly aware of the labor of artistic production, which it painstakingly codified, it rarely dreamed of foregrounding it and even less of making the preliminary sketch an end in itself. Besides Montaigne, one can cite certain sculptures of Michelangelo . . . Montaigne, bolder then Michelangelo (but his medium is different), leaves the scaffolding in place; he will even come to declare it the essential aspect of his book.

The foregrounding of memory and invention characterizes the *neoteny* or prematuration of the literary text in the *Essays;* this neoteny, while it is inseparable from the break with rhetorical production, also results from a thematicization of the unprecedented production mode of an incompletable book still seeking completion.

This phenomenon of neoteny and incompletion is analogous to what the French avant garde of yesterday called *signifiance*, production of the text, work of the signifier, and, more recently, so-called minor or feminine writing. In either case there occurred a kind of prematuration, for the text was offered to the public at a stage of its gestation, when it was still a kind of draft. The *Essays* were for most Renaissance readers deceptively similar to a commonplace-book, a pupil's copybook, or a school manual designed to facilitate the subsequent invention of texts conforming to a classical generic model. The specificity of the self-portrait escaped notice in a work written so cavalierly. With our contemporaries there is a more radical regression, since the author of avant-garde texts mimics an intermediary developmental stage, between *puer* and *infans*, so that the polymorphous signifier remains fluid, labile, its morphemes and lexemes poorly demarcated. The slippery play of equivocally semanticized graphemes becomes the norm and favors the emergence of a "paragrammatism" supposed to embody a (sexual) pleasure or at least a "drive."

Yet it must be emphasized that a reversal occurred between one regression and the other, for the Renaissance, from Erasmus to Montaigne, thematicizes the established codes and manages to destroy their arbitrariness and generality, to subvert their systematicity, whereas the post-modernist revolution does violence to a literary "nature" in order to make it avow its codes, censorship, and ideological overdeterminations. Whence the dual, apparently contradictory movement of childish regression and theorization, which is resolved by theorizing regression, marginality and insanity. This dual movement is inseparable from the lifting of the censorship that was imposed for so long on rhetoric in the name of the "natural" and "authenticity."

This prematuration (and first of all the one manifested by certain Renaissance texts) is in turn bound up with the removal of artificial memory as a treasure-house of eloquence, since this memory served to contain ready-made, prepackaged, and anonymous materials serving to edify a completed, adult work readily placed in the class of admissible aesthetic objects.

In the *Essays*, we witness as a result the discovery and foregrounding of a memory immanent in the text. Yet, *intratextual memory* still relies on the topics of humanist memory because it is the *collective* treasury of eloquence. This intratextual memory, made up of self-references, additions, and commentaries, rarely refers to what precedes the writing of the *Essays*. On the contrary, it is an invention that takes place as the book is being written and refers to its internal space. This distinguishes Montaigne's *Essays* from humanist compilations and other Renaissance collections of "essays," such as those of Justus Lipsius, Cornwallis, or Bacon, which limit themselves, *grosso modo*, to surveying the humanist topics. Intratextual memory produces its own *places* while gnawing away at those of the humanist encyclopedia, an ancient catalogue of virtues and vices. By engendering in turn an unprecedented mimesis of the uttering subject as inventor of a new type of book, this memory produces an inside, the *Essays* as well as, metaphorically, the subjectivity of the writing subject, by drawing on the outside: the treasure-house of traditional invention. A fragile and always unsettled distinction, though crucial when one considers the *Essays* in a genetic perspective.

The production of a text that refers to itself, by imitating the mechanisms of involuntary memory and, in the modern sense, free invention, results in amnesia: the self-portrait always tends further towards an autarchic economy.

The limit towards which the *Essays* are headed becomes clearer if one looks back at them from their posterity. Certain modern self-portraits are immune from the start to humanist memory and thus reveal the model of closure toward which the *Essays* were groping.

Leiris: From Simulacre to La Règle du jeu

The early texts of Michel Leiris gathered under the title *Mots sans mémoire* use intralinguistic procedures of invention that we know are analogous to those of Raymond Roussel and Marcel Duchamp, but according to Leiris himself, they also foreshadow the devices he was to use in *La Règle du jeu*. Leiris describes the writing of *Simulacre*, one of his early texts, in the following fashion:

On a blank page inscribe—disconnectedly, in the greatest possible disorder —a certain number of words that strike you as being resonant. When you feel prompted to link several of them together, circle each and construct a sentence. Continue doing this until you have exhausted all the words on the page, except (perhaps) for one or two which will supply the title . . . I view the procedure . . . as differing, after all, only slightly, from the one I use for *La Règle du jeu:* a card index (not a sheet of paper) with facts (instead of words) noted on the cards, where the actual task will be to work out the relations.[8]

The role played by the sheet of paper and the card index is analogous to that of the "backgrounds" in local artificial memory, where "words" or "facts jotted down on the cards" are *deposited*. Affectively marked "words" must be "resonant," that is, they must be charged with potential associations. This will also hold true for the "facts" noted on index cards. The work of writing consists in "comparing" and "working out relations": this is characteristic of dialectical invention, but also, according to Aristotelian tradition, of remembrance. Memory is relegated here to a secondary plane, for it is already immanent to the written traces; yet the work of invention takes shape as a mimesis of memory, as becomes evident in reading *La Règle du jeu*. A memory without a memory: textual production is conterminous with enunciation in the present, even when this enunciation is limited to producing the isolated nominal and verbal syntagms which make up *Simulacre*.

But *Simulacre* begins with an epigraph from Raymond Lully, an author known to have transformed the "arts of memory" into encyclopedic devices organized according to a spatial order. . . . *From one place to another, without an interval*, this fragment chosen by Leiris is revealing in that it alludes to Lully's chief contribution to the transformation of the arts of memory. The essential discovery of his *Great Art* consists in the spatial translation of (rhetorical) places, about which Frances Yates wrote the following:

> The figures of his Art, on which its concepts are set out in the letter notation, are not static but revolving. One of the figures consists of concentric circles, marked with the letter notations standing for the concepts, and when these wheels revolve, combinations of the concepts are obtained. In another revolving figure, triangles within a circle pick up related concepts. These are simple devices, but revolutionary in their attempt to represent movement in the psyche. (*The Art of Memory*, 176)

Leiris's method, as it develops from *Simulacre*, through *Manhood*, to *La Règle du jeu*, is a variant of the Lullian art, which tried to represent graphically the relations between concepts and to mechanically engender meaningful configurations based on the medieval *speculum*'s static and localized topical system, which in turn descended from the places of rhetorical invention and memory. Lully thus furnished the practical means for an *automatic invention* the potential of which did not escape the surrealist Leiris's attention: with Lully's devices, one no longer needs to remember in order to invent.

"To link up," "to work out relations," such is the Lullian task which Michel Leiris assigns himself in *Simulacre*, a task whose corollary is the "representation" of mental activity: one sees that the automatic method employed in *Simulacre* could further be adapted and filled out to the point of producing self-portrayal. In principle, it would suffice for the "words" to be replaced by "facts" (or things, *res*), which makes the game more complicated without fundamentally changing the combinational rules.[9] The method short-circuits memory in the ordinary sense of the word, while it engenders a memory immanent to the invention of the text. Thus, in *Biffures*, Leiris writes:

By repeating to myself certain words, certain expressions, combining them, bringing them jointly into play, I manage to resuscitate the scenes or pictures with which these signs, with crude charcoal lettering, rather than calligraphies, are associated (110–11);

and further on:

All the things I stir up, all the ideas which I hook together, trusting in words to make a chain of them (116–17);

or:

kinds of *corpuses* of facts grouped together because they are somewhat identical in nature (252);

and finally:

to effect a *convergence*, to trace paths joining up elements . . ., to group together in the same picture all sorts of heteroclite facts concerning a person, so as to achieve a book that will finally be, in relation to myself, an encyclopedic summary comparable to what certain almanacs once were, as inventories of the world in which we live, . . . or the pocket *Memento* published by Larousse. (262)

Leiris's combinational operations involve memory contents that are evoked in terms ("signs" associated with scenes or tableaux) that recall, beyond dispute, the "places" and "images" of artificial memory;[10] they still are burdened, as in Montaigne's *Essays*, with a mnemic content ("memories," *memento*) that tends to conceal the generative procedure and intratextual memory: at certain points of the dialectic development, invention brings forth narrative episodes or *exempla* analogous to those that are narratively linked together in autobiographies: these are outgrowths, or narrative byproducts, of self-portrayal.

Roger Laporte: Fugue

One must look in a book less burdened with "memories," such as Roger Laporte's *Fugue*, for a full realization of the intratextual model outlined in the *Essays*. Laporte's book in fact eliminates any memory content that is not an autoreferential symbolization arising in the course of the text's dialectic syntagmaticity. *Fugue* preserves only the scaffolding of invention and a foregrounding (through anaphora, self-citation, and commentary) of the memory processes immanent to the text, which becomes its own *intergloss* without ever referring explicitly to any other text, discourse, or "memory" anterior to the overture of the text itself: whence the metaphor of the *fugue*, a musical genre whose composition is self-referential.

Navel-Reading

Such purity, realizable only in a post-Mallarméan text, was never the aim of Montaigne's *Essays*. There is, however, a price to pay for this purity: *Fugue* being solely self-referential, it never truly manages to *captivate* the reader. It is a paradox, which engages only the intellect. In more impure self-portraits, for example Montaigne's and Leiris's, even if they conform approximately to the same model, impurity itself (borrowed memory, humanism, references to a past prior to the writing of the text, all those leftover cultural signs, collective idols, or anecdotal fetishes) is what introduces the archaeological or allegorical substance in which the reader finds objects for projection and identification. Then by a curious reversal, the text of the self-portrait turns into a *pseudomemory of its reader* and into a stimulus for the reader's own anamnesis and invention. In "Une Autobiographie dialectique," Michel Butor accurately detected this phenomenon in Michel Leiris's *Fourbis*:

> When he burrows into his memories, he awakens our own, not identical ones, of course, but comparable to his. By scratching the bark of his self, it is "our" self that he uncovers beyond his solitude. The misunderstandings separating him from himself, which he works out bit by bit, are also some of those that separate us from one another. He thus reestablishes a community or—to use a better word, one dear to him, the word on which he meditated at length in the chapter entitled "Sports Tablets"—a fraternity of minds. (*Essais sur les modernes*, 375–76)

The process of self-reading triggered by the self-portrait, the fraternal feeling, or even the illusion of identification, often noted by readers of the *Essays*—all of this is indeed encoded in the self-portrait. Not only in the narrated episodes (though these too are coded strictly enough for anyone to recognize himself in them as part of a humanist and Christian culture), but especially in what Butor calls the "dialectic," which we describe here in part under the heading "intratextual memory." It is a mistake to view this identification as a guilty "self-indulgence" or "navel reading."[11]

This navel reading (not, it is true, the only possible one) is required by this type of text, where the reader is fictively placed in the position of the writing subject since he witnesses the elaboration of the text above the writer's shoulder. The presence unto itself of the utterance, on which is built the self-portrait, arouses the latent presence unto himself of the reader, who becomes aware of himself as he is of that other talking to himself in the text without really remaining an other. This work is entirely different from the fantasized identification stirred up by the traditional novel. But this double presence unto oneself is precarious. Intratextual memory, being allergic to the encyclopedic memories of adult humanism and classical philosophy, smuggles archaic and wild contents into the self-portrait: a phenomenon homologous to the regression into *pregenre* and *nongenre* already analyzed on the formal plane.

CHAPTER 5

Archaic Memory

Anamnesis and Immortality

The memory-without-memory, whose development we have sketched from inception to purification, from the *Essays* to *Fugue* by way of *La Règle du jeu*, begins by rejecting artificial memory in order to become the archaeology of an idiolect and remain alone on stage; it takes us back to the very origins of philosophy, to that time when, emerging from myth, the notion of an interiority, or at least of the person, takes shape.[1]

Which explains the growing role played by Socrates in the *Essays*, where he becomes a paradigm of the human and Montaigne's *alter ego*.[2] Of course, Montaigne is not the only Renaissance man for whom Socrates became a master and ideal model. One has only to think of the literary stir created by Erasmus's *Sileni Alcibiadis*.[3] Yet we observe how a humanist commonplace is transformed into a structural element of the *Essays* and of the self-portrait.

In fact, in Plato, particularly in the passage from the *Symposium* which Erasmus exploited for *Sileni Alcibiadis*, duality is presented with all the dialectic resources of "contraries" to reveal Socrates' demonic character, which leads François Flahault to comment:

Socrates, the philosopher animated by the double nature of Eros, the man of remembrance, is described at length by Alcibiades in his speech; and through the anecdotes, through very concrete images, it is always the

126

philosopher's interiority that is symbolically expressed. (*L'Extrême existence*, 55)

Reason, in Socrates, is but one aspect—essential, it is true—of a more complex nature that preserved archaic traits: those that are turned toward Eros and a very different type of memory—or of anamnesis—from the one we have studied so far. According to Derrida in "Violence and Metaphysics," Socrates designates a "tautological" and "egological" Reason, which has "always *neutralized* the other in every sense of this word" (*Writing and Difference*, 314). Derrida adds in a footnote an opinion that he does not, however, endorse: "Levinas often makes accusations against the Socratic mastery which teaches nothing, teaches only the already known, and makes everything arise from the self, that is from the Ego, or from the Same as Memory. Anamnesis too, would be a procession of the Same" (314). Interesting remarks in two respects: first because what seems to be conjured up here under Socrates' name is precisely the art which he disparaged and, as a sophist, practiced: rhetoric, or at least invention nourished by a memory which is also its limit. An invention according to Bacon—and a few others— that never discovers anything new: it is indeed incapable of conceiving the other. Yet this is the rhetoric to which "philosophy" is opposed—to simplify considerably, the sequels of Platonism. But this memory-invention called *Socrates* cannot be accused here of lying; besides, it would be impossible for it to lie, since it never develops anything but the Same: it knows itself without knowing anything else. If this invention-memory *lies*, it does so by denying and neutralizing everything that is not itself, everything that is not the Self: "the World," as well as everything that eludes consciousness, and particularly forgetfulness; the latter, however seems inherent in the anamnesis process, which always implies the possibility of a major omission, especially that of metempsychosis. This critique of "Socrates" who uses anamnesis to ward off a transcendence that is Other and Ineffable, is diametrically opposed to Montaigne's. In Socrates' "deviltries," Montaigne deciphers a survival of the nonneutralized outside, of a non-sense or possession that threatens the closure of the Self and of the Same as memory, an outside liable to destroy the book produced by an *imitation* of the profane Socratic anamnesis of the dialogues. Socrates combines extreme and contradictory traits, as enumerated in the strange praise of him by a drunkenly inspired Alcibiades: Montaigne recounts these contradictions in III, XIII. One sees what separates Montaigne's Socrates from the Socrates found in the *Symposium* by philological and mythological analyses. The last words of the *Essays* condemn Socrates' "demonic status" and Plato's "divinity," casting off in one fell swoop everything that linked the historical Socrates and Plato with an archaic religious background, which Platonism finally succeeded in turning into a philosophical logos. Montaigne secularizes Socrates. He wants a human, nothing but human Socrates, which amounts to reducing the definition of ideal man to a humanism singularly closed to the sacred and to enthusiasm. Socrates' "deviltries" and "ecstasies" strike Montaigne as being the residue of a religious charlatanism regrettable in a man otherwise so purely "human."[4] But the double image, symbolized by Alcibiades' Sileni, remains fascinating, for it suggests a savage interiority, even a madness no longer intelligible to us through the notion of the "demonic." This duplicity makes *Sileni Alcibiadis* one of the textual places to which our culture stubbornly returns when it wants to modify the status of the subject and found a new anthropology. Thus Jacques Lacan would interpret in his turn Alcibiades' speech:

Included in the *object* a is the αγαλμα, the inestimable treasure that Alcibiades declares is contained in the rustic box that for him Socrates' face represents. But let us observe that it bears the sign (-). It is because he has not seen Socrates' prick, if I may be permitted to follow Plato, who does not spare us the details, that Alcibiades the seducer exalts in him the αγαλ μα, the marvel that he would like Socrates to cede to him in avowing his desire: the splitting of the subject that he bears within himself being admitted with great clarity on this occasion. (*Ecrits: A Selection*, 322)

In this reading the stress is displaced from Socrates' interiority towards Alcibiades' desire and his jealousy of Agathon, and finally towards formulating "the central articulation of [psychoanalytic] transference": Alcibiades' transference in which Socrates is "imaginarized" as the ideal of the "perfect Master" (826). Here, as in Montaigne, the demon, Eros, Socrates' interiority, seem sacrificed to the inception or description of relations of demand, of transindividual desires: interiority is but a mirage of illusion or even a magical trick. There remain only "split subjects," divided ‑because they desire, particularly because they desire to be made whole, their pieces gathered together by others, or by a text, itself divided, as are the *Essays*.[5]

If Montaigne dismisses Plato's demonic Socrates without reducing him to "wisdom" or common sense, it is all the better to steal from him deviously and textually, as a poet and as La Boétie's "lover," those traits distinguishing the dialectician from a reasonable man, those magic features that he consciously denounces at the end of the *Essays* as defects or repulsive excesses. In fact, if Socrates' "demonism" and "ecstasies" are related to Eros and anamnesis, the ideal master would also be a master of *reminiscence*, as opposed to rhetorical *memory*.[6] Eros and anamnesis represent our situation between two desires, one attracting us towards other people and the world, giving us up to imagination and duration, the other impelling us to self-containment, a return to our "seat" and resting place so as to escape from dispersion and time. This Socratic duality is also found both in the form of the *Essays* and in the tension that energizes them. The tension is between anecdotal dispersion and proliferating citations, on the one hand, and, on the other, that withdrawal into itself of a text, which, while it constitutes its own intratextual memory, tends to fold back upon itself and grant itself autonomy. The text of the *Essays* seeks a philosophic status that, in Plato, is *incarnate* in Socrates. As Flahault has said of Plato's philosopher:

It is while he is remembering that the philosopher achieves demonic and erotic status. He becomes aware that he contains divine Reality in himself and completes the long journey which, having led it from the celestial to the terrestrial world, will enable the soul, as extensively set forth in *Phaedrus*, to return to its origin, to close the cycle, which, being itself the image of eternity, obtains immortality for the soul that has completed it. (*L'Extrême existence*, 57)[7]

This analogy between Socrates and Montaigne's book invites us to see that the *Essays* undertook, beyond the dispersion which humanism attempted to gather in, a radical leap towards their origin, an origin which is also that of modern man's psychological discourse on individual interiority freed, in principle, from archaic magic. But it is in the self-portrait only that the *text* itself acquires a demonic and erotic status, since remembrance is pursued in its very web and not outside it, in what is called a "soul" or a mind. The *Essays*, which try to return to their origin and close their cycle, claim the status of immortality: thus they transcend the "psychological" message ordinarily found in them.

The maze of intratextual memory has apparently led us far afield from artificial memory and rhetoric. Yet this return to the origins of philosophy, guided by the ideal model of Socrates and by what *Sileni Alcibiadis* says about interiority, should be pursued still further, even at the risk of losing our way.

Anamnesis and the Mediterranean

Here we enter a domain where anamnesis takes on an archaic and religious sense scarcely compatible with modern psychologies. We already had the presentiment, when we introduced the paradoxes of a memory-without-memory and of an antimemory, that the self-portrait would lead us into a zone where positivist anthropologies do not wish to venture. If Eros and reminiscence are, for Plato, "the link that unites the All to itself" (*Symposium*, 202d), then one must admit that the self-portrait attempts nothing less than to effect an analogous union. No doubt it will have to borrow from what is most archaic in our culture the metaphors and emblems capable of representing such a project, no matter how obscurely conceived it is by the self-portraitist. We can already anticipate that such an undertaking is doomed to failure. Nevertheless, we shall have to follow the paths of the self-portrait where they lead, among the myths handed down to us from Greek antiquity or from its exotic and heterological complement, Egypt, if it is true that there exists what Flahault calls a:

structural homology between a cycle of the soul such as the one closed by Osiris-Horus and the soul's cycle in Plato. In both cases, the condition for transcending time is the splitting in two of Reality (or of Osiris) through which it can subsist as a memory (or as a germ) so that reminiscence (or Horus) can arise again. Thus, the terrestrial and the celestial worlds, goddess and god, the whole is united with itself by the link of remembrance or generation. (*L'Extrême existence*, 57)

The Mediterranean (or, rather its imaginary double, Mediterraneanness) is the global system for the *places* of humanist memory and "antiquity," Greco-Latin lucidity, Judeo-Christian revelation, and Egypt's initiatory and hermetic dimension converge: the Pyramids and the quest for Isis.[8]

Genius Loci. Butor: Le Génie du lieu I

This is what is suggested by such a book as Michel Butor's *le Génie du lieu I*, which describes four Mediterranean sites—Cordova, Istambul, Salonica, Delphi—and, briefly, three other towns—Mallia, Mantua, Ferrara—then, finally, Egypt. The books presents the lineaments of a self-portrait strung out along a metaphoric sequence. The *periplum* stages the writing subject and Western man as exiles from the Mediterranean matrix. But, despite the evocative power of these topographies, at no point in *Le Génie du lieu* does the discourse turn back in on the subject and the procedures of writing notwithstanding (or perhaps because of) the reference to Delphi.[9]

The description of places is, in Loyola's terms, a "composition of places," a setting or a staging. The self-portrait demands a reduplication, a "return" as Jacques Borel asserts: during this return, the mirror metaphor is engendered and the anamnesic process unfolds.

Yet this *return* implies a passage through Hades, a drowning, a resurrection after which all writing—the writing of the infinite self-portrait—will continue in the key of death. Butor's work is not, of course, closed to the initiatory "night of the labyrinth" it repeatedly thematicizes. But it does not make this passage the absolute place of origin of its return journey, which is euphemized, dispersed among fictions: "I was almost born again in this long narrow belly [Egypt] whose delta mouth sucks in, treasures and amalgamates, in slow fermentation, the Mediterranean and its passages of civilization," he writes in the *Portrait de l'artiste en jeune singe*. This "almost" makes Butor a *humanist*, as Jean Roudaut suggests: "Butor pursues not the initiatory, but the poetic path to the recuperation of psychic and mythic powers" (*Michel Butor et le livre futur*, 152). But this "almost" turns Butor away from self-portrayal whose obsession with death and survival is foreign to him, perhaps because he is overly open to the solicitations of the world in its meaningful variety. For Butor, Egypt is one Mediterranean place among others, like Rome and Delphi. Uncentered, his work is a cluster of mirrors, not the bottomless mirror of Narcissus. For the self-portrait, Osiris must be a god as *black* as Egypt, the place of dismemberment and gathering together, the space of the lost hieroglyph whose incompletable translation is the self-portrait.

One can now grasp (as Gilbert Lascault suggests in a commentary on *Le Génie du lieu* that allows cultural fantasies and "rapprochements" to proliferate) a homology between the fantastic European daydreams about the mysteries of Egypt and the mythical and archaeological encyclopedia that comes together and falls apart in the self-portrait:

To become the place of births and rebirths, of continuously displaced, threatened, and recreated permanences, Egypt must accept and privilege death and the states that are in its image. An "insidious strangeness," "a stealthy dissolution" haunts the Egyptian and the traveler; knowledge is fragmented; pleasures rot. The hashish experience reveals only death's omnipresence in ourselves, in others, at the heart of things. It corrodes our dwellings; it destroys what Henri Michaux calls our properties: our particularities and our possessions. "The aim [of Eros]," writes Freud, "is to create ever larger unities and thus to preserve: it binds; the aim [of the death instinct], on the other hand, is to dissolve compounds, and thus to destroy things." . . . In Western Europe, everything functions only by forgetting death; there, death is the primordial "repressed"; an ideology of presence, well described by Derrida, devaluates absence, traces, writing and death. In Egypt, on the contrary, there reigns a "constant awareness of the individual's transitoriness." (57–58)

Paradox and inversion: Egypt produces hieroglyphs that "phonetic" writing dissolves. These remarks help one to understand more clearly the strange omission, in Butor's evocation of Delphi, of the inscription "Know thyself": one has to have experienced the contrary of Greece (which is us, which we are), this Egyptian domain of strangeness, death and dislocation, for the Delphic task of reassembling the intratextual memory, doomed to fail anyhow, to emerge gradually in the self-portrait, as on a photographic negative.

Since Herodotus, Egypt has filled, in our conception of the Mediterranean, the function of an "upside down world" (or mirror world), the origin of arts and sciences, more particularly of *writing*: it is an integral part of our system of cultural fantasies. There is a complementary relation between the inner quest imposed by the Delphic inscription and the quest for Isis, between presence and the trace, between the gathering of the space within and the dislocation of the space without. Egypt is not the wilderness, nor the heart of darkness: rather, it is only that part of the wilderness that has already been acclimaticized, or at least admitted into Western space. Conversely, the Westerner will encounter a wildly mythical Egypt wherever death and time have dislocated buildings and left obscure inscriptions inviting decipherment: the symbols for our relation to Egypt and the Rosetta stone but also, above all, the hieroglyphic and emblematic aberrations of the Renaissance, the Enlightenment's delirious egyptology, for Egypt remains first of all, in its opacity and in that of figurative writing, the symbol of every-thing that resists the elision of the signifier and the reduction of writing to a syntagmatic transitivity.

The homology, then, between the Platonic cycle of the soul and the Egyptian Isis-Osiris-Horus myth refers us to another homology inscribed in *Le Génie du lieu*. These two homologies are the prongs of a fork, set slightly apart, which allow us to come closer to what binds the self-portrait, through a reverse chronology, to the ancient Greek texts where the concept of the *person* first appears. The sec-ond homology links the Delphic "know thyself" to the "quest for Isis," and the Greece of interiority to extravagant fantasies of Egypt. These homologues can be grasped despite the opposition that now exists between the philosophical logos and mythical discourse, be-tween the interiority that reflection, meditation, and introspection are supposed to make accessible and the allegorical tissue of myth that, to be understood, demands a detour through initiation, the word of a master and the decipherment of inscriptions in sacred characters, or hieroglyphs. This homology might be symbolized in turn by the differences and similarities that unite the Greek Sphinx to Egypt's sphinxes, the interrogator of Oedipus to the guardians of tombs.

In short, these homologies are isotopic to those that obtain be-tween two major types of self-portraits: those that, being founded, like Montaigne's *Essays*, on the places of invention, also set up an intratextual anamnesis, and those that, like Jacques Borel's *Re-tour*, while leaning heavily on the places of memory also thema-tize invention. But in both cases, as Flahault remarks, "the (textual) whole is united with itself by the link of reminiscence or generation" (Flahault, 57).

Hieroglyphs and Phonetic Writing: Vico, Hegel

The text of the self-portrait engenders itself by remembering itself. It remembers itself in order to thematicize its engendering. Thus, in its own way, it links up with the belief that interiority is anteriority,[10] especially when this anteriority burrows dizzily into the antiquity of the individual and his culture, as also happens in the theoretical anthropology of Giambattista Vico:

But the difficulty as to the manner of their origin was created by the scholars themselves, all of whom regarded the origin of letters as a separate question from that of the origin of languages, whereas the two were by nature conjoined. And they should have made out as much from the words "grammar" and "characters." From the former, because grammar is defined as the art of speaking, yet *grammata* are letters, so that grammar should have been defined as the art of writing. So, indeed, it was defined by Aristotle,[11] and so in fact it originally was; for all nations began to speak by writing, since all were originally mute. "Character," on the other hand, means idea, form, model; and certainly poetic characters came before those of articulate sounds [that is, before alphabetic characters]. Josephus stoutly maintains that at the time of Homer the so-called vulgar letters had not yet been invented. Moreover, if these letters had been shaped to represent articulate sounds instead of being arbitrary signs, they would have been uniform among nations, as the articulated sounds themselves are. Thus, in their hopeless ignorance of the way in which languages and letters began, scholars have failed to understand how the first nations thought in poetic characters, spoke in fables, and wrote in hieroglyphs. Yet these should have been the principles, which must by their nature be most certain, of philosophy in its study of human ideas and of philology in its study of human words. (*The New Science*, 97)

An analogous reverie sustains our interest in the great mythological compilations and hermeneutic strategies of the Renaissance. To be convinced of this, it suffices to leaf through Boccacio's *Genealogy*, humanist treatises such as *Theologia Mythologica* by Georg Pictorius (Antwerp, 1532), or Guillaume du Choul's historical work, *Discours de la Religion des Anciens Romains illustré* (Lyons, 1556); Francis Bacon's *De Sapientia Veterum* (London, 1609); Cesare Ripa's *Iconologia* (Padua, 1593) with numerous reeditions, translations and adaptions; Alciat's frequently imitated *Emblèmes* (1531), or Giovanni Pierio Valeriano Bolzani's *Hieroglyphica* (1536). These works can be regarded either as the description and explanation of mysterious origins, or as an inducement to reappropriate antiquity for the present, or again as the allegory of a process still unfolding *hic et nunc*, in society or the individual; they then serve as a model for a historical dialectic or a dialectic of individual development; or finally, they project intersubjective structures as well as unconscious events back upon man's origins.

Each one will find what he wants in these texts: the origin of laws, of human sciences or of poetry—everything will easily hang together—for Vico as for others: Zoroaster in the Orient corresponds to Hermes Trismegistus in Egypt, Orpheus in Greece, Pythagoras in Italy or Confucius in China (*The New Science*, 96). Vico's daydream on the origin of language and writing foreshadows a certain critique of "Western logocentrism." For this is the place (the origin of writing and language, the nature of the written) where the mythical articulation of Egypt with Greece is situated, as are the relations in the self-portrait between the imaged data of memory and the written invention which deploys them dialectically in a discourse.

The Egyptian monuments and hieroglyphs, with their archaic duality, half nature and half spirit, half sensible figure and half arbitrary sign, the body of an animal and the head of a man, the kingdom of death and the kingdom of life, half subterranean and half aerial—all these play in Hegel's *Aesthetics* the role that, in the self-portrait, we assign to places and images: sensible figures, iconic representations that propose a "mysterious symbolism" and an infinite decipherment. In this sense, all the descriptive, allegorical, emblematic, and imaged elements of the self-portrait correspond to the Egyptian Sphinx, or at least to what is still Egyptian and symbolic in the Sphinx of the Oedipus myth. But the self-portrait appears to be a combination of the Sphinx and Oedipus, a perpetual tension, always broken and always renewed, between "the uncanny monster propounding riddles" and the interpreter who solves the symbolic enigma. The self-portrait's dual nature derives from the perpetual solution of the riddle perpetually propounded by the "symbolism" symbolized by the Egyptian Sphinx. But, unlike this fragment of the Oedipus myth, where the answer to the riddle, situated between the two prongs of the choice "kill or be killed," is childishly easy and leads to the enigmatic Sphinx's immediate destruction, the self-portrait keeps propounding riddles, the way Egypt multiplies monuments and hieroglyphs, and keeps solving them provisionally in its self-commentary. In the self-portrait, the Sphinx and Oedipus are one; Egypt and Greece are perpetually present, and ambiguity reigns everywhere. To his Sphinx's question "Who am I?" the Oedipus of the self-portrait always answers "Man," thus provoking an endless debate. In fact, the Sphinx is truly half human, if one defines man as Hegel does, in the Hellenic light of consciousness, of "Know thyself." But it also has a bleaker half. Besides, as we know, this man who replies "man," who tries to get away with the generalities of an anthropology or an encyclopedia, has no clue as to "who he is": he does not even realize he does not know. So he is much more enigmatic and, in our Hellenized world, much more symbolic than the Sphinx, as a supreme hieroglyph.

There is, therefore, a profound and symbolic irony in Hegel's choice of this mythic episode to effect the passage, the progress, from enigmatic Egypt to the luminous Hellenic consciousness: for Oedipus is least of all "the clarity which shows its concrete contents through its appropriate form"—no one is less illuminated by the "light of consciousness."

In its relation to Egypt, the hieroglyph, the emblem, the equivocality of *monuments*, the self-portrait encodes the Sphinx and all it symbolizes, and what Hegel says of Egypt's "material" symbolism also applies to self-portrayal:

Now owing to this alternating symbolism [*Wechselsymbolik*], the symbol in Egypt is at the same time an ensemble of symbols, so that what at one time appears as meaning [*Bedeutung*] is also used again as a symbol of a related sphere. In a symbolism which confusedly intertwines [*durcheinanderschlingt*] meaning and shape, presages a variety of things in fact or alludes to them, and therefore already comes close to that inner subjectivity which alone can develop itself in many directions, the associations are ambiguous [*vieldeutig*] and this is the virtue of these productions, although their explanation is of course made difficult owing to this ambiguity. (*Aesthetics*, 1:30)[12]

This also is how the self-portrait functions: through the intertwining of explanation and form, in pursuit of "internal" subjectivity. The weaving of places and images (whether actually *described* or simply designated) and of their exegesis, which produces in turn other places and images, is indeed the privilege of this formation, which is always plurivocal precisely because of its inability to be totalized: only the death of the writer can complete it, while depriving him of the key to a global meaning—unless this meaning, as Oedipus asserts with the cocksureness of a sleepwalker, is quite simply "man." Besides, we know that "the man who says 'man' " surpasses the Sphinx in monstrosity, lack of understanding and plurivocity, so that the meaning he proposes immediately becomes clouded again, and explanation must in turn resort to hieroglyphs, emblems, symbols, and an equivocal exchange between the reigns of life and death.

This leads us even more deeply into that Egypt from which Hegel wanted to free us by the destruction of the Sphinx. Further? Well, no. That was an illusion, for we are back where we started; by following Hegel through Derrida's commentary, we have been imperceptibly led towards Anubis (Thoth) and his companion Osiris:

> With the answer to the riddle, Oedipus's words, the discourse of consciousness, *man* destroys, dissipates, or tumbles the petroglyph. And corresponding to the stature of the Sphinx, the animality of spirit asleep in the stony sign, the mediation between matter and man, the duplicity of the intermediary, is the figure of Thoth, the god of writing. (99) [13]

Although we only follow Derrida from a distance in his attempt to make Hegel confess his grammatophobia, we can make his comment our own: for Hegel, Thoth, the inventor of writing, is a "secondary god, inferior to the god of thought, an animal servant of the great god, the animal of man, the man of god, etc." (99), and Hegel's interpretation consequently echoes Plato's in the *Phaedrus*.

A difference that is crucial to the study of the self-portrait should, however, be noted. In the *Phaedrus*, Socrates (whom Phaedrus suspects of spinning an Egyptian yarn to support his arguments) tells how King Thamus ends up scolding Thoth for threatening the proper exercise of *memory* through his invention of writing: "Your discovery will create forgetfulness in the soul of those who learn it, for they will no longer use their memory; they will rely on external characters and will no longer remember by themselves. What you have invented is a support not for memory but for reminiscence, and you give your disciples not truth, but the appearance of truth."[14] Thoth, then, is the one who threatens memory, whose ill-devised invention jeopardizes our chances of metempsychosis and, in the long run, immortality.

The self-portrait is not merely writing but the staging of writing, and its memory, to preserve itself from disappearance and from so-called voluntary reminiscence, takes the form of a reflection on writing. In order to break the circle of metempsychoses, variants, and repetitions, it mimics circularity without, however, achieving closure. It should also be made clear that Thoth's writing is not ours, for it is composed of hieroglyphs and thus resembles the pseudowriting of artificial memory, with its *backgrounds* (provided by Egyptian monuments) and *imagines agentes* or hieroglyphic emblems, more than it does our "phonetic" writing. The self-portrait plays with these two forms of writing or, rather, it continuously destroys the former (transcoded into "localization" and "description") through the latter. But the latter remains a figurative writing, which, while challenging and dissolving the material images or Bacon's idols of the first kind, engenders in turn "images" that must be deconstructed by still more writing. The self-portrait is at once *hieroglyph* and *grammar:* its dialectic and syntax make it possible to sustain the tension between the symbol of the Sphinx and Oedipus's clever response.[15] Artificial memory (metaphor as well as rejection of writing) provides its morphology, while its syntax comes from rhetorical invention. By going beyond the fiction of a primarily oral culture which had been preserved during the Middle Ages, the self-portrait pays Thoth the homage Socrates and Hegel had denied him. Like the Egyptian temples and tombs, which, according to Hegel, are "like the leaves of a book," the self-portrait is in fact well aware that it owes its immortality as a book to the materiality of writing.

CHAPTER 6

The Places of the Return

Vuillemin, Borel, and Rousseau

After this detour evoking the archaic, through which we have been led by the ancient techniques of remembrance, it is time to analyze how certain self-portraits utilize primarily the places and images of memory. I take as my first examples Jacques Borel's *Le Retour* and Jules Vuillemin's *Le Miroir de Venise*, where the generative function of the topology is readily perceptible. It will soon become apparent that other self-portraits likewise resort to mnemonic places and images to invent their textual space, even when the dominant topical system is that of dialectical invention.

Le Retour and *Le Miroir de Venise* develop around a series of images deposited in a sequence of places borrowed from referential topographic space. Both of them are *returns*, one to the childhood house situated in a small provincial town (*Le Retour*), the other to Venice, where the author had stayed several times in the past.[1] I say the *author* because the latter and the writing subject seem one and the same in this case. No doubt, *Le Retour* designates itself as a *novel*, whereas *Le Miroir de Venise* professes to be an essay:[2] these differences are significant because they stress the self-portraitist's dismay in the face of publishing imperatives, the imperialism of the novel and respect for "proprieties." But external checks and internal indications lead one to believe that the writing subject of

Le Retour is indeed the writer Jacques Borel, even though the pro-
tagonist is designated as Pierre, and the names of places and persons are assumed names; one can also believe that, in *Le Miroir de
Venise*, the writing subject is the philosopher Jules Vuillemin, a
professor at the College de France. Nevertheless, it must be acknowledged that these books are given as "fictions," although produced by the literary matrix of self-portrayal.

Both books are marked out by a series of places, whose virtual
unity is given a priori, therefore forming a referential sequence. *Le
Retour* first covers the stages of a railroad trip from Paris to a town
in the Southwest, where the journey continues through the streets
of this town and, finally, to the childhood house whose rooms serve
as the local backgrounds for the successive chapters.[3] By a commentary in which the formal procedure reaches self-awareness as
it unfolds, *Le Retour* foregrounds the artifices of memory in the
self-portrait. Thus, the beginning of the first chapter (which, also
entitled "Le Retour," offers a scaled-down mirror image of the book's
title) is a meditation on *images* and their relation to *places:* "Images: there comes a day, even before the end [a short time before,
the total anamnesis which, we are told, accompanies drowning,
was discussed], when that is all we have left, images which one
shuffles, lines up, mixes or spreads out; there is always one missing,
as with cards laid out on a table" (11). In the appendix to *L'Espace
proustien*, Georges Poulet studies this memory topos, which he calls
the "theme of the panoramic vision of the dying" or "hypermnemic
apperception of their entire life by certain persons in danger of death"
(139), and he cites Victor Egger's formula in *Le Moi des mourants:*
"the self is total remembrance, consciousness of the past as such;
it is the series of past states of consciousness, which are held under
the gaze of present consciousness and, consequently, summarized,
condensed by processes the nature of which is rather mysterious"
(*L'Espace proustien*, 150).

It is less a question of knowing what the *in extremis* vision of
existence, or the ipseity of coming to after a faint, *really* are like,
than of describing the means at the disposal of the self-portrait to
invent or mimic these experiences. When Poulet writes that "the
visionaries in question have described their experiences, not as a
duration but as a panorama, a coextension, a juxtaposition of ele-

ments, that is, a space" (170), he is overlooking the formal constraints of writing and the weight of cultural codes. But might not
the devices of a "rather mysterious" nature that Victor Egger evokes
be the very ones that the self-portrait deploys in the Book's space?
It is no accident if Michel Leiris describes *La Règle du jeu* in these
terms: "my intention is not that of a memorialist, since I would
prefer, instead of reconstructing my life step by step, to cover it in
a single all-embracing gaze (a gaze situated in time but already
outside it, comparable to the one attributed to a man about to
drown, who sees his entire existence unfolding in a split second)"
(*Fibrilles*, 223). Nor is it an accident if Derrida wonders, in the
pages of his essay on "Edmond Jabès and the Question of the Book"
(*Writing and Difference*, 76–78), whether the *Book* is but an *epoch*
of being, "an end to which would multiply, like a final illness, like
the garrulous and tenacious hypermnesia of certain moribunds, books
about the dead book" (77). This proliferation of books on the dead
book, this intergloss which so alarmed Montaigne when he was
writing his Book, might perhaps be, according to Derrida, the herald of another epoch when the form of the Book would no longer
be the model of sense, when being would stop being a "grammar"
or the world a "cryptogram to be constituted or reconstructed
through poetic inscription or deciphering" (76). Indeed, and for
Derrida that would be what another epoch should leave in its wake:
"books are always books of *life* (the archetype would be the Book
of Life kept by the God of the Jews) or of *afterlife* (the archetype
would be the Books of the Dead kept by the Egyptians)" (78).

This deployment of life in the key of death, which at the same
time condenses duration into space, is effected by the figuration of
extended spatial metaphors (Borel's house, Roudaut's and Vuillemin's Venice, the photograph albums of Malraux or Barthes) thanks
to which arises an—anyhow very approximate—illusion of simultaneity which the book also creates. Thus, Borel's drowning man
"again sees in a flash all that he has lived since the furthest origin,
all that he has been, his life in images, a dazzling synopsis of the
whole, he sees it all again and at last he will understand everything" (9). But this drowning is the book introducing its own metaphor; its function is to prompt the reader to disregard the duration
of the reading (and of the writing) so that the book will appear

before him in its panoramic and fictionally simultaneous deployment.

The metaphor of the (incomplete) deck of cards permits the simultaneous introduction of an opposition between backgrounds and images and the discontinuity of an original disorder against which the arrangement of the self-portrait is achieved; it conforms to the model set up by Montaigne in "Of Idleness" for the opposition between imagination and writing down.[4] But Borel's meditation does not truly reach its prelude until the images become arranged against the less unstable backgrounds (staggered along a track allowing two-way transit) of the train trip and are finally disposed in the series of places inscribed in the architecture of the house (the dwelling: "what dwells" [19]).[5]

The paradox of mnemonic places appears here from the start: they are containers—designated by welcoming cavity images: "It was the dwelling place. Closed, perdurable. Protective protected place" (19); or "You will be there, and all the rest with you, all that I had once thought I could abandon or reject, all these books, all these objects, all the other images contained with them in the house's tender belly, shadowy and golden" (24); and, at the same time, contents: "of all these dwelling places, if I exclude this sordid room (le capharnaüm), . . . the only one entirely, forever contained in me, where I only need to descend to find everything, the least objects, the nooks, intact in it" (18).[6] Thus, the house, or every series of places that might be imagined as enveloping/enveloped, can become a metonymic system analogous to the one that affords the "psychological description" of characters in the so-called realistic novel. However, in this paradigmatic series, the house (my home) is distinguished from one's own body (experienced most of the time as a gift of fate: the place where heredity is inscribed) as well as from other edifices—palace, town, or museum—to which connotations of privacy are not so intensely attached and whose very form is beyond the control of the subject.[7] For if the house metonymically shapes the self of a person raised in it, it can in turn be shaped—remodeled, modified—by the adult self: this modification sometimes amounts to no more than a passing fancy, as happens with Montaigne, who never built his promenoir.[8] Two other examples immediately come to mind: Rousseau imitating the Creator by introducing rabbits on the little island next to Ile Saint-Pierre; Jung describing the tower he built at Bollingen and the meanings attached to it (*Memories, Dreams, Reflections*, 223–37).

From the beginning of the Fifth Promenade, the Ile Saint-Pierre is in fact presented as a hyperbole of the recollected home: "Of all the places where I have lived (and I have lived in some charming ones) none has made me so truly happy or left me such tender regrets as the Island of Saint-Pierre in the middle of the Lake of Bienne" (*Rêveries*, 81).[9] This dwelling is the Edenic microcosm: "I could have spent two years, two centuries, and all eternity there, without a moment's boredom" (82–83). During this *farniente* he gathers plants and herbs, carrying with him the only "encyclopedia" that belongs in such a place: the *systema naturae* that he resolved to adapt to his little Eden in a *flora petrinsularis*.

In this place, the tangible and spectacular exteriority is to such a degree abolished that the feeling of existence is all that remains: "What gives pleasure in such a situation? Nothing outside oneself, Nothing but oneself and one's own existence; as long as this state lasts, one is, like God, sufficient unto oneself" (98). But still, one has to rediscover this undifferentiated self-sufficiency in oneself by an anamnesis. Each time, the place regains exteriority-interiority, and the description of abolished places (or those to which there is no returning) restores, manifold, self-enjoyment: "Is it not the same thing [dreaming to my heart's content] to dream that I am there? Better still, I can add to my abstract and monotonous reveries charming images that give them life" (91). The relation (that is, the difference) between *places* and *images* acquires its fall meaning here. The place is but a *background*, and the compassing of oneself through imagination-memory demands a prior inventory and description of varied objects, of keenly recollected *images:* "During my moments of ecstasy the sources of these images often escaped my senses; but now, the deeper the reverie, the more vividly they are present to me" (90). One should in fact distinguish the indistinct feeling of ipseity in reverie as discourse from the ecstasy of self-portrayal. Here, as in Borel, the happiness of remembrance, which is the hyperbole of the writer's interest in his imaginary self dimly experienced as a near divine plenitude, is achieved in a description as detailed and meticulous as allowable under prevailing literary codes.[10]

Whereas Rousseau's description, encoded according to the conventions of the pastoral register, may seem rather meager to us, it still offers the virtuality of an infinite development. The writing of a *flora petrinsularis*, which remained a project, if not a reverie in itself, opens the perspective of an encyclopedic description where Rousseau's bid for divinity (or, in its euphemistic form, the Adamite dream, the Robinson Crusoe game) becomes a reality, which needs only to be sketched in. As with the palaces and recesses of memory, whose immensity and inexhaustibility are evoked in Book X of Augustine's *Confessions*, the system of places and images, whatever descriptive code is adopted, suffices to suggest memory's virtual vastness and invention's encyclopedic ramifications.

Borel, who adapted to the self-portrait the Balzacian type of description and wrote at a time when description devoured narration inside the novel itself, pushes the house inventory beyond Rousseau's rare suggestive indications. Actually Borel describes himself with more individualized particulars than Rousseau did in the *Rêveries:* Rousseau proposes the metaphor of a virtual *flora*, that is, of nature in its scientific generality as much as in its ecological specificity: the metaphor of a naturalized and potentially universal self, even though the circumstances render it specific. Rousseau chooses for his background a landscape accessible to virtually all readers and readily transposable, as is the experience of an undifferentiated godhead, whereas Borel inventories the particulars of a private house, its furniture, its library, a complex edifice (however, any provincial bourgeois home could be substituted) to which he alone has the key.

Borel also sets himself apart from Rousseau by foregrounding writing. The Fifth Reverie is an attempt to efface and naturalize the art of writing. Rousseau stresses his dislike of writing, of reading:

One of my greatest joys was above all to leave my books safely shut up and to have no escritoire. When I was forced to take up my pen to answer the wretched letters I received, I reluctantly borrowed the Steward's escritoire and made haste to return it in the vain hope that I might never need to borrow it again. Instead of all these gloomy old papers and books, I filled my room with flowers and grasses. (83–84)

The undertaking of the *flora petrinsularis* is not a "job of work" but a "recreation." *Flowers* and *grasses* rather than piles of paper and writing.

A book that would write itself—that is, not at all. The *Rêveries* have indeed been written, but the act of writing appears cloaked in a denial in the Fifth Reverie, devoted to happiness, where a deep reverie is said to "paint" things. The writer's misfortune looms fugitively—as an indirect reference to writing—in the next-to-last sentence of the reverie: "My misfortune is that as imagination loses its fire this happens less easily and does not last so long." Words that might also apply to other consequences of age.

Borel, on the contrary, constantly refers to writing and to the grammatical forms used in his description. These *asides* by Borel constitute a thematicization peculiar to the self-portrait. It binds memory to the present, to the very act of recollecting and writing, that is, to the text in its own duration.

Borel likewise thematicizes the writer as writer, as a symbol-monger cut off from *things* (the referent), action, immediate happiness, a selfish man of leisure (*otium*):

Turned towards what perhaps writing alone cannot so much bring back to me as indeed give me, as if I had not possessed anything the first time, in the contact and embrace, but only this second time, the image more alive and present than the skin, the gaze more glowing, the gesture more moving and efficient: Yes, the imperfect, you will return to it. (146–47)

Of all writers studied here, Borel is the only one who makes the house his self-portrait's principal system of backgrounds.[11] While the Ile de Saint-Pierre is central to the *Rêveries*, various places (Paris's topography reduced to its outlying districts) serve as backgrounds for the other nine walks. Twice removed from the seat of happiness and his Swiss homeland. For Borel, exile is any place other than the house through which his local memory rummages on in its meticulous inventory. Necessarily, the return will prove illusory: "There is no return, so is this what it has taught me, this book, is this then why I undertook it when I thought, complying with its hypocritical constraint, that I was rushing towards such an inextinguishable light?" (515). But this light of origin is not finally extinguished till the end of a long journey. A light, besides, which could be none other than that shed by a now lightless star: yet its source did once exist, and if anamnesic activity leads to regret rather than to a presence grasped in writing, this abolished being still survives as a trace, in the guise of written traces. If the self is now rent, exiled and captive in writing, Borel still goes on referring to a self and seeking refuge in his own dereliction. At least there was that house, that childhood: the self-portrayer is no waif; he is a dispossessed aristocrat, and if he no longer resides in the childhood house, if he must resort to artifice (to the artifice of memory, to the wiles of writing) in order to reanimate fantasy and reactivate images—at any rate he did, in *Le Retour*, piece together the simulacrum of a place haunted by absence, inscribing on each page his preserved faith: it would suffice to *merit* being, to get a tangible hold on it. If he is now barred access to presence, it is because the writer is guilty, responsible for his fall: guilty of being alive, guilty of now preventing the erosion of images "embalmed, laid out alive in writing's black sarcophagus" (514). Guilty of having assassinated memory's live images by writing, instead of managing to recapture them suddenly, like the drowning M. Vos, evoked in the book's first pages, whose *in extremis* vision, though it owed nothing to writing, yet served as a mediation leading into the written anamnesis. Like the recollected house, Borel's self now creviced and corroded by (literary) artifice, existed before and outside writing: its material are the ruins of a solid memory, of a virtual totality susceptible to archaeology. In "Problèmes de l'autobiographie,"[12] a veiled commentary on *Le Retour*, Borel shows that he is well aware of the stakes:

"the predominance of the self (and of the fictional character) in our novels and psychology," writes Jean Roudaut in his essay on *Michel Butor ou le livre futur* "is linked to a nostalgic attachment to a sole (historical and theological) center of reference." And it is true that this search for oneself or, if one prefers to put it that way, one's "true" figure, is prompted by a writer's "concern for sincerity": "the anxious or nostalgic search for a presumed unity, which, as he is unable to discover it, to fit into it or coincide with it, he postulates, hoping that it will be realized in writing by an invincible paradox, that perhaps writing will achieve, will found, this unity." (87)

Jacques Borel's self-portrait is a very complete and coherent personal variant of the vast transposition of artificial memory that humanism had already carried out during the Renaissance.[13] The same fantasy of an original plenitude of presence and language, the same return to the places (in texts or monuments) possessing a secret, the same shaken confidence in a mad venture of total reappropriation, representation, and reactivation of images, and, finally, the same recourse to a rhetoric diverted from its traditional function of persuading others: Borel's *Le Retour* is a modern variant of *Hypnerotomachia Poliphili* (1499) . . .[14]

Borel likewise examines the relation of "the confessional writer" to writing (a relation of suspicion) and to literary tradition (a relation of exclusion); he perceives as follows the equivocal (exclusion/inclusion) situation of the self-portrait and its rhetorical matrix since the Renaissance:

Such writers [the confessional ones] can resort to writing only in a very different way from the pure novelist or the poet, and they certainly do not expect the enchantment of language or fiction; nor do they tend to feel they are in any way linked to the history of literature, as does the writer who is conscious of opening a road or seeking, inventing or renewing forms; . . . if they, too, happen one day to approach beauty . . . it will only be by accident or as a by-product, so that one might say of some of them that they are, in a way, betraying literature. ("Problèmes," 81–82)

Yet, not being a poet, nor a producer of fictional narrations, but a writer turned away, a priori, from the mimesis of what is typical, on the one hand, and foreign, on the other, to the precepts of decorum which are governed by a rhetoric reduced to an essentially cosmetic function, the self-portraitist is continuously professing (aggressively or plaintively) to be an anti-man-of-letters, not a "maker of books" in the ordinary sense but, if he wants to be gloomy about it, a *traitor*. This repeats, in terms of diffused and profane guilt (for an original sin whose exact nature is not grasped by the person who only perceives its consequences) what was violently expressed in the Christian vituperation (by Pascal or Malebranche) against Montaigne,[15] though it can also be formulated in another register: that of rhetoric unconsciously disclosing the preliminary, usually concealed, operations of memory, invention, and imagination. As for the absence of beauty, as for the beauty that would

come about as a "by-product," Borel, like all who unwittingly use
and transgress rhetoric, is the victim of confusion here, unless, like
Malebranche's Montaigne, he does not say what he is thinking or
is not doing what he should do, that is, treating beauty with disdain so as to initiate an expanded poetics which would overturn
the primacy of poetry and fiction, an aesthetics that would allow
the self-portrait, as a slapdash rhetorical-argumentative discourse,
to achieve in turn some "beauty." This is what prompts Borel to
falsify his *confession* in *Le Retour* by designating his text as a *novel*,
by modifying the proper names and according the work that sweep,
that *copia rerum verborumque* in the recollected details that arouses
the reader's distrust, if he is not numbed straight off by the illusion
of reading fiction in the ordinary sense of the term. For those who,
according to a firmly rooted prejudice, believe that literature is
synonymous with *poetry + novel + drama*, the self-portrait, to the
extent that it subordinates writing to heuristic operations, to an
idiosyncratic search for truth that foregrounds the procedures of
invention and memory, is a bastard genre with a shaky balance,
apt to tip over towards instrumental description, the bare document, that is, to texts lacking in the traits that, according to Jakobson, constitute the poetic function of language. Borel considers
his work alien to the history of literature, to the inventions and
renewal of forms: this seems, of his regrets, the best grounded. Of
course, Leiris's books, Malraux's *Anti-Memoirs*, and Laporte's *Fugue* seem very different from Montaigne's and Rousseau's self-portraits, whose form they appear to "renew." But this progress is illusory, for two complementary reasons: the author who paints
himself or "confesses" is at the same time a man who lives in the
illusion of liberty, of the absence of precedent, of disengagement
(*otium*) and a writer who experiences and contributes to the death
of rhetoric. Even though, paradoxically, he has become one of its
heroes, he remains the outsider of a Western civilization completely bent on transforming the world and reveling in "communication." This man does not make history (not even "literary history"), and yet he does not experience it as a victim; he ignores it.
Unlike the novelist indebted to history in every way, the self-portraitist has no interest in the diverse conditions of man in society,
only in the human predicament and in a "hidden truth" which he

stalks through the privileged terrain of his own memory and writing. No literary model can help him in his undertaking, which always starts out from scratch, since the field of his mimesis, that is, he himself, is by definition always pristine. If then, Borel's regret is justified, it is nonetheless out of line, for the stakes of writing, as far as he and all self-portrayers are concerned, go well beyond a mere renewal of aesthetic forms. The question these writers seek to answer is posed in the face of death; it attempts to overcome death.

Borel is also aware that because of its limitless extensions and regressions, the self-portrait is necessarily prompted to question simultaneously whether it is "narcissistic" *and* whether it belongs in literature.

From Narcissus to Persephone

In a set of notes published after *Le Retour* and whose only link to this "novel" and the preceding one, *l'Adoration*, is the referential unity due to the name of the author pursuing his reflection on confessional literature,[16] Borel attempts to exonerate an undertaking that he himself suspects of narcissism. His tactics first consist in exculpating works that he considers analogous to his own:

Nerval, lingering over self-accusations that he was going round in too narrow a circle, Rousseau, Strindberg, the Pavese of *Il Mestiere di Vivere*, a certain Stendhal, a certain Proust, Svevo, and Leiris—their gaze is never, not for one moment, that of Narcissus. None of them is enamored of his own beauty, and, on the contrary, they all, like Leiris, strive to "break the circle of the self." At their own risk and peril. At their own risk, yes. (23–24)

If the gaze of these writers is not that of Narcissus, it is precisely because they *write*, and about themselves, thus wrenching themselves away from the illusion that beset those other writers who, believing that they are exempt from narcissism, are all the more immersed in it as they talk about themselves more sparingly. "Does Narcissus write?" Borel asks himself: he whom one thinks of as most narcissistic is not so. This paradox is linked to a search for truth that will lead the self-portraitist to acknowledge his own "ugliness." The more one examines oneself, the less one loves oneself: so one must avoid being enamored of one's own beauty in order to escape narcissism. But is this enough? Such revolving questions inevitably arouse the following suspicion:

Naturally, I cannot close my eyes to this either: that it is to my advantage to think that a seeker of truth, even if it is a truth narrowly limited to oneself (but is it ever that alone?) is not, cannot be, Narcissus. (24)

Is the self-portrayer, then, as narcissistic as other writers? The question matters less than the *pro domo* arguments that Borel, as a "confessional" writer, brings forward. First among these is the one dealing with the *unsayable* inherent in those moments of ipseity when the combination of *fusion* and *dissolution* leaves no room for narcissism. Moments that, in Rousseau's *Rêveries*, have not escaped Borel's attention and that, to some extent, elude the self-portrait, by nature always unhappy, fragmented and dislocated:

Fusion, dissolution: those moments that, everywhere, in the *Rêveries*, arise, so precisely localized, here, now, and seemingly outside time, motionless, that even their ephemeralness is experienced as eternity: this is when Jean-Jacques speaks of "self-love"; when, "circumscribed" in himself, he is no longer in himself, he is, perhaps for the first time, forgetful, delivered, of himself (26).

But if these moments, these states take *place* in the self-portrait, they are also absent from it, they leave holes in it; they are just as absent as is Christ's Resurrection in the Easter evangelical narrative. These are extreme moments, as elusive as orgasm and epiphany. If the self-portrayer were durably "like God," if he were God, or always enraptured and inspired, he would never write. Or, at any rate, he would not write a self-portrait. There was an intuition of this in Baudelaire, who opened "Mon coeur mis à nu" with an unsurpassable formula that intimated the omnipresent, divine center and circumference: "Vaporization and centralization of the *Self*. There lies everything" (*Oeuvres complètes*, 1206). *Everything*, true, next to which the rest is nothing, especially the rest of those notes as filled with gossip as a Parisian dinner: that jabbering, in the manner of Bouvard and Pécuchet, is the most external circumference of the encyclopedia as farce. "There lies everything": Baudelaire condemned himself to the incapacity of saying anything further, for in one swoop he had surpassed both narcissism and the search for truth, even for a lucidly joyless truth.

The self-portrait, then, sets down in writing the tension, the reversal, between a primary narcissism invested in maternal places and images and another narcissism, that of the open wound, anxiety, the confessions. Borel can indeed invoke ironically the superficial man with the euphoric mirror:

The man of smoothness, yes, of gloss—of the surface: an appearance, a surface reflected in another surface and, thus, an immutable, caressing twinhood. No crack in the mirror, nothing to grasp, nothing by which to descend, the lure of a dizzy spiral into bottomlessness. (27)

Yet he forgets that Narcissus drowns in his reflected image, in a "caressing twinhood," which does not exclude a disagreeable suffocation, nor a hypermnesia *in extremis*. Consequently, the one in whom Borel sees the antithesis of Narcissus is perhaps none other than the latter painting himself just when he is drowning in the liquid mirror:

But the one I am thinking about is the being of laceration, and he must pass, all together, through the lips of this laceration which sucks him in— all of him, lacerated himself, and his eyes wide open. (27)

The confessional writer, then, is the being of laceration: this metaphor, or rather the series of sexual metaphors proliferating around the *emblem* of Narcissus, echoes what Montaigne wrote about the confession, the disclosure of his "shameful parts," and the progress of his book since the notice to the reader that already prefaced the first edition of his book: a notice where he showed himself still bound to "public reverence," as it afterwards dawned on him:

(c) In short, whoever would wean man of the folly of such a scrupulous verbal superstition would do the world no great harm. Our life is part folly, part wisdom. Whoever writes about it only reverently and according to the rules leaves out more than half of it.

Here, in the handwritten marginal additions to the Bordeaux copy, Montaigne added and then crossed out the following (some of it is blotted and undecipherable):

My initial preface shows that I was not hoping for so much. This wisest and soundest writings of authors and the reception given to my plan have made me bolder, so that I have spurred myself to break the ice and show our———

The rest is missing.

"I have spurred myself to break the ice": this sentence, where "to spur" and "to break the ice" allow two readings, was crossed out by Montaigne in the Bordeaux copy. But the crossed-out passage does show the traits that Borel ascribes to confessional writing: *all* together, the breaking of the ice, the pricking. Of course, the pricking is not laceration, perhaps even the opposite of it: the spur. Montaigne assumes narcissism, but he surpasses it good-humoredly, being familiar with it. He incurred no little reproach for doing so.

As Borel's Narcissus envaginates himself in the laceration, he no longer is, it is true, the one who, a moment ago, empty-headed, self-satisfied, and speechless, remained deaf to Echo.[17] The one is the writer of the glossy surface, of the faultless, felicitous *copia;* the other is the writer of the lacerated fragment.

Borel's meditation on narcissism, which opposed the closed and smooth to the broken and lacerated, is like a palinode of his previous texts, smoothly bound in copious style. This meditation is written in a choppy, brutal, and sometimes slangy style, which exhibits the deliberately etched-in stigmata of the here-and-now, that is, of the fragmentary and dislocated: "Needs thinking. Not to indict writing too much. The true face in the mirror of ink, naked and tortured, surrendering itself" ("Narcisse écrit-il?" 24). Mirror of ink: this precious oxymoron, caught in a rich net of submerged clichés ("true face" where both the *Ecce Homo* and Veronica's veil seem to lurk; the sadistic connotations of "naked and tortured, surrendering itself," where "face" is reversed into its contrary), echoes a cliché of the Venetian descriptive system, and the telescoping produces a few cheeky double entendres. For instance, in a fragment of the "Venetian corpus":[18]

Venice's canals are as black as ink; it is the ink of Jean-Jacques, Chateaubriand, Barrès, Proust; to dip one's pen into it is more than a French composition, it is simply a duty.[19]

No doubt the meaning of eroticism (or the erotics of writing) and death is already inscribed in the convergence of the two syntagms that, sparingly, avoid the detour by the mirror of Narcissus and Venice: "to dip one's pen" and "black ink." But Venice and the mirror unite, locally and emblematically, desire and death, the desire that can satisfy itself in only death. The desirable, naked, and tortured face reveals itself only when the ink of death writes it off. A delicious and prolonged death for this sadomasochist, the self-portraitist according to Borel: "he must pass, altogether, through the lips of this laceration which sucks him in—all of him, lacerated himself" (27).

But the mirror of ink lures the self-portraitist to a second birth (expulsion or absorption?), to a *metempsychosis*, as much as to an agonizing torture. Would not, then, the more wretched one be the smooth Narcissus of the mute solipsism, deprived as he is of this painful and wrenching resurrection along the canal of black ink, in which, however, memory is exalted? Once narcissism has been denounced—all self-portraits do this; here Borel is not at all mistaken—one, then, should not "indict writing too much." Yet, one should shatter it, dislocate it, to seize the opportunity, and death, which speaks in the blackness of ink, would shatter itself against it.

If Borel defends the self-portrait against the charge of narcissism, it is not so much because of a penchant for paradoxes and in bad faith as owing to an intuition that jibes with the findings of philology: the myth of Narcissus cannot be reduced to its use in psychoanalysis.[20] The ancient Greeks associated the narcissus, a funereal and narcotic flower, with Demeter and Persephone, the chthonic, underworld and infernal divinities who were also the great goddesses of Eleusis, and, as Hadot notes, from the association sprang the idea of the narcissus as "an enticing, fascinating flower born of death" ("Le Mythe de Narcisse," 84). But if the narcissus is a mortuary flower, an enticement to death, it is also a living flower born of death, and its vernal metamorphosis compensates for death. The Narcissus myth is bound by a thousand textual links to the Greek attempt to conquer death by embracing, by mimicking it in the Eleusinian initiation; and this myth helps us understand why the self-portrait is less narcissistic than Persephonian: as does Venice through the diaphragm of its watery surface, the self-portrait attempts to unite the two separate worlds of life and death. Consequently Leiris placed the Narcissus myth in the middle of the chapter of *Biffures* entitled "Persephone."[21]

Why, then, do I always hesitate at the idea of a definite plunge and continue to go around in circles, instead of diving straight into this lake whose dormant waters attract me, this being the only way to avert my sterile contemplation as a Narcissus who does not move, poses as he keeps on expecting, and watches himself posing. (98)

It is necessary to take

the plunge, the liberating leap that should allow one to immerse oneself in the waters of childhood [those of "childhood memories"] which have, from this instant, become real (more real—the logic of my amplification demanded this—than they were, anyhow, in their primitive state, as markers or as mirages serving as markers). (99)

In order to recover the associations of childhood language, one must be dead to oneself in the present—in the present of invention—in the "logic of amplification." If Narcissus were to write, his writing would be that of the self-portrait: yet, Leiris's Narcissus, like Borel's, does not indulge in self-contemplation; he follows another version of the myth and plunges into the mirror of black ink in order to capture, at the cost of his life, the mirage that haunts the liquid depths; however, by entering the realm of the dead, he affords himself, against all expectations, the possibility of rebirth: he is metamorphosed into a flower of rhetoric. Narcissus attains, through anamnesis, the "logic of amplification," which is not the apodictic logic of philosophy but the looser one of dialectic, ordering the poetic invention of "childhood memories," he conjures up an intemporal paradise that combines the features of an individual's treasure-house and of a cultural system of topics.[22]

Leiris, Laporte, and Borel stake everything on writing, envisaging it in an intransigent and terrorist perspective. This writerly preoccupation was not shared by Rousseau, who tried to banish from his recollected paradise any notion of art and artifice (yet, the banishment comes about in and through writing itself); nor is it shared by Jung or Jules Vuillemin, who, while they refer to the house and town as dwellings of being, wish to exclude all properly literary problematics and to clear writing of all guilt. For, strictly speaking, Jung is not the *author* (in the modern sense, at least) of his memoirs, which were half dictated, half elaborated by a secretary, on the basis of interviews and documents,[23] whereas Vuillemin, by calling his text an "essay," declares at the outset, as Montaigne, in his epoch, had done for the first time, that his book belongs neither to philosophy nor to literature, if one limits the latter to poetry and fiction.

The Empty Mirror: Vuillemin

For the *backgrounds* for his essay, Jules Vuillemin takes the city of Venice. Perhaps because it reaches us through the evocation of Ruskin, D'Annunzio, Barrès, Proust, or Mann, the name of Venice is enough to prompt in the reader expectations of a boundless wealth and a poignant melancholy, as of a humanized, civilized Ile Saint-Pierre that would provide a Westerner, spared Rousseau's radical misanthropy, the exact mirror in which to decipher an image of himself engendered by history and soon to be engulfed.[24]

In fact, Vuillemin's book applies itself to destroying, by ellipsis and preterition, the collective store of Venetian images instituted inside our culture, so that the Venetian mnemonic system operating in this text seems to be that of an amnesic subject, almost bereft of places and images, of predicates and imaginary spaces. The book begins in this fashion:

After many years, I see Venice again as if some autumn were exfoliating it, one by one, of its charms. Time has tarnished the colors and put cracks in the canvas; less keen sensations and pondered sentiments convey to all the workings of the soul a slow inertia which I notice for the first time. (9)

Ambiguity hovers over this first paragraph as it does over the first part of Borel's *Retour:* did an actual return take place, or was it the imaginary reactivating of mnemic traces in the sequence of a fictional journey? As for the "canvas" in the second sentence, is it metaphorical? Or does it refer to Venice "seen again" in a painting? Would, then, this view of Venice belong to a set of images—those hanging in a real museum, such as the Louvre, mentioned in the following paragraph, or those of an imaginary museum that would make up, in turn, a vaster mnemonic system, where Venice would merely furnish a *background* for *images* of autumn, deterioration, decline, absence, while another city might serve as a local support for images of energy, vigor, springtime, presence?

In any text other than a self-portrait the *reality* of the return (to Venice, in this case) would hardly matter, and the question might perhaps arise from the grossest of referential illusions. But the self-portrait—by its constant reference to the present of writing and its encoding of presence: presence of "things," presence unto himself of the writer signified by the presence unto itself of writing folding back on itself in a self-commentary—allows no eluding of the question, though it always snatches away the answer.

This problematics of presence (presence of perceived things, presence of memories, and, consequently, presence of the writer unto himself) is so explicitly encoded in Vuillemin's text that the actual articulations of the device—the recourse to places and images of memory in order to create a simulacrum of a Self—are foregrounded and are commented upon inside the text. But this is done in order to deny their efficiency and destroy the illusion of the Self. Vuillemin, then, does not have to shatter his mirror, as Malraux does in the *Anti-Memoirs*, when he declares straight away, "I am not interested in myself," which implies, at any rate, that prior to this principled denial there was indeed a constituted, apprehendable, and virtually present self, which might perhaps have interested Malraux had he not been too busy politicking and writing.

Thus, returning to Venice, meeting with its places (whose series is limited here to a few brief evocations along a barely outlined itinerary), is an occasion to note how altered the images are, how diminished is their energy. This return is not a return to oneself, insofar as the self is defined as a treasury of images, as the presence of an imaginary and a memory.

The theater, which provides Vuillemin with another sketchy local system (*Le Miroir de Venise*, 10–11, 40–41, 83, 86), as well as the paternal house (15), merely confirm this waning into absence. The theater, being stripped of its illusions, has become an empty setting, and so has the house (the antithesis of Borel's house) where Vuillemin's childhood unfolded:

I spent my childhood in a village of Lorraine. Imagine a high house, separated from the one next to it by a narrow and gloomy lane, with its façade looking out on a wide street where tall chestnut trees are planted on both sides . . . My room, on the third floor, opened out on the street, and from my window that lushness seemed immense. I returned long afterwards. Everything had dwindled, except, aired out and dry, the narrow lane. (15)

A centrifugal description refusing the comforts of the maternal intimacy seemingly heralded at the beginning of the paragraph: its intent, in the last analysis, is to revoke the very foundations that make self-portrayal possible, while resorting to their devices. In fact, the village, the house, the systems of places, the backgrounds for images and metaphors privileged by the self-portrayer—all that is dismantled here, while memory is denounced as a fiction and the identity founded on memory as an illusion: "Thus we do not even feel the internal continuity of our body" (15).[25]

But if *Le Miroir de Venise* intends to dispel the illusion of a permanent self, the text is so organized as to continuously reinforce it by reminders and repetitions that unite the fragments. Thus, the reader is more struck by the illusion than by the questioning of its continuity. Besides, this contradiction is inscribed in a scattered reflection on rhetoric's maleficent powers.

They say: "Oh death!" and this figure of rhetoric provokes convulsions and sobs in the audience.

And I scoff as I say, without laughing: "I remember," on the lookout for my slow to be reborn remains.

Words have been granted the virtue of evoking ideas. But it is above all by prompting emotions and acts that they manifest—like sophists, preachers and tyrants—their force hidden from psychologists. How many motives are but manners of speaking? (14–15; cf. 52–53)

Vuillemin's reflection on the persuasive power of rhetoric, and how it differs from "the demonstration of ideas" (52) intersects his condemnation of memory's commiserating illusions (16) and of the self-reflecting word's snares (91). Actually, he is bent on dissolving the self that results from this triple illusion:

As for memory, such as they understand it, no doubt it amounts to some sort of logical construct: the word goes on, lasts, then disintegrates till death shatters it, and we add to it the fiction of the self, which embalms and preserves it. Is this not why literature plays such a large role in the cult of remembrance and suggests that the discourse on the word will shelter it from the inevitable? (94)

But Vuillemin also knows that the ways of literature do not allow an escape from literature, not even with the most radical self-criticism:

One detaches oneself; to be detached, one calls for help to reflection and the self. The self is immortal. One seeks refuge in a logical construct. (95)

And this logical construct of the self is a "fiction"—the very one Vuillemin had spun in a prior work.

In *Signification de la mort*, Vuillemin practiced an interrogation on both the Self (with a capital S) and Death, within the scope of an elegant dissertation by a good pupil who knows his classical and modern authors. This academic parody of humanism and of urbane philosophy full of ironic zest and adverse to "jargon," trivializes the gravest questions by an eloquence that makes no attempt at all to persuade or be persuaded but is satisfied simply to show the essayist's skillful manipulation of notions.[26] As in this sprightly transition: "We know now that we are mortal, but we hesitate about the meaning we should give to death. Does it reduce us to this carnal body? Does it free us from materiality and forgetfulness? Anger and fear answer this question in opposite ways" (147). Of course, the ultimate object is to establish "that death has meaning" and that philosophy's domain is "the universe of sense," a sense disclosed in a phenomenology and an anthropology. Philosophy, then, turns away from things in themselves, abandoning this to the sciences, while it is on the lookout to prevent the "sciences of man" from treating man as a thing in itself:

It diverts its attention from death as an external and organic event. Not out of unconcern for the human body, not for man's material existence, but it only considers the human body as the living unit that it constitutes with the soul in meaningful expressions. For the anthropological specificity of the human body is but its phenomenological specificity: it is the bearer of an intention. (309)

Vuillemin's project is to "suppress Nature and replace it by Man" (310) and, beyond naturalist and intellectualist fetishism, to reembrace emotion, freedom, joy. It would be easy to show that this humanist essay, because it is an *essay* and a *humanist* one, recaptures, retraces, and mimics some of the *Essays* of Montaigne, whose name is strikingly left out of this book, which, however, features a vast array of lesser thinkers. It mimics the *Essays* by a procedure analogous to the dialectic operations of rhetorical *inventio*, by the topics which it treats (animal *versus* man, death, the death of others, the passions, the virtues, etc.), and by the actual organization of a text often spattered with poetic passages in various languages, from rarely identified sources, which are used for both ornament and argument. But there remains an essential difference between this essay and those of Montaigne: Vuillemin does not come on stage, does not paint himself in it. An example of pure eloquence (this word often appears with pejorative connotations in *Le Miroir de Venise* [61, 67, 97]), this dissertation does not question its own ideology or rhetorical devices, nor does it question the status of the subject who enunciates its contents. From *man*, the first word, to *joy*, the last, here speaks, unscathed, *homo philosophicus*.

These cursory remarks, which concern a relatively early work by an author who has subsequently launched on a very arduous course, become meaningful only in relation to *le Miroir de Venise*, a palinode and surpassing of that debut. Despite the absence of direct references to *L'Essai sur la signification*, it, or similar writings, clearly are the target of the view that "oratorical art is one thing, the demonstration of ideas quite another . . . I had mixed the genres, just like a fashionable author" (52). Consequently, the autobiographical part of *Miroir* is, in line with the characteristic scheme of the self-portrait, a settling of accounts with the author's previous production.

The Self-Portrait and Humanism

The self-portrait, then, links up with the localizations of rhetorical memory. These places and images disposed in an imaginary space furnish it a topology that replaces autobiographical chronology. We have seen how the choice of emblematic *backgrounds* and *images* used by the self-portrait is itself overdetermined by the rhetorical heritage: house, town, or itinerary, the local sequence refers to the imaginary archaeology of each self-portrait, on the one hand, and, on the other, to the archaeology of the culture in which self-portrayal, more or less comfortably, takes place. The negative example of the Shereshevsky case, though very revealing in other respects, proves in fact that even a hypertrophied individual local memory does not suffice to produce a self-portrait. The latter must also be open to a cultural system of topics, must pit itself against it, even at the risk that the self and individualized memory will lose themselves in that confrontation.

The self-portrait must also set itself up as a text, that is, as a system that initiates the possibility of autoreference, palinode, cross-reference, and a memory, immanent to discourse and the book, which we have called *intratextual* memory. Yet intratextual memory questions and corrodes the encyclopedic coherence of the local recollection on which it leans. Thus, the anamnesis of the self-portrait is opposed to autobiographical reminiscence, which is always, to some degree, founded on a belief in the permanence of an individual self whose interiority is anteriority. The two memories, whose overlaps and contradictions make the self-portrait such a peculiar genre, open the self to its exteriority and the text to an unmastered intertext: cultural tradition, with its commonplaces where the readers can recognize themselves, but also with its old ambiguous myths crystallized around the emblematic figures that stand out as landmarks of an anamnesis. These mythic figures lead the self-portrait towards our culture's most haunting *speculations:* the contrast between hieroglyphic Egypt and logical Greece, the myths of Narcissus and Persephone, Socrates' dual figure, the relations between the figurative and the proper, between the subject and his other. The questions are being continuously posed and jumbled in line with variable ideological contexts.

Thus, the self-portrait links up with Renaissance humanism and borrows, unwittingly most often, the latter's *methods.* For humanism, by launching into a vast and confused reflection on rhetoric, fated itself to bring about the anamnesis of the classical treasury and the invention of modern man. Like humanism, the self-portrait discovers the subject, sets him adrift in the duration and places of a culture which, however, urges man to seek his individual place. A characteristic *double bind,* since the delphic injunction, as understood by humanism, also implies that the individual will seek in vain his position among the commonplaces simultaneously and contradictorily presented to him by memory and invention. The self-portrayer deambulates and rambles, knowing that a death has already intervened: he will never reach the end of the infinite metempsychosis that his writing demands of him, that he attempts to mimic by slipping in and out of anamnesis and amnesia, in and out of remembrance and invention.

PART THREE

Invention

Ars dialectica est doctrina disserendi. —Ramus, *Dialecticae Institutiones* (1543), fol. 8

CHAPTER 7

Compilations and the Essay during the Renaissance

Collections of Commonplaces and Topics

The self-portrait is a specific utilization of rhetorical invention, for it resorts to dialectical topics to circumscribe and mark out its metaphorical specular space. Christian spirituality, careful to preserve an ineffable transcendence, has lucidly noted the rhetorical constraints that lock the self-portrait into the *ontic* and condemn it as vanity in the eyes of those who prefer ontological epiphanies. So Gabriel Marcel writes:

I remain convinced that the closer a being is to me spiritually (the less he is for me a pure object), the less susceptible he is to being *characterized*. The same holds true for me, to the extent that I maintain spiritual commerce with myself; it is when this commerce is interrupted that I become "so-and-so" to myself. The existence of the self, then, would be linked to the impossibility of knowing oneself completely. But, then, what am I? Or, rather, what exactly do I mean when I ask myself this question? It has occurred to me to say that *I am* all the more my past the less I treat it as a collection of events indexed on cards, of possible answers to contingent questions. I am all the more the less I look upon myself as a data index. (*Journal métaphysique*, 242–43)[1]

And Roland Barthes, when he was writing his own self-portrait, also made similar remarks:

In a general way, it is not in my power to say who I am—or that I am this or that; for in saying so, I would only add one more text to my texts, with no guarantee that this text would be "truer"; all of us are *interpretable* beings, especially if we write, but it is others, never we, who have the power of interpretation; as a subject, I can never apply any predicate, any adjective to myself—except when ignoring my unconscious, which cannot be known by me. And not only are we unable to think of ourselves in terms of adjectives, but also we can never verify the adjectives that are applied to us: they leave us *mute:* they are, for us, critical fictions.[2]

These judgments are all the more expressive of an antirhetorical prejudice as there is here no question of rhetoric nor, a fortiori, of artificial memory or the "places of invention." *Being* is opposed to saying and to writing; the *one* transcends the *many:* proximity-presence cannot be expressed in terms of distance-perspective. The verb *to be* is purely intransitive and all possible predicates of the subject are deemed nonsense. The past itself must not be perceived as a sequence of events, and the question "What am I?" must remain without a specific answer. Marcel and Barthes, without ever designating their adversary, show that they are as hostile to *homo rhetoricus* as to *homo psychologicus.* But, as we shall see, Barthes himself was unable to escape from rhetoric in his self-portrait.

As soon as the self-portrait is no longer considered an unprecedented, spontaneous, sincere, and natural discourse, the pregnancy of a rhetorical matrix becomes compellingly evident.

The genealogy relating the *essay,* as it appears in Montaigne, and the Renaissance collections of commonplaces upon which Erasmus conferred a "literary" status is well known. Since Villey, modern readers know what the *Essays* owe to compilations and commentaries, to familiar letters and *moralia.* Despite the abundance of traits common to these various genres, it is useful to retain Villey's tripartite division: (1) commented examples—commentaries, glosses, annotations; (2) singular cases—"drawers" that are subdivisions of compilations "where singular cases are piled up, grouped together, catalogued"; (3) the precepts of ancient morality —dissertations on moral subjects (*Les Essais de Montaigne,* 30–37).[3] These texts, as Villey notes, "are essential elements of a genre highly appreciated in Montaigne's time. It can . . . be called the genre of 'lessons,' taking the word 'lesson' in the sense of 'reading,' which is its usual meaning" (35–36). Following this terminological decision, Villey cites the titles of the most celebrated "lessons," from those of Valerius Maximus and Aulu-Gellius in antiquity up to those of the Renaissance compilers: Erasmus's *Adages* and *Apophtegms*, Caelius Rhodiginus's *Lectiones antiquae*, Guevera's *Golden Epistles*, Pierre de Bouaystuau's *Théâtre du monde* and *Histoires prodigieuses*, and so forth; a flowering that Villey explains as follows: "Renaissance man, drowning in so many notions coming to him from both antiquity and the New World, felt the need to inventory them, to orient himself among all this knowledge. He ransacks, and sticks labels on" (36). Although insufficient, this explanation clarifies the positions of Montaigne the self-portraitist at the crossroads of antiquity and the New World.

As for Hugo Friedrich, he situates the essay among "that abundant prose literature, in an open form, which had always appeared in compilations, medleys, letters, dialogues, diatribes, etc., and had regained public favor since the fifteenth century" (*Montaigne*, 364). Friedrich is not satisfied merely to lengthen Villey's list; he explains the triumph of the open form and the taste for medleys by the influence of "diverse antischolastic tendencies of a religious, philosophic, scientific and aristocratic character" (366). This explanation does not contradict Villey's, since it also stresses the novelty of the knowledge and ideologies through which Renaissance man shakes up the authoritarian monologue of the past in order to create new discourses.

Still, it is surprising that these two interpretations—which are perhaps one and the same—should rely on shaky historical causes while ignoring a less risky explanation: in fact, one could maintain that Renaissance rhetoric constitutes the literary matrix of all the texts in question. Perhaps these two eminent critics have been deflected from this simple explanation by Montaigne's antirhetorical attitude or by a more modern prejudice.

Recent research has now furnished proof that rhetorical practice —particularly in the schoolroom context—served both as a matrix for the *essay* and as a framework for the disparate "genres" that Villey designated as "lessons" and Friedrich called "open forms" in prose. A detour into pedagogy must be made to explain the innovation of the *Essays*, for the *essay*, as Montaigne christened his work, does not result from a purely literary evolution, at the end of which the humanist compilation would be fulfilled in its own abolition: the essay is engendered by the same rhetorical practice as the other genres from which it is generally thought to be derived.[4]

This shift in point of view would be trivial if it did not illuminate the complex links between rhetoric and literature during the Renaissance, and above all if it did not allow one to specify what is different in Montaigne's *Essays* and thus define them.

If one admits that the aim of humanist pedagogy was to form moral "orators" with abundant invention and an elegant style, and likewise that the desire for *copia* triumphed over any other purpose, one gains a clearer understanding of the function of the commonplace books and the proliferation of manuals facilitating the task of young pupils as well as that of adult orators.[5] Joan Marie Lechner emphasizes that the obsession with *copia* marks and accelerates the decay of rhetoric, as understood in classical antiquity at least, and the deterioration of the traditional links between invention, dialectic and logic (*Renaissance Concepts of the Commonplaces*, 168). As a result of its having forgotten the dialectical places, the *seats* for arguments to serve in legal and political controversies and the common *topics* for many *causes*, rhetoric came to conceive of the places as "methodically arranged headings under which lessons and meditations are grouped together." The places of invention were, according to classical rhetoric, exercises in dialectical reflection, sequences of logical operations, long before they were mere catalogues of cultural clichés, or collections of quotations. The order in which these "places" are organized is often overdetermined by the praise of virtue and the vituperation of vice, as would be expected in the epideictic genre, and by extension, in the other genres of eloquence.[6]

Dialectic and Artificial Arguments

Given the degradation and disrepute of the notion of the commonplace since Romanticism, one must insist on the two very distinct senses of *locus* (topic) in classical rhetoric and, theoretically at least, in Renaissance rhetorical pedagogy.[7] Walter J. Ong has proposed an empirical division of *places* into two categories: "analytic places" and "cumulative places" (*Rhetoric, Romance, and Tech-*

nology, 260–61).[8] Analytic topics are sequences of logical operations enabling one to analyze *things* (subjects, zones, spatially conceived themes, as areas in which are lodged the ideas that must be ferreted out: the "seats" of the argument), according to codified procedures, such as causes, effects, related matters, contraries. Let us take, more or less at random, two examples of this old practice: the first comes from a medieval encyclopedia, the second from one of the Renaissance's most influential rhetorical manuals. According to Maurice de Gandillac, Raoul Ardent's *Speculum Universale* (second half of the twelfth century) is but a *summa of vices and virtues* belonging to the Victorine tradition. Johannes Gründel describes as follows the method used by Raoul to treat a *virtue*, without forgetting any of its aspects and pertinent traits in the ethical and practical context of the *speculum:*

Raoul finally discusses the virtues, or diverse aspects of man's moral behavior, related to discourse or to the five senses (*De moribus exterioribus hominis*). When dealing with virtues, he often does so according to a fixed pattern based on the following questions:

1. What is its essence (quid sit)?
2. What is its origin (unde oriatur)?
3. What elements nourish it (quibus nutriatur)?
4. What is its importance (quanta sit)?
5. Which are its species (quae ejus species)?
6. Which are its complementary virtues (quae virtus sit ex collateralis)?
7. Which vice is its contrary (quo vitium sit ex contrarium)?
8. What are its limits (qui termini)?
9. To what danger is it exposed (quibus impugnetur)?
10. How can it resist (qualiter resistatur)? ("L'Oeuvre encyclopédique de Raoul Ardent")

Our second example derives from *De Inventione Dialectica Libri Tres*, by Rudolph Agricola, completed towards 1479 and published in 1515.[9] In this treatise, all the "places of invention" are grouped together in the *dialectic*, as they would be later on by Ramus, and in the "method" which he bequeathed mainly to English-speaking Protestants.[10] As in Raoul Ardent, Agricola's dialectic still functions in the context of an encyclopedia of virtues and vices—that is, in the domain of ethics and of what we would probably call the "social sciences."

Following rhetorical tradition, Agricola distinguishes between *artificial* arguments—those obtained by art, through a technique of reasoning and intrinsic examination of the matter in question— and the *inartificial* arguments (or places) derived from testimonials—quotations, examples, documents are inartificial arguments.

Here is how one discusses courage, or any other virtue or vice, using artificial arguments (or places). One may insert inartificial arguments along the way in the form of examples, narrations, and so on. Consider in order:

The definition of courage

—its genus, species, properties;
—whole, parts;
—conjugates or closely related matters;
—adjacents, or more loosely related matters;
—acts of courage; —subjects of courage;
—efficient cause, end; consequences, and projected effects of courage;
—times and places where courage must be practiced;
—its connections, contingents, names, pronunciation;
—things comparable to it;
—analogous things;
—similar things;
—contraries, differences.

These rhetorical practices, in the Middle Ages as in the Renaissance, differ little, in principle, from those of orators of Greco-Latin antiquity. Or at least the differences by default, which one easily detects between the *topics* of the *speculum* and Agricola's school topics, on the one hand, and the topics of Aristotle's and Cicero's major treatises, on the other, are essentially the result of the shrinking social and political field where persuasion is exercised. According to many historians of rhetoric, it was that shrinking that finally brought about the decline of rhetoric and its reduction to a normative stylistics. But, by focusing one's attention on this relative decline as it occurred in the context of education, one risks overlooking an important fact in the history of culture: the topics of school invention, even while they gradually forgot the complex dialectical maneuvers required by legal and political debates, still preserved certain contents and methods that governed their utilization. Of course, these contents were relatively fixed, "commonplaces" in the pejorative sense, since they always express an old, more or less christianized, classical anthropology whose ritual divisions are the virtues and vices. Yet, even when it was limited to the invention by pupils of what everyone knows only too well, rhetoric *never* was reduced only to style. It always retained an encyclopedic and specular content, even when this content does not appear explicitly in such post-Ramist school manuals as are reduced to tropes and figures. Rhetorical invention always concerns man in society and ultimately his salvation. This anthropological content, as well as the simplified dialectic through which an adolescent can repeatedly hold forth on this or that virtue, is what will be transformed and recentered in meditation and the self-portrait.

Alongside of the dialectical places of invention, one can therefore distinguish "cumulative" places corresponding approximately to the notion of *topic*, as defined by E. R. Curtius: a store of general ideas that can be used in all kinds of compositions (*European Literature and the Latin Middle Ages*, 79). The Renaissance collections, Erasmus's *De copia*, for example, gather under more or less standard headings passages from various authors that can be used for inartificial arguments, appropriate epithets, ready-made formulas, maxims related to the thing (*res*) in question. The divisions here are generic or thematic, rather than indicative of dialectical operations. With respect to these collections of cumulative places, R. R. Bolgar wrote: "within the limits set by the demands of suitability, it was possible for an intending writer to choose from is classical models whatever struck his fancy and out of these fragments he could construct a new and pleasing whole" (*The Classical Heritage*, 272).

One must avoid a confusion between two kinds of "places," even if they are often confused in ordinary usage. While the dialectical topics of invention correspond as a rule to logical operations (opposition, inclusion, and so on), they are, above all, on the elementary level where Raoul Ardent and Agricola place themselves, basic guideposts, codified landmarks, along a compulsory route. Since antiquity, the simplest type of eloquence, encomiastic eloquence, also implemented ritual sequences: place of origin, lineage, education, corporal and mental gifts, wealth, etc.

In the sixteenth century, while still paying homage to the major manuals of invention, such as Aristotle's or Cicero's *Topics*, the pedagogues use works better adapted to the teaching of literary composition in schools: mainly Erasmus's *De Copia* and Aphtone's *Progymnasmata*, later joined by numerous modern manuals, conceived in the same spirit. This weakening of the dialectic and logical rigor of invention would finally lead Pierre de la Ramée to complete the divorce: he separates logic and dialectic from rhetoric, reducing it to composition and style.

New Encyclopedia or Grab Bag?

In ordinary pedagogic practice, then, the places of invention become mere receptacles. This displacement of the notion of *commonplace* is marked by the use, which spread almost universally among the schools, of notebooks with divisions or headings under which the student must "copy," during his readings, examples or quotations he will subsequently utilize in his own compositions. Vivès and Melanchthon, influential pedagogues, give precise instructions to this effect:

Nam et memoria adiuvabitur, cum ordine distribuerimus eas [the commonplaces] in certas classes, et haec distributio rerum inter se ordinem ostendet. . . . Optima autem in distribuendo Oeconomia erit, si sequemur artium discrimina. Cavendum est enim, ne confundantur artes, sed observandum, qui loci sint Theologici, qui sint Philosophici. Ac Philosophici possunt peti ex partibus hominibus. Ratio, Artes, Prudentia, Virtus, Affectus, Consuetudo, Corpus, Forma, Aetas, Fortuna Divitiae, Oeconomia, Conjugium, Educatio liberorum, Politia, Magistratus, Lex, Bellum, Pax. Facile est autem genera partiri, et videre, quae sententiae, quae exempla, quae similitudines, in que libet specie collocari debeant.[11]

As Lechner has shown, Melanchthon's instructions in *Elementorum Rhetorices* are typical of sixteenth-century manuals. It is therefore interesting to note that he proposes "philosophical" places, derived from the parts of man, which come mostly from the places utilized by classical orators in the epideictic (praising or blaming) genre:

Laus igitur potest esse rerum externarum, corporis, animi. Rerum externarum sunt ex quae casu aut fortuna secunda aut adversa accidere possunt: genus, educatio, divitiae, potestates, gloriae, civitas, amicitiae, et quae huius modi sunt et quae his contraria. Corporis sunt ex quae natura corpori adtribuit commoda aut incommoda: velocitas, vires, dignitas, valetudo, et quae contraria sunt. Animi sunt ex quae consilio et cogitatione nostra constant: prudentia, iustitia, fortitudo, modestia, et quae contraria sunt. (*Rhetorica ad Herennium*, III, VI, 10)

Melanchthon's "philosophical places," all of them linked to the "parts of man," are enumerated in disorder—at any rate in comparison with the rigorous progression from the without to the within proposed in *Ad Herennium*. True, Melanchthon is dealing here with a question foreign to classical rhetoric, involving the distinction between "theological places" and "philosophical places." These places are henceforth detached from the structures and function that defined them in classical rhetoric: instead of simply serving the empirical work of invention, they have acquired a kind of taxonomic autonomy in an ideological and discursive context entirely different from that of pagan antiquity.

Melanchthon considers the classification of commonplaces as a mnemonic device. He envisages memory, then, as a part of invention, rather than a distinct rhetorical function. In the context of a written literature whose contents are no longer dictated by the immediate imperatives of politics, the courts of justice and social life in general, memory becomes an auxiliary of invention; its function is to increase *copia*.

Despite the divergence between the pedagogues and the rhetoricians of the Renaissance, they all agree to prescribe the use of *libri locorum* and the organization of these commonplace books according to a number of standard headings: nor does Rudolph Agricola overlook this practice, which he describes for pupils as follows:

Certa quaedam rerum capita habeamus cuius modi sunt "virtus," "vitium," "vita," "mors," "doctrina," "ineruditio," "benevolentia," "odium," et reliqua id genus quorum usu fere communis ad omnia et tanquem publicus sit. Haec crebre iterimus, et omnia quae didicimus, quantum fieri potest, certe quaecumque discimus ad ea redigamus et repetendis capitibus illus ex quoque quae ad ea redigimus repetantur. (*De Formando Studio Epistola*)[12]

Two texts, among many others, shed light both on how commonplaces are used in teaching and on their function as a matrix for the scientific work of the period.[13]

A passage from Tabourot des Accords shows that the classification of an *exemplum* under a heading is not a simple mechanical task. Since it implies a certain dialectical activity, the distribution of the fragments of an ancient text among the places is more problematic than it seemed on reading Agricola:

> Whereas, for example, you have in Livy a speech by Lucius Quintus Concinnatus [sic], whom the Roman people elected dictator, and whom the deputies found working on his land when they came to announce his election to him. One reader will note it in the commonplace *Agriculture*, as did Cicero in his book, *Of Old Age;* another, like Livy, will note it as virtue preferred to riches. For someone else, like Cicero in his same book, it will be old age, because the people sought him out when he was old, owing to his long experience. Another will note an honest, undisdained poverty. Another, the assiduous labor of that old age; and there are more commonplaces to which this story could be fitted. Therefore, by such research, the child will learn and remember much more easily than the one who reads only for the pleasure of the story: and his judgment will be the sounder for it. (*Bigarrures*, I, IV, ch. 1, 434ff.)

A passage from the chapter "De Locis Historiarum Recte Instituendis," in Jean Bodin's *Methodus ad Facilem Historarium Cognitionem* (1572; *Method for the Easy Comprehension of History*) presents this work as an attempt to systematically classify human actions and the characteristics of civilization. According to Porteau: "it is imperative to group together, after a thought-out plan, the commonplaces of memorable deeds, so that, when one must act, one can pull out of them, as from a coffer, an abundant documentation to guide our conduct" (*Montaigne*, 136–37).

The aim of a systematic grouping together of *exempla* in places is therefore to set up a collective memory or encyclopedia. Bodin's work is divided into three books: the first treats of man, the second of nature, and the third of God. On a scientific level, Bodin's work reminds one of the medieval encyclopedic *specula*. On the school level, ambitions are more modest, although any such classification does imply an anthropology. Like Agricola, Vivès addresses children directly and places himself at their level:

Make a book of blank leaves of a proper size. Divide it into certain topics, so to say, into nests. In one, jot down the names of subjects of daily conversation: the mind, the body, our occupations, games, clothes, schedules, divisions of time, dwellings, food; in another, *sententiae*; in another, proverbs, in another, difficult passages from authors; in another, matters which seem worthy of note to thy teacher or thyself. (*Introductio ad Sapientam*)[14]

Erasmus's *De Copia*, particularly where it treats of *things* rather than *words*, fulfills the same pedagogic requirement, to which is added an encyclopedic aim: before he starts to write by himself, the pupil should, pen in hand, read all of ancient literature and distribute the newly copied fragments under such headings of invention as will enable him to cope with any emergency (in *Ratione Colligendi Exempla*).[15] In the choice of his headings, Erasmus is in fact more faithful to the ancient rhetorical model than are most of his contemporaries. He resorts to the division by virtues and vices (contraries being grouped together, since they can illustrate each other *a contrario*) and their subdivisions.[16] Faith, for example, is divided into faith in God and faith in Man. The latter is subdivided into loyalty towards friends, masters, enemies. These moral headings tend to leave a "remainder" to be distributed under different headings: old age and youth; strange and sudden deaths; each to his own taste; love and hate; monarchy and democracy.[17] Thus, collections of commonplaces, whether they are modest ones for young pupils or as vast as Erasmus's major compilations, aim to assemble the totality of individual or collective knowledge according to a taxonomy whose relative homogeneity—before the major reorganization of knowledge, first by the Ramist method and, afterwards, by the Cartesian method—describes the configurations of what passed for human *nature* and its culture.

Let us evaluate the results of this detour through collections of commonplaces. We will not dwell on their pedagogical function, though it was perhaps their most important aspect during the Renaissance, except to note that these collections of cumulative places were used not only to nourish the *copia* of the school exercises but also to effect a mutation in mimesis, which came to mean, above all, *imitation of the ancients.*

In themselves, the collections of commonplaces are not a systematic mimesis of antiquity, but the reproduction (copy) and fragmentation of classical discourses. However, the success of such printed books as Erasmus's *De Copia*, *Adagia*, and *Apophtegmata* and of many other more or less specialized compilations is also due to the fact that, because of the wealth of materials they assembled, they present a kind of general taxonomic picture of classical antiquity.[18] They are the only books that offer an inclusive image, or "theater," of the day-to-day variety of Greco-Latin culture. The eclecticism of such a view is not displeasing to the Renaissance reader: it suggests a plenitude which the moderns lack.

These compilations therefore constitute a kind of collective memory, or an anamnesis of a buried cultural past, an archaeology. They reconstruct ancient discourse in detail, with customs, proverbs, games, jokes. They delve into the diachronic thickness of language to form the lineaments of a philology.

Although, in principle, their function is ancillary and propaedeutic (theoretically, they serve to nourish prose or verse compositions modeled on ancient genres), these collections acquire an autonomous status, as witnessed by the fact that, especially in Erasmus, compilation and classification engender their own commentary. Thus, a new kind of text is produced, not a simple classified accumulation but an incipient utilization of the assembled material. The commonplace is enveloped and permeated by a "personal" discourse: it becomes the *object* of a *subject*, who, not being content with copying, also meditates on the places and impresses his individual mark on them. In Erasmus particularly, commentary engenders the *persona* of the commentator. The latter expresses in turn his opinions, his tastes, and he transmits a personal experience.[19] The collection of places thus links up with the private genres of antiquity, such as the epistle, the most striking example of which remains Seneca's *Letter to Lucilius*.

Consequently, two apparently divergent opinions, one Bacon's and the other Ben Jonson's appear to us to be complementary. According to Bacon:

The word [*essay*] is recent, but the thing is ancient: for Seneca's Epistles to Lucilius . . . are really Essays—that is, scattered Meditations, even though they are conveyed in the form of Epistles. (Preface to the second edition of the *Essays*)

While Bacon ennobles the upstart essay by finding an honorable ancient model for it, Ben Jonson complains in *Timber*, that the essay is only a grab bag of material gathered under any old heading of a commonplace book;[20] and Florio, the English translator of Montaigne's *Essays*, remarks in the 1603 preface: "Essays are but men's school themes pieced together; you might as well say, several texts."[21]

In his work *Bacon on Communication and Rhetoric*, Karl R. Wallace shows that the places discussed in the chancellor's *Essays* are ethical places, carefully chosen to fill gaps in knowledge about man, gaps whose existence Bacon denounced as early as his *Advancement of Learning*. Wallace quotes Bacon:

Now we come to those points which are within our command, and have force and operation upon the mind to affect the will and appetite and to alter manners; wherein they ought to have handled *custom, exercise, habit, education, example, imitation, emulation, company, friends, praise, reproof, exhortation, fame, laws, books, studies* . . . of these are such receipts and regiments compounded and described, as may seem to recover or preserve the health and good estate of the mind, as far as pertaineth to human medicine.[22]

In the course of successive editions of his *Essays*, Bacon works at filling such gaps by adding essays corresponding to the places in question. As a result, Wallace remarks, "only twenty-five of the fifty-eight essays in the edition of 1625 (the last one revised by Bacon) do not immediately suggest an analysis of character or of conduct" (118). This observation would be trivial, since one need only consult the table of contents of the *Essays* to see this, if Bacon, trying to establish a firmer epistemological foundation, had not consistently asserted that ethics is bound up with rhetoric. As Wallace indicates:

If rhetoric and ethics share a common end and differ only in their medium and means of operation, then it is hard to escape the inference that Bacon, if he had fully constructed a rhetorical system, would certainly have included in it his essays on character, perhaps in much the same manner that Aristotle has sketched human character in his rhetoric. (119)

It is true that Wallace's conclusions are hypothetical, though these hypotheses are supported by a tradition that makes them highly credible. Moreover, what matters here is that it was still possible during Bacon's time to conceive of an overlapping relation between ethics and rhetoric, so that, alternately, each might be contained in the other. The study of the commonplaces of invention during the Renaissance shows that rhetoric becomes increasingly anthropological and psychological as it grows more detached from dialectic. The pedagogical use of commonplaces spawns a new genre, the *essay*, where cultural and ethical generality is accompanied by a marginal meditation in which the compiler asserts, by adherence or rejection, his status as an individual judge.

CHAPTER 8

The Rhetorical Matrix
during the Renaissance

Montaigne, Bacon, and Method

Francis Bacon's *Essays* are profoundly different from Montaigne's mostly because he has no intention at all of "painting himself" in them. But, just because of this difference, the works of Bacon—the *Essays* included—enable one to define more precisely the status of rhetorical invention in the production of the self-portrait, provided self-portrayal is envisaged globally, in relation to the Baconian epistemological undertaking as a whole.[1]

The works of Bacon and Montaigne are inversely symmetrical in their relations to persuasive rhetoric, which seeks not to understand the world better, nor to call in question the stating subject, but to induce the adherence of others to an opinion. Persuasion does this by utilizing the commonplaces of a culture, according to a dialectically conducted discourse whose rules are generally deemed to be efficacious, even though they depart from the logical procedures that, in principle, govern scientific and philosophical discourses.

Although, even nowadays, the practice of "literature" often justifies itself by edifying and persuasive intentions and looks to rhetoric for the most suitable means to the desired effect, the self-portrait (even when professing to be self-praise or self-blame) resorts to a playful imitation of rhetorical procedures detached from their persuasive function. In self-portrayal, rhetoric is not a mere tool, nor a dictionary of tricks, but a structural model. Having lost its persuasive role, rhetoric provides the self-portrait with a topical structure and the metadiscourse of its invention. The point is no longer to affect others—or oneself, as in religious exercises—but to stage a rhetoric and to challenge it under the guise of the writer's questioning himself on his project and the means to carry it out, on his idiolect, and on his own status, in the text, as the writing subject. The invention of the self-portrayal is a reinvention of rhetoric, according to certain modalities specific to nonnarrative discourse in the first person: consequently it stands in a transformational relation to the other variants of rhetorical practice that cropped up in various quarters during the Renaissance and the classical period.

This is why Bacon's oeuvre—perhaps the most important of those variants before Vico's *New Science*—can also be read as a macrocosm of the self-portrait's microcosmic rhetoric or, from another point of view, as an impersonal version of the self-portrait. The *Novum Organon* and the *Advancement of Learning* do not deal with Francis Bacon, his tastes, the way his mind functions, nor even with his writing and his relations to commonplaces. But these works do treat, from a certain angle, modern European man's relations to language, to the topical system of knowledge, and to dialectic. Of course, it would be abusive to see in Bacon's works a collective portrait of Western man at the moment when he sets out to dominate the world, as it would also be perhaps excessive to see in Descartes's *Discourse on Method* and *Meditations* a self-portrait of modern man preparing to understand nature (even though Descartes does center his epistemological undertaking on an individual subject). However, the point in both cases is to invent a *method* professing to be universally applicable. These two methods—and we should not forget that the period was fertile in "methods"—produce results that, though not identical, are comparable: one is too apt to forget this when, dealing with Descartes, one neglects his physics and the pejorative connotations of the epithet *Cartesian* in the classical epoch. Bacon and Descartes both invented, through their respective *methods*, an *imaginary nature* differing less from the nature the scholastics had devised by induction and the syllogism than from the quantified nature of the ulterior exact sciences. Bacon and Descartes, like most scientists and epistemologists of the Renaissance—whether they belong to the magical or to the empirical factions—are people in a hurry who believe theirs is the definitive reform of human understanding and that they are inventing *the* definitive method. Paradoxically, as a result, their epistemological labors appear to us particularly revealing of their individual mode of thought and the cultural—in this case, rhetorical—constraints that inform them. We now know that their method is more an illusion of understanding and mastery than a viable epistemological tool. Rhetorical constraint, a polymorphous and all-encompassing *épistémè*, brings together the magicians (seekers of a universal key, who suppose there are esoteric signifieds, or attach these to certain elements of rhetoric, such as memory's emblematic places and images) and the empiricists or "methodists" who model their (heuristic or descriptive) methods on the dialectic procedures of invention.

As Hiram Haydn has shown in his fine work, *The Counter-Renaissance*, one can situate Montaigne among the empiricists, because his entire project of self-description is focused on the *particular*. Not the grammarian, poet, and jurisconsult (Man even less so, at least at the beginning), but Michel de Montaigne such as he is and not as he should be (230). Such an empiricism implies a disdain for the topos and an aversion to any orthopedic method seeking to rectify the illusions, vagaries, and insufficiencies of judgment. On the contrary, the point here is to describe what may seem aberrant to normative reason. But Montaigne, by describing his mental operations, implicitly puts himself forward as an example, if not a model. If the actual process of his individual thinking so often wanders away from the dialectic topic, can we not suspect that dialectics always is a gross simplification of thought processes? If others knew themselves better, would they let themselves be taken in by this hoax, which is not even justified by the production of new and irrefutable knowledge? And, by way of the individual, the *Essays* suggest a nonnormative description of the spontaneous workings of human understanding, which prove to be efficient in the empirical portrayal of Michel de Montaigne's mind. An invention by fits and starts is at least as good as many other methods. This amounts to a new *Organon*, modest in appearance but secretly just as ambitious as Bacon's, to which it stands in opposition within the same structure.

Yet the inverse symmetry between the works of Montaigne and Bacon is liable to escape notice, if one's primary concern is to stress the influence of Montaigne's *Essays* on Bacon's (which leads one to note that Bacon treats almost the same ethical and political places as Montaigne according to *ordo neglectus*), or if one emphasizes the contrast between Montaigne's spontaneous self-description and the impersonal didacticism of Bacon's *Essays*.[2]

Bacon's *Essays* are a (certainly major and celebrated) fraction of an immense work whose chief aim is to recast human understanding and to elaborate a new epistemology, which, departing from a Scholastic logic judged to be sterile, is modeled on the dialectic of rhetorical invention. Bacon, therefore, transforms into an instrument of scientific discovery—in the material, ethical, and political world—the procedures that used to be confined to the invention of persuasive discourses.

Conversely, with Montaigne, Pyrrhonic epistemology in its most sustained and compact form, constitutes a practically autonomous fragment of the *Essays*, namely, the *Apology for Raymond Sebond*. But, as a whole, the *Essays* aim to set up a self-knowledge and a method of self-knowledge that, in the end, make any other learning superfluous. Thus, the *Essays* founded a new, irrefutable learning, a knowledge of the *subject* of all learning, and of all ignorance.[3]

Montaigne and Bacon both tend to confuse invention and memory. Montaigne constantly disparages memory in order to turn it into a modality of his invention and something very like the self-awareness of an invention of the subject. Although less radically, Bacon also condemns memory that hinders the progress of learning, but only to turn its places and emblems into the keystones of his epistemology; thus, memory becomes something like the "repressed" underlying his method. Actually, while Montaigne and Bacon agree in thinking that rhetorical invention discovers nothing new, each produces a variant of it by inventing new places and a procedure better adapted to his respective aims.

There is also a marked opposition between Bacon's pragmatic project, which purports to dominate the social and material world, and Montaigne's idle retreat, the leisure that concentrates his uncontained writing solely on its subject, on the act of stating, and on the Book where their simulacrum is elaborated. This opposition is clearly discernable in a statement by Bacon on his own works, where a condemnation of Montaigne's *oeuvre* can be read between the lines:

And surely, if the purpose be in good earnest not to write at leisure that which men may read at leisure, but really to instruct and suborn action and active life, these Georgics of the mind, concerning the husbandry and tillage thereof, are not less worthy than the heroical descriptions of Virtue, Duty and Felicity. (*The Advancement of Learning*, Book I)[4]

Bacon's works teach, and his *Essays* are didactic in themselves. Montaigne's *Essays*, on the other hand, are concerned with describing a single mind, aloof from the world, and an idle writing devoid of didactic intent. In other words, whereas Bacon's works follow directly in the line of the humanist, rhetorical, and militant Renaissance (though set apart from it because of their disdain for virtue), Montaigne's diverges from it (though he ignores neither pedagogy nor virtue) and examines above all else its own resistance to established persuasion, teaching, and learning. Montaigne reduces commonplaces—whose persuasive effectiveness is universally acknowledged in his time—to the particularity of an undisciplined writing that runs through them to destroy them, only retaining in them that which adheres to the subject's particularities and especially to the text he is producing. Montaigne's "What do I know?" is not only the converse but also the mockery of Bacon's implicit "How must one learn?" It calls in question the imperative of learning and action, because this injunction implies the subject's alienation into generality and empirical efficiency.

Bacon's *Essays* can be read as an analogous attempt at debunking, though undertaken on the plane of epistemological generality, on the plane of humankind rather than that of the *individual* subject. Bacon revised and enlarged his *Essays* several times between 1597 and 1625. But critics concur in saying that the disorderly accumulation of examples creates confusion and a muddling of dialectic invention in each essay of his final edition, so much so that

Bacon's intentions have become decipherable only with great difficulty. In previous editions, while the development was discontinuous and fitful, the dialectic remained virtually classic, easy to reconstruct, and, consequently, more persuasive. One recognizes here an objection frequently raised against Rabelais, Montaigne, and many other Renaissance writers. The taste for the somewhat haughty *ordo neglectus* had waned. But it has come back nowadays semanticized in the register of *transgression*. It is no doubt this backlash that has provoked a new reading of Bacon.

In a book where he strives to describe the experience of the reader led through a dialectic labyrinth, frustrated of the pleasure he seeks from totalization and univocal interpretation, Stanley Fish concludes that the true subject of Bacon's *Essays* is not a collection of ethical *topoi*, but rather the very *accumulation* of examples, opinions, and apothegms; or to be more exact, how the *doxa* thinks morality. "This, of course," writes Fish, "would tend to make all of the essays one large essay in the root sense of the word—one continuous attempt to make sense of things, with the emphasis on the 'making sense of' rather than on the 'things' " (*Self-Consuming Artifacts*, 91–92). This approach—a debunking phenomenology—would prompt the reader to query himself about the validity of the examples and judgments reported by Bacon, about their internal logic and that which makes them an ethical encyclopedia, and finally to call in question the presuppositions on the basis of which such statements are engendered according to such a dialectic. The Baconian essay, then, would not prompt the reader to adhere to Bacon's values but would rather attempt to instigate a critical process. The *Essays* do become increasingly "immoral" and Machiavellian as they are revised, but Bacon is trying to show that acquiescence in a given morality, even a cynical one, is what prevents men from grasping the complexity and ambiguity of concrete situations. Accordingly, the arduous decipherment of the *Essays* would be a model for the concentration and detachment necessary to overcome errors of judgment in situations experienced empirically. Such a reflection brushes aside precedents and contests ready-made wisdom in order to embrace and master reality. According to Fish, "the essays advocate nothing (except perhaps a certain openness and alertness of mind); they are descriptive and description is ethically neutral; although, if it is accurate, it may contribute to the development of a true, that is, responsible, ethics" (94).[5] With Bacon, in the *Essays* as elsewhere, it is always a matter of freeing the reader from the prestigious influence of ancient persuasion (while imposing a new one, called a "method," or using the old arguments against potential dupes); he also contests the often specious formal coherence of discourse, which satisfies a desire for order rather than for truth. Bacon prefers the fragmentary, especially aphorisms, as "representing a knowledge broken, do invite men to enquire further; whereas Methods, carrying the shew of a total, do secure men, as if they were at furthest" (Sp. III, 405), and the *Novum Organon* designates constituted systems of thought, which create obstacles to pursuing an inquiry to its unforeseeable consequences, as "so many stage plays, representing worlds of their own creation in an unreal and scenic fashion" (Sp. IV, 55). The book and the theater, as entities that seek closure and tend to become monads, are places and metaphors for illusion, casting spells over the mind.

Yet the *Essays* never turn back on the writer himself to describe his own dialectic and the illusions from which he would free himself (or in which he would indulge). Bacon is interested in neither the particularities of individual thought, nor in the idiosyncrasy of a discourse encumbered by idols and illusions. Bacon's antirhetoric does not seek a prerhetorical, pristine sort of discourse, nor to account for the naive rhetoric of any given speaker, not even that of Bacon himself; on the contrary it reaches for something beyond rhetoric, which would be a simpler, more open Method, more heedful of the object in its particularity than of the general traits of genus or species, for the latter are but commonplaces produced by an apriorism disdainful of empiricism.

But Bacon's *Essays*, like the rest of his works (and, symmetrically, Montaigne's *Essays* despite their numerous denials of any such debt) remain indebted to rhetoric. They are a version of rhetoric, as are all Renaissance methods and antimethods produced by the explosion of the old dialectic-rhetoric: the title page of the first edition of Bacon's *Essays* (1597) bears the words "Essayes. Religious Meditations; Places of Perswasion et Disswasion." However, it is impossible to differentiate between the *essays* and the *meditations* in that thin volume.[6] All that matters is the synonymy suggested among the three terms: *essay*, *meditation*, and *place*, thanks to which the last term, a clearly rhetorical one, can be substituted for the other two. In short, an essay (for Bacon) is a persuasive and dissuasive place. One cannot conclude that the same applies to Montaigne's essays, but only that Bacon, who was as versed in the art of rhetoric as anyone was in his time, may have read Montaigne's *Essays* as a collection of commonplaces and perhaps, also, as a series of meditations. His was obviously a partial reading, which took account only of a typological classification and ignored Montaigne's subjectivist transgression.

This first edition of Bacon's *Essays* also contains a fragment entitled: "A table of the colours or appearances of good or evil, and their degrees, as places of persuasion and dissuasion; and their several fallaxes, and the elenches of them." These colors, a term to be understood in its rhetorical sense, as *colores rhetorici*, are sophisms, erroneous assertions that appear to be true and can serve to persuade good (or evil . . .). This notion is developed in Bacon's *De Augmentis* and has its place in his general reflection on rhetoric. Consequently, Bacon's *Essays*, unlike Montaigne's, confess as early as the title page their ties to this rhetoric that constantly haunts Bacon's thought, even when he strives to promulgate a new science.[7] Through Bacon, as Montaigne's disciple, and according to complex and equivocal mediations, the self-portrait is made to disclose the very rhetorical matrix it also blurs and denies. Therefore, we must examine Baconian rhetoric rather closely, even though the chancellor himself never undertook self-portrayal.

Quite paradoxically, this writer, thirsting for mastery and positive knowledge, produced a variant of a rhetorical model thanks to which those who turn away from learning and power may portray themselves at their leisure. And it is Bacon, condemning the execrable collusion of memory and invention in scientific research, who described the links between the two, though he was himself caught by the backlash of this infernal rhetorical machine. The collusion proved disastrous for scientific epistemology, since it enables one only to discover what was given a priori, but fruitful for the self-portrait, which finds there the means to deploy memory in the *hic et nunc* space of topical invention. And the self-portrait assures this monster's modest survival long after the collapse of the dialectical-rhetorical epistemology that structured the Renaissance sciences.

According to Baconian epistemology, the human mind is an "enchanted glass," full of superstitions and impostures; knowledge is vitiated by the errors inherent in judgment. These unconscious distortions, these false appearances are imposed on us by the general nature of the mind. Bacon, in the English version of *The Advancement of Learning*, gives examples of this fundamental mental defect that creates aberrations: "to the nature of the mind of all men it is consonant for the affirmative or active to affect more than the negative or privative: so that a few times hitting or presence, countervails oft-times failing or absence"; or also: "the spirit of man, being of an equal and uniform substance, doth usually suppose and feign in nature a greater equality and uniformity than is in truth." Sciences, therefore, tend to devise simple and elegant hypotheses that falsify the complexity of nature. On the basis of this denunciation of an illusory harmony between the human spirit and the spirit of nature, Bacon worked out his doctrine of "Idols" in the Latin version of *The Advancement* and in the *Novum Organon*: idols of the spirit, the tribe, the cave and the market-place (*Advancement of Learning*, 132–34, and *Novum Organon*, I, 39–68).

Bacon's method is an attempt to overcome the confusion of a labyrinthine world, a forest teeming with ambiguous forking paths. But it is also a "method to control the senses, memory and reason," as Bacon declared in *Novum Organon*. Whence the close relation between his method of scientific invention and an art of memory first set forth in *The Advancement of Learning*. This relationship is like a repetition, on another level, of the confusion evident since antiquity between invention and memory, since both of them refer to the notion of "places."

From Method to the Imaginary: Bacon, Vico, Gilbert Durand

The Baconian conception of memory is analogous to the one formulated in numerous Renaissance mnemonic works. If Bacon disdains the purely ostentatious exploits of certain mnemonic practitioners and considers that the memory faculty has been poorly studied, he still thinks mnemonics can contribute to scientific research:

This art of memory is but built upon two intentions: the one prenotion, the other emblem. Prenotion dischargeth the indefinite seeking of that we would remember and directeth us to seek in a narrow compass, that is, somewhat that hath congruity without place of memory. Emblem reduceth conceits intellectual to images sensible, which strike the memory more; out of which axioms may be drawn much better practice than that in use. (*The Advancement of Learning*, 136)

The two "intentions" of memory correspond closely with the *places* (prenotions) and *images* (emblems) of ancient mnemonics. While this *prenotion* is a less precise term than *place* in the traditional sense, Rossi reminds us that in other texts (*De Augmentis*, and in the *Novum Organon*, II, 26), Bacon refers explicitly to the elaboration of topological systems where the parts of a town, a house or the human body serve as bases to link images together (*Clavis Universalis*, 152). The works of the sixteenth and seventeenth centuries use lists, diagrams, and illustrations. In Bacon's time, the traditional places and images originating in a predominantly oral culture are supplanted, thanks to printing and its uniform reproduction of pictures and tables, by diagrams comprising emblematic figures.

Three purposes motivate numerous Renaissance mnemonic treatises; they are also found, modified to a greater or lesser extent in Baconian epistemology. The first goal is the creation of an "encyclopedia" of learning, disposed according to "trees," as in the Lullian tradition, or tables, as in the Ramist method; the second project involves producing a new artificial memory, which is organized with the aim of facilitating the founding of a "perfect science;" finally mnemonic art serves as a model enabling one to overcome epistemological confusion. Mnemonics will impose its order and coherence on the organization of the discourses of learning. This means that memory encroaches considerably on what used to be the exclusive domain of logic and dialectic, which suffer from having compromised themselves with sterile scholastic syllogisms. Instead, memory seems to offer, thanks to its places materialized in sequences and to its classifying procedures neatly disposed in space, a rigorous taxonomic model and even a pattern for logical operations. Artificial memory often appears in the role of a logical machine or *computer* program.

One cannot, then, separate scientific research from rhetorical practice, and, in the model which the latter proposes, the two distinct functions of dialectic invention and artificial memory seem indissolubly linked by their common use of places and figures indicating the operations to be carried out. This is the case with Bacon. In the new typographical culture, where diagrams, figures, table, emblems, and the like, are easily and faithfully reproduced, *place* ends up designating abstract spaces, boxes into which the tables, diagrams, or taxonomic trees are subdivided. Since the memory of real places (palace, house, theater, town, or human body) with a picturesque, tangible topology, which furnished memory *backgrounds* to ancient orators, did not completely disappear in the *methods* of the Renaissance, one sees how this memory, both as computer and encyclopedia, paved the way for the major taxonomies of the classical age.[8] Bacon is concerned with improving the sequence of places so they provide a more faithful mapping of reality. The old topical system of virtues and vices—which humanism had exploited with renewed vigor—seems to him to refer "to vulgar matters and pedantical divisions, without all life or respect to action" (*The Advancement of Learning*, 135).

The topical system, then, must be extended so as to make it account for the whole of physical and social reality: the ethical topics now are only one microcosmic domain (whose topography is delineated by the *Essays*) of the vast macrocosmic topical system of sciences and arts. In transposing rhetorical invention to new, so-called natural places, Bacon does not however produce a novel epistemology, despite his empiricism, his refusal of the metaphysical presuppositions, hypotheses and magical superstitions of his epoch. His wholly psychologizing description of procedures of nature might, on the other hand, furnish an inexhaustible collection of procedures and metaphors for writers wanting to explore subjectivity, the imaginary, and sensation, without caring whether they would influence the tangible world or increase empirical knowledge.[9] The name *scienze nuove* could be applied to the vast axiomatized topical inventions, to the speculations on the origin and ages of man, where, for example, ancient myth, metamorphosed into the diagrams of a taxonomic system, becomes mytho-logical. Since the exact sciences and, also perhaps, the sciences of man gradually detach themselves from this invention, its topology retreats into *terrae incognitae*, poetic savagery, linguistic wilds, the forest of desires, complexes, and archetypes.[10] From Baconian cosmology to contemporary studies of the "imaginary," there occurs a protracted strategic withdrawal, but the *scienze nuove*, like the Russian strategist, are always looking forward to winter . . .

As the reverse of Bachelard's "new scientific spirit," as the sciences of "Idols" in the Baconian sense, various psychoanalyses and archetypologies have resolved to show that the Idols are primary, irreducible, and that, from their obscure refuge in the unconscious, they secretly structure everything that attempts to eliminate them in the name of a totalitarian positivity. A variation on the genetic and structural intuition of Vico, in his "Last Corollaries Concerning the Logic of Learned Men":

I. 494 The results so far reached by the aid of this poetic logic concerning the origins of languages do justice to their first creators. They were rightly regarded as sages in all subsequent times because they gave natural and proper names to things, so that among the Greeks and Latins "name" and "nature" meant the same thing.

II. 495 The first founders of humanity applied themselves to a sensory topics, by which they brought together those properties or qualities or relations of individuals and species which were, so to speak, concrete, and from these created their poetic genera.

III. 496 So that we may truly say that the first age of the world occupied itself with the primary operation of the human mind. (*The New Science,* 123)

This "primary operation," this original poetics, this sensory and archetypal topics, whether posed as an *arché* towards which to return, or as a *télos* to be attained, or as an illusion to be overcome by a rigorous method, or finally as the repressed reverse of all rationality—all these are *always conceived according to the rhetorical model*. We have seen this apropos of Bacon; no further demonstration is needed concerning Vico's "poetic wisdom"; and with Gilbert Durand, rhetoric (reduced to tropes and figures) serves as a "prelogical" mediation between imagination and reason (*Les Structures anthropologique de l'imaginaire*, 449–59). But actually, Durand unwittingly models the whole *imaginary* on the various parts of rhetoric, and he deploys it according to certain dialectical and cumulative topics that are derived from the topics of invention and artificial memory.

According to Durand, "any imaginary process, even if tinged, like myth, with an inkling of discourse [i.e., even if, like myth, it is a narrative], is eventually reabsorbed into a fantastic topology whose cardinal points are formed by the major patterns and archetypes that underpin structures. Sooner or later, all mythology, all studies of the imagination, hit against a legendary, eschatological, or infernal 'geography' (448)." One realizes, then, that, by a roundabout "general archetypology," Durand creates a variant of artificial memory's localizations: he lays down the principle that *images* are disposed according to a sequence of places, a "geography" or topology analogous, for example, to the one Loyola substituted for the towns, palaces, and theaters of ancient mnemonics so as to reconstruct the meditator *in figura Christi*.[11] Consequently, under the name of a "fantastic topology," Durand reinvents the places of memory among which he distributes the images—for example, the emblematic images borrowed from the Tarot cards—serving as signifiers for other sets of images, the so-called archetypes of the imaginary: "it is a kind of spatial and qualitative game that one is describing, and this authorizes us to name the major parts of our work with terms borrowed from the symbolics of the Tarot" (449).[12]

Durand's book, then, resembles the mnemonic works in the Lullian, cabalistic, or Neoplatonic traditions of the Renaissance: it is a "theater" analogous to Giulio Camillo's *Gran Theatro delle Scienze*, in the latter's dual aspects as an encyclopedia and a *clavis universalis*.[13] Like the Renaissance magus, Durand does not separate the spatial topics, descended from memory, from invention's dialectical topics, whose assigned task is to produce a taxonomy, called an "isotopic classification" in the jargon of archetypology:

These categories, which are just as topological (qualitative spatial polarizations) as they are structural, are perhaps the model for all taxonomic categories, and the affective and spatial distinction that determines the naming of the regions of space probably serves as a model for the entire mental process of distinction making. (450)

Although justifications for this statement can be found in the works of Durkheim and Mauss on "primitive forms of classification," it would seem less arbitrary if it did refer to the history of rhetoric and the semantic evolution of the word *topos* in its contexts. Of course, to reduce dialectic and its subtle distinctions to a qualitative spatial system of topics is to leap over a good many intermediate stages; and, above all, it diminishes the fecund ambiguity of rhetoric, where memory's spatial topics act, so to speak, as a matrix for invention's logical topics which exploit in turn the dialectical virtualities of the spatial system, thus continuously producing discourse and metadiscourse. Moreover, this ambiguity does generate new variants of the topical structure, among which one might henceforth place Durand's archetypology alongside the literary self-portrait and Western religious meditation.

But the main interest of Durand's book—which is much more perspicacious in this respect than Jungian and Bachelardian psychoanalyses—lies in that it reinscribes rhetoric in a mediating position between the imaginary as nature and discourse as culture. It is not necessary to share Durand's ontological or ideological preference for the "luxuriance of imagination" or his aversion to "syntactic and conceptual aridness" (451), which are the antithetical options between which rhetoric is supposed to act as a mediator: only rhetoric's role concerns us here. Accordingly, one can overlook the semantic vagueness that surrounds Durand's use of the word *rhetoric*, since the macrocontext is deeply steeped in the very substance of rhetoric, that context having indeed been *invented* by a rhetorical matrix. This is why the following statement, despite its gross misunderstanding of Aristotle, accounts rather accurately for the status of dialectic in the invention of such topical texts as the self-portrait, meditation, or "archetypology":

Contemporary epistemologists argue endlessly on the interdependence of logic and mathematics. And they have come to align them both with the Aristotelian principle of exclusion. Had they only questioned themselves on the relations with rhetoric of these two formalized syntaxes! They would have realized that rhetoric includes Aristotelian logic as a banal subdivision and that, far from being parallel, rhetoric exceeds the narrowness of logic by using a host of bastard devices derived from the functioning of fancy. (451–52)

Without reducing formal logic and its principle of exclusion to the status of a by-product of rhetoric's virtualities, or without ad-

hering to a restrictive sequence—Fantastic > Rhetoric > Logic—
we agree that there is indeed a logic of tropes: it, rather than the
dialectic and enthymemes of invention, is what is evoked here. We
know, we have relearned from the work of Rosemond Tuve, that a
logic produced the "images" of Renaissance poets and, possibly, all
poetic "images" before the divorce between the modern *imagination* and logic.[14]

During the Renaissance at least, there never was any question
of separating dialectic and rhetoric from poetics, and the self-portrait teaches us that the invention of an "imaginary" results from
a series of dialectical operations the text describes in its metadiscourse, thus undermining the *imaginary* effect in the modern pejorative sense of the word (Sartre, Lacan). Rhetoric, then, resorts
to what Durand calls "a host of bastard devices derived from the
functioning of fancy," but one should likewise underscore that fancy
uses bastard procedures of logic. And so on: Leiris's dialectical *bifurs* produce a poetry that they hasten to undermine while producing images . . .

Any formalized description of the imaginary (even within the
self-portrait) is condemned to become a variant of the "old rhetoric": this relationship is the more evident in Roland Barthes's self-
portrait as he is reluctant to acknowledge it. But this reinvention
of rhetorical invention (in the self-portrait or in archetypology)
confirms that any rhetorical invention is a topography, an extended spatial metaphor, a hunt through places. Durand reduces
the "signifying process" to a metaphoric displacement engendering
the spatial form of the imaginary, "the imaginary of antidestiny"
(453); but he also writes: "rhetoric, like logic, is expressed and
thought in terms of spaces" (453). The same holds true for anthropology, for the imaginary, and for the self-portrait's microcosm. And
Durand's anthropology ends up being an "isotopic classification of
images" (474–73), a topic of fantasy and therefore a variant of the
Baconian tables, where the dialectic and cumulative topics, marked
off with emblems borrowed from the tarot, are deployed. There
looms, between the imaginary of Durand and contemporary self-
portraits (certainly those of Leiris and Borel, but others as well,
despite adamant denials), an inversely symmetric relation to rhetoric, a relation that repeats, while inverting it, the one that ob-

tains between Bacon's philosophy and Montaigne's self-portrait. The main difference lies in the fact that the modern topical encyclopedia and treasure-house of invention have shrunk down to the dimensions of the individual psyche. Modern invention is deployed *ex analogia hominis*, whereas Montaigne's self-portrait and Baconian epistemology are antagonistically situated with respect to the macrocosm, either because they declare the latter unknowable and fall back on the subject, or because they attempt to know and master the macrocosm while operating *ex analogia universi*. A microcosmic rhetoric—already reluctantly outlined in Montaigne—replaced the Baconian macrocosmic rhetoric which the rise of the exact sciences made obsolete.

Within the limits of their respective epistemologies, Montaigne and Bacon strive to disenchant the world, to defuse its prestiges and deconstruct the subject's illusions. With Montaigne and Bacon, invention never seeks to use the powers of rhetoric to produce the wondrous or the fantastic. Both undertakings, for all their divergences, aim to dissolve fantasies and idols, to liberate the mind. Conversely, the self-portraitist and the modern fantasmologist, with their indebtedness to surrealism and psychoanalysis, seek in rhetoric a mediation opening up to them the fantastic and the marvelous, the paradise of the *figurative* without a proper sense, to a "language" prior to the "impoverishing" social pact, with its binding linguistic norm, communication, and "logic." Rhetoric has become a long, patient practice, doomed to drag on through distinctions and *bifurs*, aiming to fashion an ersatz for poetry, and to fashion a precarious sham of the marvelous that preceded Babel, our lost birthright, which can also be named "the plenary world of the fantastic." And the self-portraitists who condemn the imaginary, those who are not interested in themselves, such "Jansenists" as Vuillemin, such Protestant iconoclasts as Barthes, *mourn the loss of it.* Durand aptly foretells the dilemma Barthes would thrust upon himself throughout his self-portrait:

For, in short, the reproach leveled by so many modern thinkers at the symbol is "that it is made for me" (Barthes, *Mythologies*, 232). And, in the final analysis, this antimythic position strikes us as being singularly situated in that regime of the imagination which finds the intimacy of the self despicable and loathes the entire conception of any nonobjective reality, that is, any reality which is not distant, separated from the understanding that thinks it. (428)

But, in the self-portrait, the myth and symbol made for me are made and unmade by me, with the collaboration of the rhetoric that mediates between a "regime of the imagination" and the practice of writing. In Barthes, this will engender a fragmentary, aphoristic ensemble, a nontotalized anti-Book—after the manner of Bacon—which is also a Book of the Self, the theater of an imaginary and a fantasized topics.

We now see what links the self-portrait to methods of the Ramist and Baconian type: one and the same rhetorical matrix, which turns into an epistemological model here, and there into a series of places— corresponding with "essays," "reveries," or "fragments"—it structures the dialectical and imaged invention of the microcosmic subject. And this rhetorical matrix—a metalanguage and an explicit code of communication—engenders the dominant metalanguage that one detects in *methods* as well as in the self-portrait: rhetoric reinvents itself through the project of knowing nature, or the writing subject. This is why there are perhaps "natural" novels and naive autobiographies, but no self-portrait that does not contain in itself its own theory, even if only by implication in the very choice of its system of places.

The rhetorical matrix common to method and the self-portrait also explains the archaism of the semiotic ensembles mobilized in modern self-portrayal, which seems condemned to making new patchworks out of bits of discourse discarded since the Renaissance. Even in productions as revolutionary as Bacon's *Novum Organon*, the Renaissance itself was cluttered with ancient residues, with old fragments reputed to be the receptacles of a lost secret and potency: a confused, entropic semiotics encrusted with hieroglyphs, emblems, and allegories. These signs would come back to haunt modern discourses, insofar as those are variants of rhetoric and they track down the mystery of origin in their last lairs: the fantasmatic, the poetic, the unconscious, the "body."

CHAPTER 9

Self-Portrait and Metamorphoses
of Invention

Antique Invention: Michel Leiris's Manhood and Psychoanalysis

A modern genre, the self-portrait has an archaeology. It has one because self-portrayal uses the procedures of invention and rhetorical memory: a two tiered archaism since the self-portrait's rhetorical matrix is historically inscribed in the Renaissance, which refers in turn to a mythic antiquity, where Roman or Hellenistic features are hardly distinguishable from classic or archaic elements, forming as in a museum that imaginary synchrony that one might call the *Antique:* Pompeii jostles Babylon, Alexandria is in the room next to Troy. The self-portrait also has an archaeology because its invention often consists in running through places furnished by individual memory. But the self-portrait's memory is a compromise between the individual's and that of his culture, and, consequently, it ties in with the practice of ancient mnemonics in its use of Antique images, figures, and places.

The invention, in the present, of a discourse "about" the writing subject is intimately bound up with the recapitulation of a culture whose source and model still is Renaissance humanism. Yet this invention is not purely and simply a repetition of humanist invention, which was a collective undertaking aimed at creating a norm for Western man and a cultural past meant to replace an individual's biography and family as he is emerging from the barbarous condition of childhood. Unlike humanism, the self-portrait seeks to be an individualized patchwork using for its own purposes bits and pieces borrowed from the vast humanist system of which the subject partakes as a "cultured" man. It is no longer a question of standardizing the individual's memory to fit a cultural model but, on the contrary, of working with fragments that do not conform to the stereotype and out of which the subject can fashion an idiosyncratic ensemble of metaphors where he will find himself (again) or get lost. The self-portrait, then, makes the Antique (among other available *collective pasts*) an element of its individual mythology, which is presumed to account for a unique present and a personal particularity; but the Antique mytheme tends to worm its way into that uniqueness; it haunts the present and dispossesses it of its presence. Through the self-portrait, the Antique breaks into the present, asserts itself as being "truer" than the contingency experienced in "life" or writing. The process is parallel to the one that runs its course through language, for if the individual attempts to appropriate his language to turn it into an authentic self-expression, he soon realizes the etymological dimension of the lexicon of his choice; so there he is, dispossessed by the etymon, just when he thought he had achieved the authenticity in his own, present, enunciation. He finds himself forced to fashion his "own" etymology or to transmute his dispossession into a superior authenticity. The relations between self-portrayal and the Antique duplicate those of rhetoric with the self-portrait, for rhetoric and the Antique are inseparable on the imaginary plane.

Analysis can dissociate rhetoric from the imagination of the Antique, provided one is aware of the uses of rhetoric and of its functions in a given historical context: witness the adaptation of rhetoric to the contemporary linguistic, sociopolitical, and scientific context by Kenneth Burke and Chaim Perelman. Once can also surpass the nebulous myth of the Antique, thanks to a diversified historical and philological knowledge of antiquity. But this demythologizing—this scholarship—is powerless against those mythic constructs, that, contemptuous of rhetoric as a theory of persuasion, disregard antiquity as a subject of historical knowledge while attempting to account for the human psyche and constituting a post-humanist anthropology centered on the speaking subject, his "unconscious," his desires and dysfunctions. Rhetoric and the Antique return piecemeal through the discourses of speculative psychology and anthropology, serving to explain the subject's absence unto himself and to fill the gap discursively. The discourses on the individual human subject cart along a strange amalgam, full of extreme ingenuity and radical ignorance that reminds one of the several "renaissances" of the High Middle Ages, when Western barbarians tried to apprehend the mysterious secrets of ancient art and eloquence with which they might master chaos.

The Antique, then, is classical culture as it appears in the dream of a Romanized and Christianized barbarian, who finds an erotic charm in each fragment, each imaginary reconstruction of the object of his desire, despite *moralization*, censorship, and other fig leaves. Beside the infinite resources of its Olympus, the Antique proposes a choice of episodes, figures, attitudes and masks transmitted via the school, the theater, the plastic arts, and so on. This multiplicity of media reinforces a confusion between the *lessons in morality* and the promise of pleasure, connotations that are closely interwoven in the notion of the Antique. In this sense, nothing is more *Antique* than *fin-de-siècle* neoclassicism, à la Alma-Taddema, a horny fantasy haunted by Mallarmé's and Debussy's fauns, Gustave Moreau's *Sphinx and Oedipus*, Strauss's *Salomé*, Pierre Louÿs' *Aphrodite*, and Cleopatra's innumerable avatars . . . Evidently, the Antique was a purveyor of pornographic visions for so-called "cultured" people, at a period when eroticism had to wear the veil of culture to appear in good company.

Yet this bourgeois Antique remains a variant of Renaissance humanism: fantasized and imaginary invention still finds its nourishment in the humanist encyclopedia. The Antique never is mere transfer of knowledge. Everyone has to construct the version that excites him or accounts for his frigidity.

This is what Michel Leiris undertakes when he starts tracing the lineaments of his personal mythology. In "Michel Leiris ou la psychanalyse sans fin," J. B. Pontalis has aptly traced the dual movement through which Leiris conjures up and rejects images of the Antique: "the double (here the mythological self) is destroyed by an unflattering inventory, while the confession frees him from the malaise of a confused existence: masks, even when they are wrenched off, the fabulation of being nothing." Pontalis adds this footnote: "Leiris rightly recognizes that Freudianism 'offers everyone easy means of rising to the tragic plane by taking himself for a new Oedipus,' and, at another point, he singles out the natural tendency of Leiris's memory to retain 'all that can serve as a basis for a mythology' " (*Après Freud*, 318).[1] But, in *Manhood*, Leiris's mythological double is constructed around allegorical, emblematic, and mythological images, analogous to those that Freud and Jung reinvested with signifieds and affect in order to designate "complexes," unconscious configurations, to formulate hypotheses on the "dream work" and its function, and also, more generally, to label the stages and accidents of psychological growth.

The anachronistic and figured underside of the present is foregrounded while the story of the individual and the future as the horizon of a project are reduced to the intention to write a book and to the story of its writing. In this regard, Pontalis speaks of a stagnation and an insistence, which would be "the face and reverse of a single desire" (321). But what is of interest to the self-portraitist, as a writer, is the process of construction and deconstruction of places, the classification, inventory, interlocking, and unlocking of images, rather than the specific contents of memory, which become mere markers in the invention of the text. This is why the mnemic contents tend to conform to cultural and mythical stereotypes (without ever reaching such a limit). The activity of associating and deciphering symbolic elements produces the impression of insistence or stagnation for a reader who envisages this kind of writing either from the point of view of narration or—which perhaps amounts to the same thing, in the end—from the point of view of insertion and success in an active life.

Whatever his original project and need of confession, the self-portraitist pursues his task as the most conscious of writers, fascinated by the procedures that he thinks he is inventing, that he implements, and on which he obstinately theorizes. These procedures refer nevertheless to a double archaeology: that of the subject himself and that which inheres in rhetorical practice. And, in this sense, the self-portrait is the doublet of psychoanalysis rather than its offspring, despite what Leiris asserts in *Manhood*. For their respective metadiscourses and theories are born of the same matrix. It would, then, be just as correct to say that Jacques Lacan writes in the margins of Michel Leiris, as to suggest, as does Philippe Lejeune, that Leiris writes in Lacan's margins. In fact, the psychoanalyst—as the theoretician or inventor of a discourse on the "truth of the unconscious"—just like the self-portraitist, goes through a series of commonplaces concerning the formation and analysis of semiotic systems, whose principal elements derive from the humanist tradition and from the Antique, in the imaginary and fantasized sense.

As a case in point, there is the celebrated article, "The Function and the Field of Speech and Language," where Dr. Lacan seems to comment upon the literary invention of his friend Michel Leiris:

Hieroglyphs of hysteria, blazons of phobia, labyrinths of the *Zwangsneurose*—charms of impotence, enigmas of inhibition, oracles of anxiety—talking arms of character, seals of self-punishment, disguises of perversion—these are the hermetic elements that our exegesis resolves, the equivocations that our invocation dissolves, the artifices that our dialectic absolves, in a deliverance of the imprisoned meaning, from the revelation of the palimpsest to the given word of the mystery and to the pardon of speech. (*Ecrits: A Selection*, 70)

Of course, by presenting psychoanalysis as a practice that solves, dissolves, and so forth, all the signs thanks to which Renaissance esoteric thought—with a Pico della Mirandola or a John Dee, for example—undertook to reconquer the magic powers supposedly held by antiquity, by becoming the Horapollo and Poliphilo of neuroses and hysteria, Lacan promises more than Leiris himself thinks he can deliver. But the hieroglyphs, blazons, labyrinths, charms, enigmas, and the rest (one would willingly add *emblems* to this list) are in fact part of the gear deployed by Michel Leiris in his self-portrait, and his work, moreover, concerns hermeticism and equivocations, about which one is hard put to decide whether he "solves" them or whether he maintains them with all of rhetoric's resources to produce an adorned *copia*, of which the Asianism of his double, Dr. Lacan, would be, as it were, the playful hyperbole. For dialectic certainly does not absolve artifices; it *is* an artifice, and would only absolve itself by ignoring or silencing itself. There is, indeed, no question here of absolution or pardon, but rather of rhetorical invention, writing, style: the point is, in short, to speak as a book, to transform the speaking subject into a Book.[2] The point is to produce an extended metaphor, where what is said of the book-vehicle will apply to the psyche-tenor, and vice versa. Just any book will not do, of course, since it must contain a missing chapter. Not an obvious gap, nor a patent incompleteness: no, the absence of the chapter will have been skillfully camouflaged, the narrative continuity, the coherence of the discourse will have been pieced together, and great skill will therefore be needed to detect the fraud and reconstruct the truth.[3] But, in order to produce the simulacrum of this book with its censored chapter and to assert the cryptographic power of psychoanalysis, one will resort to a lexicon marked by a long liturgic, exegetic, and thaumaturgic use: in short, a religious Cabala (more Christian than Judaic, more Greco-Roman than Hebraic, with Leiris and Lacan at any rate). But, also, metaphors will have to be drawn from archaeology, paleography, epigraphy, philology, etymology, mythology—all the historical and linguistic disciplines derived from Renaissance humanism's global attempt to decipher classic and Judeo-Christian antiquity.[4]

This is why Lacan's famous description of the *unconscious* can be read as a variant of the Renaissance humanist project, or as a description of Leiris's undertaking in his self-portrait or, finally, as a contribution to the metapsychological theory that appears in turn to be an application to the individual subject of procedures devised in the Renaissance in order to decipher the lost secret of the ancients:

The unconscious is that chapter of my history that is marked by a blank or occupied by a falsehood: it is the censored chapter. But the truth can be rediscovered; usually it has already been written down elsewhere.

Namely:
—in monuments: this is my body. That is to say, the hysterical nucleus of the neurosis in which the hysterical symptom reveals the structure of a language, and is deciphered like an inscription which, once recovered, can without serious loss be destroyed;
—in archival documents: these are my childhood memories, just as impenetrable as are such documents when I do not know their provenance;
—in semantic evolution: this corresponds to the stock of words and accep-

tations of my own particular vocabulary, as it does to my style of life and to my character. (*Ecrits: A Selection,* 50)

We said: *humanism,* and this may suggest a pious respect for the ancient treasury, perhaps even a mystifying, or at least a mythological intention. But Leiris's or Lacan's version of humanism openly aims to demystify, dispossess, exorcise. In this respect, it is closer to the work of biblical exegesis, or rather of the higher biblical criticism that preceded and accompanied the age of Enlightenment, an age—must one remind oneself?—overshadowed by its interesting half, which thirsted for myths, esotericism, hieroglyphs, and all kinds of mysterious inscriptions. Lacanian psychoanalysis also, like Leiris's self-portrait, hesitates between its fascination with the mysterious and its will to dissolve it. This is particularly manifest in a vertiginous syncretism of metaphors borrowed from many domains of the "sacred," including Christian sacraments: "in the monuments" and "this is my body"; through the words of the Consecration and Last Supper, what is signified, of course, is that hysteria is inscribed in the body, which becomes subject to a semiological, or even perhaps a semiotic, reading. But, conversely, one ought not forget that Western semiotics, as concerns its modern origins, is inseparable from the debates surrounding the question of the Eucharist during the Reformation: a "symbol" or "real presence," transubstantiation or consubstantiation?[5]

Thus, the discourses of both psychoanalysis and the self-portrait are bound to an intertextual and cultural network: the fragments of semiotic systems from which these discourses borrow their *images* and metaphors inevitably refer to larger configurations. Whoever refers to a *monument,* an *inscription,* and the like, does not avoid the clichés of the Antique; and the writer who borrows figures from the Bible, from liturgy, necessarily risks triggering the return of another semiotics. He who writes *hermeticism* is carried away by the notorious "flood of mud," from which Freud extricates himself no less soiled than Jung. In fact, the occult is hardly distinguishable from the Antique: they arouse the same desire for that which dream emblems and Pompeii's volcanic dust conceal.

This explains Freud's passionate interest in Jensen's *Gradiva.*[6] Freud experienced, of course, an analytical and conscientious fas-

cination, rather than a vague reverie prompted by the many ancient statuettes lined on his desk, the very one upon which he wrote
up his cases, *Dora: An Analysis of a Case of Hysteria* for instance.
One reads over his shoulder:

In the face of the incompleteness of my analytic results, I had no choice
but to follow the example of those discoverers whose good fortune it is to
bring to the light of day after their long burial the priceless though mutilated relics of antiquity. I have restored what is missing, taking the best
models known to me from other analyses; but like a conscientious archaeologist I have not omitted to mention in each case where the authentic parts
end and my construction begins. (27)

These same steps are taken by Leiris in his self-portrait, and it is
difficult to see how such a "restoration" would differ from rhetorical invention, which persists in exploring a *place* according to an
ancient method, in order to produce a text worthy of the classics.
Certainly, it is a question of constructing and not of interpreting
in the ordinary sense of "transcoding into another descriptive system." Above all, this involves an invention, the weaving of a text
among given elements and place-markers. According to Freud, the
psychoanalyst and archaeologist "have the undisputed right to reconstruct by adding and associating vestiges" ("Construction in
Psychoanalysis"). Pleading this "undisputed right," one of Freud's
commentators, Catherine Backès-Clément, asserts that Freudian
archaeology or "history" challenges the deceitful continuity of the
personal or cultural myth ("Continuité et construction historique"). Freudian historical reconstruction seeks truth, and it breaks
down the factitious continuity of the imaginary, the "repetition of
fragments unaware of their own fragmentation, thinking that they
are wholes, myths, fantasies; combinatory systems unknown to
themselves" (81). The breakdown of a factitious continuity: perhaps this aptly describes the clinical practice of Freud and other
psychoanalysts in general; but, on the other hand, as regards the
aberrations imputed to the imaginary, one comes across them rather
easily in psychoanalytic *theory*, at least when it borrows its fragments and combinatory systems from the Antique and rhetoric. It
is in the analogy between an archaeological "construction" and an
analytical "construction" that this misprision lurks, with Freud as

with Lacan. Of course, the extended archaeological metaphor may be an unimportant part of psychoanalytic theory, a simple heuristic procedure for a rough definition of ideas in a domain that can only be expressed figuratively. Yet one must agree that this analogy is of no great help in establishing the new, unprecedented character of Freudian theory and method. If psychoanalysis is *like* an archaeology, inevitably it is *like* a modality of Renaissance humanism. For this reason, one has no trouble detecting the denial in the following paradoxical apology of Freudianism:

From history one passes to imaginary prehistory, the immemorial time of origins, marked by the figure of the Ancestor of Hero, the first one to slay a mythic father. But the Freudian system lacks a definition of culture, and there lies the reverse of analogical thought. The danger is all the greater as it is easy to consider psychoanalysis itself as a *version* of the culture from which it depends . . . But, on the contrary, psychoanalysis, as Freud would have it, is not a version according to a cultural matrix, but a *subversion* of this matrix: otherwise, it would be an interpretation, and not a construction. ("Continuité mythique")

Let us suppose for an instant that the aim and effect of the psychanalytic experience is to subvert in the patient such cultural elements as he has internalized and with which he has constructed a myth whose approximate coherence is reputed to be purely neurotic and imaginary, since psychoanalysis succeeds in deconstructing the myth in question. But this certainly does not mean that psychoanalytic theory avoids as a result its status as a version (however "subversive") of the products of the cultural matrix. Unless one were to postulate that the notions of *version* and *subversion* (generated by an evident rhetorical device) are radically heterogeneous. But can subversion become, in such a context, anything but an unorthodox or paradoxical version, a "transgressive" variant of the discourses produced by the cultural matrix? Using an analogy not out of place here, is the New Testament a perversion of the Old Testament? That depends on the point of view (Judaic or Christian) adopted. But no one could claim that these two texts do not coexist in a transformational relation; nor that an entire (Christian) culture has managed to produce endless commentaries on the basis of its belief in an allegorical link between the Old and New Testaments.

Certainly, one can prefer the "truth" of the discontinuous, of the fragmentary, to the coherent error of myth and fantasy; further, one can think that psychoanalysis aims to fragment, dissociate, deconstruct, in order to produce a truth beyond the grasp of "culture," in its mythic and ideological constructs, or of an individual subject indulging in his personal myth or bogged down in his neurosis. Yet one can wonder whether psychoanalytic theory and the self-portrait—respectively on the levels of anthropology and self-knowledge—do not both operate by alternating figuration and interpretation, mythologization and demystification, and whether the two tendencies are not inherent in the dialectic of invention in these two genres. But one must go even further: are not these two versions, if envisaged as subversive versions of the culture that produces them, to the very extent that they aim and manage to be subversive, symmetrically blind to the blindness they denounce in culture? By disclosing the "truth" of the unconscious, by revealing that the subject is reduced, in the last analysis, to the ways of his enunciating and inventing, are not these discourses both blind to their rhetorical matrix and its semantic content, which we have called the Antique but might also have named the *humanities?* This scotomization is continuously threatened by the frequent returns of the rhetorical and the cultural, now swathed in a mythic construction bent precisely on concealing the matrix of which it is born. In a sense, then, one would be going round in a circle, advancing at one end and regressing at the other: it is tempting to think that what motivated the Freudian and post-Freudian condemnation of Jungian psychoanalysis is not so much its having abandoned the sexual theory (after all, the Lacanian theory that has been so well received in French literary circles also departs from Freud's sexualism) as its having transcoded into the code of the unconscious the esotericism of the Renaissance; and this return threatens to reveal the humanist and rhetorical foundations of psychoanalysis in general. Once again, let us reread a key text of Lacan's:

Take up the work of Freud again at the *Traumdeutung* to remind yourself that the dream has the structure of a sentence or, rather, to stick to the letter of the work, of a rebus; that is to say, it has the structure of a form of writing, of which the child's dream represents the primordial ideography, and which, in the adult, reproduces the simultaneously phonetic and symbolic use of signifying elements, which can also be found in the hieroglyphs of ancient Egypt and in the characters still used in China. (*Ecrits: A Selection*, 57)

The amalgamation of rebus, pictogram, and writing, and also of hieroglyph and ideogram, is reinforced here by reduction of the dream work to a "rhetoric" limited to figures and tropes. An amalgamation already carried out by the Renaissance and perpetuated in modern esotericism and "mimologism."[7] Besides, in his haste to produce a magic formula, Lacan minimizes the ambiguity of the *Traumdeutung*, where Freud compares the interpretation of dreams to deciphering a figurative writing of antiquity, such as Egyptian hieroglyphs. According to Freud, the interpreter's task resembles more that of a Champollion (or of one of his less fortunate predecessors) than the simple decipherment of hieroglyphs by an Egyptologist well versed in their code. Yet, Freud's text is equivocal, for it also leads one to understand that, for the modern Egyptologist, hieroglyphs remain polysemous; they would comport indeterminate traits whose only "sense" is to determine the meaning of other signifying elements. These traits only have to assure, as determinatives, the intelligibility of other elements. The plurivocality of dream elements has its counterpart in those ancient systems of writing . . .[8] Consequently, one can wonder whether, with Freud and Lacan, the obscurity of the text, like the indetermination that one ascribes to hieroglyphs, is due to the nature of hieroglyphic writing, as we know it since Champollion, rather than to the convergence in psychoanalytic discourse of two symbols of the mysterious and secrecy: the *dream* and the *Antique*. With Freud, as with Renaissance humanists and perhaps even still with Lacan, the hieroglyph symbolizes the *true* sense, arduously and precariously deciphered, easily mislaid, always mysterious, whose interpretation demands the intervention of a possessor of pyschoanalytic knowledge and power.[9] Like the Sphinx, the hieroglyph designates the place where the enigma is disclosed to the one who knows: if Pharaoh dreams in hieroglyphs, if Egypt *dreams* emblematic knowledge, Joseph certainly had to intervene to open up to discursivity the opaque Egyptian signifier and to decipher the hidden meaning that heralds and effects the liberation of the Chosen Ones.

Whether dreams have "the structure" of a rebus, pictography, a hieroglyph, or an ideogram is, after all, of little importance: what matters is that the dream work is supposed to hark back to archaic signifying practices that preceded or transgress the dialectic or logical categories of discursive and conscious thought. In the *Traumdeutung* section devoted to the study of representation, Freud shows that dreams are incapable of saying: *because, if, either-or, although, just as,* and so on. Dreams share these limitations with pictorial emblems. The interpretative work must, then, restore the conjunctions that articulate logical and dialectical operation.[10]

This is another way of saying that psychoanalysis operates in the same way as dialectical invention: both seek to produce a text that is dialectically structured and (according to the criteria of its own versimilitude) persuasive, by using syllogisms and enthymemes acceptable to the reason of a being moved by desires. It forces the orderly disposition of the representative and linguistic content of a dream (of *dreams,* to be more exact, since the interpretation of a single dream presupposes that an encyclopedia of oneiric symbols has already been compiled, that these have been classified under headings furnished, in Freud's case, by the modalities of sexual desire), according to a specific dialectic that must pit itself against Aristotelian topics—if only to show how far removed the latter are from dream thought.

The object discourse (the dream) and the metadiscourse of pyschoanalysis are copresent in the text of the interpretation, which is indeed a construction; but the same holds true for the orator's text, which is not a simple *interpretation* of the topoi (for example, virtues and vices) furnished by a cultural encyclopedia. Each produced text has one or several specific functions, since the interpretation of a dream can hasten the treatment of a given patient or contribute to the theory of dream interpretation. But, in both these cases, the discourse has a double bottom: its given datum (the dream text) is diverted from its initial function (satisfying an unconcious desire, protecting sleep), which was inscribed in an archaic semiosis and referred in turn to an archaeology, the exploration of the subject's early childhood. As it gets caught in the construction of the interpretation, this archaism is placed at the service of the present through a therapeutic or persuasive ("scientific") dialectic. But this dialectical invention is itself subordinated to a constant reference (even if it is indirect and unconscious) to an archaeology, to the Antique, since the interpreter fantasizes himself in the role of Joseph, or of Champollion; the interpreter of dreams unwittingly repeats the humanist's undertaking, shares his desire for the magical power which decipherment confers, and borrows from him the dialectical procedures supposed to give access to this hidden power.

Surely, the *Traumdeutung* inverts a Renaissance text such as *Hypnerotomachia Poliphilii*,[11] for it is *in a dream* that Poliphilo progresses through a landscape strewn with monuments, inscriptions, emblems and hieroglyphs. But, Poliphilo is seeking amid these vestiges Polia, his mistress, whom he will embrace in his dream and lose forthwith upon awakening. The *Traumdeutung* is just the opposite of the dream of a naïve, love-sick, deciphering pilgrim. But the allegory of Poliphilo and the *Traumdeutung* share a desire, and it is Poliphilo who can psychoanalyze Freud here, just as Freud would have no trouble in psychoanalyzing Poliphilo: what is at stake here is a desire for the Antique, a desire to decipher the Antique whose meaning is pleasure: it is the locus of forbidden pleasure, a pleasure suggested by mysterious inscriptions. Whereas *Hypnerotomachia* is pure leisure, Freud's pleasure is the reward of long labor. The modern hermeneutic no longer seeks pleasure in dreams, for he has succeeded in replacing this illusory voluptuousness, erased upon awakening, by the hard-earned, though more assured, pleasure he derives from his interpretative labors, as he gazes upon the row of ancient statuettes that decorate his desk, transporting it through time, turning it into a Ptolemaic hypogeum or a little syncretic Renaissance temple. Freud's Gradiva is always stepping towards a villa of Mysteries, or towards a brothel.

"Since childhood I have attributed to everything *classical* a frankly voluptuous character," writes Michel Leiris in *Manhood* (26). Ancient, voluptous, and allegorical figures are the first skeins from which Michel Leiris will unwind the invention of his self-portrait. The differences between the Antique and the "personal sacred" whose *places* are the landmarks of *la Règle du Jeu* (these were sketched in "Le Sacré dans la vie quotidienne," an essay dated 1938), are in fact due less to a disparity between the given places and images than to the way this given is constructed, invented, interpreted, allegorized.

But in *Manhood* Leiris does not set the Antique apart from allegory; he finds them both equally voluptuous. This affinity also ties in with Leiris's penchant for hermeticism and his habit of "thinking in formulas, analogies, images—a mental technique of which, whether I like it or not, the present account is only an application" (25). Evidently, then, the "mental technique" on which the rhetorical invention of *Manhood* rests is a simplified version of the dream work, as described by Freud. Except that Leiris's text contains some metadiscursive elements: his own theory and an embryonic interpretation.

Between an avowed predilection for allegory and emblems and his evocation of a marmoreal, voluptuous, and cruel antiquity, Leiris introduces the images of Cranach's Lucrecia and Judith, around which he disposes figurations of his criticism. The double figure is doubly desirable, since these naked ancient women, with their sanguinary attributes and hieratic poses, also are allegories: they are indeed very equivocal, perhaps even contradictory allegories, for ordinarily Judith and Lucrecia signify temperance (Sophrosyne), whereas in Leiris they evoke castration and suicide, the anguishing ties between sensuality and death.

It is on this inscription of ambivalence (recalling that of dream representation, according to Freud) in Leiris's self-portrait that we must dwell for a moment. Undoubtedly, the Antique differs from *Playboy*. The Antique comes down to us through Renaissance images and texts (about which there is nothing clandestine) or through reference books and school manuals, the vehicles of official culture. Yet Leiris, as a child, discovered in these pedagogic instruments a source of voluptuousness that the adult writer seeks to recapture through writing.

The erotic suggestiveness of these virtuous heroines, Judith and Lucrecia, owes much to the art of Cranach, for whom the Antique is at once a semiotic system serving to teach virtue *and* a voluptuous dream. Panofsky in fact considers that Cranach was not unaware of the neo-Platonic philosophy of love originating in the Florentine milieu whose magus was Ficino (*Studies in Iconology*, 129). When, as an adult, Leiris borrows entries on Cranach, Judith, and Lucrecia from the *Nouveau Larousse illustré* to paste them in his self-portrait, he mimics his gestures as a child leafing through this encyclopedic dictionary in search of ancient voluptuous pictures and of information on the mysteries of sexuality. Finally, a volume devoid of openly erotic suggestions, such as the sixth-grade history textbook, could also become a source of sensuality for him, simply as a manual of *ancient* history: "My memory furnishes various elements to illustrate this circumstance [suggestiveness of the Antique], such as the photographs of monuments, busts, mosaics, and bas-reliefs decorating the ancient history text" (26). Young Leiris's antique reverie, which the invention of the text attempts to bring to life again, reproduces in many ways the dream of Poliphilo, for whom ancient vestiges are the landmarks and stimulants of an amorous quest. Albert-Marie Schmidt may have underestimated the equivocalities of the Antique in Colonna's book when writing in his preface to *Le Songe de Poliphile:*

This tirelessly repeated experience [the pleasure Poliphilo derives from contemplating the breasts of Polia, his mistress] so absorbs him that he considers it decisive to the point of disparaging his former passion for the relics of antiquity: this proves that their solicited reproduction is not, whatever anyone says, the essential merit of the *Hypnerotomachia*. (xxvi)

The old stones, the worn inscriptions, are the other side of one and the same desire, one that is already very complex in the Renaissance but becomes more and more so as textual and iconographic meditations multiply. Reconstructing the erotic suggestiveness of the Antique is also, for Leiris, an archaeological probe into his adult fears and desires; it produces as well, in the present, an archaeology of his own writing after having incurred an irreparable loss, homologous to that caused in our culture by the ruin of antiquity. From then on he has to reconstruct stone by stone, one inscription after another, what had once been a child's happiness, an unproblematic pleasure. But the inscriptions remain lacunary, the images mutilated. The writer can only attempt to put together a fragmentary encyclopedia, through a system of places forming an incomplete mosaic: the essential element has been lost through the lacunae, though it is the lacuna itself that is unsettling owing to an excess of meaning:

I have always been attracted by *allegories*, enigmatic lessons in images which often are alluring female figures powerful in their own beauty and in all that is disturbing, by definition, in a symbol. (24)

Not *uncertain*, nor vague, but "unsettling": it is the body of the allegorical signifier that excites Leiris. In this respect the modern self-portraitist differs little from the semioticians, and a fortiori from the painters and poets of the Renaissance. Neoplatonic emblems, for example, provide access to the Idea through sensual signifiers and cultivate a confusion between sacred and profane love. Besides, for these Neoplatonists, Eros himself can be a god of death, thus anticipating the amalgam of sensual pleasure and death that is characteristic of *Manhood*.[12]

The sensualism of Renaissance mnemonists led some of them to reveal a fact that otherwise remained latent: since "unsettling" or frankly sensuous images were easier to retain than abstractions, a certain Guglielmus Leporeus Avallonensis proposed a frankly erotic mnemonics in his *Ars Memorativa*.[13]

By inventing in the places of the Antique, Leiris's self-portrait smooths the way for the erotization of "rhetoric" and for the "rhetoric of desire" that asserted itself in Lacanian psychoanalysis and in the writings of his epigones, as well as those of "avant-garde writers" and "desiring semioticians" of the 1970s in France. Leiris harked back to Renaissance semiotic theories and practices. The *rhetoric of desire*, which implements the "places of the body" by using such figures as metathesis, anagram, anaphora, aphaeresis, and apocope—in short what was called "plural writing," "the text," or "amorous discourse"—is tantamount to a desire for an eroticized rhetoric, as opposed to a hypothetical normative, asexual, and academic rhetoric. So that, while developing the *place* of the Antique in the erotic register, while linking antiquity to nakedness and cruelty, Leiris could also write:

Nothing seems more like a whorehouse to me than a museum. In it you find the same equivocal aspect, the same frozen quality. In one, beautiful, frozen images of Venus, Judith, Susanna, Juno, Lucrece, Salome, and other heroines; in the other, living women in their traditional garb, with their stereotyped gestures and phrases. In both, you are in a sense under the sign of archeology; and if I have always loved whorehouses it is because they, too, participate in antiquity by their slave-market aspect, a ritual prostitution. (*Manhood*, 30–31)

Leiris manages here to generate an extended metaphor of rhetoric and humanism. The museum's classical feminine figures, like the emblematic women of the brothel, fascinate because they are stereotypes and relate to archaeology: through the women ritually offered up to desire in the bordello, one also possesses those whose effigies make the museum exciting. The living women are coveted only because they remind one of the ancient figures: thus, one must *invent* them—as does the text of the self-portrait in its relation to archaeology—so they will conform to the archetype, without which there is no desire. The Leirisian fantasy of a sensual pleasure provided in a museum by a beautiful impassive stranger (67) is the very fantasy that keeps haunting the series of rhetorical places, with their "shady" and "petrified" allegorical images, the strange impassibility of their topics, their fortuitously sensuous labyrinth. This pleasure appears paradoxical to whoever forgets that the self-portrait is a furtive and delightful practice and that it privileges "certain forgotten nooks" of the museum, in order to make them "the theater of hidden lewdness" (67). The invention of the self-portrait is a misappropriation of the museum for lewd purposes, with an added touch of masochism perhaps. But this hidden lewdness is disclosed in the theater of the book, which reveals how anyone can derive his own private pleasure from what belongs to everybody. The communicability of the self-portrait is due as much to the universality of the topics as to the generality of the Leirisian fantasy. If one cannot do without the museum, the cultural encyclopedia, then one must learn to take one's pleasure in them. For such cultivated men as Leiris and all self-portraitists, culture, rhetoric, and the commonplaces are metamorphosed into brothels, and their private pleasure is bound up with ritual prostitution, the stereotypy, banality, and impassiveness of the desired objects. The archaeologist-self-portraitist derives his sensual pleasure—and his suffering —from the imagination he shares with Renaissance humanists; the reader in turn locates the fantasy of his own pleasure in the public places of culture.

This prurient imaginary museum is perhaps a perversion of museums, of the official culture and encyclopedia: but one may wonder whether the modern idea of the museum, as the locus of an uplifting mass pedagogy is not a truncated, very elementary, equalitarian, and compulsory version of what the museum, the encyclopedia, and rhetoric represent for the writer who, since the Renaissance, has been looking there for vices as well as virtues. For the writer has always managed to retain a certain wilderness and to procure his own pleasure from what belongs to all people: language, commonplaces, the museum. Whereas for others, culture is an instrument of standardization, the self-portraitist uses it as a chance to invent a difference that brings him alternate joys and sorrows.

The Invention of the Savage: Montaigne, Leiris, Barthes

The *Antique* and *savagery* evidently are antithetical places. But one cannot deal with either without referring to the other. Invention in the self-portrait, more manifestly so with Leiris than elsewhere, plays with this complementariness: clear proof of this is found in the transitional text entitled "Le Sacré dans la vie quotidienne,"[14] which is the generic template for *la Règle du jeu*. But this text did not yet formulate the difficult anthropological problem of the relationship between the savage and the self, between the most remote and the closest.

Still one should keep in mind that the savage (like the barbarian) is a topos inherited from ancient tradition, which one can exploit "artificially" with the help of dialectic, while adding "inartificial" proofs along the way, such as examples borrowed from ethnography and personal observations. This topos, already found in Tacitus' *Germania*, rests on an implicit comparison between Greco-Latin culture and what lies outside it, negatively defined as barbaric: "They use neither images nor temples; war and plunder are their livelihood; they do not appreciate the value of precious metals, etc."[15] But, as a result of this comparison, the savage belongs to the Antique, either negatively or, according to a paradox that will in turn become an important element of our *doxa*, positively: savage = antique, or, at least, "worthy of the Antique," as well as *naked*. More generally, it can be shown that the archaeological undertaking of the Renaissance is indeed the matrix of modern cultural anthropology. Scholars had to recognize the *difference* of antiquity and to start describing it historically and archaeologically as a culture different from modern culture before Renaissance travelers and writers could find exotic humanity a subject fit for study and reflection.[16] Ethnography on the whole was, for a long time, conceived as an archaeology: the transformation of the "savage" into a "primitive" says so clearly. This helps to understand that, turning to the otherness of what he calls the "unconcious," the psychoanalyst should also have taken a long detour through the Antique and that certain humanist philological practices should have served him as a model in his attempt to decipher the etiology of disorders.

The self-portrait's ethnology, like its archaeology, deals with the Other only to say something about the writer himself; that he too is Other, savage, ancient, and that he feels more at home with what is radically different from his present, his surroundings, his own culture. It will probably suggest this by a paradoxical approach to the commonplaces of the cultural encyclopedia of his own period, class, and milieu. Montaigne ascribes to savages an ancient bravery, an aristocratic disdain: a savage chieftain incarnates the gentleman in his essence, in his natural nakedness. Inside Montaigne there is a naked savage who is not unaware of what he is, since the Tupis described in Thévet, in Léry, those portrayed to him by his reliable servant, as well as the Indian chieftain whom he met in Rouen but who had to remain mythical for want of being able to communicate, revealed so much to him that he inscribed this baring of the self at the outset in the notice "To the Reader." Likewise there is, in Leiris, a Dogon initiated in the secret language, a bush Dogon, as well as two savage women who match Judith and Lucrecia, the ancient heroines, in the register of prophecy and prostitution: Emawayish, the Ethiopian (whom Leiris first mistook for a reincarnation of the Antique)[17] possessed by the *zars*, and Khadidja, the Algerian prostitute of Beni-Ounif (*Fourbis*, 181–239), also caught in a paradigm of the Antique, out of which also arises Joseph, the interpreter of dreams, as well as Invention, that binds all these figures of otherness together under the aegis of rhetoric:

Rebecca, Agar the servant, Naomi, Rachel (rediscovered in the deck of cards, together with Judith, Grecian Pallas and Argine, the unknown creature no one even bothered about): beautiful women with insidious names who, in the Hebraic legend, confront a comical Potiphar's wife and . . . result from a touching inventive capacity, whose iridescent products are also signs of recognition. (238) [18]

This invention goes round in circles, yet does not produce a center. It is a game of cards—of index cards, with Leiris or Barthes—from which several deals may result: the text of the self-portrait is one of them, our reading another. An encyclopedia of places opening up a thousand directions. It is under the heading "The Ethnological Temptation" that Barthes suggests a homology between ethnography, the description of a culture, and self-portrayal:

the ethnological book has all the powers of the beloved book: it is an encyclopedia, noting and classifying all of reality, even the most trivial, the most sensual aspects; this encyclopedia does not adulterate the Other by reducing it to the Same; appropriation diminishes, the Self's certitude grows lighter. Finally, of all learned discourse, the ethnological seems to come closest to a Fiction. (*Roland Barthes by Roland Barthes*, 84–85)

By perceiving the "ethnological book" (for which, according to him, his own *Mythologies* is a model) as a privileged encyclopedia (or a counterencylopedia that does not falsify the Other by reducing him to the Same), Barthes discloses to others, and tries to conceal from himself, the hidden form of his self-portrait. Of course, he rejects the analogical, mythical order adopted by Leiris. He struggles against invention of a taxonomical coherence. Denial alone appeases the ethnological and encyclopedic temptation: the haphazard classification of index cards and fragments hardly forms a circle. Perhaps. On the other hand, Barthes's self-portrait comprises an index, about which the author writes: "the index of a book is not . . . only a reference tool; it is itself a text, a second text that is the relief (the remainder and roughness) of the first text: what is delirious (interrupted) in the reason of the sentences," without realizing that it is only too easy to turn such a statement around: the index is the reason (the analytical table, the synoptic description) of what is delirious (savage and Antique) about the fragmentation of the encyclopedic text. It is the *method* of the text, which transforms it into a catalogue of commonplaces. But this methodical index could hardly be prepared by the self-portraitist himself, who appears as early as Montaigne's *Essays*, very busy shuffling the cards to prevent an archaeological reconstruction, to deny a museumlike order.

As a micro-encyclopedia and micro-ethnology, as a delirious or erotic specification of the encyclopedia, the self-portrait seeks in ethnology a guarantee and model for its savage otherness; but it can never reduce the otherness of the center, which is the Other, lost and locatable solely through the figures, the emblematic fragments of the Antique. If this lightens the certainty of the Self, it is because the self-portrait is like a phantom encyclopedia that haunts the encyclopedia of commonplaces. It pledges itself to an absence of index and plan, while acknowledging that it is made up of the infinite possibilities of cross-referencing among the "contents" that its spontaneous invention, guided by desire and analogy, keeps transgressing, fragmenting, and reorganizing in a fantasied order. But the reference of the two *specula* or encyclopedias (the self-portrait and the cultural vulgate) to rhetoric, as a combination of invention and memory, enables one to perceive that the circle of fragments never had a center, only a desire to say something and to continue expressing itself. With Barthes, this is revealed through an examination of the archaeological substratum or pre-text of the self-portrait, since *Roland Barthes by Roland Barthes* is indeed a rewriting in the erotic mode of the "Aide-mémoire" on "ancient rhetoric" (1970), which had explored the *taxonomical identity*, the *socio-logic* of Western civilization. Barthes, then, refashions Renaissance humanism, being driven to do so by the desire to bring to light what *constrains* all discourses, including those whose invention progresses "by minute destinies, by amorous fits" (*Roland Barthes by Roland Barthes*),[19] and to smash the "stupid" topical grids, which have "no bearing on 'life' and 'truth' " (*Aide-mémoire*, 207, n.1).[20] It was necessary to journey through this desirable and cursed antiquity in order to be back with oneself and to transform the topoi into places of pleasure and laceration. It is the fantasy of furtive enjoyment in the museum, designated here by the notions of *text* or *writing*, which conceals here the notion of a dialectical *invention*. We shall see, as we analyze Roger Laporte's *biography*, that the reduction of the self-portrayal to a dialectic of invention is doomed to fail because the latter is inseparable from an encyclopedic *speculum*.

A Poetics of the Self-Portrait: Fugue by Roger Laporte

In this short book (1970),[21] a kind of "discourse on method" for the self-portrait, Roger Laporte combines the practice and theory of the self-portrait. This discourse on method does not, of course, aspire to the universality of a scientific epistemology: consequently it would be *out of place* to raise objections against it, to propose amendments, just as it would be impertinent to contest Montaigne or Leiris when they theorize their practice within the very self-portraits. But, unlike Montaigne or Leiris or all other self-portraitists, Laporte eliminates from his "biography" (a term he distances from its ordinary meaning and uses ironically to baffle the reader) everything that forms the cumulative topical substance (so diaphanous, for example, in Jules Vuillemin) of other texts of this type. This radical revision is asserted, in the first lines, by a transformation of the self-portrait's fundamental question, "Who am I?" whose variants "What do I know? Where am I? Whom do I haunt?" imply, each in its own way, a substantial answer that must comprise the description, or at least a taxonomy of a kind of "content" or referent outside the text that we are reading (the characteristics and culture of Montaigne, Nietzsche's hygiene, Leiris's obessions, Borel's house, and so on). Laporte transposes the question onto the self-referential plane of writing: "What is it to write?" (12). Since it is impossible to give a direct answer to this question, whose verb is both intransitive and impersonal, one "must approach it in a roundabout way playing the game which children call the 'Chinese portrait.' Let us transpose this game for our own purposes. I know the name: a book, but nothing besides the name of the thing to be guessed, and yet I can query, even answer the query as though I knew the ultimate reply to it" (12). This beginning serves the triple function of producing a *copia*, of sketching the lineaments of a metaphoric-ana-logical system that admits of subsequent modification, enlarge-ment, or obliteration, and, finally, of introducing in the text the notion of play (the virtual network of figures where this notion can be inserted), which implies rules of the game to be formulated while playing.

Before going any further in our analysis of the idea of a "Treatise on Play," so suggestive and charged with connotations for anyone studying the self-portrait, yet so clearly *dated*, one should note that the rules of the Chinese portrait are no sooner evoked than they are violated. If the first question, "What about this book, then, if it were a treatise on physics?" (12), is according to the rules, since the point here is to guess the characteristics of a *kind* of book, the next two questions, "And what if I were an explorer?" and "If I were a historian?" veer the interrogation towards the *author*. Such a shift is legitimate only if *book, author, life,* and *work* are all one, as the figurative use of the word *biography* led us to believe from the cover and the very first lines of the book.

One can now see what kinds of problems the reader of this book is faced with: first, problems concerning the text and how it functions; second, problems suggested by the silences, the exclusion from the text of any "autobiographical" contents. Each sentence would require a juxtalinear commentary, since each statement is already a query with a theoretical bearing on the practice that has just begun. Subsequent reading will confirm this hypothesis, prompted at the outset by a paradoxical assertion: "although there can be no question of writing an autobiography, nevertheless I shall provisionally, as a pointer, call this work a biography" (11). This paradox announces an "anti-auto-biography" which differs greatly from what Malraux calls his "antimemoirs." Anyone wishing to comment on *Fugue* sentence by sentence, sequence by sequence, would be led to elaborate a theory of the theory, or simply, as is more likely, to paraphrase Laporte's text, which is already, and remains, a metalanguage.

Whence the temptation: to refuse to obey the rules of the game which, if one submits to them, stipulate that one must follow the syntagmatic deployment of repetitions and palinodes, the commentaries that sentence by sentence and sequence by sequence constitute the theory of the practice and the practice of the theory through successive alterations, or at any rate the playful mimesis of such an activity. The immediate consequence of refusing to play is that the reader would miss precisely what is specific to *Fugue:* the (sometimes erratic) development of the game, the (surprising, falsified, sabotaged) operation of the "writing machine," the pivoting of the "mobile," the struggle between the writing and the "counterwriting," with gaps and displacements that dislocate, articulate, and give play to this discourse that erases and uncenters itself as it progresses. This summary—anticipating the very first pages, fictitiously the only ones we are supposed to have read—has already cut them up, reduced them, done them in.

But this critical cutting up, or, rather, this locating of notions and articulations in the text—in short, this refusal to play Laporte's game—is perhaps justified when the text itself asserts: "On the one hand, I propose to discover the implicit grammar of the mind, though on the other hand I intend to contest all rules, even those some future grammar would invent" (86); nevertheless, it categorically rejects heterogeneous critical constructs: "As for the new genre I seek, there is no more need to theorize on its practice in another book" (96). That remains to be seen.

A series of metaphors: a treatise on the game of writing, a model summarizing the work, a writing machine, a writing-rereading program, a "mobile" supposed to represent the mind, a grammar of the mind, a combinatory activity, the (loom) frame—these do seem to share, despite the rather heteroclite array of vehicles, a common tenor: a coded matrix or, in other words, a rhetorical invention.[22] Thus, Roger Laporte's undertaking and the one being pursued here differ only on the following points. In order to constitute itself as theory, *Fugue* limits itself to observing an individual practice, that of the writer ("himself"—this formulation deliberately betrays Laporte's clearly stated intention not to separate theory from practice, especially not to assign, by right or in fact, any primacy to the latter), whereas I am analyzing here a varied corpus, while manifestly not playing the game of self-portrayal. Moreover, Laporte's book evacuates without managing entirely to eliminate them, as we shall soon see, the mnemic traces and the cumulative commonplaces, in order to devote itself as exclusively as possible to using and studying the dialectical places of invention. Consequently, one can "reduce" Laporte's procedures to the anachronistic practice of the old rhetorical invention, of which the theory elaborated in *Fugue* now appears as a resurgence through the barrier of antirhetorical censorship.

It is this repressed material (a ghost in the productive machine) that finds its way, despite the obstacle raised by a lacuna (the unconscious), into the following passage from the sixth sequence:

the manuscript that I am trying to reconstruct is disfigured, forever mutilated by the loss of a single fragment: to write is to go on a wild chase, a
quest for Isis, in order to find the missing fragment, a desperate attempt to
catch up with what was lost, to recover what eludes me and gets away.
(72)

This passage designates the origin, the end, and the resumption of
what we call, perhaps awkwardly, *self-portrait.* One cannot but
recognize in it one of the fantasies that haunted Renaissance man
confronted with the fragmented and lacunary vestiges of antiquity,
those gaps that the immense editing, assembling, and classifying
work of the humanists attempted to fill. Turned around, trimmed
down, and centered on the writer, they would give rise to Montaigne's *Essays,* where the transformation of the *corpus* into an analogon of the writer's own body takes place. This always vain and
open-ended attempt at gathering will eventually be placed by Laporte (at the end of his eighth sequence, 125) under the sign of
Freudian Eros, an Eros that lingers rather complacently, though
not permanently, at the narcissistic stage.

But one can also decipher here a reverse movement that undermines the subject's narcissistic illusions and language's referential
illusions, as it seeks a new understanding of the symbolic order by
showing the function of a lack (Osiris' missing phallus, the object
of Isis' quest) and of castration; a "nothing" must be absent from
the symbolic body for it to become articulated in the unconscious,
an unconscious conceived of, in Lacanian fashion, as autobiography's missing chapter. According to this reverse reading, the impossibility of "biography" becomes evident: Laporte's own, certainly,
but even more so the impossibility of autobiography, which he
had ruled out at the very beginning to grasp the Ariadne thread of
writing.

At the cost of sacrificing the "subject" and the "story," *Fugue*
achieves the paradoxical success of having formulated its theoretical apparatus without denying what erodes it, and even seeking
the dissolution of its theory. *Fugue,* the birth travail of a "new"
genre, underscores what separates the self-portrait from narcissistic
constructions (autobiography, journal, memoirs, and the like) in
which some have seen the end product of humanism, whereas the

latter obscurely defined itself, since the time of Petrarch, in relation to a lack and to hermeneutics as a quest for Isis.

But to get back to the passage cited above, one might bear in mind the rhetorical context of such metaphors as the chase, quest, and the search: we know that they traditionally designate the labor of Invention of which Laporte's work is a kind of imitation.

Fugue differs from the other texts analyzed here by its deliberate amnesia, or rather by the fact that its memory encompasses only its textual space, for the writing subject never tries to recollect, by any procedure whatsoever, what in him might have preceded the writing of the initial word of the text. The writer presents himself as absolutely contemporaneous with the writing of his "biography." This resolutely intratextual memory merely pushes to the limit a constitutive feature of the self-portrait, one that was already implied in the paradoxical intemporality of Book X of Saint Augustine's *Confessions*. The amnesia blotting out any prior referent is one of the rules of Laporte's game, linked to the writing-rereading of the whole text before starting each new sequence, yet it is not properly theorized in the text. Besides, this rule limits the scope of *Fugue's* theorizing, which, in principle, cut itself off from any cultural heritage. It thus condemns itself to entertaining the illusion of inaugurating a radically new genre: an "ellipsis of *diegesis*" for the benefit of *discourse;* a refusal of the *outside* equated with the past and the rest of mankind. This banishment, attempted rather than achieved, becomes visible in the blurred, distorted, intertextuality ("Treatise on Play") between *Fugue* and Michel Leiris's self-portrait, and with Descartes's *Meditations* through a reference to the famous "evil genius" (93), or in the reversal of Blanchot's assertion "the writer has no dwelling where he can persevere in his being other than the universe-book," which becomes here "writing never erects a dwelling, never establishes the steady presence of a home" (60). A careful reading would enable one to multiply the examples of transparent *denials* of context other than the one already revealed in *Fugue's* text.[23] Invention does not attain here a solipsism in which the only "dialogue" allowed under the rules of the game would be the meditative soliloquy of a divided subject. The impossibility of absolutely casting out the intertext never is clearer than at one of *Fugue*'s crucial points of articulation, when at the end of the seventh sequence (100–2), the temptation to abandon the project, a "blank period," a moment of despair, the feeling of pointlessness suddenly give way to "the exhilaration of a festive day" (99), and further on:

> so once emptiness had been articulated with emptiness, I knew that all had been accomplished, that since I could not write, I had been granted the chance to say: nothing has happened to me, other than this nothing that has secretly become a bright enchantment reserved for the morning of the resurrection. I alone know this, the text does not bear witness to it, but at present it is urgent for me to work: I must write so the work, a glorious tomb, may be raised to the memory of nothing. (102)

The reference to the Gospel narrative of Easter is obvious. It transposes Christ's Passion, and the empty sepulcher guarded by the angel and the joy of Easter into the register of *writing*. Death and resurrection: this is the fundamental topos of spiritual auto-biography, of the quest for truth, such as initiation to the Isiac mysteries or of the several "conversion" narratives that Pierre Courcelle has shown to be the antecedents of Saint Augustine's *Confessions*.

The topos that generates confessional autobiography is inscribed in this self-portrait although it is apparently alien to the Augustinian tradition and to Christianity: the place where the text is engendered contains, as in a watermark, the double figure of the suffering and the risen Christ, which turns *Fugue* into a variant of Christian meditation. It is therefore important to specify the contextual function of the Easter topos and the symbolic link connecting the writing of the self-portrait with the Resurrection.

What occurs in *Fugue*, as in the Gospel narrative, is indeed a *nothing*: a gaping hole (the stone rolled to one side), an absence (of the body, of the text), an articulation "of emptiness with emptiness," which, however, tenders a "chance" (a notion borrowed from Georges Bataille, who refers us, through his *Sur Nietzsche: Volonté de chance*, to the author of *Ecce Homo*), the "bright enchantment reserved for the morning of the resurrection" (102). A new work[24] and a new discourse are breaking through here. Louis Marin described them as: "This word [the angel's] is the other of being, the *other-body* in the place of the dead body; it is not 'here and now' in the empty place. It is the other-body of the exchanged word, the historical universal" ("Du Corps au texte"). No doubt this commentary seems out of place when applied to Laporte's text, in principle so hostile to the historical Universal. Yet, this book also purports to universalize writing in a concrete practice, to articulate the singular with the universal workings of the mind by taking advantage of this *blank period*, which can also be called a death and a resurrection, since this event was first signified to the Holy Women, though unintelligibly, by the sight of the empty sepulcher. For Laporte the *work* itself, after this "loss" (first experienced as grief, made more acute by the absence of the *body*), must be turned into a "glorious tomb . . . erected to the memory of nothing" (102).

The "writing machine" that produces this type of paradoxical discourse in self-portrayal takes us back to psychoanalytic discourse with this *nothing* which Laporte also designates as the missing fragment of Osiris, the detached phallus, which, according to Lacan, enables the "symbolic" to be articulated; a *nothing*, a "glorious tomb," around which every self-portrait turns out to be structured. A twice empty tomb: language can neither express nor immortalize, nor even mummify the writer's own body, still alive at the moment of writing and usually already dead at the moment of reading; self-portrayal can only turn the writer's body into narcissistic fantasies of the fragmented body, transforming the now obsolete question "Who am I?" into Breton's query, which will remain current so long as a self-portrait has readers: "Whom do I haunt?" A Mallarméan tomb no doubt, one whose emptiness is due to the very nature of language, it is also a place of resurrection, as each reader elicits again the reply of the evangelical angel, who reiterates to every visitor a promise of resurrection. "The memory of nothing": this amounts to accepting without reservations the disappointment caused by the irremediable absence of the writer from his text and his illusory presence to the reader; this instigates an exchange inscribed in all testamentary literature, of which Laporte's *cenotaph* also is a version. The self-portraitist signs a binding pact with the reader, who grants him immortality.

A testament, indeed, bequeaths the *properties* of its maker on the explicit condition that the deceased's will shall be done. Since the deceased is henceforth absent—that is, incapable of exchange (through dialogue, just as through other "dealings")—he imposed on his heirs a scrupulous interpretation and complete submission to his testamentary dispositions, in return for which they will received certain *benefits*. Fully aware that it creates and imposes the "rules of a game," the self-portrait resorts to all the resources of the symbolic and figurative so as to overcome, especially on the side of death, the boundaries of the "proper," or, rather, to blur them. Consequently, the encoding of the self-portrait is especially fussy and scrupulous, for it performs a function analogous to testamentary dispositions; yet the self-portrait is not addressed only to immediate survivors (since it can be published while the author is still alive), nor solely to direct heirs, but to all posterity.[25] This deliberate stipulation of rules of the game, by analogy with a testament, inscribes the self-portraitist's own death, as well as the survival of language and that of the readers.[26] Yet Laporte's self-portrait is literally "erected to the memory of nothing," since it aims to be amnesic: in principle, nothing in it is prior to the writing of the text, except the mother tongue itself (which is also contested: "Shouldn't I set upon my mother tongue and, above all, my own style?" [155]). But this amnesia, hardened and theorized, harks back to Montaigne's own and to his privileging of invention in the *Essays*. It has therefore a foreseeable consequence: in Laporte's empty *tomb*, an encyclopedic topical system cannot be deployed. Since Laporte emphasizes exclusively the places of dialectical invention, the memory places are reduced to a sketchy mnemonic system within an extended theatrical metaphor (162), which, in turn, metamorphoses into the metaphor of a labyrinth towards the end of the book (165).[27]

Topics of invention, however, proliferate in *Fugue;* they produce a series of spatial metaphors, as well as an incipient allegorization and dramatization. The "idea of a unitary field [is] replaced by that of several spaces" (123), and these various elements combine into the description of a metaphorical stage or *theater*, where the following allegorical figures are displayed: Eros (or Philia), Sophia, the reciting spectator, and his double, the actor-director; on this stage "Some abstract dionysiac spectacle finally takes place" (165).

In Laporte's self-portrait, the Renaissance Memory theater becomes a theater of Invention.

Fugue's dialectical invention rests on a system of binary oppositions, but in the later versions of this system there crops up a mediating term, an articulation through *loss*, through *nothing*, and so on:

First of all, we find the over simplistic image of the literary game that comports, on the one hand, a mobile etching its pathway and, on the other, a literally confusing outside. (37)

If the first image is "over simplistic," it still does display the essential traits of the opposition between a "productive machine" that engenders the *within*, and the *without* whose main semantic feature emphasizing the break and opposition is linked to the prefix *dé*—of "*dé*router" (confuse), "*dé*vier" (deviate), "*dé*construire" (deconstruct)—and the preposition *counter*—as in *counter*writing. The metaphor of a literary game sketches in a poetics loaded with rhetorical and alchemical recollections. Here is the first formulation of this poetic art:

It happens as though the work were the place where a within and a without confront each other, where writing confronts counterwriting, an adversary that it would be unfair, however, to consider an enemy of the work, for without it the work would become geometrized, crystalized into a Treatise, which, though perfect, would nonetheless mean, for the work sublimated into an *oeuvre*, a mortal immobility. Counterwriting is inseparable from suffering and is thus life bearing. (38)

Perhaps it would be superflous to analyze in detail a poetics so classically "modern," suspended between a deliberate "rhetoric" and an abandonment to unconscious drives and whose personifications are so clearly figures for biological maternity. Still, one should specify that the "without" is also a limit of the "within," for "the writing act . . . is . . . always acted upon at the heart of its activity" (39). Furthermore, *writing* and *counter*writing are quite obviously in a complementary relation to each other, like *animus* and *anima*, law and transgression, male and female, and so on, so that in the final analysis, it becomes impossible to "distinguish the mode of production from its subversion, for it is all one to speak of subversion and displacement" (91).

There comes a moment, then, in the development of *Fugue* (92), when the allegorical confrontation of writing and counterwriting ceases to be productive: inventing a text by the dialectic of contraries. The two adversaries, by dint of having collaborated in weaving and puncturing the text end up resembling each other, like a white pawn and a black pawn on the chess-board. This is when the episode of a "textual death" and resurrection occurs, engendering in turn a new poetic art, where "loss," "emptiness articulated with emptiness," "what is missing," "disappearance," (103) are turned around to become "chance" and "feast."

It would be easy to show that this variant of the poetics derives, on the theological level, from the model of conversion and resurrection, and, on the level of literary ideology, from Georges Bataille's variant of surrealistic poetics, a variant that is imbued with sacrificial Christianity.

The space of the work becomes (112) the place of confrontation, not only of two accomplice-enemies, but of three protagonists, namely, "work," "loss," (which may by *chance* bloom into a *feast*), and "savagery." (113) The distribution and articulation of these agencies, together with their anthropological, religious, and psychoanalytic connotations, are more suggestive than the first topical system, frozen in an allegorical confrontation.

By considering the opposition between the notions of *work* (a new version of the writing machine, of the program, of gathering Eros) and *savagery* (a variant of counterwriting and the "without," to which are added the dimensions of *language* and the "death instinct," which transcode "primitivism" and *savagery* understood as fear and desire that possess a civilized white man), an opposition mediated by the "loss-feast" (variants of utopia and uchronia) borrowed from Christianity and the Lacanian concept of the symbolic, one can now formulate more clearly the implicit and scrambled poetics that have produced, among other writings, Montaigne's *Essays* and Leiris's self-portrait. The opposition between work and savagery also enables us to clarify the function of cannibals in the *Essays* and of (phantom) Africa in the works of Leiris. Savagery, indeed, is what *haunts* the writing of the Western self-portrait, or what "possesses" it. It is not a "without" simply opposed to the within, but rather, as Montaigne indicates in his notice "To the

Reader," a *limit* in the dual sense of that towards which one tends (for example, the total nakedness of the natural state) and that which is interposed (the *interface*) between the within and the without, a mediation never absent from the very movement of invention.

Thus, there arises the question of the "subject" and of knowing what it becomes in this tripartite system, where according to another version: "two camps share literary space: the thought that plays [counterwriting, savagery] and the thought that works [writing, work], separated and united by the emptiness of the interface" (117).

This interface causes a problem. For the emptiness is precisely that place where metaphysical thought, the metaphysics of the sign, situates the "subject": "the dividing line between the two camps is drawn through the one who says I" (161).[28] It would be superflous to dwell on this "subject," properly split and cleft by emptiness articulated upon emptiness, if Laporte had not designated the cleavage as an impossible utopia-uchronia, which evokes the impossible and sovereign situation of the risen Christ "in" his body of glory, a situation that metamorphoses the empty sepulcher into a scriptural catafalque. Laporte admits this contradiction: "Fearing that the crack might become a break, wishing to finally find his own unity, the one who says I often tries to reconcile the two adversaries, but every attempt is in vain" (161). An impossible reconciliation according to *Fugue*'s own rules of the game and the dominant antisubject ideology of the time, to which one who says I does not adhere without sliding back into metaphysics; yet this backsliding furnishes him the occasion and means to carry out or botch his paradoxical undertaking. In fact, the self-portrait takes advantage of the ideological ambiguities surrounding the sign, since it thematicizes the *dislocation* of the writer's own body and that of writing, of the hieroglyphic signifier and of the discursive signified. If Laporte wins something at this game, it is because he wants to "stay in a safe place" rather than let himself go completely, adrift in savagery or yielding to the mutism of the cleft that would swallow up his writing.

But if Laporte knows full well that the self-portraitist places himself somewhere short of a passionate acceptance of the subject's disapperance, still this does not make him a caricature of Cartesian man, so smugly assured, as we are told, of an ontological certainty of his "ego." The self-portait precedes and survives the transcendental subject, for it is not constituted through a *metaphysical meditation* but by a dialectical invention, where loss and splitting are implicit in the always inconclusive and fragmentary attempts to totalize: self-portrayal turns to its own account the counterwriting of the cultural intertext (the classics, Holy Writ, humanist writing) as well as *savagery*, whether that is understood to be an "image of the savage" or a threat from the "death instinct."

We may conclude that the "treatise on the writing game" outlined by Laporte is nothing but a rhetorical art, a specialized theory of invention enabling the self-portaitist to stake out a safe writing place in the face of unbearable threats. Having studied Laporte's literary accomodation, we shall now examine the consequences of a radical refusal of rhetoric and of compromises of writing, for another writer who, tempted by self-portrayal, encountered what he judged to be insurmountable objections to its demands. Jean Prévost's short *Essai sur l'introspection*, in its lofty opposition to both metaphysics and rhetoric, presents *a contrario* a theoretical approach to the self-portrait, which is in a sense more rigorous than that of self-portraitists themselves. This absence of self-portrayal may therefore be considered as the most incisive criticism of the self-portraitist's literary *games*.

An Impossible Invention: Jean Prévost

Jean Prévost's *Essai sur l'introspection* (1927) clearly belongs to the French literary and philosophic movement of the beginnings of the twentieth century that made "sincerity" and revealing the way "the mind really works" its supreme goals, while rejecting the "artifices" of formal logic and rhetoric.[29] But Prévost's essay is just as opposed to the metaphysical idealism of philosophers as it is to the epistemological confusions of the literati. His rigorous insistence on the epistemological obstacles to introspective (and automatic) *writing* sets him apart from his contemporaries and leads him, perhaps unwittingly and certainly much against his will, into the domain where rhetoric once ruled: the domain of the commonplaces.

His poetic commitment also prompts him to demand a rigorous distinction between verisimilitude and truth, between literature and science or philosophy.

For this reason, Prévost cannot endorse the scrupulous illusions of a Jacques Rivière who, while opposed to the centrifugal lie of the self as cultivated by Barrès, tried, by means of introspection, to create his soul *such as it was*, a hidden entelechy whose murmur is hardly audible beneath the verbiage of the self:

in my utmost depths a low, continual meditation—of which I shall know nothing if I don't make an effort to know it; it is my soul. It is weak and, as it were, ideal; it barely exists, I feel it as a possible and distant world. (*De la sincérité envers soi-même*, 22–23) [30]

Prévost on the contary wants to describe more precisely, more scientifically the obstacles to the practice of what is called, with excessive simplification, introspection. Not only the aporias denounced in the neoclassical period under the heading of vanity,[31] nor even the resistances that Karen Horney recognizes in the free association practice of self-analysis (*Self-Analysis*, 111),[32] but the specifically methodological and epistemological difficulties inherent in the *writing* or invention of so-called introspective texts. As a result, Prévost achieved observations—or cautionary warnings—closer to Montaigne's in "Of Idleness" (I, VIII) than to the facile Bergsonism of the moderns:

An inactive but continually watchful man sees parading before his gaze a series of thoughts detached from present action; if he does not let himself drift, he can control, and with amusement, follow them. These trains of thoughts are one of the subject matters of introspection; rather than observe them directly (for these spontaneous states would combine in the mind with the observation, and thus necessarily be modified) one should rather call them to mind, compare them and try to discover by what laws they are formed and succeed one another. (26)

Prévost even emphasizes that the (written) results obtained by an inquiry devoid of method and epistomologically vitiated do not at all correspond with what pseudopsychologists think they obtain: on the contrary, the understanding is circular and tautological, for the text thus produced only rediscovers what the essentially literary culture of the investigator had provided to him in the first place:

For I believe that most of those who think they practice introspection and offer a vast field to their inner vision are grossly mistaken, they do but mimic unwittingly the minds of others, or let the residues of others combine at random without contributing anything of their own. (59)

The remedy finally proposed against these Baconian idols and the methodological confusions of all the psychological schools of criticism by Prévost is perhaps a little naive, but it has the merit of simplicity: let us resort to "bodily introspection" and describe our body's internal sensations. This way we shall escape metaphysical contradictions, as well as the alienation caused by an unwitting imitation of others in idealistic introspection: "It is . . . in the resources and sensations of this body that one must seek the principle of our own individuality." (81)

Prévost's bodily option enables him to specify:

I think the most total impression of *self-knowledge* one will have will share all the data of bodily introspection, when unimpeded by digestion or hunger, numbness or irritation, feeling one's blood circulating throughout oneself but not excessively, our mind composes from all these data a tempered and subtle harmony. (112)

And further on:

Here one might reiterate the remark of Cebes in *Phaedo* and think the feeling of our soul is the feeling of the body's harmony; but this would carry us too far into metaphysics. (114)

Yet, the *cogito* of Prévost—one of the first French intellectuals to praise sports, for whom physical harmony resulted from regular training—is but an impoverished version of the *cogito* of Maine de Biran, whose youthful raptures came from "a mode of union, a more harmonious correspondence between body and soul: the inferior part communicated to the superior one the equilibrium and quietude it enjoyed, and the superior part communicated to the inferior peace and bliss" (*Journal*, 3:240–41).[33] This, of course, harks back to Rousseau's ecstasy in the Fifth Reverie.

Prévost's undertaking is presented as a "game" (of which he gives here only brief, actually rather banal, examples). It is not unrelated to the—infinitely richer, though unscientifically oriented—exploration of the body practiced by Henri Michaux (in *L'Espace du dedans*) or Jacques Brosse (in *Inventaire des sens*). Any introceptive and coenesthetic inventory (of which Prévost's text offers a mere sample, thus eluding these constraints), however naive the investigator, cannot avoid running through topics, the simplest one being the "places of the body" or the five senses. As a result, the *method* followed turns out to be a variant of Baconian *invention*.

But Prévost is hostile to rhetoric: one of his main reasons for condemning introspection, as it was practiced at his time, is that it resorts to *commonplaces:*

> It is said, and rightly so, that the reader must be able to recognize himself in any literary creation but at the same time he must recognize *another* than himself; remaining sympathetic, he must also observe and learn. Literature's *commonplaces* also belong to philosophy; any commonplace on the inner workings of the mind is a part of introspective psychology. (64)

While these remarks, where "introspective psychology," "philosophy," and "commonplaces" are amalgamated, may appear rather off-handed, at least they foreground—if only to mark it with a negative sign—the notion of *place*, while stressing that "introspective psychology" is a collection of literary "commonplaces." Furthermore, Prévost inveighs here against "most psychologists" rather than writers: he reproaches pseudoscientific idealistic psychology for cribbing its findings from literature and repeating "commonplaces in technical language." Prévost, then, does not indict "subjective literature," so much as he accuses a pseudopsychology of "practicing bad literature and bad science" instead of examining its epistemological foundations.[34]

> Introspective psychology would provide the rules, limit the terrain, and produce the most general results of a game for which the direct, sincere portion of literature would serve as an exercise and testing ground. (64)

Thus, having resorted to notions that have since become obsolete or unfashionable in France, Prévost opposes literature to psychology in terms where one catches a glimmer of a rhetorical preoccupation. Unlike his contemporaries, who always overlooked the specificity of the discourses used in "introspection," Prévost discreetly alludes to *composition*, persuasion, and the search for effect peculiar to literary discourses:

One difficulty is that literature and psychology do not seem to judge by the same rules: literature chooses and composes internal realities to achieve the greatest possible effect, and the reader then judges according to the unity and truthfulness of his emotion; psychology seeks a specific truth, and the reader exercises his acumen to determine whether his experience, or some average of his experience, corresponds with the impression the work gives him. (65)

This is certainly rather confusing and in fact somewhat embarrassing. We are now far enough away from the time when Prévost was writing to perceive readily what lurks behind such an opposition: the malaise that still persists as a result of the collapse of the barrier separating *truth* from verisimilitude, which entails the following ideological chiasmus: literature sometimes exceeds verisimilitude in the name of an untamed savage imperative, whereas science has to limit itself to the norm and the average. Truth is to be found in mediocrity, in generality; it is therefore convincing without being moving. On the other hand the emotional impact of literary persuasion is distinct from its truth-value; it is produced by an internal coherence or verisimilitude. But isn't literature in a sense "truer" than "science," even if it is excessive, ab-normal, and unverifiable? Clearly, this precarious opposition threatens to collapse, insofar as it rests entirely on a desperate attempt to maintain (while abolishing it) the opposition between truth and verisimilitude inherited from the Aristotelian tradition. In other words, the introspective "psychology" in question by no means steps outside the rhetorical, nor even the literary terrain. The opposition lies, indeed, between a dull "scientific" literature that wishes itself to be normative, normal, and generalizing and a literary literature that is violent, excessive, transgressive, and provokes an emotional response in the reader while remaining somehow plausible. The opposition between the norm and deviation, between the proper and the figurative is fully operative here, right in the midst of an ideological confusion that tends to blur the difference. Consequently, even though Prévost strives to extricate "good" introspective psychology from literature, his essay never succeeds in seperating legitimate science from literary invention.

Since he tries to conceive of truth as extradiscursive while being unable to renounce literary discourse, Prévost is led to deplore the fact that literature manages to mimic what escapes authentic experience and produces "imaginary, invented experiences," which are nevertheless plausible. The example chosen by Prévost, of an "imaginary" and "invented" experience (these epithets are used pejoratively here) is extremely interesting because it is a crucial topos. On the one hand, it refers to an archeological substratum of self-portrayal (metempsychosis, initiatory conversion); and, on the other, it evokes Christian meditation which also derives from this archaic model: Christ's death and resurrection, the writer imagining his own death as a fall into sleep, a descent to hell, and so on:

For example, it is impossible . . . to observe the mind in its fall into sleep. Yet, one can find among words, among images, an impression *equivalent* if not faithful to the vague memory we retain of this fall. Will such a description be valid? Will it teach us about what is within us? And what then is to be said about a purely imaginary description, such as the fall of the mind into death? Only its impossibility often dissuades us from believing in it. It seems that the simplest course for introspective psychology is to reject these impossible experiences, since it considers truth—the kind of aesthetic impression which it calls truth—the rule of its game. (65)

The problem here is our inability to overcome the truth/fiction opposition within an axiological context where fiction, provided it admits that it *is* fiction, is no more nor less valued than the truth. Prévost did attempt to overcome this opposition by introducing the notion of play: let us play at introspection and write the rules of its game. But this resolves nothing unless, like Iurii Lotman, one resorts to the concept of a model that enables one to articulate and hierarchize the notions of play, fiction (or art), and truth, which are mutually exclusive in discourse:

It is precisely play, because with its biplanar behavior, its possibility of conventional transference into situations and realities unavailable to a given man, that enables him to find his profound nature . . . to an even greater extent, art carries out this mission altogether essential for man.
By creating for man a conventional possibility of speaking to himself in different types of language, by coding his own self differently, art helps man to resolve one of the most important psychological questions: the determination of his own being. (*La Structure du texte artistique*, 107–8)

In this perspective, the function of "purely imaginary descriptions," such as the "fall of the mind" into sleep or death, is clear enough. If a game and the pratice of religious *meditation* are in-

deed a sort of "game," it is not the conventional aspect of the situations proposed to the player (Christ's Passion and death; "one's
own death") that can cause a problem, but only its specific content. Anyone may accept or reject the proposed models, but neither
modelization per se nor the conventional transference it implies,
can be challenged, so long as one admits the generality of play
among humans. One would have to uphold an extreme Romanticism, a terrorism, ideologically averse to all play, to any modelization, and therefore, to any rhetoric, to deny that any player can
thus discover his "profound nature." There is no contradiction between the strictly individual (the profound, the genuine, if one
prefers) and the conventional: the games or ludic situations coded
into a given culture do not necessarily obscure the undivided transparency of "pure and authentic" subjectivity. Individuality and
subjectivity are indeed games peculiar to certain cultures.

Imaginary descriptions, then, whose status seemed so equivocal
to Prévost that he wished to exclude them from his search for psychological truth, appear to be a conventional coding enabling one
both to store data and to produce new knowledge in the context of
a given culture. The objection to modelization leads one to believe
that the art of self-portrayal only apprehends what is conventional,
since, according to Valéry's strong expression, it is "the theater of
residues" (Essai, 69), or the "general place of culture" (68). It would
necessarily miss the "individual." Against this objection, we again
appeal to Lotman's skillful interweaving of generality and individuality:

Any "individual" fact, any peculiarity in the artistic text results from the
complication of the fundamental structure by complementary structures.
It arises as an intersection of at least two systems, receiving a particular
meaning in the particular context of each. The more norms interact at a
particular structural point, the more meaning this particular element will
carry, the more individual, the more extrasystemic it will seem. What is
extrasystemic in life is reflected in art as polysystemic. (120–21)

This paradox—so difficult to accept in general—may seem particularly shocking in reference to "personal literature," where individual revelation ought to prevail over convention in principle
at least. Accepting the validity of Lotman's paradox leads one to

consider self-portrayal as any other personal genre, to be a literary work of art; it also entails that this kind of literature, insofar as it aims to multiply the effects of individuality, must be exceptionally complex, since its fundamental structures, the places of memory and invention will be intersected at numerous points by complementary structures. It would seem, then, that any analysis that first attempts to reveal the existence of one or several systems of places in the self-portrait must also become more complex, as it turns back to those structural points where the effects of the individuality strike one powerfully on a first reading.

Conversely, any analysis of the self-portrait that overlooks the encyclopedic systems of commonplaces, either out of ignorance or ideological prejudice, must end up piecemeal, if not completely meaningless; such an analysis would indeed miss the point of the self-portrait as a work of art as it retained only the transgressive features of the system, in order to transcode them hurriedly into such extraneous cultural codes as "psychology," "psychoanalysis," or some "deconstructive" version of ontology.

The merit of Prévost's book is that it clearly manifests its choice, not through the criticism of a preexisting text but, rather, in its assertion of the impossibility of writing a text for which the *Essai sur l'introspection* stands in the guise of admission of failure. After having rejected any cultural commonplace, Prévost recounts several attempts that, given another strategy, might have led to the successful writing of an "introspective" text.

In order to prove this, one would have to cite an entire chapter of the book, where Prévost explicitly rejects that which Leiris, for example, welcomed and sought in his self-portrayal (ch. 5, "L'Introspection à la dérive"). But the crucial difference between Prévost and Leiris is that the former strictly dissociates introspection from writing, while the latter relies on dialectical invention to carry out the process. As he distinguishes between the purely introspective procedure and the verbal account of it, Prévost must resort to an extratextual memory in order to remember the contents of conciousness, whereas Leiris regards memory essentially as a result of intratextual invention. A passage by Prévost entitled "Unavowed Language" proves this point:

It seems to me, as I questioned my memories [of introspection], that every verbal or language impression had disappeared from them. But certain words resisted being written, and others I had to choose were often less logical, often not so suitable, it seemed to me later on, to my thinking at that moment; sometimes the words came of themselves; I did not at all feel that I was *choosing them, just as when one describes an external object, nor of finding them by chance: it was as if they were dictated to me;* when I hesitated I felt the reality, *while I had thought them,* of these forgotten, unknown, invisible words: remembering them, I made an effort, as if to cite from a book I would have read while falling asleep.

The sound of these unavowed words was more supple than in expressed language: I felt, as I wrote them, one after another, a kind of embarrassment, due to the demands of their structure, of their normal use, which I had forgotten during introspection, and which were protesting under my pen. In order to verify this observation, I had only to read a few pages from a dictionary or a strict author, like la Rochefoucauld; having become more stringent about the value of words, I returned to the terms and concepts of my introspection, only to judge they were deformed. (72–73)

I got bogged down in the difficulty of writing everything; building sentences or mere punctuated series of words without grammatical linkage would recreate other links between these words, risking the falsification of my memories. To write the words (or the series of clotted words) without linking them in any way, would falsify everything even more, making them rough and dry, whereas on the contrary, when they had taken place, they were too liquid to have taken shape, to be distinguishable from one another. One would have had to run words together, to paint certain series in certain colors shading into each other, in order to mark the different states of mind, that, being as arbitrary as these colors on paper, had summoned and collected these words in my thought. (74)

In principle, then, all that Prévost had to do was to ignore a methodological obstacle, to surmount a resistance he considered (perhaps rightly) to be an epistemological aporia, in order to tilt his poetic project, as Leiris did, over to the side of poetry. For Prévost, the distances separating the time of introspection from that of writing and, further, the chasm between introspective consciousness (which, he says later, degrades one's judgement, makes one sink into dreams and the sottishness of ecstasy [78]) and the writing conciousness (which he knew to be a divided conciousness, where the subject cannot grasp himself) is impassable; Prévost believed that any attempt to reduce this distance in writing leads to mystification: the mimesis of the introspective drift would be a fiction, a lie. Between the linguistic regime of this twilight ("a book I have read while falling asleep," which echoes the Proustian metaphor in the overture to *La Recherche*) and the regime of the waking state—of the day after—there is an incompatibility accentuated here by a reference to such norms as the dictionary and La Rochefoucauld.[35] The terms and concepts of introspection are "deformed," they are monsters, "too liquid to take shape, to be distinguishable from one another." In introspection, the signifier plays tricks, and words are slippery entities: Prévost cannot, should not, fit them in the normal lexicon and syntax. And he is careful not to cross over to another syntax, as he censors a monstrous, grotesque, chimerical, and fantastic lexicon.

This attitude is in keeping with the one adopted towards the experience of the fall of the mind into sleep; except that Prévost then recognizes some literary, if not scientific, value to the words and images that give an impression "*equivalent*" to our vague memory of that fall. According to Prévost, "the rule of the introspective game" says that such an equivalence—which can also be called a mimesis and a model—is off sides.

The stakes in this game are anything but trivial, since Prévost adopts a position that sets the limits of literary introspection, and, correlatively, of self-portrayal. Leiris's entire undertaking, from his surrealist language games to *La Règle du jeu*, is founded on the transgression of the limit, in principle impassable for Prévost, between endophasia and writing—a transgression thanks to which what was lost on one side will be recovered elsewhere, as literature, if only the writer will agree, even implicitly, to resort to commonplaces and weave at first between written words and then between "facts," those "fictitious" links that do indeed betray the experience of language and memory that precedes writing.

As is revealed by his obstinate refusal, Prévost had a keen awareness of rhetoric's hold over the texts that claim to offer a transgressive mimesis of the "prediscursive": rhetoric ineluctably imposes a betrayal of "introspective conciousness," a betrayal in the direction of the typical, the general, the communicable. No wonder, then, that anyone can recognize himself in self-portraits, despite whatever violence may have been done to syntax and lexicon.

Prévost's objections to this betrayal also enable us to clarify, in the light of Lotman's theoretical statements, the reasons why the self-portrait must be envisaged as a work of literary art and not as a psychological, historical, or sociological document whose ideological coding would be a mere matter of "expository writing" rather than *writing* in Barthes's intransitive sense of the word.

Functionally, the self-portrait is indeed a kind of game for the writer and for his readers, according to Lotman's assertion that "play gives man the possibility of a conventional victory over something invincible"—death in this case. It is a function shared with philosophy as it was understood by Socrates and Montaigne; it is also that of religious meditation, the *artes moriendi*, and the *Imitation of Jesus Christ*: they all impose "playful" practice and, therefore, assume a psychopedagogical function. The self-portrait's game in the face of death remains incomplete insofar as it refuses definite rules, the loss of self, the reduction of oneself to a playful conciousness that playing the game imposes on the player so he may, without damage, "pass" or replay a hand and, as a result, acquire some know-how. Self-portrayal does not really teach one how to die, although it sometimes overestimates its own didactic, or at least autodidactic, capacity.

But it does teach the writer to *modelize* his own death; Lotman tells us that play is "like an activity" while art "is like life." Among all other literary forms the self-portrait has this particularity, that it is both "like life" and "like death," which it systematizes and foregrounds.

It situates death exactly in the initial fringe or limbo that Prévost refuses to cross and that all self-portraitists must enter: they indicate it by means of the topos of "falling asleep" or "death and resurrection." This symbolic death marks their accession to the symbolism that cuts them off from their own "true" body, their "true" introspection, their "true" self, as they enter, perhaps unwittingly, the sphere of "equivalence," mimesis, invention, writing, silence, and immortality—that is, the pleasure of literature. In the final analysis, the lesson that Prévost teaches us, in spite of himself perhaps, is that he did not want to die to the world in order to accede to literature. This lesson can also be understood as a refusal of representation, a refusal that could be transcoded in the protracted ambiguity of "deconstruction." Prévost's book, then, stands, so to speak, as the obverse of the works of those such as Leiris, Laporte, and a few others. It is a book that does not wish to become a *Book*, in Mallarmé's exalted sense of the word, and therefore undermines the modern myth that sustains the endless undertaking of self-portrayal.

Invention in Relation to the Book: Leiris's La Règle du jeu

In the course of his analysis of the *mimetic motivation* of language as found in the works of Leiris, Gérard Genette remarked that the game of the author of *Biffures* rests on an opposition between the social and the private, the collective and the autonomous (*Mimologiques*, 352). And in an introduction to an explication of a chapter in *Biffures* entitled "Alphabet" (an explanation in which he examined the verbal network encompassing the name Esaü, with its disquieting diaeresis),[36] Philippe Lejeune concurred with Genette insofar as he situated the erotic connotations of the diaeresis in Leiris's self-portrait within its ambiguous contextual relationship to the Bible story:

A doubly ancient history; relating the origins of the world and how the law was given to us, this history also marks a child's origins, since it is one of the first books he read. Just as with ". . . reusement!" [". . . tunately!"], it deals with learning language, but also with learning about the law. One says "Moïse" [Moses] and not "Moisse." Thy fathers . . . and thy mother shall thou not covet. The structures of language and those of kinship correspond. There are rules of the game. At the same time that the Bible is full of diaereses, it is full of strange family stories. And perhaps they are the same thing. (*La Pacte autobiographique*, 292)

Perhaps this genetic approach is a little too rapid. But we will retain the main point: in his mosaic,[37] Leiris manages to regress sometimes from "Moïse" to "Moisse" as well as elsewhere from "heureusement" (fortunately) to ". . . reusement" (". . . tunately"). In *Biffures* we find both *Moïse* and *Moisse; Moisse* was a *moiïque* (ego-ideal) or imaginary Moses, while *Moïse* was indeed the Moses of the Decalogue. Let us note in passing that these language-bound word games are played under the aegis of a very French muse, in an idiom common to Leiris, Genette, Lejeune, and to the author of the present lines: in short, a familiar idiolect. Of course, there are rules, but there is also some play in them, for the "Alphabet" chapter in *Biffures* plays with two systems of places: *L'Histoire Sainte*, the Sunday School textbook, which combines narration and illustrations like the Stations of the Cross, mediating between the Passion narrative and the "composition of places" of a spiritual exercise; and the elementary school *Histoire de France* textbook, whose sequence of textual places combines with those of the childhood Bible. Leiris reveals here a specifically French and Catholic education, *normal* for a child of his class and time. Without this normative topical system Leiris would be unable to explore intelligibly the idioms or gallicisms of his cultural idiolect. There is play *because* there are rules. The commonplaces mediate between Leiris's private linguistic quest and French bourgeois culture. Anyone who needs explanatory notes to follow Leiris's course through the "Alphabet" and the rest of his self-portrait; anyone who does not immediately recognize the analogies between BAIR, CASTLES, CAUDA in *Manhood* (64) and the MANÉ, THÉCEL, PHARÈS of *Biffures* (65), is a barbarian:[38] to read Leiris and to realize what is peculiar to him, such a barbarian must undergo an apprenticeship in French culture, with its families, its version of the "mess of pottage," and its clichés about the Gauls.[39] Conversely, each self-portrait must inevitably be a rich ethnographic document for the foreigner (in the cultural sense), provided he can detect the interplay of the norm and the exception, of the cliché and the idiosyncratic variant.

According to Genette, the passage from ". . . reusement!" to "Heureusement!" at the begining of *Biffures* reveals two facts simultaneously:

Adult language reveals all at once its internal and its external relations, its systematic structure and its social function. *A contrario*, therefore, the child's language displays retrospectively its essential characteristic, its *autonomy*: the speaker's autonomy with respect to other people, since he was speaking to himself, without addressing anybody else, and the autonomy of each verbal element with respect to an as yet unrecognized linguistic system. (*Mimologiques*, 352)

Extrapolating from this analysis, Genette interprets all of Leiris's works, to the extent that they are produced by linguistic games, as an effort to remember or reconstruct a "lost linguistic paradise": "The work is, for him, a *quest for language;* and obviously this paradoxical situation can be understood only if the language sought for is in some way hidden or lost" (353).

This quest may be understood in the first place as a recollection of the language of childhood. Rather than a spontaneous anamnesis, it is an "artificial reconstruction," which Leiris also calls play. A play in the second degree rather than the simple repetition of a child's game. First came the child's authentic and euphoric play, the memory of which is almost erased; now we have the adult's play, which dodges the linguistic norm and involves an element of simulation and make believe. Genette underscores ambiguity in the practice of Leiris as an adult who no longer believes in the magic of the Word, yet still clings to—or yearns for—a residual credulity. Leiris knows full well that it is impossible for him to restore, sometimes even to *revive* by the artificial breathing of the text, that part of the game which is not entirely dead in him and still shows some signs of life through such verbal revelations as *teta-ble,*[40] *the names of unheard of beings who would people a world outside our laws. (Biffures,* 21) This requires an irritating, prolonged, and disappointing search, accompanied by an emotion analogous to "the suffering that the quest for the absolute causes in those who persevere in this quest, thirsting, and yet without faith." *(Biffures,* 22) In brief, a heuristic alchemy, a great game rather than a *magnum opus,* since the ludic consciousness combines detachment and seriousness: it asserts without believing in the truth of its assertion. A game, finally, whose magic etiology is as easily found within our culture as it is in Leiris's biography. Desire without faith, quest without a Grail . . . this enables Leiris to distinguish (while still equivocating) between the illusion of *presence* and the labor of *invention:*

If I want to give substance to this present moment—to this very *presence* —suddenly it eludes me, grows blurred; and all I can say about it—unable as I am, and for quite good reason, to challenge it directly (when I would like to cry out to it at the top of my voice . . .) —all I can invent to lead it or bring it back into reality turns into the idlest chatter: I line up sentences, I accumulate words and figurative language, but what gets caught in each of these snares is always the shadow and never the prey. *(Biffures,* 23)

If there is a "double game" here, as Lejeune puts it (*Le Pacte autobiographique* 291), this duplicity is simply attributable to *rhetorical invention*, which is evoked, further on in same passage, by the ancient metaphor of the hunt. No doubt this illusion without illusion (which Genette clarifies from the point of view of mimologism) is indispensable to Leiris in order to override the epistomological scruples that blocked Jean Prévost and reduce his book to a recognition of the conditions of impossibility of the self-portrayal. Only rhetoric enables the writer to disregard truth's *non possumus* without sliding into lies or, worse, into naiveté. Rhetoric is a game, as equivocal as one wants it to be and capable of making the player uneasy, for its field is not truth, but rather the possible and the verisimilar. There is then much lucidity, though not due to a knowledge of rhetoric, in Leiris's assertion: "Whether I hunt the present instant that flees from me, track down a memory turned to dust, or stalk imaginary objects that seem to hide behind false windows of words painted in trompe l'oeil on the façade of my mind, I am always hunting for the same quarry" (*Biffures*, 23). Interference between metaphors of the hunt and those of the theater produces the composite image of a theatrical chase staging itself. An involuntary avowal of rhetoric. But a rhetoric that is unaware of itself is likewise unaware—though not entirely in good faith—of being forgotten to ontological presence: it does not wish to know that its *own particularity* lies in producing trompe l'oeil and make believe.[41] Leiris comes very close to grasping the status of his writing, after having admitted that the confusion is perhaps insurmountable, when he is obliged to note: "when all is said and done, the conventional aim which I assign to myself hardly matters. I always hunt in the present"; and further on: "this tense race which, having become its own object, constitutes . . . this strange series of resonant vibrations whose vague perception fascinates me" (*Biffures*, 23).

The final paragraphs of the second chapter of *Biffures* therefore realize in an exceptionally copious variant, the cliché of rhetorical invention as the hunt in a *place* ("a memory, precisely localized in the past") located in the imaginary time-space of memory. As dissimulation and revelation, memory adorns itself with the classical theatrical metaphor that ultimately yields to a system of mnemonic places and images ("words painted in trompe l'oeil"). This theatrical hunt is in a way a metarhetorical place, the place of rhetorical invention; an individualized and *ad hoc* variant on the ancient cliché—*memory, treasure-house of invention*. Moreover, this transformation of the cliché brings about a peculiar inversion of the ends and means, since the new rhetorical model appears devoid of any persuasive goal. Traditionally it is the *catch*— a well-argued, well-composed and well-adorned discourse—that enables the orator to persuade and to please at one and the same time.[42] On the contrary, Leiris indulges in an intransitive hunt, his only aim being to take a stroll and capture the presence of writing rather than its meaning. Heedless of past experience, or of any persuasive project whatsoever, Leiris realizes that the pleasure of writing, which may yield to disillusionment and to painful consciousness of artifice (*Biffures*, 19), is linked to *local* invention and bound up with a contextual memory. One invents only what has been previously stored, classified, cataloged (in the card-file box). Invention is less a gift of the imagination than a product of labor and art. Leiris's anamnesis, therefore, cannot be a spontaneous remembrance. It is a dialectical operation, during which a text is produced that is also a mimesis of the process of remembering: what we call a "memory," "a souvenir," in the trite and autobiographical sense is only a side-effect and by-product of the dialectical procedure. Anamnesis is a fiction. Neither truthful nor naive it is, seen from the point of view of being and truth, a lie, a stylistic flourish. As a consistent enemy of rhetoric Jean Prévost resisted the perverse pleasure of transposing what Leiris calls "a strange series of resonant vibrations whose vague perception fascinates me" (*Biffures*, 23): the presence of these vibrations commands attention precisely when rhetorical writing takes charge of and betrays the endophasic murmur which is like the shadow, the etymological phantom, and the excess of manifest discourse. Leiris's writing develops as a compromise behavior between the two—the price that invention has always had to pay for access to the *copia*, the fullness of discourse.

This artifice, which the antirhetorical terrorists denounce, can also be called *art* and, more specifically, literature. Even without the knowledge and against the wishes of the self-portraitist art can effect a mediation between the faculties of the subject (who consciously seeks truthfulness, authenticity, remembrance) and the cultural tradition. Rhetorical art *composes* these dispersed agencies, without, however, reducing them to a unity.

By realizing a variant of the rhetorical topos of *invention* by means of the descriptive system of the hunt, Leiris subordinated memory to invention. Anamnesis is nothing more than a textual effect, and the metadiscursive excursus where the cliché of the hunt is deployed therefore functions as the *memory of invention* within the text it produces.

The illusion of presence-in-the-present-of-invention ("for when I hunt I always hunt in the present") becomes problematic in turn, since the metaphor of the hunt points to a series of artificial or artful operations of which this particular chapter of *Biffures* is the result, as are the other parts of the book where Leiris "prospects" a "rather special layer of memories," namely, the dialect of his childhood. The present in question here is not really that of the writing of a paragraph engendered by the topos of the hunt. The entire contextual system, the entire self-portrayal that spans so many years is likewise in that "present." But the hunt and the present belong to the catalogue of the commonplaces: the hunting metaphor therefore mediates between the "present of writing"—a necessary fiction for the self-portrait—and another fictitious present, the one inscribed in all practice of rhetorical invention, a conventional present which the disclosure of the procedures involved imitates: this present is illusory, a conjurer's effect; it masks its fictitious status just when it seems to be disclosing it ingenuously.

The self-portraitist practices the hunt-invention "always in the present," due to an artistic decision indissociable from the self-portrait's topical structure. Autobiography, on the other hand, forming itself along the factual thread of its narrative recounts the contents of meaning: it does not foreground the process of its invention or "remembrance."[43] Of course, in both cases, the desire for presence is thwarted or, at least, is sated only in terms of artistic convention. Thus Leiris expresses his disappointment in contradictory terms: while he knows that he uses rhetoric, he deplores its being

mere rhetoric: "I line up sentences, I accumulate words and figurative language, but what gets caught in each of these snares is always the shadow and not the prey" (*Biffures*, 23). Illusion and its
destruction both have a crucial function in the process of invention. Leiris's fertile error lies in his inability or unwillingness to
recognize that the snares of his writing were themselves the only
possible prey of his rhetorical hunt. Through this Hamletian torment of being or not being, as with "the play within the play" of
Hamlet, Leiris reluctantly reveals his choice in favor of dramatic
staging, eloquent ineffectuality, bullfighting flourishes: the killing
is always deferred *sine die*. The dialectical system of traps and topoi of invention that makes the self-portrait a "writing machine"
also makes the writer a reluctant and contradictory man of letters,
whose ideology remains militantly hostile to the art which he practices. If Leiris's works are a *quest for language*, foregrounding the
passage from the autonomous to the systematic, from the individual to the collective (and vice versa), this other real language must
remain an elusive prey of which Leiris's invention will never deliver more than a shadow.

This enterprise, though doomed to fail, is stubbornly pursued in
all its ambiguity, and, as Lejeune noted in another context, "we
recognize the ambiguous mental gesture which manages to combine decomposition and recomposition within the same act, in
Leiris's attitude towards psychoanalysis and ethnology, and what I
shall call his methodological "subversion" of them. An instability,
a crawling that consists in moving forward clutching every possible
point of support" (*La Pacte autobiographique*, 256). These ambiguities, these "subversions" are inherent in the initial overlooking
of the aporia so lucidly analyzed by Jean Prévost. To exploit an
anthropological *topical system* is incompatible with achieving a
science of man, since any such topics will engender verisimilar or
paradoxical statements, but never will it yield any new empirical
findings. The fact that Leiris's observations (as self-portraitist) converge with the assertions of the speculative "sciences of man" merely
suggests that the latter were produced according to the same
"method," that is, by practicing a kind of rhetorical invention that
does not bother to take any empirical resistance of reality into ac-

count. It is not surprising then that Philippe Lejeune could note in turn a structural "homology" between Leiris's individual concept of the "sacred" and Lacan's notion of the "language" of the "unconscious." They all came out of the same topical matrix.

The self-portrait—that of Leiris singularly—is a personal and self-reflective variant of those rhetorical and speculative "human sciences" for which Bacon and Vico gave us the model. These are "sciences" whose main task is to define and deploy the "ages of man" from an initial hodgepodge (*méli-mélo*) until the exhaustion of an omnivorous dialectical invention. After running up against the falsifications effected by physical anthropology, ethnography, historical linguistics, and so on, the major anthropological speculations have sought refuge (like the theologies they were devised to supplant) in domains closed in principle to any empirical verification, and their critique of empiricism resorts to a sophistry that draws on all the resources of persuasion.

It is entirely possible that, as Lejeune asserts, Leiris intended his self-portrait to mediate between poetry and science (*La Pacte autobiographique*, 261). But the self-portrait is only a meeting place for the general (a topical system) and the particular (self-reflective invention in the first person), a compromise between impersonal (philosophic) discourse and personal discourse (opinion): and as it seeks "truth" through the "probable," self-portrayal gets away from the equivocal noetic status of literature.

By drawing attention to the index cards used by Leiris and to the passage from juxtaposition to combination in the formal evolution of the self-portrait from *Manhood* to *La Règle du jeu*, Lejeune pointed, perhaps unwittingly, to the cumulative and dialectic places of Leirisian invention. Leiris's rhetorical practice becomes quite evident if one examines the transformation of "Le Sacré dans la vie quotidienne" into *Biffures*, a much expanded variant.

This important short text presents, according to Lejeune, "the equivalent of a series of initial index cards" that have been classified but not yet linked together. Lejeune further specifies:

Nevertheless, this classification work resorts to a system that defines by opposition, along a sequence of binary forks which correspond both with an effort to reconstruct a child's mental structures (just as an ethnographer attempts to reconstruct the logic peculiar to the thought system of the group being studied) and with a process that develops the text through continual alternatives, this being a process that will often be used in *La Règle du jeu*. (275)

Whereas one may doubt the soundness of this assimilation to the ethnographer's practice (at best Leiris's method imitates it playfully and poetically), Lejeune's description is nonetheless valid. "Le Sacré dans la vie quotidienne" constitutes a series of *index cards* (or *exempla*) that will be developed in different ways in *La Règle du jeu*: whether by the *glossing* that provides the characteristic *copia* of Leiris's self-portrait, or by corrections, resumptions and recalls, or even by proliferating metadiscourse dealing with the dialectic of invention. But one should also note that, generically, the 1938 text is an *essay* that sets out to answer the question: "What makes up *my* 'sacred?' " The answer to this might be given either according to a hypothetical-deductive and empirical method or rhetorically, as the writer wends his way, according to the Ramist kind of "method" pertinently described by Lejeune, through the topos of the "sacred," a way that implies using procedures of invention and, correlatively, memory procedures. I doubt that the latter method can result in any anthropological advancement even if such reasoning, which Bacon termed *ex analogia hominis*, always bears the stamp of a certain anthropology and of the individual who applies it. In principle, empirical knowledge follows other procedures. "Le Sacré dans la vie quotidienne" is a literary essay based on a rudimentary dialectic. Its invention consists above all in a topical classification of *exempla*, analogous to the one found in Renaissance humanist compilations. The text bears no trace of a rhetorical elaboration that would eventually achieve a "praise of the sacred" or a "vituperation of the profane" or produce a chapter of some hypothetical *New Science*. The binary dialectical method serves to sift through a certain subject matter in order to unravel and deploy it, rather than to use it for some persuasive or demonstrative purpose. The text of *La Règle du jeu* would later be elaborated according to a subtle dialectic, which one might metaphorically call *braiding*: it is an intransitive invention that describes its own procedures, comments on them and describes their idiosyncrasy. An examination of *Biffures* will enable us to understand the evolution of Leiris's invention.

The "Alphabet" chapter of *Biffures* contains a variant of the last paragraph of the preface to the 1939 *Glossaire*, where one could already read:[44]

By dissecting the words we like, without bothering to follow etymology or the accepted meaning, we discover their most hidden virtues and the secret ramifications that spread through language, channeled by associations of sounds, forms, and ideas. Language is then transformed into an oracle, and there we have (however tenuous) a thread to guide us in the Babel of our mind.

The variant found in *Biffures* is inserted within a system of *places* furnished by Genesis, as told to French Catholic children. This results in plainly visible interferences between the code of the reflection on language and the biblical code, whereas such interferences, in the preface to *Glossaire*, only appeared through a toponym trivialized as a catachresis: Babel. Here is the text from *Biffures:*

Once the mighty waters of the deluge are reabsorbed, the mainland reappears and other punishments arise. Ruin of the Tower of Babel, which I imagined similar to the labyrinth represented in one of the boxes of the game of goose [sort of conical tower around which runs a helicoidal ramp]; this is followed by the "confusion of languages," a spiritual muddle [*brouil-lamini*] in which men—playing blind man's bluff in a maze of mumblings, each entangled in the jumble [*capharnaüm*] of his own thoughts—speak but no longer understand one another. (57)[45]

Both the above passages also appear to be variants of a section of *Manhood* entitled "Old Age and Death," where the series of images is a reverse of the one found in *Biffures.* In *Manhood* a sequence of "boxes" analogous to those in the game of goose (it is an early type of cartoon strip, an "image d'Epinal" that emblematizes "the colors of life") furnishes its background to a series of images that represent the ages of man in the form of an allegorical "progress." But the initial box, denoting earliest childhood and corresponding with the *méli-mélo*[46] color, evokes for Leiris a lost paradise, the one whose loss was noted by Genette, together with the attempt to recover it through language:

Finally the only one of the images which I retain as truly charged with meaning is that of the *méli-mélo*, because it expresses marvelously the chaos which is the first stage of life, that irreplaceable stage, when, as in mythical times, all things are still poorly differentiated, when the break between the microcosm and the macrocosm not being entirely consummated, one floats in a kind of fluid universe, as if in the womb of the absolute. (*Manhood*)[47]

Méli-mélo, "muddle" (*brouillamini*): the two sides of the same "heureuse" (fortunate) confusion, one from before the fall (*Felix culpa*, . . . *reuse* fall) the other one from after. Between the two: Babel. The Jumble (capharnaüm) of our thoughts,[48] the Babel of our mind. Labyrinth, language: Ariadne's etymological thread. "Speak but no longer understand one another": each one must orient himself through the muddle, towards the initial hodgepodge. This is what Leiris's self-portrait tries desperately to do. But the harmonious match between the microcosm and the macrocosm, on which are founded Paracelsian magic, the *Hieroglyphic Monad*, and Lully's *Great Art*, has been shattered; men's possibility of understanding one another has vanished and each one is now shut up in his own idiolect. Yet Leiris's self-portrait is spared the curse of Babel as much as possible precisely because it places each *image* peculiar to it, each of its tussles with its own glossary, within the background of a commonplace. The self-portrait results indeed from a *humanistic* or civilized compromise between the most general and the most particular: between the idiosyncratic connotations of *Hodgepodge* (*méli-mélo*) for example, and the commonplace of the "ages of life"; it individualizes such *topoi* as the homology between the microcosm and the macrocosm; or it rewrites the commonplaces of myth and history: the labyrinth and Ariadne's thread to the Tower of Babel, the Bible story, and the history of France, and so forth. And it is this interference between the general and the particular that produces a mimesis of a childhood memory, since, during its process of acculturation and education, childhood is a hodgepodge that blurs the general and the particular. Childhood undertakes a partial, singular, and "subjective" decipherment of the system of cultural places from the point of view of another coherence, an intimate and unconscious coherence that is perhaps provided by one's own familial arrangement.[49]

Leiris's self-portrait is nothing other than the discovery and revelation by one cultivated individual of the degree of acculturation, participation, and *resistance* of his personal microcosm to the virtual macrocosm which anthropologists call a culture. Leiris also

discloses the ambivalent relations connecting his linguistic microcosm to the macrocosm of the French language.[50]

The idea of a microcosm lies at the core of Leiris's understanding
because it mediates between mediation's inner forum and the order
of the world and language; it modelizes the relations of the solitary
writer with his readers through the agency of the French language.
Such is the function of the microcosm in this classic development
of the *desert* cliché:

> Place of conjugation of being and nonbeing—or of fullness and emptiness
> —the desert, at the same time as its bareness deprives me, exalts the feeling
> that I have of my presence and makes me—as at certain times when I write
> —feel alone in the world, nothing (when I face this nothing) seeming to
> exist for me, if it is not in terms of myself, like a dream invented by me,
> affecting only me. In this place of meditation, which is the natural desert,
> just as the desert that still surrounds me sometimes when I sit down to
> write, I do not believe that I am any more detached or any purer than
> when I participate in the habitual tumult, nor do I ruminate with distress
> on the idea that I am separated; but instead I think of myself as having
> really become a *microcosm*, as if the world were reduced to the ideas which
> I manipulate, or to the inert exteriority which I see belonged, in all its mad
> diversity, to me, to a solitary being, with no living intrusion preventing me
> from incorporating it, so that everything would be summarized in me.
> (*Fourbis*, 186)

From the time of his early text on John Dee's *Hieroglyphic Monad*,
entitled "La Monade hiéroglyphique" (1927) Leiris's imagination
was haunted by a wish for a mediation between his microcosm and
the macrocosm, by the desire for an isolation that would be neither
a break nor a separation. This is the dream of every self-portraitist:
it reinscribes culture at the core of solitude; it links up with the
esoteric tradition through which the self-portrayal's monad is rein-
serted within the entire analogical system; and it enables him to
regress towards the Renaissance magic of Paracelsus, Cardano, and
Dee, "those who believed in the possibility of a transcendent science, without the bondage of utilitarian purpose but truly capable
of providing the 'place and formula.' The microcosm of contemplation would then correspond with the macrocosm of an active life."
(*Brisées*, 16)[51]

As a result, Leiris's linguistic paradise is split in two: the childhood paradise—chaos or labyrinth[52]—on the one hand, and, on the

other, the paradise of a certain Renaissance, which is in turn a resurgence of the Hellenistic period where one may fairly see the quintessence of the *Antique*, since Alexandrian culture was already a rerun of Greek antiquity within a hellenized Egypt.[53] Leiris discovered the esoteric counter-Renaissance at the same time as he adhered to surrealism. This Renaissance stands as the reverse side of the modern period, on which every esoteric quest, every hieroglyphic reverie has been inscribed: it sums up the many avatars of "mimologism," analogy, and symbolism.

That is why the latter part of the chapter, which Gérard Genette devoted to Leiris's "Cratylism" may enable us to gather together the preceding remarks, even if his conclusion deals only with one side of the self-portrait. Genette writes:

Convention is by definition contractual and social; the mimetic motivation is "deep," "secret," refuses collective constraint. Ludic in the most aggressive sense, it is capricious and rebellious. Hermogenes is the man of the city, that is, of consensus. His adversary having become a "poet"—but wasn't he one from the beginning? "—sets himself apart, willingly or not (we know that Socrates pushed him a bit), from the city. He turns to exile and shuts himself up in what he decides to be the truth—"his" truth—of language and the world. A stranger henceforth to all ordinary *communication*, he launches on an exploration of his inner universe and lexicon, from which he brings to light strange verbal objects, take them or leave them, bearing his mark, and imposing it without a debate: *Cratylus spits out his style.* (*Mimologiques*, 374)[54]

Spitting out his style, Cratylus exalts, but it is a regressive euphoria: as he indulges in his pleasure, he is turning away from reality. He displaces the compromise. This may well be Leiris's choice in *Glossaire:* my glosses ossuary. But looking over the continuation of his oeuvre, one notes that the self-portraitist's constant dilemma, and the reason for his self-laceration, is the impossibility of being content with the necessary choice between Cratylus and Hermogenes, between the desert and the city, between rhetorical persuasion and being shut up inside his own (for that matter equally rhetorical) truth. Leiris surrounds each of his Cratylian utopias with copious written developments in an exoteric and civil style to which a Hermogenes would have nothing to object.[55]

The linguistic paradise (not the initial one of early childhood, when language is said to be an erotic mode of expression, but the second paradise that comes with youth, when Leiris placed all his trust in the actual efficacy of "poetry") consisted in believing that by exploring his inner lexicon a writer would come upon the hidden truth of the city and the universe, whose locks he learns to spring by manipulating the alphabet.

This is what is suggested by the opening to the "Alphabet" chapter of *Biffures*, where, by pursuing certain ramifications of the clichés accumulated around the notion of a *sign* and combining them with the paramount esoteric commonplace of "the world as a cryptography," Leiris brings about an encounter between the *throw of the dice* and the *alphabet*, which immediately calls to mind Mallarmé's poem, and his projected Book. In short, Leiris's text reactivates those avatars of Cratylism which one calls symbolism and surrealism, the belated variants of Renaissance Cabalism. But Leiris has lost his belief in poetry,[56] so that he finally had to become Hermogenes in order to write *Manhood* and *La Règle du jeu*, and to inscribe his "poetic games" within prosaic commonplaces as his disillusioned metadiscourse warded off the temptation of resuming his initial play with the Cabala, and with "poetry" in the elevated sense that wholehearted Neoplatonists reserve for the products of "frenzy."[57]

Dialectical Topics and Bifurs: Leiris

Philippe Lejeune, summing up the passage from *Fibrilles* (225–57) where Leiris treats of the "art of autobiography," noted that the "autobiographical text is, as Leiris himself admits, an ersatz for poetry . . . and perhaps, at the same time, for dialectics" (*Le Pacte autobiographique*, 293). If one rules out painful connotations, *Ersatz* is indeed the right word: a substitute, an understudy, an artifice, as opposed to generous Nature's gifts.[58] An ersatz for poetry would then be a text invented by (rhetorical) art. Leiris is a rhetorician[59] who consciously, conscientiously implements the resources of invention and style. An artist, in short, but one who is continuously dreaming of the impossible moment when his imitation of inspiration would turn into revelation, as frenzy and thunderbolts ripped open the curtain of discourse. Yet the writer produces, come what may, poetry that is civil, profane, civic, dependant on the commonplaces of the City. Like Rimbaud, Leiris did return a cripple from Abyssinia though without the same "furious eye." Besides, he moderately partakes of political life, so that his self-portrait may be considered a copious, settled, leisurely, and, in the original sense, bourgeois (or civilized) variant of *Une Saison en enfer*. Damnation here becomes the small change of negativity, stylistic flourishes, and scruples, which *Fibrilles* turns into a leit-motif, precisely when the self-portraitist, glancing back towards the opening of *La Règle du jeu*, notes that his undertaking, except insofar as it is difficult, does not differ essentially from that of an orator whose "role is to move, not in order to ignite an innermost fire in others, but in order to lead towards an exalted goal, those whom he will have touched" (267).[60] Having verified that he has readers, that he does "communicate," that his *art* is effective, that he helps "such as are less sure of themselves to know themselves a little better," the self-portraitist is tempted to assume his eloquence seriously, to make it more democratic and thus attain to deliberative oratory: "Having opened my mouth to make myself heard, am I not obligated to substitute some *heureusement* for my overly singular or too abrupt . . . *reusement?*" (226). A peculiar question, unless Leiris is seriously thinking of addressing himself to the masses and of rejecting his mandarin past: in fact, has not *La Règle du jeu*, from its very first words, substituted *heureusement* for . . . *reusement?* The text has consistently pursued the dialectical ramifications of . . . *reusement* (and inventoried the Leirisian idiolect) by means of the collective language to which *heureusement* belongs. While ". . . reusement" pertains to an idiolect, Leiris's philological enquiry is carried out in French. But it is perhaps less difficult than Leiris suggests to cross the distance between idiolect and language. Actually, his microcosm is not at all cut off from the linguistic macrocosm. The fact is that all Frenchmen understand perfectly the adverb *reusement*, for we've all said and still sometimes say "reusement," and we have all misread something like *Moisse* for Moses. There is nothing esoteric about common slips of the tongue, childish solecisms, and malapropisms. As Leiris himself notes, "At least one myth has been forever destroyed: that of the rebellious writer, so marginal that, strictly speaking, no longer is he a writer" (*Fibrilles*, 88). The writer and his most intimate idiom are located in a language, in a culture, even though he may experience this immanence in a spirit of rebellion, in sorrow, or in madness. There is no such thing as a "secret language," and the ersatz for "poetry" is simply called literature.

It remains to be examined whether Leiris's invention resorts to an "ersatz for dialectic." Certainly, if by dialectic one understands Hegelian dialectical reasoning, as Lejeune, a faithful Sartrian, seems to do, or even the Platonic dialectic that enables one—just as frenzy does—to ascend from lower terms to a unitary transcendent term and then return to the lower term so as to invest it with the spirit of the transcendent term. In that case Leiris's dialectic is indeed deficient, a poor imitation that would fool hardly anyone.[61] But if by *dialectic* one understands a method serving to inventory, organize, and retrieve memory contents in order to produce a probable discourse, which for persuasion's sake resorts to the slightly fallacious magic of the enthymeme, clearly then Leiris's method is authentically rhetorical and dialectical in the Aristotelian tradition. It is, after all, the most widespread sort of dialectic used in literary works, in persuasive eloquence, criticism, ideological and political discourse—wherever opinion strives to pass itself off as Truth by yielding to or paradoxically transgressing verisimilitude.

Unlike other dialecticians, Leiris, believing that he implements unprecedented procedures, discloses his maneuvers and describes his strategies, so that some sections of *Biffures* read as if they were a treatise of sorts on rhetorical invention.[62]

Let us examine in this respect the chapter entitled "Tambourtrompette," where Leiris explains what he means by *bifurs* and erasures (*biffures*), distinctions and bifurcations, throughout a *topical* invention whose special function is to engender the text of dialectical metadiscourse. Leiris produces an individual, playful (as should be the case for a "rule of the game") variant of ancient dialectic of which Cicero's *Topics*, for example, offers a rather rudimentary version. The difference between Cicero's *Topics* and Leiris's *bifurs* is homologous to that which separates *heureusement* from *reusement*. In fact, the procedures enumerated by the Roman orator were no more his than was the Latin language itself, and he knew them to be entangled in a vast network of collective signs and norms: a code of laws, kinship structures, and so forth. Dialectic is supported by a cultural agreement upon which rests the acceptability and efficacy of the legal or political discourse. And finally, the dialectic procedures implicitly refer to the entire tradition and practice of rhetoric. This enables Cicero to dispatch very swiftly what seems to pertain to common knowledge.

Leiris's *bifurs*, on the other hand, initially are *facts* of his idiolect, traits of his microcosm, before becoming "switching points, connecting possibilities that are discovered among words and end up as a permanent system of relations" (*Biffures*, 257) or "the slip (no sooner made than crossed out) at the instant when one says to oneself "it's my tongue that got twisted" (257). This outlines a distinction between "things" (or "cumulative places") and dialectical places (or logical operations), the former being in a way raw material (recorded on index cards), and the latter, the manner in which the information is processed. But it is in fact an individual topical system, made up of singularities and opinions as well as an idiosyncratic logic: the passage where dialectic (designated by the *bifur* lexeme) is dealt with in *Biffures* will give a sufficient idea of the kind of invention that produced the text of *La Règle du jeu*.

As *reusement* resulted from an aphaeresis, *bifur* is produced by the apocope of *bifurcation*.[63] This removal of syllables signifies that the lexeme belongs to Leiris's idiolect, and designates it *ipso facto* as a *bifur* in the first sense (a fact recorded on an index card): leaps, faltering or shifts of thought caused by a flaw (256); the apocope or the aphaeresis are the (missing) signifiers for such a flaw.[64] In addition, one must point out that *bifur* is homophonous to *biffure* (crossing out) and that the aphaeresis or apocope results in a way from crossing out of one or more syllables. Moreover, because it jointly belongs to two separate idiolects, that of the railways and Leiris's own, *bifur* also suggests that the Leirisian idiolect is like a network with numerous switching points.

While *biffure* is a good French word, verifiable in dictionaries, the same does not hold true for *bifur*, which can pass on first sight for a slip of the pen and remain without a signified, even for French readers who are not railroad workers. This difference enables Leiris to resort to the first dialectical place described by Cicero, the definition (*Topics*, V, 26 *sq.*): "definitions are made by enumeration [*partitio*] or by analysis [*divisio*]: by enumeration when the thing

[*res*] in question is, so to speak, divided up amongst its parts . . .
Analytic definition includes all the species coming under the genus
which one is defining."[65] Besides, by the end of *Biffures*, a definition of *bifur* by enumeration has already taken place: in fact, this
enumeration makes up the entire text that comes before the manifest attempt to define *bifur*.[66] The difference between a Leirisian
bifur and Leiris's book *Biffures* lies in the fact that the former designates the dialectical mode of production of the latter. As he defines *bifur*, Leiris is also defining *Biffures* and *la Règle du jeu* (the
rules of the game) as a whole. In so doing, he is perhaps defining
as well the self-portrait in general, which appears therefore as the
genus (in the logical sense) or genre, of which *bifur* is a species.
Cicero defines these terms as follows: "A genus is a concept [*notio*]
pertinent to several classes [*differentia*]; the species [*forma, species*]
is a concept whose class characteristic can be referred to as the
head, or, so to speak, the source of the genus" (VII, 31). And, re-
solving curtly Leiris's incurable dilemma, Cicero adds: "Orators and
poets often go so far as to define by comparison, and by using metaphor, with a certain suaveness" (VII, 32). This is in fact how Leiris
proceeds when defining *bifur*. He accumulates metaphors: railway
network, switching point, braids, nodes, curvature, warping. Of
course, Leiris's work makes little of a distinction that Cicero stresses
rather obscurely, between *partitio* (enumeration) and *divisio*
(analysis); but this is a license that rhetorical tradition grants orators and poets, and no one can find fault with Leiris's dialectic,
since he is the best, (as was Montaigne, in his own case), indeed
the only expert of the thing (or *res*, or *quaestio*) in question. This
is why Leiris can pile up metaphors, thus avoiding the realization
that *bifur* is, in fact, the Leirisian idiolect equivalent of rhetorical
invention: he remains a captive of the Romantic ideology according to which *invention* is more or less synonymous with imagination and creation *ex nihilo*. Leiris stubbornly ignores that invention is nothing other than the implementation of dialectical topics;
whence a fertile confusion as to the nature of his own practice.

The bulk of my work, therefore, ends up consisting less in a discovery, an
invention, and an examination of these nodes, then in a meditation that
zigzags along the thread of writing and, "bifur" after "bifur," proceeds
from one theme to another (the latter being arranged, little by little, into

more or less separate bundles, though they are juxtaposed in chapters and linked together to constitute so many successive episodes of a capricious point-to-point race which I would have to run over hedges, streams, ploughed fields and other obstacles on the roughest of terrains). (*Biffures*, 259–60)

The opposition of invention of the nodes (places), examination of the places (dialectical procedure), and *meditation* complicates things unnecessarily; despite Leris's striking historical and structural intuitions, if classical Christian meditation is indeed a transformation of rhetorical memory and invention, by depreciating *meditation* and overestimating *discovery*, Leiris here loses sight of the fact that his "point-to-point" race is for the sake of a virtually endless chase, just as is the case with Montaigne's.[67]

Moreover, his hostility to the dialectical procedures which he cannot do without also causes Leiris to make a curious omission in the metadiscursive passage where he describes his invention in *Biffures*. As Cicero noted after his remarks on *definition*, numerous arguments are drawn from *notatio*, or etymology, a place of which Leiris is well aware since it fills the pages of *Glossaire, j'y serre mes gloses*. But Leiris's etymology is an oracular procedure that would be out of place within the context of prosaic invention, "the toil of setting file cards end to end," which ignites "no poetic fire" (264).[68] Besides, the neological lexeme *bifur* does not seem to lend itself to the Leirisian kind of etymology, while it clearly points to the third place of invention according to Cicero: "The place embraces circumstances which are, one way or another, closely linked to the thing in question." The first subdivision of this topos is that of *conjugation*, which the Greeks called *syzygy*, a procedure close to etymology, which resorts to (preferably "etymological") affinities between words: between *bifurs* and *biffures*, to be sure, but also between *rectilinear* and *curvilinear*, or between *official* and *officious* (258). In these phonetic or other resemblances or differences, a bifurcation is inscribed, and therefore a possibility of launching discourse in a new direction. But these "convergences" and "disjunctures" can also take place in the things themselves (258); this is quite correct provided that by *thing* one means *what is in question* (*res, quaestio*); and by *things* (with an explicit referential twist) one will designate the examples (*exampla*) used in the course of an argument. Those *things* thus come under the place

of *similitude*, which, according to Cicero, enables orators and philosophers "to make mute things speak, to conjure up the dead from
Hades, to narrate impossible events, so as to strengthen an argument or to weaken it . . . and they work many other wonders" (X,
45) This is the context where one might encounter "trumpet-drums"
and the other wonders around which, much later, Leiris would invent a long section of *Frêle bruit* (323–79).[69]

Dialectic Invention and Forgery: Barthes

The dialectical device of conjugation (resemblances between words)
is no doubt one of the topoi best adapted to the production of self-
portraits. Roland Barthes has shrewdly analyzed its use in his own
texts. And yet his antirhetorical bias and the delightful thrill of
appearing old fashioned lured him into believing that "thinking"
preceded his writing ("I produce to reproduce, as though I had
thoughts and represented them with the help of materials and rules"
[*Roland Barthes by Roland Barthes*]). But what Barthes calls his
forgery is nothing other than rhetorical invention translated into
his own idiolect. And the use of syzygy (denotation/connotation:
readable/writable: *écrivant/écrivain*), which contrasts like-sound-
ing terms borrowed more or less scrupulously from "Science," serves
quite simply to say *something*, which is indeed—as Barthes himself acknowledged—the very function of rhetorical invention. The
other "figures of production" (more traditionally, topics or falla-
cies of invention) enumerated by Barthes—"evaluation, nomination, amphibology, etymology, paradox, climax, enumeration,
whirligig"—have no other role, and one could easily show that
these "figures," as he calls them, all have one or several equiva-
lents among the traditional topics of invention. Besides, Barthes
lucidly described the rhetoric of his discourse, whether it aimed at
persuasion or self-portrayal; it is, he writes, "a double discourse
whose mode in a way exceeded its aim: for the truth is not the aim
of its discourse, and this discourse is none the less assertive" (*Roland Barthes by Roland Barthes*). One could hardly characterize
persuasive or sophistic discourse more accurately in its deviation
from the discourses of theology, philosophy, science, and so forth.
Yet, to admit this rhetoricalness would get one caught in the end-

less play of *doxa* and paradox, and it would be confessing to sophistry, an impossible admission in a cultural context where (rebellious or established) verisimilitude tries to pass for truth at all
cost or to deny truth value to any assertion. A striker out of predicates, such as Barthes, is reluctant to have his name on file as a
rhetorician.[70]

Barthes's self-portrayal aims to blur its rhetorical matrix and fi-
nality. Thus: "He remembers more or less the order in which he
wrote the fragments; but where did this order come from? According to what classification, to what sequence? He no longer remembers." . . . *reusement*! Henceforth the system of places being blurred,
it may be deemed fortuitous, and alien to the rhetorical network:
"Alphabetical order blots everything, represses all origin. At certain points perhaps, some fragments seem connected by affinity":
but "seem" only—one should refrain from searching for substance
behind this appearance and from reconstructing its topical system.
Barthes was already warning himself in his "Précis" on "ancient
rhetoric" (1970): "The passion for classification always appears to
be an ill-timed futility to those who do not empathize with it . . .
yet . . . the taxonomic option implies an ideological one: something is always at stake in the place of things: *tell me how you
classify and I'll tell you who you are.*" Consequently, he adopted a
defensive strategy in *Roland Barthes by Roland Barthes:*[71]

the important thing is not to link up these little networks, to avoid their
slipping into a single large network that would be the structure of the book,
its meaning. It is in order to stop, to divert, to divide this descent towards
a destiny of the subject that, at certain moments, the alphabet calls you
into order (that of disorder) and tells you: *Cut! Pick up the story in another
way* (but, likewise, one must sometimes, for the same reason, smash the
alphabet).

Barthes's procedure is therefore the exact reverse of Leiris's: it is
the same one deliberately turned inside out. No sooner "rediscovered," rhetoric has forthwith "fallen into ideology," it has been
surpassed by the advance of "something else." Perhaps, but isn't
Roland Barthes by Roland Barthes a personalized version of the *précis* Barthes so aptly called an "aide-mémoire" on "ancient rhetoric?" Yet it says nothing about artificial memory, nor about the
"properly theatrical" part of rhetoric (*actio*): in short, nothing about

the *hypocritical* parts of rhetoric, those where the self might stage itself framed by a far too revealing set of topics. But we recall that rhetoric has already fallen into "ideology" in the eyes of Montaigne, who decided it had been overtaken by something else, which he called the *essay*. The illusion of surpassing rhetoric opens up the space where all self-portraits are written. The writer knows only too well where the trap lies. Unlike Leiris, who connects his network Barthes scatters his. May Isis not hasten to stick the pieces back together!

The corpus: what a splendid idea! On condition that one is willing to read *body* in *corpus:* either because, in the set of texts set aside for study (those which make up the corpus), one seeks not just the structure but also the figures of enunciation; or because, with this set, one has some love relationship (without which the corpus is but a scientific figment.

In the case of *Roland Barthes by Roland Barthes* the corpus is Roland Barthes's entire previous opus (*hoc est enim . . .*) where the reader is urged to seek, following the author himself, the figures of enunciation; are these figures different, then, from the *figures of production?* They do seem to promote what, on the same page, Barthes calls a *dramatization* (of science) marked by a mode of enunciation that would be neither tight-assed nor "affected," nor "indifferent," that is, a cordial utterance. In short, Barthes favors all rhetoric shared with the theater, and orators with actors: "expressive" gesticulation, voice modulation, the allurements of body and corpus.[72] Between dramatized enunciation and theatrical eroticism (see "Eros et le théâtre," 86), there lies an erotic discourse with which the reader and analyst ought to have a "love relationship."[73] One is immediately reminded of what Plato said about the sophists and the questions Socrates put to Gorgias. But it would be quite a mistake for the *lover* to answer such questions, allowing himself to be led by the nose, since he would risk seeing his art put in the same bag as cooking, fashion, and sophistry.

Such an amalgam is likely to distress anyone who would mistakenly attempt to look at these things from Socrates' supercilious point of view or from that of his innumerable serious disciples: these haughty epigones almost managed to stick the rhetor with a "political superego," to impose upon him a tight-assed reverence for the ontological *doxa* of his intellectual milieu.[74] Of course, it is usually held against the rhetor that he is *nobody*, or, in turn, that he is multiple, elusive, diverse, fluctuating, whereas the philosopher hunkers with his cogito, or his ontology. With Barthes, as with all rhetors, there is only a *text*—which "*figures* the infinity of language: without knowledge, without reason, without intelligence" —and then there are *masks:*

All this must be considered as told by a character—or rather by several characters—in a novel. For the imaginary, fatal matter of the novel and the labyrinth where one who speaks about himself goes astray, the imaginary is taken in charge by several masks (personae) staggered according to the depth of the *stage* (though no one is behind them).

Novel or theater? A *book* in any case, or perhaps a *text*, that is, according to the above definition, a discourse that is opposed to literature as, with Aristotle, rhetoric is contrasted with poetry; an infinite invention and an elocutionary disappearance. There is no one behind them, since each mask is negated in the course of infinite regression to be replaced by the next mask. *Larvatus prodeo.*

As Barthes's discourse always is rhetorical, it is even sometimes tempted to persuade, and it may succeed in doing so. This does not concern us here, no more than it does to know whether or not the Pyrrhonic arguments of *The Apology of Raymond Sebond* are persuasive. For the self-portrait makes no attempt to persuade; it discloses, more or less, the tricks of persuasion; it foregrounds them allegorically. Just like every other self-portrait, *Roland Barthes by Roland Barthes* is a specialized or idiosyncratic rhetorical treatise that reveals—perhaps unwittingly —to what degree the self-portraitist's *idiorhetoric* partakes of general rhetoric: it is an inventory of more or less trumped-up places, the dialectic procedure of a more or less fallacious invention, and ultimately the denial of any topical system. *Roland Barthes by Roland Barthes* is indeed the Book of the Self: "the book of my resistance to my own ideas: it is a recessive book (which goes backwards and also, perhaps, steps back to look)." No matter what these ideas (or places) may be, they necessarily belong to everybody, to a culture at any rate, or to a subculture (call it a counterculture). The entire movement in Barthes's book consists in his self-distancing and in showing how his

difference generates the substance of his text. Barthes has to emphasize this distance, especially regarding rhetoric, for without a
distance, there would be no Self (to be denied), but only an impersonal "writing machine." Barthes's problem, in *Roland Barthes by
Roland Barthes*, is the converse of that tackled by Leiris, for the
latter has stacked everything on self-portrayal, where Barthes (like
Nietzsche or Cardano) leans on his other books, books that do indeed communicate, that are seductive, pleasant or annoying. In
short, his books exist and cause their author to exist. Barthes can
indulge in the luxury of dispersing himself because he fears that
readers will pull him together just a bit too tightly as they analyze
his corpus. Leiris, on the other hand, never seems sufficiently grasped
by the reader, he can never be sure that others fathom his depth,
or gather his *disjointed members*. This is why he must *invent himself* in the course of an immense dialectic, as his *idiorhetoric* mimics the common procedures of classical rhetoric, but sometimes the
most disreputable ones.

For it is possible, after all, that Leiris's topics of invention in the
"trumpet-drum" sections of *Biffures* and everywhere else in *La Règle du jeu* are indeed among those treated in Aristotle's *Rhetoric*,
but they are the fallacious arguments, or *elenchi* against which
Francis Bacon intended to arm the readers of his *Essays*. These are
suspicious but damned useful topics, without which a self-portrait
—among other works—could never be written. An enumeration of
these topics includes:

1. To conclude an argument, as though one had completed one's
   reasoning, without having, in fact, effected this reasoning.
2. To play on words having illogical, fortuitous similarities.
3. To state something about the whole that is true about certain
   parts only, and *vice versa*.
4. To become indignant.
5. To use a single, unrepresentative example.
6. To take the accidental for the essential.
7. To argue from a consequence.
8. To argue *post hoc, propter hoc*.
9. To ignore crucial circumstances.
10. By deceptively confusing the particular and the general, to de-

lude one into believing that the improbable is probable, and vice versa.

11. Etc.

It matters little that the self-portraitist is no more scrupulous in his choice of topics than, say, the theorist of psychanalysis, the political ideologist or literary critic. These topics are efficacious— and fair enough.[75] As for Leiris, he does not try to be convincing, nor even to convince himself of anything but the usefulness or futility of his self-portrayal. By so doing he produces a text, he writes a book that will eventually be judged according to aesthetic criteria. Since the relation to Truth is not up for debate here, let us not confuse genres. But how can one avoid mixing them when one is obsessed by the myth of the *Book?*

CHAPTER 10

The "Book," the Opus, and Their Theater

Leiris and Mallarmé's "Book"

It can be asserted with certainty that *La Règle du jeu*—and indeed, any self-portrait, despite patent individual differences—is a book that seeks to achieve the status of the BOOK, in the exalted sense given to this word in France after Mallarmé.[1]

Leiris, at any rate, ascribed his reading of Mallarmé's "Book" to a crucial locus of *La Règle du jeu*: the reader/writer was in the hospital, gradually coming to after his ultimate gambit, an attempted suicide (*Fibrilles*, 165, 168, 176).[2] The commentary of this reading of the "Book" thus neatly integrated into a "resurrection" narrative. Besides, while Schérer's reconstruction of Mallarmé's "Book" was to Leiris a windfall, it did not drop down at all like an erratic rock, without warning, into the convalescent's bed and book. No one could have been better prepared than Leiris was to come across "Mallarmé's prodigious and preposterous notes on the famous 'Book,' which he had made the very aim of his life, even if he never actually wrote it and seemed to have conceived it as the total work that seems to sum up and justify the universe" (*Fibrilles*, 165). We already know that *la Règle du jeu* is haunted by Mallarmé's "throw of a dice"; long before Schérer's edition, what Leiris knew about Mallarmé's "Book" had metaphorically oriented from a distance all his own labor, at least since *Biffures*. Consequently, Mallarmé's notes gave Leiris a shock of recognition while providing a broader perspective:

Docile to Mallarmé's teachings I shall make the idea of the total book my target and trying with this concatenation of narratives and reflections— already a snake biting its tail, since self-justification is actually what most moves it—to achieve a work that would exist as a closed, complete, and unchallengeable world; such might also be my way of eluding subjectivism, thus soaring above it instead of choosing to crawl out of it from a ground level exit. (*Fibrilles*, 168)[3]

Leiris's reaffirmation of his fidelity to the Mallarméan lesson is not devoid of ambiguity—an ambiguity that concerns precisely the relation between the mythical notion of a Book, as a total, encyclopedic, and self-justifying work, and the subjectivism of Leiris's contents, a "concatenation of narratives and reflections." This has to do, once again, with the way microcosm relates to the macrocosm, and, more generally, the many to the One. Mallarmé sought the One. In Mallarmé's "Book," the subject is supposed to disappear into "elocutionary impersonality," whereas Leiris is just one among many subjects who write, a mere individual. Another capital difference: *La Règle du jeu* is indeed a *book*, a book that bites its own tail, whereas Mallarmé's *magnum opus* exists only as myth, or in the volume put together from scraps by Schérer. In either case, it is merely a "Book," in quotation marks, a virtual object; and its *mana* is that of a specter that is haunting because of its very lack of substance. Chaos, ruin, or dust: this insubstantiality evokes a virtual Hermes Trismegistus, whose powers are proportional to the elusiveness of his secret. Mallarmé's notes conform to a discontinuous and approximate mimesis of cabala, or the "cabalistic." The Mallarméan system's majesty actually rests on a solid cultural cliché, which can also produce the myth of *Superman* as well as Alcibiades' Socrates: according to this cliché, a mean, even a ridiculous appearance can conceal demiurgic powers. It follows from this that the glory of "the Book" is inversely proportional to the futility of Mallarmé's fashion magazines, incidental verse, and even the mediocrity of the notes testifying to the poet's great ambition. Under the appearance of Stéphane, a man of letters living modestly on the Rue de Rome, there hides an impersonal *One* whose

Book was finally to abolish Chance. His secret would necessarily follow him to the grave: "Myself alone, the only one," he writes *in extremis*, in his "Recommendation as Regards My Papers," "might extract from it [his *Nachlass*] what there is" (*Le "Livre" de Mallarmé*, ix). Schérer's commentary forms, in all its purity, the Mallarméan myth of the "Book" that has haunted Leiris as well as so many other modern French writers:

> To be sure, this is in certain respects a subjective, circumstantial, discontinuous work. But its greatness comes from the total Book towards which it is oriented. The summits of the published work bask in a strange light, the invisible source of which is the last and unfinished work. They are lit by a reflection of the absolute. Therefore, what could be called Mallarmé's failure assumes a necessary character. The occultist traditions, whose influence on his thought were so strong, always taught that any fragmentation of totality is betrayal and fall. The truly pure work must always be total, and only the Book into which the world would eventually turn is a true book. The intellectual sun must not become fragmented, but it is by pursuing it that Mallarmé created all he wrote. (*Le "Livre" de Mallarmé*, 142–43)[4]

In a way this myth turns the cabala on its head: the Mallarméan bible is yet to be written, even though it is virtually present already in the manifest work that it orients both as a hidden presence and an unaccomplished *telos*. With this work (*opus absconditum*) and the "sun" that guides it, one may therefore perform all the wishful operations of a neocabala.[5]

What one calls Mallarmé's "Book" is a modern variant ("modern" to the extent that it claims to abrogate previous revelations and also in the sense that it refers to an origin only in order to obliterate it) of the various attempts, made during the Middle Ages and Renaissance, to seize upon a universal key, to resuscitate the *prisca theologia* and to conjure up a manipulatable totality. In short, it endeavors to fashion a "true" simulacrum of the universe, which in turn is supposed to confer absolute power upon the one who operates it.

The most interesting effects of modernism on the Mallarméan "Book" are observable in its dual regressive movement. While the Judeo-Christian theology of the Book implies its reality and totality, the modern Book must remain fragmentary and virtual: not just unfinished (that is, conclusionless, unpolished), but an embryo, faltering, the roughest of all drafts; the scarce notes developed by Mallarmé deal mainly with packaging and distribution, except when they dwell on the dream of an infallible martingale. The "Book" formulated the rules of the game in which, however, no hand is ever played.[6]

To the extent that it remains entirely private and dodges the resistances of collective language and society, Mallarmé's game is an adult mimesis of a children's game, comparable to the one that generated the juvenilia of the Brontë family, but evidently Mallarméan play is not a child's game, it is childishness. In this respect, Mallarmé's project falls short of the text written by Leiris; it lingers over the unsayable reverberations of a childish ". . . reusement." Mallarmé's "Book," as it has reached us, greatly resembles the children's complicated sports forecasts related in La Règle du jeu, which definitely is an "adult" text.[7]

Mallarmé also lingered over an adult fantasy, a writer's dreams of glory, who imagined himself before the public, reckoning the fame and riches that a huge circulation of his "Book" would bring him; all this under the cover of a denial, since he claimed his work would be *impersonal*. Yet Mallarmé's notes remain hyperbolically personal, making sense only to him, the only one. This is a variant of a Romantic theme found several times in Balzac—the "unknown masterpiece," Gambarra's uncommunicable genius, the quest for the absolute—a theme with deep roots in the mythology that nurtures occultism and alchemy. We also recognize in Mallarmé's "Book" an avatar of the dreams and disappointments of Giulio Camillo Delminio, whose Theater of the World was one of the Renaissance's esoteric oddities.[8] Giulio Camillo's failure caused Frances Yates to exclaim: "Poor Camillo! His theatre was never completed; his great work never written!" (The Art of Memory, 132). When asked to explain his work, Camillo would stammer, but he did claim to be in possession of a "solar virtue" that, when it shone on lions, made them as tame as sheep. François I protected Camillo among many other scholars. The "theater," or at least the scale model of a Vitruvian theater he had built, passed for "a work of admirable skill, and anyone admitted to it as a spectator will be capable of discoursing on any subject no less profoundly than Cicero" (132).

According to a witness, this "theater" was a large piece of wooden furniture "marked with many images, and full of little boxes; there are various orders and grades in it. [Camillo] gives a place to each individual figure and ornament, and he showed me such a mass of papers that though I have always heard that Cicero was the fountain of richest eloquence, scarcely would I have thought that one author could contain so much, or so many volumes could be pieced together out of his writings."[9] The differences between Camillo's theater and Mallarmé's "Book" are plain: Camillo's only aim was to produce *copia*, according to the literary values of the period—and he loved ornament. His Ciceronian rhetorical machine was supposed to supply everyone, without effort, the resources of invention that in Cicero were the result of genius and hard work. The actual text—and the infinite virtual text supposedly produced by Camillo's theater—was provided by Cicero or was an extrapolation from the texts of Cicero, the summit of Latin eloquence. The productive machine was also a memory, an encyclopedia of learning, a microcosm, as witnessed by the presence of numerous *images* derived from the visual procedures of rhetorical memory. This attempt to make a great Renaissance dream come true may be considered a variant of Lully's Great Art, now deployed in the three-dimensional space of a "theater:" the ultimate gadget of *Homo Rhetoricus*. Presumably, this "machine" never functioned outside the dreams and sales talk of its inventor.

We know that, from Roman times, the theater either as an edifice or a dramatic performance often served as support for artificial memory: thus the meshing with the polymorphous metaphor of a *theatrum mundi*. We may remember Camillo mainly for his dramatization of literary invention, his theatricalization of rhetoric's power: the Orphic dance of Camillo in front of his sideboard *cum* library foreshadows the dance Mallarmé would in turn dream of performing in his domestic theater, before a filing cabinet of his own invention. A performance during which he would reveal himself as the Operator of the "Book." Schérer imagines the staging as follows:

He operates in a simple setting, such as is feasible in his own apartment. There are chairs for the guests. Perhaps there is a table on which he can place the sheets of paper he does not use. The chief piece of furniture stands

against the wall facing the spectators: a sort of lacquered bookcase . . .
with diagonally slanted compartments . . . This arrangement makes much
clearer the permutations from one compartment to another which the
operator will have to carry out . . . The machine is ready to start. The
operator insisted on its being transparent. (71–72)

This manual paleocomputer could, in principle, produce, if not
an infinite, at least a very abundant text: Schérer, estimating that
the device was capable of 9,864,100 permutations, adds that "The
Book could therefore easily acquire, with a few basic elements, a
huge outer volume" (87). It goes without saying that the machine
could produce all "genres," including the (new) one that consisted
in performing the proliferation of text before a select audience. A
proliferation that would have fed the "sole" and vertiginously polysemous "Book."

With Mallarmé, as with Camillo, the fantasy of an absolute rhetorical machine (whose 'pataphysical and Faustian aspects no longer
escape us since their good-humored adoption by the Parisian work-
shop of Potential Literature)[10] took itself seriously, as though the
proliferation of discourse and a quaint operative arithmology were
finally expected to spring a lock in the Absolute, to keep Time in
check, to control Chance, and unify multiplicity: in short, it would
abolish rhetoric by pushing it beyond hyperbole, or by making it a
tame demiurge of the impersonal One.[11] With the lack of seriousness that characterized him, Jorge Luis Borges satirized this cabalistic dream by "operating" the Library of Babel and the Babylonian
Lottery. But, to be sure, he did not liquidate this dream, for the
One haunts French culture, and what modern writer does not secretly wish to become both the impersonal operator of the "Book"
and a Stéphane (a Fredericus, or a Michel comparable to God), by
manipulating his own lot of file cards, like a divine conjurer? Such
an impersonal operation would nevertheless confer immortality upon
the operator of the machine: *It* works but *I* sign.

Mallarmé's "Book" marks therefore a double regression: towards
the esotericism of the counter-Renaissance, from which Mallarmé
derived a dream of absolute power and of wealth bestowed upon
the Magus; and towards the ever-in-progress-but-never-written text,
the zero degree of writing that never achieves anything beyond an

embryonic magma, potentially containing the All: a child's dream translated into the language of esotericism; as the alchemy of the Word. The evidence of mere lead *proves* the virtuality of gold. Who would *truly* want to complete such a work? What prestige wouldn't a Raymond Roussel, for example, have achieved had he managed to incarnate his *glory* in a "How I shall write (some of) my books," instead of revealing to the world the dubious products of his Great Work? Roussel madly squandered the incomparable benefit of the doubt.

By his double regression, Mallarmé inaugurated a tradition of modernity: he is the first "conceptual" artist and, as such, Marcel Duchamp's predecessor. His machine remained at the stage of fantasized sketch, existing only by virtue of its nonrealization. With less ambition and fewer inhibitions, he would only have been a René Ghil, at best a second Marsilio Ficino sporting a Lavallière and addressing Orphic hymns to the chandelier in his living room.[12]

Yet one should seriously examine the paradoxical impersonality claimed by the "Book," when the author in the trite sense of the word, contemplates putting himself on stage. On cannot settle for the hypothesis of a naive contradiction, or that of a ploy by the artist merely seeking publicity. Mallarmé's thinking here proves to be very coherent indeed. In fact, the whole set of notes on the "Book" is overdetermined by an anti-Romantic decision (Romantically signified by the crisis of 1862),[13] an antisubjective but Hegelian choice, a turning point that, through Stéphane's negation, marks a return of rhetoric. Phillippe Sollers's analysis of Mallarmé's choice starts out well:

This remark is attributed to him: "I believe the world will be saved by a better literature." If the remark is authentic, it is not, in his mouth, a witty outburst. He had given up suicide ("Having fled from suicide victoriously . . .") precisely because of the deception it harbors: true suicide could only be literature. It implies the *sacrifice* of him who writes, a sacrifice "with regard to personality," which is unique of its kind. There is in fact no subject per se (so that one cannot suppress it by killing oneself), since the subject is the *consequence* of his language. Therefore, this language must be pushed to its very limits in order to find out what it is about and *what* is in question in us. A most difficult undertaking, considering that one immediately discovers the extent of unconsciousness which is one's very ground. *(Litterature et totalité,* 72)

This analysis is debatable in that Sollers postulates a *uniqueness* for Mallarmé's "sacrifice," a sacrifice heralding the world's "salvation" through literature. This is a crucial point, since Sollers, in his indisputable fidelity to Mallarmé, shows his reluctance to give up a conception of history, language, literature, and "the subject," which one must term theological and even monotheistic, or at any rate Hegelianly philosophical. By stressing the uniqueness of the Mallarméan sacrifice and "salvation" through literature, Sollers seeks to settle the (unique) history of writing and the subject about one given point in time and space, meant to replace Bethlehem, Jerusalem, and so on.

Homo Rhetoricus

But if we reread Sollers's text in a perspective less clouded by messianism and a transcendental conception of history, we soon perceive that it contains an adequate description of the consequences of Mallarmé's unreserved choice of the rhetorical attitude, that is, of impersonality. As Richard A. Lanham notes in his study of the "rhetorical ideal":

The rhetorical stylist has no central self to be true to. In the Arnoldian, highly serious sense of self, he boasts no self at all. At his center lurks a truly Ciceronian vacuity. He feels at home in his roles and to live must play them. When he poses . . . rhetorical man is an actor and insincerity is the actor's mode of being. (*The Motives of Eloquence*, 27)

Therefore all modes and genres are potentially available to this rhetorical man, who may indeed choose not to adopt any of them. For him, conventions—for example, the opposition between verse and prose—are only the means to attract different types of attention. All is verse, nothing is verse. No style is too decadent, excessive, or obscure. It would strike him as naive to try and push "language to its limits" in order to know *what* it is about and *who* is in question in his discourse, for the sole purpose of going to the limit would be to fill a rhetorical void and displace philosophy's anxious questions onto what Sollers calls the very ground of the subject. Insofar as it surrenders to language and rhetorical invention, the "elocutionary disappearance of the poet who yields his

initiative to words" cannot gain him a foothold either beyond or
on this side of language. Rhetorical man does not appear as a subject—or rather, he disappears in the elocutionary act: in the case
of writing a generic and stylistic gesticulation foreign to any hierarchy; and in that of speaking, a declamatory elocution, a his-
trionic performance of the (masked or unmasked) body, a mimicry,
dance, chant, or conjuring, with which the orator abolishes himself (his self) in his discourse and gesture—a *charlatan* (in the
Spanish sense, among others) illuminated by the living-room chandelier or by the sun itself. He does not, as a god or a father, *create*;
he *invents*, like a polymorphous demiurge. He could not care less
about Truth, about his Truth, all that matters is knowing that all
is here in appearances, always already and forever belonging *elsewhere*.

This is made evident in (at least most of it) an "unclassifiable"
book such as *Foi de fol: Récit drôlatique enchevétré de plagiats et
d'exemples* by Bernard Teyssèdre, where the narrator assumes the
personae of a Sophist (Gorgias) and of Erasmian Folly, as the very
ground of the self is removed from under what might at first pass
for a book of the Self or a self-portrait. This unlimited proliferation
of rhetorical gesticulation pulls the self-portrait out of its orbit and
breaks up the Book by subjecting it to the generic and modal at-
traction of the Menippean satire, or of the anatomy.[14]

The Self-Portrait, Menippean Satire, Anatomy:
Bernard Teyssèdre's Foi de fol

Like Robert Burton's *Anatomy of Melancholy*, Teyssèdre's book reveals that there is no hard and fast distinction between an anatomy and a "self-portrait." The difference lies in the choice of a
certain unreserved rhetorical attitude that is sustained throughout
the book and confers a kind of modal coherence upon its farrago of
plagiarisms, pastiches, and collages that comically sum up the humanist tradition in accordance with the three fictional durations
specific to self-portrayal: the time of a culture, the time of a life,
the time of an invention.[15] *Foi de fol* displays its own generic and
modal hesitations—and its own fears of confusing the reader too

radically—in an interpolated chapter (the "analyst's letter to the editor") where another persona (another aspect of Folly, dubbed the *analyst*) presents a serious, philosophical, and antirhetorical critique of the book and of the inventor's personae. It is no accident that this same section very lucidly and exhaustively discloses the author's thwarted desire to write a self-portrait. An allusion to Michel Leiris (via a quotation from Jacques Lacan) underscores the theoretical resemblance between the aims of *Foi de fol* and those of *La Règle du jeu*. But since the place has already been occupied, these aims will have to be achieved in a different way, though not without a preliminary meditation upon the ontological status of the word:[16]

Thus *I* am the word. But what am I "in person" but a horizon opened by the life that was mine onto a culture that goes well beyond me . . . The word is the man in me to whom I speak; and yet I myself, I am not the Man . . . If the part that belongs to the novel, that is anecdote, fades out, then what remains is the *word itself, as the order of words in time* . . . Therefore, the inference should be avoided that the word would be in one person alone because the word would have spoken in person according to a disquieting assertion of the Word in the Bible, "I am the one who is." (24–25)

There follow remarks on the temporal division of speech events and the distinction between three elements of enunciation: addresser, addressee, allocution. This metadiscursive excursus along with its accompanying bibliographic references, reflects the current cultural *doxa*; it would lead the reader to expect a serious, orthodox, if somewhat breezy, theoretical text, in the manner of the French 1960s.

But the bibliography also contains reference to Christophe's classic comic strip, *L'Idée fixe du Savant Cosinus*, inserted between a work by Heidegger and the *Discourse on Method*; this incongruity suggests a very different—playful, if not satiric—relation to culture, which is confirmed by a musical metaphor: "Fool's Faith [*Foi de fol*], a polyphony for mixed chorus, with the instrumental accompaniment of plagiarisms and collages, against a backdrop of idiocy" (27). After this, one can no longer read as a ritualistic *captatio benevolentiae* the repeated assertion in the text that this book is a failure; it testifies to an ultimate discord between the seriousness of self-portrayal and comical Menippean form, between the philosopher and the Sophist, between the linguist and the 'pata-physician, between idiocy in the etymological sense and folly in the ordinary one.

One may read the commentary in the "analyst's letter" as a re-fusal to give in to idiocy, a hesitation about being considered a nutcase (or instead of, picturesquely, for a "fol" in a *sotie*) and as an attempt to narrow the gap between an Anatomy and the kind of discourse suitable to a Parisian intellectual in 1968. One may also read this "letter" as another *mask* of Folly, that of psychoan-alytic and linguistic madness. This metadiscourse, which is stuck on and localized at the threshold of the *anatomy*, is heterogeneous to the duration of the book, because of a generic or rhetorical in-compatibility that blocks the speaking subject's ability to plunge into the carnival, to be dissolved in it, so long as the very serious, very antirhetorical will to grasp "who I am" subsists. In *Foi de fol*, Teyssèdre is unable to let go entirely, to efface the speaker, to erase the reference to a truth of the masks, to dissolve a persona into Menippean anonymity. Therefore, this book also attempts to put the subject together again through an initiatory journey.

Teyssèdre's superb failure results from an incompatibility sym-metrical to the one that in a sense empties Book X of Saint Augus-tine's *Confessions*. Augustine's progress and initiatory path diverge from those narrated in the *Satyricon* or Apuleus's *Metamorphosis* because he is addressing God, not because of the intrinsic narrative events. Allocution to the Word results in the strange evasions of Book X and in the "elocutionary disappearance" of Augustine, which occurs just when he is about to tell "who he is." Saying "who I am" would be part of the folly of the world, which stands con-demned in the knowledge of God. Augustine the rhetorician must overcome rhetoric; he must reject its emptiness and its masks so that he may be filled by the Word whom he is addressing. The end of the *Confessions*, therefore, turns to a commentary on God's rev-elation in Genesis. If God dwells in the depths of my memory, rhet-oric is abolished; and the self-portrait of Augustine, of the sinner, in order to avoid a relapse into rhetoric, must be transformed into a meditation and a prayer that sanctify rhetoric. For self-portrayal to sustain its rhetorical soliloquy, it must steer a cautious course between the comical uncenteredness of the Menippean mode, and the God-centered vacuity of Christian meditation.

Hamlet's Soliloquy

Elocutionary disappearance: provided the divine word has withdrawn into silence, then disappearance of the speaking subject must be accomplished through the exhaustion of rhetoric. This is what Mallarmé seemed to suggest as he imagined himself gesticulating before the book-producing machine, operating its drawers, its slips of paper, and its arithmology in a seriously idiotic performance of infinite "intertextuality." This withdrawal of the center, this refusal of a norm and a zero degree, dramatizes voice and style with an eccentric show that undermines everything that philosophers and "deconstructionists" glumly ruminate about: presence, signs, and the logos's ontological privilege. Rhetorical man, on the other hand, shuffles his conceptual cards and performs a number, one little act among the many possible ones: that which Mallarmé called, perhaps ironically, a *better literature.* Mallarmé, the discrete poet, dreamed of being at once everyone and noone, a mere *it* that discourses, plays, mimics, makes an encyclopedia, and is screwed in the end by an encyclopedia. But *it* is not a representation. On the contrary, *it* is the universe finalized as a "Book," and everything that exists imitates *it* imperfectly, just as the cabalist's world does the Torah.

To be sure, Mallarmé only dreamed this culmination, this cosmic disappearance of the speaker. Sometimes, on the contrary, his rhetorical show shrinks down to mere soliloquizing, actually nothing more than one of those vaudeville acts which "café-concert" audiences used to love: comedians decked out as soldiers or fauns would recite monologues filled with salacious fantasies involving nannies and buxom nymphs in flesh colored tights. Or else Mallarmé turns to Hamlet, about whom he writes: "The play, a culminating point of drama is, in Shakespeare's works, a transition between the previous multiple plot and the future monologue or drama with one's Self. The hero—everyone else an emptiness, he strolls, that's all, reading in the book of himself, a high and living sign—denies others by his glance" (*Oeuvres*, 1564).[17] Evidently the rhetorical idea does not necessarily lead to the subject's "elocutionary disappearance"; on the contrary, it can turn the speaker into a *Sign* with a capital *S*, whose haughty self-sufficiency makes others into silent satellites. Let us pause for an instant over Mallarmé's admirably equivocal text and the veiled re-cognition that comes about at this point: the subject is a theater; he (the Self) *is*—and is not—what is in question; the hero becomes the theater-book that he is, where he is. He transcends the many as he achieves the status of the One in soliloquy, meditation, self-dramatization, self-persuasion. The Hamletian hero brings about the subjectivization of rhetoric, which leads, at first, to the denial of other people. Our hero is alone at last. But his solitude is a dramatic fiction, which exists only for the spectators contemplating it in the darkness. A soliloquy, after all, is spoken to be overheard by others, or by God. Having become the Sign, our hero needs to be recognized as such. Between a Hamletian hero and an orator there is but one difference: the former does not have to address himself directly to the public. The soliloquist moves the audience by *moving himself*.

"He strolls, that's all," like Montaigne pacing in his tower, like Rousseau wandering, like all self-portraitists who slowly explore their memory places. Yes, strolling is an essential attribute of the soliloquizing hero: it is the master metaphor for rambling invention, of which Hamlet gives some celebrated examples in his monologues while reading, as Mallarmé put it, in the book of himself.[18] A written or unwritten book, whose writing is a stroll, reading it aloud is Drama: Mallarmé managed to preserve its virtuality, along with that of the theater. He finally chose not to choose between the *elocutionary affirmation* inherent in rhetoric (which, however, produces an empty subject unable to resolve by himself the question of whether to be or not to be, since he exists only in so far as he poses the question in every tone and at every opportunity) and the *elocutionary disappearance*, which is in turn inherent in the rhetorical choice, since the latter implies that the subject (who asks himself if he is or not) is not a "whole subject," a Sign *for Himself*, especially when he creates an illusion for the spectators whom he invites to watch him walking on the stage, shuffling his papers, lining up his file cards, inventing his text, reading in the book of himself. And yet, from another point of view, that of philosophy or theology, it is still possible to discourse on the transcendence of this subject, or on the very ground of the Self; at this point there arises again a need of the Other; God, other people, the unconscious, language, that which the subject is not, but without which he is not. The Sign of which Mallarmé speaks, if it is neither a result of theatricalization nor a mere simple dramatic motif, must be integrated forthwith into the infinite chain of signs, and only a theology would confer upon it the singularity, the supplement of being that are implied by a capital letter. If he is not Himself God or a sacramental presence, the host in a monstrance, then he can only be a sign among signs, existing only as a play of difference and resemblance. He can be situated anywhere in the Book, but the Book that contains him (and that he potentially contains) is in turn but one book among other books. There is no *Book*. The encyclopedia is a mirage, for the circle cannot be closed, the library grows and effaces itself continuously. Only a work of art such as a book can be declared—if somewhat arbitrarily—finished. Life and death are contingent, without an overture—in the musical sense— or final curtain. The book, the theater, the self-portrait are not metaphors of the self and life, but illusory compensations for their contingency. Hamlet is, if you will, a *Sign*; but for William Shakespeare, Stéphane Mallarmé, or Friedrich Nietzsche, despite the latter's *Zarathustra* and his self-divinization, it is another matter entirely.

Thanks to Schérer, we know that Mallarmé's "Book" was supposed to create "modern myths" and that its principal "theme" is that of a summons: "what happens when a personage hears his name called?," when his name is "uttered?" (131). The following answer, different from that proposed by Schérer, is imperative: when someone hears his name called out of nowhere, he is transported into the Bible (or into hagiography), he becomes a peer to Abram-Abraham and to Lot, and the event takes place in a version of Genesis 11, shortly after Babel and the dispersion. By analogy, Mallarmé's "Book" presents itself as a Bible still to be written, a reverse Torah, the one that was dispersed after Babel. This conclusion is, in a way, as trite as it is inevitable: a commonplace. Mallarmé's project has already been masked in a book that consumes many other books in the fire of rhetoric: Rabelais' *Panta-gruel*.

Mallarmé's Lesson

One can now ask what subsists of "Mallarmé's lesson" in *La Règle du jeu*. Of course, Leiris wants his book to break out of subjectivism, and it is the book's closing upon itself ("the snake already biting its tail") that must objectify it: thus, the book would become "a closed, complete, unchallengeable world"[19] wherein the alchemical emblem is easily spotted. One hesitates to take too seriously this conception of *La Règle du jeu*, though Leiris's work refers frequently, as does Mallarmé's, to the occult and to alchemy. And yet, the emblem of the ouroboros is placed in a context where the hero has just evoked his own descent into hell and his own resurrection, thus inevitably recalling the alchemical analogy between Christ and the philosopher's stone and, even more so, between the stone and the rock of the sepulcher: dare we borrow from Jung his analysis of this alchemical and theological nexus?

Without knowing it, the alchemist carries the idea of the *imitatio Christi*, a stage further and reaches the conclusion . . . that complete assimilation to the Redeemer would enable him, the assimilated, to continue the work of redemption in the depths of his own psyche. This conclusion is unconscious and consequently the alchemist never feels impelled to assume that Christ is doing the work in him. It is by virtue of the wisdom and art which he himself has acquired, or which God has bestowed upon him, that he can liberate the world-creating Nous or Logos, lost in the world's materiality, for the benefit of mankind.[20] (*Memories, Dreams, Reflections*, 355)

To be sure, Leiris no longer "believes" in alchemy, nor even in the alchemy of the Word. He does not, in any straightforward sense, practice the *imitatio Christi*. But, in an interview of 1966, he revealed his interest in Loyola's *Exercises*,[21] which he placed in the context of anamnesis. *La Règle du jeu* is, in a way, a protracted denial, during which alchemy, meditation, esotericism, and *imitatio* are handed over to rhetorical invention and *copia*. As *bifurs*, they are inscribed and effaced in the same movement, *manifestly* relegated to the role of a picturesque stimulus, as becomes evident in the examples of the "marvelous" discussed at length in *Frêle bruit.* Nevertheless, invention and even the *bifurs* become exhausted:

With such additions, what would I do but dilute the sauce like a trickster chef? For I would either be talking about things that have dazzled me, but to which I attach no meaning that might enable them to play anything but a decorative role here, or—regarding certain things—I would simply repeat what I've already said, all that I can say about them during this kind of long march that long ago stopped claiming to be a quest for the Grail. (355)[22]

A long march or a snake biting its tail? The enumeration of *places* of the marvelous in *Frêle bruit* and the setting up of the mnemonic images (for example, the knights of the round table, and, among them Lancelot who, like the biblical Judith is a court figure in French decks of cards) extend and close the series of places and images first used in *Manhood*. After emphasizing the role played by emptiness, absence and lack in most of "these examples" (347), Leiris discusses theatricality at length, with special reference to Wagner and the esoteric Mozart of *The Magic Flute:* such theatricality is all the "poetic truth" of which *La Règle du jeu* is capable. Its inventory, its deck of file and playing cards never manages to detach itself from "subjectivity," to encompass the macrocosm, even though Leiris's method presents and visits, exploits and glosses all the places where certain "magi" claim to have found their springboard for a leap into the absolute.

But theatricality, for the common herd as well as for an entire philosophical tradition, implies emptiness, absence, a lack —that is, unreality, insincerity, "rhetoric." Yet Leiris himself is reluctant to retain only the pejorative connotations of theatricality.[23]

Opus, Theater, Opera

References to the theater, and especially to the opera, are so numerous in the works of Leiris that one need not dwell on them. These references, with their repetitions and leitmotifs, constitute one of the main patterns of Leiris's self-portrait. But isn't the opera (analyzed by Leiris in "L'Opéra" ["Opera, Music in Action"][24] an essay that might well be an "out-take" from *La Règle du jeu*), a metaphor for an ideal self-portrait? For what strikes Leiris most in

the lyric spectacle is a lack of centrality, as well as spatial dispersion:

One sees the music caught in the net of a space affirmed each time in a new
way by the operation of a scenic mechanism, and at the same time one
feels that it eludes this network and, by thus setting the vibratory space in
which one is immersed, constitutes the miracle of the opera. (284)

And further on:

This stretching out of the normal scenic framework, these manifest intru-
sions of the drama in the orchestra, or the doubling of the latter to create
another level of sound, and institute a "music within the music," just as
there exists a "play within the play." (285)

Opera, then, is comparable to a baroque edifice as the latter is
to *La Règle du jeu*, particularly since *Hamlet* (which, together with
L'Illusion comique, Leiris considers to be a privileged example of a
play within the play), already mentioned in *Fourbis* (29) to evoke
the "wings" of certain memories, especially those "of a slightly
theatrical character" (20), which Leiris is known to prefer—*Hamlet*, then, with its unresolved double plots and illusions, can pass
for the very sign of baroque theatricality. Add to this the fact that
Fourbis underscores the theatricality of memory, precisely at the
point where Leiris evokes active backstage forces that strive to
transform the places covered in *La Règle du jeu* into "the stations
of a kind of initiatory journey."[25] *The Magic Flute* repeatedly serves
as a metaphor enabling Leiris to group together all these elements,
as does Wagner's *Parsifal* and its quest for the Grail.[26]

One should of course add that *opera* is the plural form of *opus*:
a theatrical, public, and eloquent version of the chamber alchemy
passionately practiced by Leiris, although he does not believe in its
outcome. The most significant aspect of this global metaphor resides in its embodiment of Leiris's attempts to turn duration into
space, and, more precisely, of his wish to reduce the multiple plots
and thematic repetitions of opera to a set of spatial constructs, grids,
or networks. For Leiris the "miracle of opera" consists precisely in
its ability to capture the duration of music in the nets of a system
of devices, which, however, music transcends to convert them from
"vibratory space" structured by couplings. Music "hollows out and
sculpts theatrical space in the same way as the disposition of a

baroque edifice enlivens its geometry and opens up perspectives"
("L'Opéra," 284); in short, operatic music works in the same way
as do the *bifurs*, which hollow out and enliven the textual space
of *La Règle du jeu* to create the fiction of an unfixed simultaneity,
of a circumscribed animation: in the same fashion, we speak metaphorically of the "movement" of a building. The contradiction
between immobility and motion is resolved when we realize that
the semblance of movement is created when the stroller moves about,
or at least when the visitor's glance roves over the edifice. When
we reflect on the paradox of a theater serving as a mnemonic system, although the encyclopedia of places is presented all at once,
it must nevertheless be deciphered in a sequence that produces a
hidden hieroglyph along the "stations of a kind of initiatory voyage," perhaps along the Stations of the Cross: such would be the
case in a baroque edifice built according to the principles derived
from Loyola's *Exercises*.

Leiris's theater, unlike Mallarmé's, is not wholly imaginary. It
is a theater dispersed and distributed throughout the text for which
it may, furthermore, serve as a global metaphor. *La Règle du jeu*
measures its successes by its own theatricality. But does Leiris put
himself on stage in the guise of Hamlet reading in the book of himself? He does often invite us to visit backstage, to watch the promp-
ter's box and to observe him manipulating the *file cards*, which are
like his orchestral score. But the scene lacks theatrical magic, and
the hero fails to become a Sign. Rather than writing itself, the Book
is being written, and the monumental edifice crushes the drama.
We know that, for Leiris, returning to writing after an interruption
is like awakening, going through a "curtain of clouds," a painful
raising of the curtain (*Fourbis*, 7–8). The stage lies on the other
side. *La Règle du jeu* is *not* opera. It is in turn the negative and the
parody of an opera: an alchemical theater that transmutes neither
the base matter nor the operator himself; it is mnemonic theater
unable to produce either a "universal key" or an efficient magic; it
is a lyrical drama devoid of miracles, since whenever the marvelous shows up, it is anatomized—for self-portrayal lacks the poem's
immediate and living intensity. *La Règle du jeu* imitates a baroque
theatrum mundi, on the stage of which a comic illusion fails to
take hold.

The disenchantment of Leiris's theater can be easily explained: by shaping a series of rhetorical places into a serious soliloquy, Leiris deprived his text of the euphoric vacuity of rhetorical play. He also eschewed the satisfactions offered by tragic seriousness, neurosis, and even psychosis, which, in a sense, testify to the sufferer's transcendence. Leiris's anguish, constantly dispersed in rhetorical places, always seeks a recentering in a sincere, scrupulous, and sadly antirhetorical enunciation. A grand opera's potentialities yield a Hamletian soliloquy, more closely related to Laforgue's wan irony than to Shakespeare's robust ambiguities. Alone as he conjures up and negates imaginary attendants, Leiris delivers his "To be or not to be" in such a paradoxical fashion that, far from achieving "a marriage of contraries" that would come about with completion of the alchemical *opus*, he keeps finding himself. Such dilemmas produced by a lame examination of contraries, are never solved though they produce an abundant text which in itself is resolution enough in the uncomfortable predicament of Buridan's ass: yes *and* no. Ethnology or self-portrayal?[27] Suicide or nonsuicide? Renounce *La Règle du jeu* or continue it? Such an issue never resolves itself either in Pyrrhonism or certainty:

In my quest for some token of agreement, I have nothing to gain by discarding my pen if the passage from garrulous to taciturn behavior means only that I have substituted, for a certain verbose manner of churning oneself, another equally indulgent and more confined manner, without even the appearance of an issue that the soliloquy represents. But, being as far removed from the hermetically stitched mouth (a standoffish queen) as from the mouth that babbles its inexhaustible monologue, what mountains must be moved to succeed in formulating a song that would work its way outside me and resemble those airs that have accompanied certain minutes of my life that I consider crucial! (*Biffures*, 268–69)

The failure of this operatic dream is inherent in the actual realization of the "Book." Conversely, Mallarmé, who merely dreamed of being the *operator*, never risked stepping on stage or writing the Book. Whence his absolute success—for believers at least—but his was, in the proper sense, a *utopian* prowess: Mallarmé who avoided getting caught in rhetorical places, on the stage or in the space of the "Book," was a Magus on the installment plan.

Leiris's achievement is of another order. If he did not produce what Rimbaud called a *fabulous opera* with *La Règle du jeu*, if he did not manage to hypostatize himself on a magical stage, he did succeed in *disposing* commonplaces into a model of his—and our own—inadequacy with regard to those places. He lets the willing reader cross the footlights and go backstage, to square himself in his own culture's imaginary theater, or rather, to realize how out of place, how ill at ease, he is on the stage. For the theater metaphor impersonalizes. It is one of the devices, in *La Règle du jeu* as elsewhere, that initiates communication with the reader, forcing him to become in turn the spectator, the actor, and the text. It also is one of the metaphors the self-portraitist uses to designate or discover his own intentions, so that the stage on which he fancies himself alone is in fact crowded with fellow self-portraitists; his soliloquy merges with a kind of chorus. Thus Barthes: "The vital effort of this book [*Roland Barthes by Roland Barthes*] is to stage an image-system. 'To stage' means: to arrange the flats one in front of the other, to distribute the roles, to establish levels, and, at the limit: to make the footlights a kind of uncertain barrier" (105). And while Jules Vuillemin, in *Le Miroir de Venise*, seeking to dismiss theatricality along with eloquence as he grapples with rhetoric in a theatrical Venice, comes to accept eloquence, so long as it acknowledges that it is but a play.[28]

On the whole, the theater metaphor (because its descriptive system includes the personae, the mask, scenery, the stage, footlights, the wings) is a double of the metaphor of the Book: *theatrum mundi = liber mundi*.[29] But one face of this Janus is turned towards the private and autonomous (the book of oneself) while the other designates the public and the collective. The one can be content with remaining an idiolect while the other mediates a passage towards the language of culture. *Moi-sse* indisputably belongs to Leiris's own *Book*, but Moses is, *inter alia*, the title of an opera by Rossini.

Invention as Antimemory

André Malraux's Miroir des limbes

1. THE ANTI-MEMOIRS. At the start of his *Anti-Memoirs* Malraux
declares:

Almost all the writers I know love their childhood; I hate mine. I have
never really learned to re-create myself, if to do so is to come to terms with
that lonely halfway house which we call life. I have sometimes managed
to act, but the interest of action, except when it rises to the level of history,
lies in what we do and not in what we say. I do not find myself interesting.
(2)

It would, therefore, seem idle to seek a self-portrait in the *Anti-
Memoirs*. Yet the self-portrait is defined neither by complacency
nor by confession. Self-portrayal resorts to rhetorical *inventio*, to
the artifices of memory, and to a metadiscourse whereby the text
questions its own generation. So visible are these characteristics in
the *Anti-Memoirs* that one is tempted to see in them only mechanical transitions between the narrative episodes that give the *Anti-
Memoirs* their anthropological character. But these two aspects are
inseparable in the self-portrait, for the topical structure of a *return*
(not necessarily a return to the paternal or maternal house, barely
evoked here by a writer born of his own action and books) appears
here under the guise of a journey back to the *places* where the

images and meditations from previous books are inscribed. This journey serves as a fictional device whose zero degree might feature the writer in his study, leafing through his own books. Such a procedure would, however, sacrifice another characteristic of "Malraux," as he appears through his books: the writer as a man-of-action. Malraux has reduced to one of its terms the dichotomy formulated by Nietzsche in *Ecce Homo*, at the beginning of the sections entitled "Why I Write Such Good Books," which indeed seems to have provided a model for the *Anti-Memoirs*. In that passage Nietzsche declared: "I am one thing, my works are something else." The very form of the *Anti-Memoirs* asserts that "Malraux" does not want to be anything other than his works. Perhaps this choice was revealed most clearly in an anecdote that portrays Nietzsche himself: in *The Walnut Trees of Altenburg*, the fictional Walter Berger, who is accompanying the mad Nietzsche on a train traveling through the darkness of the Saint Gothard Tunnel, suddenly hears him chanting *Venice*, his last poem, in a voice momentarily freed from insanity. Walter's commentary sums up Malraux's oeuvre: "In the prison of which Pascal speaks, men succeed in drawing from themselves a response, which, so to speak, imbues those who are worthy of it with immortality. And in that carriage . . . the infinitudes of the starry sky have seemed to me to be as far outshone by man as our own petty destinies are outshone by the stars" (28). But the man who eclipsed the star-clustered sky, the poet of *Venice* and *Zarathustra*, is also that pitiful, insane, paltry man who, in *Ecce Homo*, so indelicately described for us his psychosomatic symptoms and his diet, thus disclosing what separates a sententious invalid from the sovereign Zarathustra. Nevertheless, the question of the relation between the man and his works is insistently raised in the *Anti-Memoirs*, even if only in respect to those superimposed pathological liars Clappique, Mayrena, and Malraux himself, who was certainly not unaware of the doubts expressed by commentators as to the authenticity of the adventures elevated to the epic plane in some of his novels. The *Anti-Memoirs* clarify none of this. On the contrary.

This book is therefore the self-portrait of a fictional personage, of a persona engendered by its fictions, whether they be novels or conversations with famous people that unfold like dialogues of the dead.

On the semantic plane the self-portrait is defined by what turns out to be the mainspring of the *Anti-Memoirs:* the subject's double confrontation with his own death and with Man in general. The *Anti-Memoirs* consequently foreground some characteristics that remain more muted in other self-portraits, where they conform to the structural invariant already revealed by our analysis of the other texts.

Malraux's "I do not find myself very interesting" does not mean that the self (a cluster of private properties or predicates revealed to the Subject through introspection) does not exist for him, nor that he finds it unknowable or hateful. Malraux is not torn by the paradox of Vuillemin, for whom one can detach oneself from the Self only by designating it, by affirming it, though reluctantly, as a "logical construct." Malraux is interested in the features of the individual only insofar as they reveal an anthropological structure: a relation to death particular to a given culture, and this indeed makes him a self-portraitist. This is confirmed by the contrast between *resemblance-realism* and *convention-idealization*, which Malraux develops with respect to pictorial portraits and self-portraits: "Although nobody now believes that the object of the self-portrait, or even the portrait, from the effigies of the Egyptian sculptors to the Cubists, was simply to imitate its model, people still believe it of literary portraiture. (6). Malraux shares this belief with all other self-portraitists. As he criticizes factual realism based on true and contingent occurrences, a realism that developed historically against convention and idealization, against praise and vituperation governed by traditional conceptions of the virtues and vices and their effect on the city, Malraux takes up again the classical commonplaces, and through them he rediscovers the topics of rhetorical invention. Consequently, it is not simply out of modesty or moral censure, but under the constraint of a coherent discursive system, where conventional verisimilitude eclipses anecdotal truth, that Malraux eliminates the tittle-tattle, "the cheap titillation we expect from the irrational" (6). The choice of a style is not determined by a vague aesthetic decision, nor by the desire to build a heroic effigy: Malraux is sketching an anthropology. In fact, the choice of certain topics is based upon an anthropological choice:

If Man becomes the object of a search and not of a revelation—for every prophet who reveals God reveals Man by the same token—there is a great temptation to drain him dry, to assume that the more copious the memoirs and journals the better we will know him. But man can never plumb the depths of his own being; his image is not to be discovered in the extent of the knowledge he acquires but in the questions he asks. The man who will be found here is one who is attuned to the questions which death raises about the meaning of the world. (7)

This anthropology is evidently opposed to that of a Maine de Biran or an Amiel, indirectly alluded to here, through Gide: a tradition of the exhaustive introspection and meticulous diary keeping; it is also opposed to the scientific anthropology that strives to describe empirically the characteristics of *homo sapiens* in all his diversity.[1] As a result, Malraux situates his anthropology alongside those of prophets and founders of religions; and throughout his *Anti-Memoirs*, this representative of the agnostic West keeps interrogating present and past Eastern religions. But this interrogation, just as the one he addresses to real and imaginary museums, does not lead either to a hackneyed ethnological relativism or to symbolic syncretism. Malraux's man, like the man of the self-portrait, is defined by the questions he puts to himself—"What am I, who am I, where am I, what do I know?"—more than by the particular answers he may invent to soothe or prolong his anguish.

In Malraux, the approach of one's natural death does not deter death's questioning of the meaning of the world. Unlike Montaigne, whose first question (queries about the death of young men and Stoic reflections on suicide) resemble those of Malraux, the latter grows old without become inured or hardened. As Riffaterre has judiciously remarked: "With others, dialogue confronts the illusions of the past with the disillusions of the present. I am unable to discern the slightest disillusion in these confrontations wherein Malraux superimposes his present onto his past" (*Stylistique structurale*, 293). In this case we are dealing with the present and past of a writer who, since his early works, has not modified his questions, his style, nor the meaning that he initially projected onto the world and art. This statue is erected and his work completed: the *Anti-Memoirs* might merely be the literary analogon of a small museum or mausoleum if the closure of the text on Malraux's effigy were not repeatedly violated by quirkiness (*le farfelu*), that combination of humor and objective chance that skews lines, poses tragic questions ironically, and pushes ajar the door to the hypogeum.

Is all this enough to make the *Anti-Memoirs* a self-portrait? In the Introduction I cited Riffaterre's opinion that the *Anti-Memoirs* "rest on analogy (the method of superimposition is itself identical with metaphor); therefore they are poetry" (296). We now know that this nonnarrative "analogical" discourse is related to "poetry" and particularly to metaphor (among other tropes and figures) through the topics of dialectical invention and the procedures of artificial memory. While these observations instill caution in our theoretical handling of the content of poetry, they do not allow one to make a definitive announcement about the *Anti-Memoirs*.

As it happens, the preceding pages on Malraux were drafted shortly after publication of the *Anti-Memoirs*, at a rudimentary stage of my research on the self-portrait. No doubt they would have been dropped from a subsequent rewriting if Malraux had left it at that. I have retained them because they testify to a dual expectation: the vague anticipation of a "continuation," which the *Anti-Memoirs* did not explicitly promise, and the hope of an empirical confirmation of my own initial hypothesis about the self-portrait's open topical form and symbolic contents. The publication of *Lazarus*, followed by the rearrangement and redistribution of Malraux's last text under several collective titles and ceasing only with the death of the author, in many respects fulfilled this expectation.

2. LAZARUS. Rather than touching upon or "filling out" the portrait of Malraux outlined in the *Anti-Memoirs*, *Lazarus* hollows it out, for the book is arranged so as to imitate the neuromotor troubles that it uses as a pretext: "a sleeping sickness has afflicted me; my legs repeatedly refused to respond and I fell down, as in a fainting fit but without the loss of consciousness" (9). This twilight state (an "I-without-self"), mimicked by the very structure of the book, only incidentally and episodically produces a narration, which

unfolds fictionally in the presence of enunciation. While each self-portrait has death for its horizon and more or less explicitly encodes death and resurrection so as to abolish autobiographical memory, in the sense of a trite narrative remembrance, *Lazarus* squarely locates the key episode at the center of the book, which is organized around a vanishing self and its dis-location:

Our bearings are almost as much a part of us as our limbs; my body has disappeared with them: no more body, no more "I," nothing surrounding me, an agonized consciousness which does not suggest the approach of death, although it is not the consciousness of normal life. (82)

The mimesis of this dizzying loss that foreshadows death strikes us, on the structural plane, as a motivation of the textual procedure initiated in the *Anti-Memoirs*. For want of a central *place* (center and hollow, approached death and resurrection, and space between, all at once), the imitation of involuntary memory in the *Anti-Memoirs* only succeeded in producing an anthology of variant episodes from Malraux's earlier novelistic and autobiographical works. The *Anti-Memoirs* were most successful in portraying the writer as an unreliable narrator.

Within the framework of *Le Miroir des limbes*,[2] it is only when we reach *Lazarus* that we achieve a clearer understanding of the function of the *Anti-Memoirs:* the places deployed in the *Mirror* (references to earlier works, rewritten narrative episodes, narrated events) serve to constitute a series of backgrounds (*loci*) in the mnemonic sense. *Lazarus* mentions them allusively, at every turn, as a precisely arranged and oriented space that suddenly fails the self-portraitist. Against these backgrounds (textual patches of some scope) removable emblematic *images* stand out: clothespins, a prison camp, the sign of a glove merchant in Bône, Ganges funeral pyres, the antitank pit, cyanide: these refer to "experienced" as well as novelistic episodes, and they supplement or revise Malraux's previous writings.

These *images* have indeed the virtue of emblematic allusiveness: they conjure up instantly in the present of the *Lazarus* text vast portions of Malraux's novelistic works and point up what in them is still relevant to the self-portrait. Having set up his system of backgrounds and *imagines agentes* in the *Anti-Memoirs*, Malraux is now free to play with a mimesis of "memory without a memory": in fact, by summoning one another and grouping themselves analocally, the images can in turn summon or dismiss their *backgrounds*.

Yet what, in the strict sense, pertains to memory or rewriting is pushed back to the periphery. The beginning of *Lazarus* revises the episode in *The Walnut Trees of Altenburg* where Major Berger takes part in the first test of combat gases on the Russian Front; and the end of the book alludes to past novelistic episodes and as yet untold heroic anecdotes, which alternate with a dialogue on death reminiscent of philosophical dialogues commonly found in Malraux's novels; this dialogue also recalls Plato's *Phaedo*, and Montaigne's *Essays*, Christian meditations on death (*Artes Moriendi*), Saint Augustine's and Rousseau's *Confessions*, and the like.[3] But owing to such dense intertextuality, to which are added references to the deaths of Socrates and Jesus, the personal experience of death becomes exemplary of dying in our culture. The individual death of the modern West is contrasted with Oriental and medieval death: the light demise of men who live out myths, believe in metempsychosis, or have faith in a beyond. These are the very ones who never wrote self-portraits, yet the modern Western self-portrait keeps reactivating or evoking their comforting beliefs.

Thus Malraux's invention is a version of Montaigne's "humanism," even though it does place death under the modern sign of fraternity, of a revolt against the death of others, of death embraced to spare other people; but it so happens that this self-sacrifice again assumes a classical dimension: it is the "*No* of Antigone and Prometheus" (12). The story of the combat-gas testing on the Vistula, which is told several times with variants, bespeaks first of all Man's revolt against the Scourge:

That day, the semi-beast hailing from as far as Evil, from the depths where Man was born, discovered, as it slobbered, the challenge of Prometheus. Perhaps invested by death, I seek refuge in the narrative of one of life's most enigmatic convulsions. There the individual does not exist. (13–14)

What a paradox, for the modern reader, at least, that, sometimes, in the face of death, the individual should not exist. The whole of *Lazarus* is set up in order to stage such a paradox: "Death is not to be confused with my demise." (102)

In order to approach this paradox, to determine its emergence in the *Le Miroir des limbes* and the meaning that it has in the general context of the self-portrait, one must first uncover the contextual necessity that governs the appearance of Socrates' name in *Lazarus*. This occurrence had been prepared from way back by what must be termed an *essay* on the quirkiness of memory: "My memory never applies itself to me without effort"; and further on: "I don't remember my childhood" (123). Malraux has a more sustained interest "for the mechanisms of memory" than for the latter's contents, which he relinquishes to psychoanalysis (123–24). To elucidate these mechanisms, or to mimic them at least, Malraux will subsequently resort to a metaphor, the photo album containing "illustrations for a study on me." The device compels him to reinscribe in his text the backgrounds and images of artificial memory. Realizing that such images, in their broken sequence, cannot constitute an (auto)biography, Malraux sets forth the features that differentiate (auto)biography from self-portrayal:

Images do not make up a biography, nor do events. The narrative illusion, the biographical work are what create biography. What, if not moments from his own biography, did Stendhal set down? Everyone articulates his own past for an elusive interlocutor: God, in confession; posterity, in literature. One has no biography except for other people. (125–26)

This would be banal if Malraux did not succeed in elucidating metadiscursively the most paradoxical feature of self-portrayal: it is a *lack* that might well amount to a lack of "Self." Therefore, having noted that "images are arranged analogically here," Malraux is led to write a few lines further: "Me. Unexplainably, this personage, who obsesses me sometimes, does not interest me here" (127). The explanation is to be found not in this familiar motif, of which many variants are found throughout Malraux's writings (besides, *obsession* transcends *interest* and leads beyond autobiographical and narcissistic discourse), but rather in the discursive model that generates *Le Miroir des limbes*, a work whose title is so apt.

By contrasting *Lazarus*, which he supposes to be an unnameable sort of discourse, with biography, Malraux is prompted to set "memories" against "consciousness of existence," self-knowledge against consciousness-without-memory. *Memories* ("the assessment of life, the vertiginous past of drowning" [128]) are opposed

to *images*, just as the narration is to *description*. The former implies an ontological continuity:

the proximity of agonies submerges the "Who am I?" and makes it point-
less. Would this be false in solitary agony? This tourism in the archipelago
of Death is unaware of any sequence of events, lays bare but the most
unformed and intense consciousness, the convulsive "I am." But not beyond the other question: What is the human adventure?" (134)

Description, on the other hand implies a presence unto oneself in
the present of writing. But this consciousness without a memory,
stabilized in images, is deeper than ordinary consciousness: what
the textual mirror reflects is not a Self but rather a Limbo, evoked
very briefly and incidentally as it were, much further in Malraux's
book, in the context of a dream narrative:

I make my way over a leaden ground, through the pipes and tile debris over
which wanders a host of shivering coats without a body, between fences
with endless perspectives; a companion, guessing at my anguish despite my
silence and pointing vaguely at this limbo, murmurs: "It's nothing, sir, it's
the unconscious . . ." (234)

A consciousness without a memory, a consciousness of existence
bound up with images, in no manner amounts to a narcissistic epiphany. It opens onto another stage, another space, which is at once
that of Death and of the unconscious, *nothing*, in other words.
Nothing, just like death (that aspires, 155). But terrifying, too, hor-
rible: "Deep down in me, mine, as is my own heartbeat. A sacred
horror dwells within us, waits for us just as mystics say that God
awaits them" (154–55); and further on: "No religion, no experience has told us that terror is within us" (155) Not a consciousness
of nothing but instead individual consciousness's *nothing*; yet, it is
also *Limbo*, that is, a space between, "something else," rather than
death itself, in which consciousness would be completely abolished, rather than a presence unto oneself in the present. Consequently, concerning his experiences of dislocation and disorientation that echoes at the beginning of Proust's *A la Recherche de
temps perdu* Malraux writes: "Neither sorrow, nor memory, nor
amnesia—nor dissolution" (142), and he interprets the dream-met-
aphor of "coats without bodies" as an "I without self; a life without identity" (143).

Knowing oneself, telling about oneself is out of the question. It is at best a matter of not losing oneself entirely, of eschewing suicide. Malraux gives one to understand that the meditation goes beyond the Socratic dictum "to philosophize is to learn to die" from *Phaedo* (130), which Montaigne would make his own, and beyond Rousseau's ecstasy in the Fifth Reverie (130). The reader is thus prepared, as Malraux's text winds its way through these canonical places, to encounter side by side Socrates condemned to death and the suffering Christ. Socrates first appears during the central meditation around which all of *Lazarus* is organized, and which serves to justify the writing of the *Anti-Memoirs* (129). He is encountered again in the opening of the third chapter (158), which is a variant on the main meditation.

Yet just as Montaigne rejected Socrates' "ecstasies and possessions by his daemon" (III, XIII, 856), Malraux refuses his "cock and bull theory about the soul" (158): "Thoughts about death are always more or less empty, like those of Socrates when he tries to prove the existence of the soul" (178). But Malraux also juxtaposes the serenity of Socrates' pious last words—"And tomorrow do not forget, Crito, that we owe Aesculapius a rooster" (158)—with that of Jesus on the Cross—"Woman, behold thy Son—I thirst—It is the end" (158), which confronts with the heartening anguish of the cry reported by Saint Mark: "Lama Sabachtani," the penalty for the *love* introduced by Christ as, without effacing death, he gave a meaning to the life and death of those who were born and have died in vain:

Not believing in the Redemption, I have come to think of the enigma of the atrocious as no more fascinating than the simplest act of heroism, or love. Yet, sacrifice alone can look torture in the eye, and the God of Christ would not be God without the Crucifixion. (160)

The central part of *Lazarus*, then, is a rewriting of the *Phaedo* and the evangelical narrative of Christ's Passion. But it is not a "meditation on death" in the Christian sense. Besides, Malraux dismisses this kind of exercise as a mere meditation on the "places of the body": "Those feet used to run, those hands used to open, neither will ever move again; those eyes will never look again" (179). Yet Malraux's text is also a reflection on the corpse, on the transformation from self to cadaver. Such a reflection, in the manner of *Phcedo*, opens onto metempsychosis: the very separation of body and soul that enables Indian culture to domesticate death. Malraux's interlocutor, his physician, proposes an explanation that draws on the notion of the unconscious: though he notes it for the record, Malraux certainly does not endorse it:

Our relation to death is part, of course, of a belief, but I've asked myself, from the first time I lay dying, if for one's unconscious this belief is not the transmigration of man into his own corpse. Think about it. Man has clung damned hard to the idea of metempsychosis. He still sticks to it in Asia, and elsewhere too. (193–94).

As does the encounter between Christ crucified and Socrates condemned to death, Malraux's borrowings from the evangelical narratives and Plato's *Phaedo* clarify the meaning of "mirror of limbo": the textual mirror reflects an interim, suggested also by the name of Lazarus, a descent into Limbo, Hell, or Hades, such as the one described by Socrates in *Phaedo*. But this textual reflection also is a resurrection of sorts. Malraux explored limbo, the space in which the self-portraitist anticipates his transmigration into his own corpse. Malraux is not taken in by such metaphors of writing as the "body of the letter," or body-corpus, and, while relying on the work of art to "efface the starry heavens," he is well aware that he shall not avoid his own demise just by surmounting death. The myth of the Risen One (Lazarus, Christ) underscores the paradox of self-portrayal that assures *nobody's* survival, so that no one is ever reflected in its limbo, least of all in the particularity of a unique and irreplaceable body. Yet the writer's own body does seek through self-portrayal a revenge against the philosophical logos that keeps substituting impersonal *death* for his own demise.

PART FOUR

Writing Incarnate

CHAPTER 12

The Body, Locus of
Enunciation

Even when he devotes himself systematically to introspection, as Maine de Biran does throughout his "anthropology," or when he resorts to a phenomenological approach, as do Sartre or Merleau-Ponty, even when his experience and reflection do not set aside his physicality but, on the contrary, are nourished by a sustained attention to internal perception and the insertion of his body in the world, the philosopher still aims at generality.[1] He wants to correct the deviations from the norm that his singularity has introduced in the line of argument, and the René Descartes who designates himself as *I* in the *Discourse on Method* and the *Meditations* is a mediator towards a rationality with universal implications. Of course, it may seem to us that the generalizing purpose of the philosopher, or even that of the psychologist, is vitiated by unsurmounted idiosyncrasy and can be reduced to the symptoms of a narcissistic pathology or to the modulation of a neurotic configuration. But that was not the conscious purpose of the philosopher as philosopher and that is what matters here. Similarly, the psychoanalyst is more willing to discuss his patient's deficient body image than his own fantasies of dismemberment, and the "historian of the body" habitually does not mention his own quartan fevers. On the other hand, the sick, stage performers, modern poets, athletes, and most people often hold forth about their bodies without aiming at universality.

But the self-portraitist's relation to his own body is more complex and more paradoxical, for while self-portrayal is obviously not reducible to a description of the writer's body, he cannot ignore it either. As the only genre where writing is ineluctably led to raise questions about the *locus* of its own production, about the incarnation of the word and the resurrection of the body, self-portrayal contrasts with the philosophical logos. It is situated somewhere between opinion and reason, between individual incarnation and commonplace. The question of the relations between *places* and *body* arises globally in the body-corpus metaphor, and piecemeal through the symbolic images around which the self-portrait disposes its topical sequence.

The Places of Resurrection

In "Du Corps au texte," his commentary on the evangelical narrative of the visit of the Holy Women to Jesus' tomb on the third day, Louis Marin sought to link the absence of the (dead and risen) body with the symbolic order and the transformation of a universal topography. Marin's study, which is grafted onto a narratological analysis of the evangelical story ("Les Femmes au tombeau"),[2] shows that the connection between the designation of the *place* and the (dead or absent) *body* is an "essential moment in the transformation of the signifying experience into a discursive communication." After having reflected, without any specific reference to rhetoric, about the various meanings of the word *place*, Marin adds:

> That the place should be a *tomb*, and the absence that of a vanished *corpse*, this leads to the transformation of topography into a topical system, of the physical place into the place of speaking within history's semantic dimension. The narrative emergence *of* and *in* the symbolic order can now be interpreted: it is carried out in a figure that must be deciphered. Hence the temptation of allegorism. ("Du Corps au texte," 925)

Could it be that the narrative of the Resurrection, transformed within the self-portrait into that of *my* own resurrection, is the archetype of a type of discourse that, no longer being simply narrative, brings about the transformation of a topography into a topical system?[3]

As a result, the body and the places, indissociable from the allegorical figures that mark their course and designate them, may be seen as an attempt to overcome the distance separating the book from the body and textual space from imaginary speech. In the metasemiotic register characteristic of such an approach, Marin furthermore concludes that the angel's paschal message, like the message of the evangelical text, leads through the space of interpretation, towards a *message of the message:*

This discourse on reality as the reality of discourse: a common, historically vivid word, because it is openly plural, because its sense is the very possibility of sense. This word is the other of being, the *other-body* in the place of the dead body: it is not "here and now" in the empty place. It is the other body of the exchanged word, the historical universal. (928)

Self-portrayal as we study it here likewise postulates an *other-body* and a historical universal. Here perhaps lies the consequence or the cause (depending on whether one envisages the encoding or the decoding of the texts) of the figural presence of a suffering or resuscitated Christ in the self-portraits written in Christendom:[4] these literary monuments are empty tombs from which the true body has fled. They are the other-body, whereas the real one, that of the flesh, of topography, and of experienced space, has been turned into a topical system and into typography: "This is my body," says the writer, as the priest does, while showing mere signs. Let us, then, come back to the linkage between the notion of place in Marin's text and that of place in the context of rhetoric:

What is a place? A fragment of space provided with a unity of its own, an inhabited or visited space, a dwelling: a house, a temple and a tomb are places, as are a dining room, a room or garden, and a palace. By place is meant the relation of space to the function or qualification of the being who is indicated and exposed in it, in his absolute individuality; in other words, the relation of space to the only possible epiphany of Being in space: the body. Place is a body-space, the return of space to its pre-objectivity in the sense of an experience of its nascent significance, its return to its originality. (924)

This is not so different from what Cicero has already said, when discussing the disposition of *images* in the *places* of memory: "But these forms and bodies, just as all that we happen to look at, need a seat, since a body without a place is unintelligible to us" (*De Oratore*, II, LXXXVII, 358). The difference between *objective space* and *place* (or body-space) is similar to the one that is at work in self-portrayal: it intersects on several levels the opposition between *universal discourse* (logos, philosophy, science) and individual opinion, speech, an act, language incarnate. The ancient mnemonic arts had anticipated this transfer by prescribing the permanent inscription of *backgrounds* in the memory, by means of a frequent physical perambulation in real places—a temple, palace, forum, or city—forming a referential unity that insured the homogeneity and stability of the individual's memory. It is this autodidactic perambulation, transposed into self-portrayal, that gives rise to such intimate mnemonic places as the *dwelling* and its subdivisions.

These places, insuring the unity, interiority, and individuality of the self-portraitist in his metaphoric and metonymic relations to his own body and environment, achieve meaningfulness through the progress of literary invention. This is where an exchange between what is most individual and most general, between *my* house and *the* house, between *my* body and *the* body, between the *proper name* and the *common name*, between the individual place and the commonplace takes place. The evangelical narrative of the Passion-Resurrection, a course so often evoked by Christian meditation, so frequently *imagined, represented,* and adapted to individual visions and anguish, offered from the very outset these two complementary sides, these two indissociable functions:

Thus, now and henceforth, the places belong to narrative, that is, to that discourse (of which they are the primal and fundamental moments) to which experience can be referred by the discourse that says it, the networks of proper or common names spaced out along the narrational act within the narrative enunciation. (924)

Yet, the places of self-portrayal are much more than "primal and fundamental moments." They are not just the markers or pauses of a narrative: the places encompass and structure—whether at the level of individuality, through specific descriptions, or at the level of generality, as with the commonplaces of invention—the entire self-portrait. It is certainly correct of Marin to assert that "the places signify precisely the point where signifying experience accedes to cultural-discursive signification" (924). With respect to the specific place mentioned in the Resurrection narrative, the empty tomb where the holy women meet the guarding angel, Marin further adds:

"It is a place only in the incipient narrative: a narrative place, a place of discourse, a topos" (925).

Unexpected as it may be in that context, the use of *topos* in the strictly *proper* sense of the word, is nonetheless overdetermined by strict rhetorical usage: the tomb in question became part of the narrative only because it already belonged to a set of *resurrectional topics* that is characteristic of both the evangelical type of narrative and of self-portrayal: there must be a topos of the empty tomb, of the body that is absent and preserved in glory, in order for the gospel narrative to designate a particular tomb, the scene for an event that is verisimilar in context, and that is presented as *trustworthy*.

Marin knew that the status of the evangelical Resurrection narratives is equivocal: they claim to be the telling of a real event located in time and space, deriving its meaning from History: for the believer, the Resurrection orients the sense of History. From the point of view of Aristotelian poetics, these narratives, as they are taken by the believer, avoid a poem's highly equivocal noetic status: *mimesis of the typical* is foreign to them. But, since Christianity is founded on the Resurrection, one cannot say either that the Gospel is an ordinary veracious *historical narrative*. Without their becoming typical or general, the Resurrection narratives avoid the pure contingency of the particular. To account for their status, then, Marin proposes a novel category, the *possible*, which he sets outside the Aristotelian dichotomy of truth and verisimilitude. This category would encompass what is ordinarily called the *mythical*: "*fundamental narratives*: these narratives of the past, in the sense of the basic 'historiality,' define the very conditions for the possibility of any discourse" (916); and further on: "the fundamental narratives are the possible, because they are narratives and because they are narratives of the discursive operation *per se*" (917); and finally: "In truth, the Resurrection narratives tell the circumstances of the advent of the event of experience in language and discourse and how this advent becomes communication" (917). If the narratives in question are "figurative discourses on the foundation of language," which "cannot hold the speculative discourse without which no theory of language and discourse can be thought," one might suggest that such narratives imply and encompass the

articulations of the figure and the concept, of truth and verisimilitude, of the named place and the topos, of experience and discourse. This can also be shown by resorting to the opposition between mimesis and rhetoric. For, if the Resurrection narratives do
indeed transcend the opposition between poetry and history in order to attain the *possible*, defined as a myth anchored in a particular topography, such narratives open up the possibility of a topical system centered on the *other-body*; so that these narratives,
which transgress categories, now turn out to be the narrative homologies of self-portrayal, itself a figurative and spatalized discourse on the foundations of languages in one's own body, opening
up the possibility of all discourse that is modeled on the body-space
and that offers, as does the narrative of the Resurrection, food for
thought and interpretation rather than a speculative discourse. Both
the evangelical narratives and self-portrayal as confirmed by the
status and function of *description* in the self-portrait, fail to conform to the dichotomies set down by Aristotelian poetics.

Let us then go along with Marin and say that "the place signifies
. . . the point where signifying experience accedes to cultural-discursive signification," with the proviso that this passage from experience to sense will take place in discourse only if the culture
provides the means for it to occur, particularly in the form of a
topical system containing the virtuality of the *place* and *experience* in question. The place-topos, then, is the point of passage between cultural meaning and an experience that signifies only to
the extent that it already is potentially discursive. Inside any given
culture, every discursive realization dialectically modifies the potential relations between the commonplace and the referential place,
between experience and signification. There is evidence of this with
respect to "inhabited spaces" and "visited spaces": in order for the
dwelling or the *Venice* of signifying experience to accede to discursive signification in self-portrayal, the writer must have a domestic
or Venetian topic at his disposal to play with, or that can toy with
him, which he can reactivate or transgress, but which he cannot
altogether ignore since in the absence of topics the experience would
not achieve significance: indeed, no signifying experience, no modelization, no didactic play would have taken place at all.

Necessarily, the same has to be said of one's own body as a place-topos. For Louis Marin, "the place is a body-space" (924) and the word of the Resurrection angel designates the place of Christ's absent body: this word is "the other-body in the place of the dead body; it is not 'here and now' in the empty place. It is the other body of the exchanged word, the historical universal" (928). Can this be said of all "written-bodies," of texts that always designate the absence of a body "here and now" and eventually propose an other-body for a dead body? This would amount to stating that the written body, the *other-body* of one's own body was to begin with, in the case of self-portrayal, a discursive place about which all that has already been written regarding the dialectic between "signifying experience" and "cultural discursive signification" remains valid. An exchanged word, a historical universe: the self-portrait already inscribes this paradoxical universality in the places of the other-body-space of Montaigne's *Essays*; it does so doubly, first by means of a *mise en abyme*, for one may consider the hole in Book I (ch. 29), where neither La Boétie, his *Contr'un*, nor his sonnets can be found, where a mere reference reveals an absence, as a metaphor of the empty tomb, next to which the angel Michael is pointing to the resurrection of his friend in the *Essays*, in this other-body, in this single body and cenotaph crafted for two men united by a friendship that was as divine as is poetic fury.[5]

But the ecstatic other-body of self-portrayal is itself, in turn, a place and, if one prefers, a *body-space* of a particular type, since it aims to encompass all other named places, thus becoming the encyclopedic totalization of invention. Unlike narrative, which can limit itself to designating a few places by name, the very nature of self-portrayal condemns it to exhaust all places, whether by describing them, that is, by at once specifying and universalizing them, or by means of an encyclopedic invention whose dialectic deals with each place in turn and connects it to other places by analogy, contiguity, antithesis, and so on. But the standard opposition between description and invention does not hold up under scrutiny: one cannot say that description "is a mirror of reality," any more than one can say invention merely produces a *speculum* of cultural cliché's and accepted ideas. In both instances, there occurs a spatialization with multiple modalities, the most fundamental of which certainly seems to be the invention of a transcendent mediation between the *body* and the *corpus*, through which there can occur an imaginary transfer from one to the other. Let us examine this hypothesis.

CHAPTER 13

Body and Corpus

Leiris: Manhood

"Midway in life", Leiris begins *Manhood* by reworking the old topic of *mediocrity*. The writer describes his own body by reference to an ideal of which, owing to deficiencies or excesses, he falls short. Medium build, adult masculinity, *aurea mediocritas:* classical humanism furnished him with plenty of clichés. Leiris would always be torn between this representation of manliness in the prime of life (the committed man, responsible, true to his *word*, an upright artisan of language), which he never manages to match, and his immature refusal of paternity, his nostalgia for childhood, his feelings of being small, the little Michel.

Leiris first defined himself in comparison with other people, speaking of himself as one might talk about someone else, real or imaginary. It is to the extent that he can capture an image of himself reflected by others, or under the gaze of others, that the Leiris of *Manhood* introduces himself to the reader. This is why he first describes himself as a body, as his own body perceived in a mirror, front view, profile, or back, from the points of view sometimes provided by a tailor's mirror. Leiris is a man for whom fittings have been frequent and traumatizing experiences. Hence the importance attached, from the very first pages of *Manhood*, to a configuration described by the author as a "very straight nape of the neck." One would be tempted to deem this personage an unsuccessful dandy; his failed attempts to correct his "humiliating ugliness" result in the dismal remark: "ordinarily [I] consider myself thoroughly inelegant." Instead of a dandy's haughty hieratic pose, all he can manage is an insignificance that is the opposite, since an insignificant character is readily deciphered, provided someone should pay the slightest attention to him.

Leiris's anguish is that of a man without a shadow, who believes that he is entirely obvious, without mystery or interest for others, but nevertheless opaque and obscure in his own eyes:

> there are doubtless things that escape me, and most likely the most apparent among them, since perspective is everything and a self-portrait, painted from my own observation, is often likely to leave in obscurity certain details which for other people would be the most flagrant. (4)[1]

So it is a question of maneuvering between what is too clear (insignificance, easily classified and catalogued) and what is too obscure: what for me is located at the back of my head, like the nape of my own neck and may be unexpectedly revealed to me, but that usually requires an invention resorting to reasoning and analogy, contortions before the mirror so as to skew my point of view. A darkening of what is too clear by inserting it in an obscure semiotic network provided by esotericism; a clarifying of the obscure through clusters of metaphors and analogies, a dramatic display of allegorical entities, which finally enables one to see it "in the round," as it were. Thus is produced the imaginary of *Manhood* or, better still, its *imagery*.[2]

By giving the body a "soul" and the soul a body, Leiris multiplies and superimposes the meanings of signifiers at first seemingly univocal (the body, appearance, habits); he also reduces the number and connotations of signs that are meant to capture the floating, equivocal, and shapeless signifieds making up "subjectivity," the unconscious, and things forgotten. The course, then, is oriented between two poles: the pole of symbolism and that of allegory. In order to charge the insignificant—primarily, one's own body, familiar acts, the anecdotal—with symbolic resonance, there must occur a superimposition of several codes; and these, with their intersections and varied shifts, create an aura of uncertainty and mystery around banal and too readable appearances. Hence, from the beginning of *Manhood*, the recourse to astrology, physiognomy, and palmistry. To explore and structure the obscure, Leiris uses allegorical figures and the description of a stereotyped iconography, such as a sequence of folk images from a broadside entitled the "colors of life," or the complementary figures of Cranach's Judith or Lucrecia, which gather a web of relations among eroticism, death, and *castration*. These are used as a discursive network capturing emotions that could pass a priori for being utterly unsayable.

Girolamo Cardano: De Vita Propria

Leiris reactivated old semiotic systems that make the body meaningful, and, while he was about it, he reinscribed the problematics of the body, as it arises in the self-portrait, within a vast discursive and ideological context, inside which not only abnormalities but all relations between mind and body, between signifier and signified, between clear and obscure, became intelligible without ceasing to be mysterious. Indeed, Leiris's archaizing esotericism led him to turn *Manhood* into something like a modern variant of a Renaissance self-portrait, Girolamo Cardano's *De Vita Propria Liber* (*Book of My Life*), where the author describes his own body as follows:

I am a man of medium height; my feet are short, wide near the toes, and rather too high at the heels, so that I can scarcely find well-fitting shoes; it is usually necessary to have them made to order. My chest is somewhat narrow and my arms slender. The thickly fashioned right hand has dangling fingers, so that chiromantists have declared me a rustic; it embarrasses them to know the truth. The line of life upon my palm is short while the line called Saturn's is extended and deep. My left hand, on the contrary, is truly beautiful with long, tapering, well-formed fingers and shining nails. (19)

Cardano's gait is scarcely more harmonious:

Because I think as I walk, my gait is uneven, unless something claims my attention. My feet are moved, and often my hands, even, make gestures at the bidding of my restless mind. The very diversity of my concerns, the circumstances that befall me, nay, the very disposition of my body, influence my going. (77)

The cause for these somewhat buffoonish incongruities, which fall just short of congenital monstrosity, can be traced to Cardano's astrologically and obstetrically disastrous birth:

> Besides, to return to the horoscope, since the sun, both malefics, and Venus and Mercury were in the human signs, I did not deviate from the human form. Since Jupiter was in the ascendant and Venus ruled the horoscope, I was not maimed, save in the genitals, so that from my twenty-first to my thirty-first year year I was uanble to lie with women, and many a time I lamented my fate, envying every other man his own good fortune. Although Venus was, as I have said, ruler of the whole nativity, and Jupiter in the acendant, unfortunate indeed was my destiny; I was endowed with a stuttering tongue and a disposition midway between the cold and the harpocratic—using Ptolemy's classification—that is to say, gifted with the kind of intense and instinctive desire to prophesy. In this sort of thing—it is called prescience, to use a better expression—as well as in other methods of divining the future, I have been clearly successful at times. (5) [3]

In this self-description, medical semiology is barely distinguishable from astrology, divination, or even the version of humoral psychology Cardano ascribes to Ptolemy and on which he had written an astrological commentary. No part of his own body is insignificant, while his habitus is completely decipherable. Cardano's conduct and appearance are interpretable despite some blurring of the signifiers, which is due to nearly monstrous incongruities. But since the system of astral influences that produced him was intelligible, Cardano has no problem understanding himself body and soul: for instance, his ten years of sexual impotency was a vexation rather than a mystery. Nor is there anything unexplainable in the gift of prophecy that compensates in some sense for his stuttering and his unfortunate sex life. The subject's body, which utters embarrassed or prophetic speech, turns out to be as intelligible as is the rest of nature. Cardano is not one of those individuals who, understanding everything else, is devoid of self-understanding; his sick body is as amazingly transparent as the buoyant physical health from which Nietzsche derives such satisfaction in *Ecce Homo*: the subject's extraordinary status finds expression in his singular lucidity regarding the needs and workings of his own body.

Cardano's ill-assorted body conceals a hunger for glory and perenniality: *The Book of My Life* was written to define and incarnate its modalities. Cardano ends his essay by asserting that his desire for immortality is *natural*.[4]

One recognizes in Cardano's book a procedure typical of the "essay" and profane meditation, particularly since its dialectical elaboration along a series of commonplaces eventually leads to a personal assertion of opinion and to a description of the particulars of the writer. The whole intertextual scaffolding seeks to display and justify an individual choice. Furthermore, this meditation is falsified and skewed from the outset by the narration of a prophetic dream that conjured up for Cardano, at a crucial point in his life, "a second road, a road to glory." Cardano was thereupon blessed with a perfect command of the Latin language, something he had never before achieved.

Thus, hunger for posthumous glory, anticipating the day when one's own body passes away, is indissociable from that transitory body, the locus of astounding phenomena and strange needs: its yearning for physical pain, for example, without which Cardano is engulfed in intolerable anguish. He consequently prefers illness to good health and does not hesitate to inflict upon himself such physical torments (twisting his fingers, pinching his flesh) as enable him to carry on his scientific work. The body, for the advent of one's glory, must be martyred.

Cardano wrote *The Book of My Life* in 1575, when he was seventy-four. By then, as a mathematician and physician, he was famous in all the learned circles of Europe. There was nothing extraordinary at the time, when *glory* was a literary commonplace, about asserting one's desire for immortality.[5] According to Burkhardtian interpretations, the quest for glory and immortality was essential to "Renaissance Man" to spur him on. Cardano's assertion of his superiority then, is true to type. Less typical, however, is an immodest disclosure or, it is not clear which, a humble avowal of the contrast between the fame he finally achieved through his exceptional scientific work and his wretched shameful life spent until the age of forty-three in a confused and indolent state attended by poverty and disgrace. Of course, a Romantic, taking literally such oxymorons as "harmonious monster" and "mad genius," would see in this disproportion the normal distinction of an exceptional being; and the thesis that Cardano is "baroque" might also be easily sustained in accordance with one or the other of the innumerable definitions of that Protean term. In his *De Utilitate ex Adversis Capienda* (1561), Cardano had already formulated for himself a characterology enabling him to analyze the paradox of professional achievements founded on handicaps or vices.[6] One can therefore analyze his *Book of My Life* with references to contraries such as appearance and reality, grandeur and pettiness, the weak body and the mind triumphant. But this might entail missing the specific relations obtaining between the body and the corpus in such a text, whose paradoxes are traceable to the imperatives of self-portrayal as much, or more, as to the categories attributed to the baroque, although both can be traced back to elementary topics of invention.

Cardano's astrological observations led him to believe that he was destined to die before the age of forty-five. But a "new life" began for him when he was forty-three: "That was the moment when, induced by my age and by my disposition, by the anxieties of the past and the opportunity of the present, I made a new beginning, turning away from pleasure" (ch. 10, "On the Course of My Life," 37).

Thus Cardano has already died and he was born again. not so much in a glorious body as fated for a glory that would do violence to his own body. This rebirth does not prevent him, in his self-portrait, from enumerating, nor from recounting his innumerable disputes, his imprisonment, the affronts and torments inflicted upon him by the misbehavior of his sons, along with the triumphs of his medical career. He wants to proclaim his own truth, to make himself known as a "teller of the truth, an upright man and indebted for my powers to a divine spirit" (291). Cardano's *vita nuova* differs from his old life only insofar as he accumulates claims to glory through his scientific works. But the "divine spirit" had to intervene before the scientific work became possible.

Whether guardian angel or a being analogous to Socrates' *daemon*, the writing of *The Book of My Life* embodies, so to speak, a "spirit" that stands as the only plausible explanation for such premonitions and scientific intuitions as were bestowed upon Cardano in his second life (ch. 47, "The Guardian Angels," 240–47). This "guardian angel" is Cardano's secret, the hypostasis of his furor in a Platonic sense, the principle that enabled him to take a mysterious qualitative leap from the plane of his wretched life and miserable body to that of glory, the force that transmuted his plodding observations and modest erudition into the illuminations to which his medical cures, his mathematical discoveries, and all his scientific overtures testify. In short, Cardano in his elevation to glory, becomes just the opposite of Alcibiades' Sileni: precious drugs constitute his outside, his appearance for the world and posterity, whereas his inner self remains misshapen, grotesque, devoid of intrinsic worth; *The Book of My Life* is relentless in its disclosure of hidden wretchedness.

Nietzsche: Ecce Homo

The arrangement of Cardano's book reverses the usual relationship between without and within. In this respect, there exists a homology between *The Book of My Life* and Nietzsche's *Ecce Homo*, since the latter also contrasts the contingency of the writer's own body with the necessity of ecstatic inspiration. A microcosm of each author's literary corpus is concealed at the center of each book. Cardano cites his bibliography and Nietzsche comments on his own works, so that if the rest of their respective oeuvre were to disappear, that much from each of them would remain. The chapter order of such books as *The Book of My Life* and *Ecce Homo* serves to encase their nutritious marrow (their "substantifique moëlle" as Rabelais put it) within the bone of habitus, just as a body encases and protects a soul. Both books are bodies the soul of which is a *corpus*. But then, in order to attain immortal glory, why should anyone bother to fashion an analog of the mortal body? Nietzsche's book makes the interdependency between self-portrayal and cultural motifs of incarnation and Resurrection startlingly clear.

Before adopting the title *Ecce Homo: Wie man wird, was man ist* (How One Becomes What One Is), Nietzsche tried out several other possibilities, the traces of which can still be found among his drafts.[7] The symbolic coordinates of literary self-portrayal are conjured up and summarized in the various versions of the title:

1. *Der Spiegel*
   Versuch einer Selbstschilderung [crossed out] *Selbstabstraction*
   (The Mirror—Attempt at self-description [crossed out] Self-Abstraction)
2. *Ecce Homo/In Media Vita*
3. *Fredericus Nietzsche/De Vita Sua*

Two of the discarded titles (1 and 2) clearly indicate that Nietzsche never planned an autobiography, a confession, nor in Abelard's sense, a *Historia Calamitatum*, but a *synchronic section* (*In Media Vita*), a descriptive, fragmentary, heuristic undertaking (*Versuch*), in the very sense denoted by Montaigne's use of the word *essay*. Most striking is the hesitation regarding the word *Selbstchilderung*, which implies a mimesis, a representation (also implicit in the *mirror* metaphor). However, the mirror, as an encyclopedic *speculum*, also implies a generalization of the particular. The book is not about a mere individual, it fashions a model, the model of a man who puts forward a new anthropology, a new encyclopedia. The crossed-out word and the recourse to *self-abstraction* clearly points to the abstract, thematic, and conceptual intent of the book, at loggerheads with the concrete denotations of *mirror* and *description*, which cannot fail to arise as soon as the writer attempts to capture his own features *hic et nunc*. *Self-abstraction*—for Nietzsche's reader this word is completely devoid of any pre-existing meaning—designates precisely a type of self-portrayal organized around a number of "commonplaces of invention" and giving rise to an encyclopedic metadiscourse. In fact, this is what—among other things—the final subtitle appears to suggest, as though Nietzsche had said: by commenting on my own texts, I will be showing you how I managed to be what I am. One's *assets* (the available capital, as represented by one's previously published *opus*) are credited here to one's *being*, through the dual process of citing and commenting on one's own texts: interpretation revives these vestiges of the past, now in danger of becoming frozen in otherness. But "how one becomes what one is" also recycles what was discarded by the second title, *Ecce Homo/In Media Vita*, that is, a conversion and retreat that create the possibility of becoming what one is, and of accounting for it, *Nel mezzo del cammin di nostra vita* . . .

The four titles (including the one finally retained) are divided into a title and a subtitle; and by superimposing all four of them (in actual fact, only three, but the juxtaposition of different subtitles changes the significance of *Ecce Homo* in the two instances where it appears), we have:

1. *Der Spiegel*
2. *Ecce Homo*
3. *Fredericus Nietzsche*
4. *Ecce Homo*

What first attracts one's attention is how the *mirror* is transformed into *Ecce Homo* within the religious paradigm of self-examination, confession, and the medieval moral *speculum*. Nor should one overlook the Latinization of the first name in the third title; its function, clarified by the other versions, is to create a linguistic distance within which mirroring could take place, a looking at oneself in a mirror plainly denoted in the words *Der Spiegel* while it is merely suggested by *Ecce Homo* and its reference to Christ mocked by his tormentors. Matched with that of its twin book, *The Antichrist*, the finally adopted title, *Ecce Homo*, yields additional connotations: what seemed at first a title borrowed from painting, recalling a fairly common identification with the mocked Christ among Lutherans during the Reformation, exemplified by Dürer's famous self-portrait, turns out to be a trangressive bid to displace at once Luther and Christ and to obtain recognition as the new martyred God-Man. Richard Samuel, while vainly trying to turn *Ecce Homo* into an autobiography nevertheless rightly observes that although there are few autobiographical elements in Nietzsche's book, its beginning is set in the year 1879, when Nietzsche at thirty-six, and utterly depressed, resigned his professorship at Basel. Nietzsche's father had been thirty-six at his death. "I am, to express it in the form of a riddle, already dead as my father, while as my mother I am still living and becoming old," he wrote at the very beginning of the first section of *Ecce Homo*[8] (222). A riddle indeed, but one that the rest of the book seems to contradict given Nietzsche's deliberate identification with his "Polish" father, while the "German" mother stays in the shadows; that enigma, however, is overdetermined by Nietzsche's identification with Christ, even though it is a negative and antagonistic one. As an extension of his father, Nietzsche is dead, just as is Christ himself. They are dead in order to descend to hell and rise from the dead. No other self-portrait resorts so visibly to the cliché of death and resurrection: this is how one becomes what one is. The experience of death/ resurrection is what opens up the field of literary self-portrayal; and it also engenders a *glorious body*. *Ecce Homo* erects, about a literary *corpus* and a glorious body "in perfect health," a monument such as is needed to mark the geographically located inspiration of Eternal Recurrence. The "locus" of this monument is indicated in the first section of *Ecce Homo* devoted to *Zarathustra*: "six thousand feet beyond man and time" (295). It would be fitting here to examine how the specific "referential" locations in *Ecce Homo* (Sils-Maria, Èze, Rapallo) tie in with *Zarathustra*'s atopia. Inspiration, place, and specific time, all of which are inseparable in *Zarathustra*, are three modalities of the *revelation* of an anti-Gospel. The named places amount to an anti-Bethlehem, an anti-Jerusalem. But there are no referential places (not even Lake Urmi and Persia) in the completed *Zarathustra*. On the other hand, Nietzsche's self-portrait stresses the uniqueness and reality of the body, of the place, and of the time when the eternal recurrence is revealed to him. There is a crucial difference between the incarnation of Friedrich Nietzsche and Zarathustra, his timeless poetic myth. Besides, the revelation of eternal recurrence creates a gulf between Nietzsche and all other men (even those who are Zarathustra's disciples). Nietzsche is unique and selfless, if the self is indeed a passive synthesis of habit and memory, the ground from which bad repetition stems. He is unique because he is both Dionysus and all of history's heros: all times and places come together in this infinitely multiple and pseudonymous being, who soars to greater heights than history, "six thousand feet beyond man and time," and thus realizes in one leap philological humanism's dream of assimilating the power of all illustrious men and of all ancient divinities. In his self-portrait and in his madness, Nietzsche finally fulfills the pagan Renaissance: the great Pan has come back to life and the usurping Christ has been dismissed.

Consequently, there is a *before* and *after* to Nietzsche's incarnation: the before—with its morality and philology—is of no account; the after—where health and physiology are all that matters—is transfigured. Moreover, the before was alienated in books and discourses by other people; the after is selfish, to all intents and purposes devoid of any books except the ones Nietzsche has written. Those are in turn reiterated in *Ecce Homo*, a text that gathers together all that is worth keeping, worth passing on to posterity.[9]

Thus, because of their consubstantiality with ethical values, with the virtues and vices, the traditional contents of the topics of invention are left out of *Ecce Homo*. These cumulative topics, tainted with idealism, are transvalued into a series of places that are to the topics of Christian humanism as the anti-Socrates is to Plato's Socrates and the Antichrist to the Christ of the Gospels.

These new topics reformulate the main themes of Nietzschean thinking in order to apply them directly to the writing subject and his own body: the first two chapters of *Ecce Homo*, entitled "Why I Am So Wise," and "Why I Am So Clever," are subdivided into brief sections that make up a *hygiene* and a *physiology*.

The second section of the first chapter ascribes good health to an inborn physiological soundness; midway through the section, there occurs a description of the *well-turned-out-person:*

What is it, fundamentally, that allows us to recognize *who has turned out well?* That a well-turned-out person pleases our senses, that he is carved from wood that is hard, delicate, and at the same time smells good. He has a taste only for what is good for him; his pleasure, his delight cease where the measure of what is good for him is transgressed. . . . He is strong enough; hence everything *must* turn out for his best. Well, then, I am the opposite of a decadent, for I have just described *myself.* (224–25)

Self-knowledge is transferred from the ethical to the physiological plane, so that the classic *ne quid nimis* becomes a matter of hygiene. There is a transportation here to the biological plane, rather than a dismissal of the ontological and ethical opposition between seeming and being: an unwholesome appearance can mask a "fundamentally healthy" reality—witness the ability to cure himself of such a seemingly diseased being. Good and evil are a matter of physiology: "A typically morbid being cannot be made healthy again, much less make itself healthy." The old Lutheran predestination is transferred from the plane of grace to that of somatic propensities.[10]

Whence the importance Nietzsche confers upon hygienic precepts, which he deals out with the assurance and inflexibility of a dogmatic catechist: what is good for Friedrich Nietzsche must govern the lives of the chosen ones. For the remainder there is no salvation. The second chapter, setting forth "Why I Am So Clever" is ordered around tenets of the new hygiene:

Answer: these small things—nutrition, place, climate, recreation, the whole casuistry of selfishness—are inconceivably more important than everything one has taken to be important so far. Precisely here one must begin to *relearn*. What mankind has so far considered seriously have not been realities but mere imaginings—more strictly speaking, *lies* prompted by bad instincts of sick natures that were harmful in the most profound sense—all these concepts, "God," "soul," "virtue," "sin," "beyond," "truth," "eternal life."—But the greatness of human nature, its "divinity," was sought in them. (256)

We find here a distinct, term-by-term opposition between two topical systems: while the new supplants the old, the opposition is articulated around a *change of method*. Topic, method: Nietzsche is the direct heir to the Renaissance, particularly Bacon, for whom his admiration was so great that he credited him with the works of Shakespeare. Between Bacon's theoretical output and "his works" as a playwright, Nietzsche perceived an opposition-complementarity analogous to the one inscribed in his own works, between the polemic texts of *Human, All too Human* and the sublime poetry of *Zarathustra*.

Ecce Homo then becomes the textual locus where an exchange of status between Nietzsche's corpus and his own body takes place. The change of method amounts, one might say, to the somatization, the incarnation of the corpus. As the corpus is about to be completed, Nietzsche makes a spectacle of his body in a textual ostension that results from a *performance*, and a transubstantiation: *Hoc est enim . . . Corpus meum:* the whole ambiguity of this venture is crystallized in Nietzsche's passage from German to Latin, the key to which is found in his discarded tentative titles, *Ecce*

Homo heralds a departure, an *upswing:* Nietzsche wanted to leave behind the species of a new Eucharist.

Roland Barthes by Roland Barthes

Roland Barthes's self-portrait,[11] like the books Nietzsche and Cardano wrote about themselves, is organized as a commentary on the author's own works. It also includes a bibliography and a brief curriculum vitae. This happens to be a coincidental homology, for *Roland Barthes by Roland Barthes* actually is the result of a wager and a fortuitous convergence between the structures of self-portrayal and the well established features of a popular series of critical literary biographies called "Ecrivains de Toujours." The title of the series (Writers of All Periods, as well as Forever Writers) reveals the exceptional status of the authors to whom its many volumes are devoted: immortality. Each study bears the title *X by Himself,* preceded by the name of the author of the commentary, with the exception of the book on Roland Barthes, which is entitled *Roland Barthes by Roland Barthes.* The fiction according to which a commentator, as it were, lets the author he is discussing speak for himself here becomes reality: the two names on the cover are identical. Yet in contrast with the other volumes of this series where each great writer is presumed to introduce himself through excerpts from his works, *Roland Barthes by Roland Barthes* contains not one passage from Barthes's earlier publications. Unlike the works of other immortal writers, Barthes writings are supposed to be present in every reader's memory, or they are considered to be so closely woven that excerpting passages would be barbaric treatment—that is, unless self-commentary is deemed a sufficient summary. However that may be, this omission can best be explained by the fact that, in this case, commentator and he whose works are being commented upon are one and the same, by the lack of distance between subject and object, not to mention commercial considerations.

Most of the "Écrivains de Toujours" are dead white males. The book devoted to each of them bears witness to the writer's posthumous glory. Actually, the "Écrivains de Toujours" formula tends to minimize the anchoring of a text within its own time period, to be oblivious of the scant duration of human life, and therefore to stress both the transhistorical perenniality of great works and their eternal "modernity." Each volume dealing with a living contemporary author is a gamble on posterity's willingness to grant so-and-so (or at least his works) an afterlife. Moreover, in an attempt to overcome the academic dichotomy between the "man" and his "works," the series, whenever possible, would present the author by means of an abundant iconography. Writers since Daguerre are represented by pictures from their family album, generously scattered through the critical text. *Roland Barthes by Roland Barthes* is no exception to this rule.

We now understand how *Roland Barthes by Roland Barthes*, thanks to contingent imperatives, became a self-portrait conforming to the model furnished by Cardano and Nietzsche: the writer's aspiration to glory and immortality is *guilelessly* inscribed in the series' general title. Barthes has therefore been spared the exertions observed in Cardano's and Nietzsche's writings: the proof that "I write such good books," that "I am so clever," that I am "inspired" stands right there on the cover: the writer is thereby given leave to be both modest and ironic inside his own text. Witty euphemism is the only way out of such a ticklish situation. On the other hand, immortality, glory, and the writer's relation to his own body are certainly what the undertaking is all about. A writer erects his own monument under the pretext of being his own commentator:

> When I pretend to write on what I have written in the past, there occurs . . . a movement of abolition, not of truth. I do not strive to put my present expression in the service of my previous truth . . ., I abandon the exhausting pursuit of an old piece of myself, I do not try to *restore* myself (as we say of a monument). I do not say: "I am going to describe myself" but: "I am writing a text, and I call it R. B." (56)

A brilliant restatement of the myth of transfiguring one's own body into a corpus that is being reasserted (by rereading and commenting upon it) while it is being transformed into a perennial text now called *Roland Barthes*. This suggests, under the pretext of dismissing the myth of Isis and disdaining monumental restoration, a threefold cutoff: a break between the present and antiquity; a severing of the penis that metamorphoses it into a unlocatable symbolic phallus; and, finally, a separation of one's *vita nuova* as a self-portraitist from one's previous life. This triple abolition seeks to settle the text in the present and to center it on the present of the subject of enunciation. Still, the recourse to a denial ("I do not . . .") certainly shows how fragile this assertion is. The disclaimer draws attention to a return, a regression at the core of the self-portrait: it courts these dangers as it wards them off. Thus *Roland Barthes by Roland Barthes* is at once a rewriting and an unwriting: it wrangles with certain "classical" and "modern" texts by other writers, as well as some of Barthes's own previous texts. Moreover, certain fragments of *Roland Barthes by Roland Barthes* are the palinode of some other fragments copresent in the book itself. This microcosm displays a whole array of features inherent in self-portrayal in general: Montaigne's *Essays,* for example, already rewrote and unwrote certain texts by other writers, as well as themselves. Rousseau's *Rêveries* challenge his *Confessions;* Saint Augustine flushes out the first nine books of the *Confessions* through Book X; Jacques Borel's *Retour* is a palinode of *The Adoration.* In the second part of *Fugue* (after the symbolic death/resurrection) Roger Laporte unwrites the first part, which in turn deleted such previous self-portraits as Leiris's *La Règle du jeu.* The case of *Anti-Memoirs* and *Lazarus* comes under the same paradigm: in both these books there is a partial rewriting of Malraux's previously published novels, though *Lazarus,* by means of the topos of death/resurrection, cancels what, in the *Anti-Memoirs,* was still a spectacular heroization, a narcissism of memory. *La Règle du jeu*—in the run of titles given to successive volumes: *Biffures, Fourbis, Fibrilles, Frêle bruit* (Deletions, Odds and Ends, Fibrils, Faint Noise)—encodes the notion of cancellation and that of metathesis or anagram (in a minor mode), so that the work as a whole becomes a system of permutations in which not only all of Leiris's previous writings, but also, with each new volume, the earlier ones, get recast, and, in a sense, abolished. Nietzsche, however, because he did not cancel out his "good books" which he was content to comment upon and boast about, remained blocked as it were at a particular point of the constructive/deconstructive process during which the self-portrait is engendered. For, while he did cancel out the books of other writers, all his own are recapitulated in *Ecce Homo.* He now believes that he is in sole possession of the last word, which transcends his terrestrial self-portrait; as his own evangelist Nietzsche holds the secret to Nietzsche's Ascension. Barthes, on the other hand, demurs, "what I write about myself is never *the last word*" (120); and elsewhere, after the passage cited earlier on:

> I do not say: "I am going to describe myself" but: "I am writing a text, and I call it R.B." I shift from imitation (from description) and entrust myself to nomination. (56)

But, caught like all self-portraitists between *description* and *nomination* (although he chooses to cloak the first term in denial), Barthes merely repeats, magnifies, and extends to his entire text the naming operation, which Nietzsche confines to the microcosmic invention of his title when, overriding the cancelled *Selbstschilderung* and the surpassed *Selbstabstraction, Fredericus Nietzsche* ends up becoming *Ecce Homo*, the ultimate degree of metaphorical abstraction and nomination: to be consistent with his unwillingness to describe himself and thus become *man*, Roland Barthes would have to write "Roland Barthes" around his own picture a thousand times.

Barthes would return, elsewhere, to the system of description, *after* having brought up and denied the possibility of a literary mimesis of his own voice, of his several voices, and particularly of a "voice *without rhetoric*" (67), Barthes's emphasis. Rhetoric and description are mentioned and denied at one and the same time. They both are in the retinue of death: "voice is always *already* dead," writes Barthes, thus underscoring that ideologically and stylistically he is here allowing Derrida and current *Doxa* to do his thinking for him.[12] And yet the articulation of three essential topics of self-portrayal is made manifest by this very obeisance: death implicit in textual resurrection; the ineluctability of an impossible description; and the necessary *periplum* through the places of rhetorical invention and memory which are laid waste, transcended, and crossed out in this process, as are the "places of the body" or those of one's own voice:

> Whereby we may understand what *description* is: it strives to render what is strictly mortal in the object by feigning (illusion by reversal) to suppose it, to desire it *living*: "as if alive" means "apparently dead." The adjective is the instrument of this illusion; whatever it says, by its descriptive quality alone, the adjective is funereal. (68)

This is extremely well put, for the sentence also contains its opposite: the funereal adjective is unavoidable insofar as it builds a cenotaph that the subject describing himself erects for himself in his own lifetime, as a subject who is already dead in his writing, in his retreat and his withdrawal from life.

Consequently, with Nietzsche, Barthes, Borel, and the other self-portraitists, self-description is present as it were, under a deletion; it is always a first impulse, soon squelched and that must nonetheless be protracted; otherwise the author would have to settle for writing a meta-self-portrait, as is Roger Laporte's *Fugue*, where all that survives is the blueprint for a productive machine and a description of potential workings. Barthes notes elsewhere that to write a self-portrait is writing in the second degree, where "I write that *I write*," while the first degree would be "I write." (70) And, quite rightly, he underscores that such writing, with its language that thinks about itself, is corrosive. But this corrosive agent feeds on what it corrodes, the impossible description. The self-portrait is an infinite and infinitely self-destructive text, where description survives only insofar as it is dismantled, fragmented, shamed, or at least undermined; and the second degree, in turn, spawns several others. One might think that Barthes, like all other self-portraitists, persists, so to speak, in ramming in a door that was opened long ago by Saint Augustine, only to realize immediately that this superfluous violence generates the very text of the self-portrait. Barthes himself is prompted, of necessity, to say as much:

I shift from imitation (from description) and entrust myself to nomination. Do I not know that, *in the field of the subject, there is no referent?* The fact (whether biographical or textual) is abolished in the signifier because it immediately coincides with it: *writing myself* . . . I myself am my own symbol, I am the story which happens to me: freewheeling in language, I have nothing to comparte myself to; . . . to write on oneself . . ., it is also a simple idea: simple as the idea of suicide. (56)

Quite a modern idea, with its extreme Hamletism and perhaps, because, casting the shadow of a bull's horn over the text, it mitigates a self-indulgence henceforth threatened by death. But there is more to it than that, for even the most fashionable of self-portraits, according to an enunciation whose referent eludes the writer when he endeavors to refuse *imitation* in conformity with prevailing fads, nevertheless is the place where the writer, who may have coddled or despised himself before taking up the corrosive self-portrayal game, dies unto himself.

Still, there are a few extant self-portraits, Barthes's among others, even though their texts have been generated by the inexorable process Barthes calls *suicide*. This would be unintelligible if it were solely a question of the "field of the subject, [where] there is no referent." It must be that the topical organization of the self-portrait makes up for the elusiveness of the referent without saturating the field of the subject. Barthes knows this full well but says it elsewhere, under the heading of the "fragment" that allows him to glimpse faintly the topical imperative of his undertaking. Hence this observation: "To write by fragments: the fragments are then so many stones on the perimeter of the circle: I spread myself around: my whole little universe in crumbs; at the center, what?" (92–93). Further on, there occurs the inevitable palinode:

I have the illusion to suppose that by breaking up my discourse I cease to discourse in terms of the imaginary about myself, attenuating the risk of transcendence; but since the fragment (haiku, maxim, *pensée*, journal entry) is *finally* a rhetorical genre and since rhetoric is that layer of language which best presents itself to interpretation, by supposing I disperse myself I merely return, quite docilely, to the bed of the imaginary. (93)

Thus, Barthes is going round in circles; and, having already asserted that the (imaginary) referent was missing from within the field of the subject, he suddenly discovers the imaginary ensconced (as its referential content) in the fragment, as a "rhetorical genre"; and thereupon, if only to make it scamper off, he starts the rhetorical hare from cover. Everything that might serve to clarify the conditions inherent in Barthes's undertaking is present in his text, but whenever these signs, which are so clear to the reader, loom up before this Oedipus blinded by his ideology and coiled round the corpus that makes him a writer, he misinterprets or disdains them.

The fact that Cardano, Nietzsche, and Barthes had reached an earlier or later stage of their lives when they wrote their self-portraits can be disregarded here; what mattered is that at this point in their career they considered that their oeuvre was completed or that its published part already ensured their immortality. This situation is diametrically opposed to that of writers whose oeuvre (whose claim to glory) is just about coextensive, in duration and amplitude, with their self-portrayal. In this latter type, exemplified by the *Essays* or *La Règle du jeu*, metadiscursive stock-taking and self-commentaries become an integral part of the text, whereas in the former, the previously concluded works stand apart, as a citation, a pre-text, or a foreign body, or rather, as an already dead and transfigured body that has passed on to the other side of mortality. But the corpus-body also motivates self-portrayal, where the writer's own mortal body, whose abnegation allowed the advent of a glorious corpus, is at least inscribed and represented like an actor who takes a curtain call in person, after having well served the intemporal *persona* whose mask he was wearing. The analogy among Cardano, Nietzsche, and Barthes breaks down at this point. For the last words from *Ecce Homo*—"Have I been understood?—*Dionysus versus the Crucified*" (335)—are the obscure heralding of a metempsychosis, the reincarnation of a dead god, the demise of the Risen Christ, while Cardano has words only for his fear of death, for his hopes of eternal life and lasting glory, and Barthes becomes ever more revealing about himself as a desiring body.

The *in extremis* featuring of a writer's own body in this type of self-portrait (in what is at once an *apologia pro vita sua*, an anticipated funeral eulogy and a gospel in the first person) remains as problematical as the symbolic death and resurrection that the self-portraitist inscribes in his text. Nietzsche, having reached "the lowest point of [his] vitality" at thirty-six (his father died at that age), goes through darkness before he is reborn with *Aurora* (222). Cardano experiences his own metamorphosis at forty-three. Barthes is in his sixties when he discovers that "his word-as-mana-is the word 'body' ". (*Roland Barthes by Roland Barthes*, 130) Henceforth there obtains a *concordia discors* between the oeuvre and the ailing body, which nevertheless discloses its concealed vigor in the lucidity of an inspired mind and in the euphoria of writing: the oeuvre has ideally displaced the body, whose resurgence in self-portrayal makes a last minute protest. Exploited and mistreated to make the work possible, the body is not content with being transfigured into a corpus: it takes the upper hand and claims its pains, its desires, its somatized hysteria, its mortality, against the writings that despoiled it as they fabricated the myth of transfiguration.[13] The body denounces literary glory: its function is that of the mummy which has been brought forth in the middle of a banquet. *Ecce Homo* also signifies: you are not Dionysus, nor an unflagging Zarathustra; you are but *this*, a sickly, a desiring, and a mortal body.

Nietzsche's self-portrait reads less as a denial of his identification with Socrates and Christ, in their most defenseless predicaments, than as a scarcely veiled affirmation of *imitatio* as a turning back to a grotesque truth that underlies the transvaluation of all values as it undermines it. A suffering body forsaken by the Spirit so that all may be accomplished; a comic body stilled by the hemlock that finally puts an end to its dialectic. *Ecce Homo*, especially as it turns morality into hygiene, cannot conceal beneath the bluster of the First Man the lament of a sick body protesting against glorious hypostases, sublimation, and soaring metaphors: incarnation is here and now.

The self, like self-portrayal, is an *ante mortem* mummification; Self material is produced by the folding back of language upon itself, thus hindering communication and squelching transitive discourse, whenever speech is drawn back to the place and manner of its production in an attempt to foreground them:

If language is not the same kind of fact as the ones it describes, is this not because when language reflects upon itself, it creates between facts a continuity, a unity of staging that gathers or lights them up? (Vuillemin, *Le Miroir de Venise*, 104)

And yet, conversely:

Speech is wondrously attuned to the world that it represents; for it passes on with the world, and both let go at once of one another. But, whenever it talks about itself, it brings everything to a halt, abusing time and begetting the weaver. (105)

This movement, a clotting, or rather a concretion, this faulty communication, brings forth the speaker as a parasite of speech, as an object analogous, all things considered, to a foreign body, such as a kidney stone that will painfully beget the speaker's own body.

Unless it is, inversely, a body-part that has been removed: Roland Barthes relates how, from high up on his balcony, he once discarded his own rib, "a sort of bony penis," which the doctor had returned to him after a pneumothorax operation. Now, this gesture of Barthes's, this jettisoning of a part of his own body piously deposited in a *secrétaire* among other keepsakes, seems to symbolize the actual writing of his self-portrait where we can read:

And then, one day, realizing that the function of any drawer is to ease, to acclimate the death of objects by causing them to pass through a sort of pious site, a dusty chapel where, in the guise of keeping them alive, we allow them a decent interval of dim agony, but not going so far as to dare cast this bit of myself into the common refuse bin of my building, I flung the rib chop and its gauze from my balcony, as if I were romantically scattering my own ashes, into the rue Servandoni, where some dog would come and sniff them out. (*Roland Barthes by Roland Barthes*, 61)

By dint of sniffing, the critical hound eventually discovers that this humorously immodest anecdote celebrates the death and resurrection of the body, the transfiguration of the writer's body into a corpus, within his self-portrait where many other memories, removed from a *secrétaire* get thrown to the wind, so they should live on less secretly and less precariously. Barthes hated/loved self, just like his rib, must be cast to the readers so it will become a book as it is being dispersed and thrown away. For the Self and the removed rib are scraps, the consequences of a parasitic infestation (tuberculosis), the products of a language sickness, the necrosis of memory: what originally was a euphoric and silent body or language freely flowing without a subject become hypostatized as laughable *simulacra*.

The Self is a lapse that calls for endless exploration and treatment. Either the healthy body is silent or its satisfied murmur escapes notice: one becomes aware of such paradisiacal happiness only when losing it. By the same token, the universal word circulating through an unblocked network does not spawn any self-conscious speaking subject, any subjectivity, or any Self. The same applies to a memory that assimilates and recalls properly: it does not draw attention to itself. But a snag in the process causes a precipitate to form:

On this return to Venice, an abrupt change seems to take place in me, so that, though I haven't noticed them before, thousands of slight modifications are rallying suddenly to form a mass. (Vuillemin, *Le Miroir de Venise*, 99)

This precipitating *mass* (the body, the word, memory) is the Self; some writers may enjoy describing it as they try to redeem this first fall by a second fall into scribbling and accumulating predicates. On ideological (on ontological, on ethical) grounds, some writers, Vuillemin and Barthes for instance, stand opposed to this unbearable reification of the Self, that already *dead* precipitate. The flow must be restored, in order to eliminate this pathological concentration. Therefore, the pathological discourse that produces bits and pieces of the Self, much as stones are found in the kidney, finds expression in a network of corporeal metaphors: in Montaigne and in Barthes, a bared body delivered up to the gazes of the public a tired member, an old and sick body that no longer assimilates or excretes adequately in Montaigne, Vuillemin or Barthes.

But, as the reader soon realizes, there is a contradiction in these metaphors: excessive *stasis* is inseparable from excessive motion. When language becomes blocked, there results an uncontrollable elimination, a logorrhea. The fact is that this blocking is due to mirror effects between an object (an imaged) language and a meta-language; for the latter "lays bare" the former and stretches it out in an endless series of specular duplications.

Like Leiris's body frozen up by his tailor's mirror, or a malfunctioning digestive tube, the self remains suspended metaphorically between reflection and excretion, between retention and incontinence. The self-portraitist's Self, being at once a *calculus* and a *passage*, resolves itself into an interminable book. Jules Vuillemin proposes a treatment in words that combine an exacting ethics of self-control and a regimen calculated to avert logorrhea:

As it reflects upon itself, language is spontaneously carried away, it feeds on itself and partakes of infinity; the expression of feelings rather than feelings themselves, is being expressed; and there is no end to this game.

Moderation alone can cure this anxiety; a temperate and prudent language, even a stark language, is imperative here. (*Le Miroir de Venise*, 91)

On the other hand, Nietzsche writes, "Only my sickness brought me back to reason" (*Ecce Homo*, 242). Viewing his own genius as a euphoric excretion, he had already asserted of the person who does not know what is for him a propitious place and climate: "His animal *vigor* has never been great enough for him to attain that freedom which overflows into the most spiritual regime and allows one to recognize: *this* only I can do." Nietzsche's next paragraph prolongs the equivocation of that unique *doing:* "The slightest sluggishness of the intestines is entirely sufficient, once it has become a bad habit, to turn a genius into something mediocre, something German" (240).

The Body and Opinion

Thus, to paraphrase Barthes, the self-portraitist sets out to discourse about his truth on the basis of an economy that is the one of his own body. Even though, unable to be silent about the body, the self-portrait cannot pass for the philosophy of the body, much less for a philosophical corpus: whence the failure, on the part of the commentators, to formulate a philosophy or philosophies of Montaigne's *Essays.* The self-portrait is born of a rent in the warp of sense, a breach of attention through which a duality manifests itself in various ways: the duality of the body and the soul, of reason and the passions, of sense and sensibility, of the signified and the signifier. The self-portrait attempts to overcome it. While the fault, through which the body and the phonetic or graphic materialization of language becomes manifest is part of ordinary experience, yet, in most instances it is deemed to be a malfunction, something that one strives to efface, to reduce to insignificance, just as one does a slip of the tongue that threatens the intelligibility of speech and inopportunely attracts attention to extraneous determinants:

As I followed the thought of the other, I grasped a certain conception that was developing through the articulations and starts of discourse. But even if, in keeping with the nature of discourse, it was required to agree with the facts, the argument itself never wrestled with things; only the intelligible sense of a memory or a transcription of experience that alone concerned the sense of the words. Riveted to a theme, attention sought the universal; and, in proportion to the rigorous repression of opinion, the contingency, materiality and historicity of language were annulled. The other and I had both been eliminated from the scene of ideas, ideas that were just as indifferent to our bodies and feelings as to our respective interests. Completely absorbed as I was in the sense of the words, the voice, having achieved a supreme self-effacement, I did not even notice that this sense was being *expressed.* (Bruaire, *Philosophie du corps*, 25)

Quite evidently then, philosophical dialectic claims to be an abstraction, and it also expects to keep at bay all the concrete modalities of communication and, a fortiori, of persuasion. On the other hand, persuasive dialectic has been understood, since Aristotle at least, to be a *pragmatics*, attentive to all the material and emotional circumstances of interchange emphasizing through tropes and figures the sensible, the opaque signifiers and corporeality, in order to vest itself with the power that attends the exaltation of passions and desires. This is the dialectic to which the self-portrait resorts, an "impure" dialectic. The other one, however, the dialectic that is supposed to structure Socrates' argumentation, is known to have consistently failed, especially when using ordinary language, to attain the level of abstraction it aimed for. But, in philosophical dialectic, a precarious discretion of the body tends to obtain even when the concepts with which it deals are those of the body, language, and communication, even when the argumentation has to do with self-knowledge. And yet, on closer examination, is there, in this respect, such a radical difference between rhetoric and philosophical discourse? Even though rhetoric takes the body and corporeal expression into account in *pronunciato*, it never reflects on a body that writes here and now, on this very topic, nor on the particular body of a given orator; for his gesticulation, mimicry, and voice modulations are coded and more apt to travesty or make up the body and efface its particularities, than to put it in charge of its own individuality and "defects."[14]

Thus, with philosophy and rhetoric, as well as with linguistics, logos, generality and communication prevail over incarnation, which is always seen to be lacking, an insignificant anomaly. Nowhere is this dissociation more remarkable than in Erasmus' *Alcibiadis Sileni*, which turns into a norm the striking discordance between Socrates' grotesque body and the harmony of his universal discourse. Consequently, Alcibiades desires Socrates' body to the extent that it is beautified by the logos. Claude Bruaire's historical survey of the status which philosophy has assigned to the body since Plato yields many variants of the belief that, when attributed to an individual body, thinking is but an opinion, an alienation in individual life, hysteria, and neurosis; it is subservient to becoming and the appetites of the senses:

To purify, divide, and strip language so as to get through to the perfect intelligibility of the eternal Idea, that was the sole recourse of this lofty request for the absolute. Inevitably, another alienation came to replace the one that was vanquished: the single subject—as much of a stranger to divine thought as the latter is to man's personal life and the natural world —was not only dispossessed of himself and reabsorbed into the wretchedness of his own body, but also, finally, abolished in universal extension a random expression of impersonal Substance. (85)

Thus, on account of a decision that has to be considered perverse and transgressive in this (however diluted and unthought) ontological context, self-portrayal must initially fall into opinion, into the relative, the perishable; properly speaking, it is an idiocy. Montaigne was no doubt as fully aware of this fall as was Augustine, Pascal, or Malebranche, and he did not become resigned to it straight away; or, rather, the foolishness did not strike him with full force until it had become his last resort. What Montaigne still had to show was that the thinking claiming universality and seeking to triumph over alienation in "one soul and one body" is self-deluded: philosophy is in turn an opinion, yet unaware of being such. Having lost everything, a stranger to the body, to individuality, philosophy is thus doomed to think about death, and to miss it in its unthinkable contingency; it is undermined by time and corruption, from which it turns away so as to transform them into concepts. Universal thinking "having no determined body, *has no within and no without*" (Bruaire, *Philosophie du corps*, 75): it is, in its turn, exposed as an imposter. For this reason, it is correct to say not only that Montaigne is not only a philosopher, but also that his undertaking is one long effort to rid himself of philosophy, to undo bit by bit the universal discourse of philosophy while building an *analogon* of his own body in the *Essays*. If wisdom consists in transcending one's own fate, in masking the contingency of one's own death, if, in accordance with the Platonic formula, "to philosophize teaches one how to die," what the self-portrait has to offer could hardly be termed wisdom—unless one were to stretch the denotation of this word to the point of encompassing an opposite meaning. For, as Bruaire remarks, philosophy is adamant:

He who carries out effective, active, inner thinking, is indeed reflecting. But he who reflects upon himself from within himself loses the hope of rejoining the absolute reflection of unique and eternal Thought; and this is why the first step of wisdom is a negative one that places him who thus reflects outside the game, off sides, a step that silences his insular opinion, which inevitably expresses his individuality and his own body: only in such a way will the truth that is sufficient unto itself arise in the stripped and mute soul. (85)

Just as that initial step is difficult for the average man to take—supposing the common man to be less alienated from his own body, more complacent about the insularity of his own opinion—so the reverse step, that must be taken to attain nonwisdom and non-knowledge and bring one back into one's own body, proves to be arduous for the man of culture and the philosopher, who recoils from it as leading to desublimation, to a regression. In his own way, Jean Prévost corroborated this with his refusal to portray himself. Such a regression is abominable to the man of faith, as confirmed by Saint Augustine, the convert who, in Book X of the *Confessions*, resolutely strikes out in the sole pursuit of God and produces what we take to be a negative self-portrait: only a non-converted Augustine, indulging fully in opinion and in the desires of the body, might have wished to fill in, to embody the vast abstract spaces of memory. For the Augustine of the *Confessions*, who is not a philosopher nor a theologian, but who is not a self-portraitist either, remains poised on an impossible threshold. The Incarnation happened elsewhere, at another time; only the relation to another Body, to another Death, and to Resurrection—that alone gives meaning to Augustine's refusal, or to a choice of a threshold that sums up the Christian's condition. This is borne out by a tradition of spiritual meditation that culminates with Loyola's *Exercises*.

But, even Montaigne, setting out in quest of himself, and becoming resigned to having to explore his own memory, does not do so without reticence, without reversals, without censures, nor without first ridding himself of all borrowed memory, of that place without an inside or an outside where the play of universal thought is timelessly staged. For that thought is indifferent to such an incommensurable event as constitutes for me my corporeal supervention at a moment in time, at a given place in space.

Clearly, "Cartesian dualism," with its philosophical implications and vast cultural consequences, projects far beyond the problems addressed here. Consequently, in a study devoted to the self-portrait, there are frequent encounters with Descartes and one cannot, in connections with his *Meditations*, elude the question as to whether this work is a kind of self-portrait. Two answers readily come to mind: the first one is that Cartesian meditation is a reflection with a universal intent in which the *I* seeks the status of any thinking subject, rather than a deliberate fall into opinion and a choice of the singular. The very word *meditation*, charged as it is with religious connotations, suggests that a recourse to images, even if it is a mandatory passage for the meditator, must nevertheless lead to ecstasy and self-detachment.[15] With respect to Loyola's and Rousseau's texts, we have drawn attention to the transformational connections that occur within a single discursive structure, rhetorical memory and invention, with the procedures of meditation. Whenever the Christian exercitant resorts to *places* and images, even to those of his own body, he does not think of them as an end, but rather a means and, on the whole, as a stop-gap. On a philosophical plane, the same could be said for Descartes himself. Consequently, it might also be said that a meditator turns to his own body and memory only so that, on good grounds, he may dismiss them. In a commentary that is developed in a manner completely foreign to rhetoric, this enables Claude Bruaire to conclude:

Thus, I do recover my subjective body through reflection; but the latter brings me back to myself by distinguishing me from that body, by releasing me from the purity of spontaneous, unconditional and absolute judgment, that is, from the only singular substance in which I am as one with myself. Sensible experience, with Descartes, fails to coincide with the substantial "I"; and furthermore, the equivocal status that makes it mine but does not make it me, is what determines the whole Cartesian doctrine of the body. (90)

It might be said, in reply to these remarks, that the metaphysical reflection which the Cartesian thesis comports might have been tainted by the very rhetoric to which it resorts; and the singularity of the body in the extension might have prevailed with such force that the *Meditations* would slide back into self-portrayal.[16]

Freed from mimetic ingenuousness, from the tangles of representation and the snares of *ut pictura poesis*, we now become aware that in self-portrayal, the question of the writer's own body is improperly framed within the context of specularity or pictorial "self-portraiture." Besides, the philosopher views the relation between body and language in theoretical discourse as an aporia:

if the body becomes meaning, if, in order to appear, by virtue of an immanent reflection that metamorphoses being into a concept, the idea arises from nature, how might that which has become, how might language that has come to pass inside the body, recognize its own place of origin, the place that, because of its very essence, it conceals? How can language that takes itself for a theme revert to the body which it ravishes and denies? Conversely, how might the body become unmasked, how might it let itself be said, if what is said inevitably envelops the body and, as it were, uses up the latter's mute materiality? (Bruaire, *Philosophie du corps*, 169)

But the reader of self-portraits will note that, though his words suggest an impossibility in the form of a question, Bruaire indicates a new course. In fact, owing to the self-portraitist's inability to capture his own body through description, can it not be said that he lets his body speak for itself precisely insofar as he takes language for a theme and *describes his own language*—insofar as self-portrayal always is at once both discourse and metadiscourse? The body manifests its presence as an obstacle, through a lapse, a faulty operation of linguistic and conceptual communication. But indeed, it cannot be said that this passage of Bruaire's addresses in any way the question of self-portrayal; it deals, rather, with linguistics, that scientific folding back of language upon itself, which the philosopher criticizes in these terms:

I cannot think and grasp the words of my own thinking simultaneously, for they can be apprehended only through reflective attention, and reflection, per se, as an act, cannot be reflected upon. Whence, since thoughts are both the subject matter of the philosopher and a theme for research, they are inevitably reabsorbed into spatial or synchronic linguistics; furthermore, they become petrified in a juxtaposition of empty structures, in the system of a structure of structures, in that indefinite relaying of copies for which there are no originals, in which there is no thinking subject, for the latter is denounced as a myth engendered by ignorance. (170)

In this instance, as in all others, the philosopher's position is that of the generality of reflection; and he reflects upon the generality of linguistic science, which is presumed to evacuate the subject who speaks and thinks. But Bruaire's critique of structural and synchronic linguistics, which he believes to be spatial and petrified, echoes, through its use of negative metaphors Sartre's dismissal of the unconscious and the imaginary, a critique that does not spare the spatial and linguistic models (the Freudian topics and Lacanian structures) of psychoanalysis. If, according to Sartre's thinking, imaginary spatialization is inseparable from the postulation of a (psychoanalytic and/or linguistic) unconscious,[17] and if this spatialization always leads to splitting and fragmentation of the thinking-speaking subject, to its final evacuation, the issue is certainly of consequence for philosophy insofar as it deals with the transcendental subject, and for the sciences of man. But, since self-portrayal is such that its essential aspects elude both science and philosophy, it could hardly be included in this condemnation; nor could it be destroyed by the incompatibility between two types of discourse which, moreover, concern it only insofar as self-portrayal itself becomes an object discourse and a document, or when, at risk to itself—that is, betraying its own purpose—it ventures into philosophy and science. On the other hand, there are enough grounds here for both the possibility and impossibility of self-portrayal.

Conclusion: The Way
of Self-Portrayal

While at first self-portrayal may seem to be an attempt to answer the preliminary question "What am I?" it soon appears that the process is of such complexity that it cannot be reduced to such an obvious query. On further consideration, the interiority and exteriority of the question, and its variants, become themselves problematical. Self-portraits are written after the writer has already fallen into a formless and disoriented space, created by a loss of certainty. For Montaigne, the fall results from the death of La Boétie, the friend on whom he had relied to insure his own oneness and truth. Poetry and efficacious language withdrew from Leiris before he decided to imitate them painfully and artificially in the prosaic work of self-portrayal. A mimesis without illusions and a chancy attempt to return home, self-portrayal is an odyssey towards a submerged Ithaca. The writer's task consists in conjuring up, without any magic tricks, a textual simulacrum of the lost mirror-place.

Many are those who plan to write their memoirs or autobiography and who, with that end in view, collate documents, take notes, and check their old diaries. Some, finally, set their hands to the actual writing of a narrative. Not to mention the innumerable "autobiographies" that have been written "with the help of" a ghost writer: this is not likely to happen with self-portraiture.

But does anyone ever actually undertake to write a "self-portrait?" Would it not be more correct to say that self-portrayal is the post-facto recentering, deployment, and reworking of one's idle and formless writing that initially wandered off aimlessly into the vague field of fantasies, glosses, and jottings? Such is the case with Montaigne, for his first essays, the first that have been presented in a more or less united form, are notes taken at leisure by an idle reader and marginal scribbler. The case of Leiris as a self-portratist is analogous, if one considers that "Le Sacré dans la vie quotidienne" is a kind of "essay" that now seems to foreshadow the self-portrait, since the latter is extant and gives meaning to the former. No self-portraitist, stupid or admirable, devises the plan of painting himself, at least not at the outset; and the understanding, insofar as it becomes crystalized and stated in an actual text, is only one more step in a much more elusive and complex enterprise; "painting oneself" perhaps is just one negative moment of that endeavor, or at least an unstable and fleeting moment, since the proposition inverts itself with the realization that the subject cannot paint himself and thus ends up in dispersal and in the effacement of the subject's predicates: what remains then is intransitive *writing* rather than a mimesis of the self. In this sense it is true to say that Narcissus does not write, or that he ceases to be Narcissus while writing his "self-portrait." Writing per se is soon called into question; and there arises a *cogito* of writing that replaces that of being. Not the *I write therefore I am* to which autobiographers and authors of diaries cling, but rather, in Roger Laporte's formulation: *What is it to write?* or, *What is the status of myself in writing?*

"Who am I?" "What am I?": these are quintessential metaphysical and philosophical questions. As I could hardly find the answer to them within myself, through introspection and self-analysis, the reply must be sought elsewhere, outside: through revelation, through anthropology, or in the eyes of others. If I desire to be someone, *so-and-so*, I also want to know who I *really* am, outside the roles imposed on me, the lapses of memory, and the unconscious. I want to be like others, like such an Other; or, conversely, to be different from those others, from such an Other. The autobiographical writings produced by minorities, for example, or by feminists, seek substantial identities, definitions by opposition. Whether by assent or resentment the question "Who am I?" always implies that an answer is within reach: only a few obstacles have to be removed in order to apprehend it. You would not be seeking yourself if you had not found yourself already. Such a discovery can only be ideological or dogmatic. The faith that seeks itself is answered in advance with quiet assurance: *Tolle, Lege.* Evidently the question "Who am I?" becomes nagging only if it has not, so to speak, been answered in advance. Saint Augustine himself underwent numerous metamorphoses and suffered many disappointments before he was granted the overwhelming assurances that enabled him to escape from the labyrinth where he was seeking the answer to that question. To ask oneself who one is, one must no longer be what one was: one must have lost certitude and penetrated into an anxiety that can also be called "freedom of choice."

The self-portrait goes beyond this anxiety and such beliefs, no matter how confused they may be, for self-portrayal is bound to corrode and leave behind "Who am I?" the earnest, rather lumpish, and subordinate question of a slave desperately yearning for emancipation, searching for roots, and attempting to turn his former abasement into dignity: it is the question of someone querulously soliciting power. In short, a worldly, political, and neurotic question. Self-portrayal, on the other hand, modulates and nurtures the unease of certain individuals who making up a minority far smaller still than any sexual or social minority, separate themselves from the dominant class and sex to which they belong by right: they exile themselves, at least through their writing, and withdraw to a powerless retreat—which may be accounted by the many to be haughty, uncivic, and guilty; their seclusion is inextricably bound up with their position with respect to rhetoric.

Rhetoric is not only a civic art, but an art of mastery as well. Together with the art of war, it was for a long time the only art that freemen were willing to practice. Military leadership and speech-making (as can be gathered from old and not so old historical accounts) obviously complement each other. Efficacy, rather than justice, is the aim of both rhetoric and the art of war. Neither a rhetorician nor a soldier would believe that a just cause triumphs in politics and war because it is right. He who said so would be a hypocrite. Whenever conventional armies are routed, whenever subtle enthymemes fail it is because guerrilla warfare or blatant arguments are more efficacious in the circumstances. The Sophists were aware of this—whence their enormous success and also the obloquy heaped upon them by the "virtuous" powers that nonetheless filch their weapons. For the Sophist, the politician's amanuensis and his guilty conscience, is interested in power for power's sake; and, unlike the politician who must get himself elected or at least create a façade of legitimacy, he serves any master and makes no bones about it; granting him recognition and honors would give the game away. Rhetoricians are ostensibly excluded, along with poets, from the polity of the just, from Plato's Republic, for example. And yet a rhetorician is only a technician, at best a technocrat, a specialist in communication, an advisor in what is understood to be civic virtue by those who are in power or maneuvering to gain power. But in what way can the self-portraitist, a voluntary exile in his own retirement and powerlessness, be likened to a Sophist? A curious paradox.

Even if self-portrayal is initially faced with the temptation of asking "Who am I?" as is the case with Leiris in *Manhood* and with the earliest chapters written by Montaigne, even when he tries on the role of a diplomat or that of the commander, the self-portraitist will soon abandon the question unless a much more radical anti-Socratic bent such as that of Barthes has preserved him from the *vulgarity* of this question, to which other people hold the answer and on which they have the last word. Perhaps he will remain haunted by the question, as the psychoanalysts claim is the case with all their clients. So the self-portraitist will attempt to get around the nagging question. As a last resort he may even reach for the *other* answer that can be obtained without resorting to other people, to metaphysical axioms, to religious or political dogmas, the answer that says: "I am this fragmentation, this scattering; I am that which lies beyond asking 'What am I?' " He does not say, "I am *not* what I am," since this would be tantamount to postulating an essence transcendent to reified hypostases; it would amount to positing a desire or even a liberty that consumes its predicates along the way. On the contrary, he proclaims: "I am this appearance"; I am, for instance, my "styles," my "writing," my "text"; or even, more radically, I am style, writing, text; I am a textual and stylistic histrion, wild in my dispersal; I am lawless folly, heedless of any center or norm; my *personae* are eccentric and uncentered rhetorical gesticulations, pure rhetorical impetus cut off from ontology and indifferent to virtue.

At any rate, these two movements, unreconciled and untotalized, are found in self-portrayal. Even if it begins as a quest for an essence of the self, the essence soon slips through the self-portraitist's fingers; if he started out denouncing the illusion of the self, he will soon turn about and hit upon crystalizations that will make the question of the center rise again at the very periphery he thought had been annihilated by centripetal forces. On a microcosmic scale, the ambivalence of self-portrayal duplicates the paradoxes of contemporary cosmology. This is another way of saying that self-portrayal occupies the no-man's land that has always separated rhetoric, born of sophistry, from the metaphysics of authenticity that obstinately sets reality against appearance. Self-portrayal is a hybrid: across many mediations it has inherited the axioms of sophistry, relegated to the impure and uncertain purview of action and discourse: reason and justice are bracketed by self-portrayal. But self-portrayal does not and cannot forget the philosophic edifice and edification from which it is excluded and to which it lays siege. This filiation, as well as the equivocation of self-portrayal, stands revealed in that Nietzsche, the new Sophist or anti-Socrates, wrote a self-portrait whose title virtually echoes the Protagorean tag: "Man is the measure of all things."

Montaigne, however, was intensely interested in *arete*, in virtue and gentlemanly education. Yet the Renaissance ideal of a "man for all seasons" is open to the charge of opportunism. Erasmus was charged with duplicity, Bacon with Machiavellianism. The rhetorical Renaissance and the baroque ethos rested, in many ways, on a juggling with predicates. Circe and the peacock symbolize the magic of a power that is justified only by the limitless play of appearances.

If Montaigne referred less frequently to Protagoras (he does so several times in the *Apology for Raymond Sebond*) than he does to Socrates and Plato, his Pyrrhonism is no less scandalous than is the absence of any center in the sophistical flitting about. In either case, the only Being that remains is that of a Protean polymorphy.

But another paradox crops up at this point: for while sophistry is chiefly concerned with the means of persuasion, beginning with language itself, it is also a radical skepticism that seeks to undermine all philosophy, any impersonal, disembodied, and universal discourse on essences; it refers all things to the speaking subject and his perceptions. If all discourse is *incarnate* individual opinion, why then raise the question of a missing center? The subject, each and every subject, is a center and a source. A speech event is always performed by an individual in context. But the subject is not himself ontologically stable or safe: such at this moment, at another time different, he is not amenable to totalization. The subject is nothing but the sequence—without a last word other than the latest utterance—of his own discourse, appearances, and *personae*, with no vanishing point to hold them together. On such a stage there is neither a homogeneous perspective nor a unique Mallarméan Hamlet standing by himself; there are only attendants.

Self-portrayal is the discourse of attendants. Nowhere is this more evident than in the text where Nietzsche's claim to self-divination forces him to refer to the great protagonists of Western culture, Socrates and Christ. The self-portrait cannot escape the realization that, if the philosophy and theology incarnate in Socrates and Jesus cease to underwrite ontology and history, then there are only attendants left on the stage of the world. The surviving protagonists now are impersonal entities, collective constructs such as ideology, myths, and culture. Whence the attendant self-portraitist's discovery that insofar as individual discourse resists the illusion of transcendent coverage by it, Truth is proscribed to a neutral limbo.

Has the neutral, as Roger Laportes claims, been a dimension of thinking barely explored from Heraclitus to Maurice Blanchot but one that "will someday lead to an entirely new way of answering the question "what is thinking?" ("Le Oui, le non, le neutre," 590). While it is audacious to make Heraclitus the first thinker to have "thought neutrally," there is little doubt as to the intent of such an attribution: along with Heidegger, Heraclitus has been turned into the very symbol of a philosophy that seeks salvation through its own scuttling. Heraclitus has supplanted Socrates as *the* philosopher, because, in Heraclitus' fragments, the reader rediscovers the *cheerless obscurity* of a philosophy yearning for poetry and infused with rhetoric. However, it would be more plausible to attribute the neutrality of thinking, together with all its radical consequences, to those who, having forgone obscurity (even prestigiously Sybilline obscurity) and cheerless truth, embraced the joyful clarity of unknowing—the Sophists.[1] According to Plato's *Gorgias*, the purview of the rhetorician is the probable, as it is perceived by the senses and structured by the two mothers of error, *phantasia* and *mimesis*. And the sophistic approach draws meaning from the pragmatism and the will to power brought to bear upon the world and imposed on the city. Now Leiris constantly questions himself about efficaciousness, about *commitment;* he keeps wishing to turn his private and playful discourse into revolutionary violence, into political mastery. He would like to know what he wants, or to want what he thinks he knows, and impose it on others. He often proclaims political opinions that are hostile to his own way of life and socioeconomic status and are even more inimical to his idle mode of writing. Yet he persists in writing a self-portrait that uses up his philosophical and political fantasies. These wishes are fictionalized, dramatized as they turn into operatic arias, while the writing itself, attentive to its music, to its own dialectic and places, marks time. Here the sophistry of the probable becomes a prolonged uncertainty, a display of impotence, a dialectic with no exit. But such already was the case with Montaigne's *Essays*, since the "domestic and private" intent of that work ignored most of the author's actions and frustrations in the field of politics. It has been said of sixteenth-century authors of memoirs (diplomats, politicians, soldiers) that they "sketched in a minor key what Montaigne set out to do in a masterly manner" and that they did so because, in those disastrous times, "the self, whose interiority battens on the corpse of a political and social machinery that has been subjected to all kinds of mutations and cataclysms, constitutes the elementary unit of knowledge in a world whose collective structures are constantly being called in question" (Dubois, *La Conception de l'histoire en France au XVIe siècle,* 168). Thus, self-portrayal is linked to political, military, or diplomatic practice by a complementarity, and also by an opposition that is transcended by their recourse to the devices of persuasion.

The self-portraitist cannot fail to recognize that he is a variant of the man of action, nor that the text that produces and undermines his self is a microcosm of the very social forces from which he withdraws in order to write. Instead of setting his subjective truth against the lies of the world, he recognizes that rhetorical sophistry operates in the contradictions of the written self as it does in the intractable violence of society.

Jules Vuillemin is a philosopher who has chosen a position of methodological exile amid the impersonal rigor of the logic and mathematics, as well as the author of a self-portrait that is a reflection on theatricality and eloquence, on the rectitude of language, the maladies of the word, and of silence. He listens to "contrary voices" within himself: "I can, anyone can create for myself a violent and unified self, but, when I listen, the unity demanded in the name of the law is no longer there" (107). Conscience is a forum that is tumultuous, divided, foreign to the general will and divine right, a forum on which only an arbitrary violence could impose unity.

The self-portraitist, in his own text, is a man of retirement, of peaceful meditation, even if he has merely shut his door against the uproar of the city. He seeks his own seat, he wishes to survey the premises and leaf through his picture album in order to find himself. But he soon finds out that there is no way back and that the old home has been torn down. There is no Grail for his quest, nor any quarry for his hunt. Unlike the Sophist's, his eloquence is for the most part without effect, except to exhibit itself as such, to become an end in itself, and to cultivate its own opaqueness; it exercises its violence against the person the writer imagines himself to be. To know oneself is to know the means of knowing oneself, and even more those with which one can *efface oneself* beyond eloquence: eloquence has retreated from the self-portraitist who is a Sophist in retirement, a man of the world who has given up worldly affairs and has no world except the book, his universe-catafalque. Thus, in the name of all self-portraitists, Vuillemin can write: "I searched myself badly. I saw the games of language coming apart, and I forgot them so as to seek the cause of their decomposition within myself" (77). For the end of that writing machine is also the death of the subject.

This is why these peculiar rhetors must meditate on the deaths of Socrates and Christ. But their Socrates and their Jesus differ from those whom philosophy and theology have turned into *the* philosopher and into Christ Pantocrator. They are not champions of dialectic nor the scourge of the Sophists and the Doctors of Law, but rather the victims of their own eloquence, orators whose rhetoric falters; powerless to persuade assemblies, their former victories sentence them to death. The Resurrection of the One and the metempsychosis of the other have not yet become accomplished facts. If the self-portraitist measures himself against Socrates and Christ—or if he contrasts himself with both of them, as Nietzsche does—he must become the artisan of his own resurrection and of an anamnesis much more radical indeed than that of autobiographers. He has no other hope, no other place than his text.

Autobiographers and memorialists want to be remembered for the life they have led, for the greater or lesser deeds of which they tell. The memorialist is first of all, *somebody*, someone of importance who recalls his part in certain affairs. The self-portraitist on the other hand, is nothing but his text: he will survive through it, or not at all. He is, above all, a writer, and only a writer. Malraux differs from other self-portraitists discussed here in that he has a "biography" to some extent separate from what he wrote. But a biography of Montaigne's adult life would essentially be a transformation of the *Essays* into a narrative.[2] It is difficult to imagine that this would not also be the case with Leiris, Borel, Laporte, or Barthes, who are all, in a strict and entirely nonpejorative sense, men of letters, and whose self-portraits are free-standing texts rather than a mimesis of past deeds. Cardano, Nietzsche, Vuillemin, or Barthes have, respectively, become something other than a physician, a pamphleteering philologist, a logician, or a "structuralist" as a result of their writing self-portraits that call into question their status as subjects who have also produced other books, of which their self-portraits are either a palinode or a hyperbolic panegyric. Such praise or blame is manifestly rhetorical: it hollows out the eponymous center so as to restore it to the culture from which it wanted to "set itself apart"; and, in this process, the center is scattered in the dictionary, dispersed in the encyclopedia. What remains after self-portrayal is not the physician, the philosopher or the semiotician, but rather the staging—each time different, displaced, and to some degree unforeseeable, but always immediately recognizable—

of some major places in an impersonal, transhistoric, and anonymous topical system. No longer a mere *theatrum mundi*, a mnemonic or alchemical theater, but on the contrary, the very drama of writing, a passion of the logos, a rhetorical opera.

Are we then talking of writing and of a *cogito* radically different from those to which we have become accustomed over the past two or three centuries? Undoubtedly, if the dominant mode of writing is made up of mimetic narratives, of narratives always based at once on two fallacious arguments, namely *post hoc, ergo propter hoc* and *the interior is the anterior*. If epics, dramas, novels, and elegiac poetry such as Wordsworth's *Prelude* and Lamartine's *Poetic Meditations* stubbornly remain our primary literary models, then, yes, of course, self-portrayal is *something entirely different*, despite first appearances and the reemergence of narrative within it, precisely because the self-portrait is based both on a different relation to writing and on a spatialization that deploys the interior as well as the anterior in a topical exteriority. As Blanchot says:

Someone is still present when there is no longer anyone. When I am alone, I am not there, nobody is there. But the impersonal is there: the outside that prevents, precedes and dissolves any possibility of a personal relationship. Someone is the faceless He, the one of which one is a part . . .

And further on:

In this region that we try to approach, here has collapsed into nowhere; and yet nowhere is here, and dead time is real time in which death is present, comes but keeps on coming as if, by coming, it would sterilize the time for which it can come. The dead present is the impossibility of realizing a presence, an impossibility that is present, that is there as the double of the present, that the present carries and conceals within itself. (*L'Espace littéraire*, 22)

That shadow—is it death or rhetoric? Or both at once? For rhetoric is what robs "presence" of its presence. It precedes, encompasses, and invests the subject; and self-portrayal records that dispossession. It is not a stage in a historical dialectic towards "more consciousness" that turns into a knowledge of the unconscious, which estranges the subject from himself. Instead, in a calmer and more essential way, it is the other possibility, the one that scoffs both at progress and at those who disparage progress; at the in-

crease of liberty and at those who contemn it; at growing enlightenment and its deconstructors. Self-portraits are always short of
and beyond what is now "being thought" by the majority, in the
midst of the city and of history: on the contrary, they embody the
absence of time, or, more properly, an interval of time, the mimesis
of an interspace, of a loss-awakening; and also of a corpus-body
henceforth present-absent in its hypogeum:

This is the time of the body that awakens, that is still new, neuter, un-
touched by remembrance, by signification. Here there appears the Adamic
dream of a total body, the dream marked by Kierkegaard's cry at the dawn
of modernity: Give me a body! The division of being into a body, a soul, a
heart and a spirit is the basis of the "person" and of the negative language
that attaches to it: the total and impersonal body. ("Drame, poème, roman")

Let us turn around Barthes's sentences and reverse their sequence: the awakening of self-portrayal to the impersonal entails
an *examination* of a topical system: body, soul, spirit, faculties,
memory, and invention, and it must erode the topics by its "negative language," as it erases the predicates and journeys through
places towards the impersonal—that was already Saint Augustine's undertaking at the dawn of the Christian era. Such an undertaking now abuts against nothing; it gets no answer and no
guarantee from God.

A paradox defines the self-portraitist: he has no interest in himself, at least not any longer, or, more properly, he is too essentially
interested in himself to waste much time on describing the space
within, or defining his own personality, or characterizing the individual. Rhetoric provides him with the means to transcend all
this. Ever since Saint Augustine swept beyond *memoria sui* towards
another Memory, the self-portraitist has been drawn through the
within towards a *Without*. And the body he inscribes no longer is
the mortal, voluptuous, suffering body perceived in coenesthesia.
It is an impersonal body, that is to say, either a cultural body, a
corpus of impersonal places, or the promise, the illusion of *hoc est
enim*, and of *Ecce Homo*.

Self-portrayal is writing on the outside and from a Without that
dispossesses the "inside" and yet does not settle down to a position
of mastery; self-portrayal generalizes exteriority, impotence, and
anxiety, because it proves to be a strangely mystical kind of writ-

ing, a writing of religious preoccupation and composure. Self-portraitists are the peculiar anchorites of modernity and their sophistic meditation, the last avatar of Western ascesis, is the way of those who, having lost old beliefs without adopting a new faith, persist in travelling the *via negativa*, while resisting any certitude about the world and the subject. In contrast with the Oriental yoga of emptiness, the self-portrait proclaims the dispersal of topics, the absence of a center, and nobody's text.

Notes

Introduction

1. In *Le Pacte autobiographique*, Lejeune's definition was extensively qualified. Complete citations for the works referred to in the text and notes can be found in the bibliography at the end of this volume.
2. English original in *Columbia Forum* XI, 4, 1968.
3. Antonin Artaud, "Correspondance avec Jacques Rivière."
4. In relation to the temptation and ultimate impossibility of attributing substantial predicates to oneself, Marcel Raymond very aptly mentions that "language still bears the imprint of a (in a medieval sense) 'realistic' philosophy." And he cites a passage from Stendhal's *Henry Brulard* where that author dismisses allegorizable predicates: "I don't know what I am: good, bad, witty, stupid. What I know perfectly are the things that cause me pain or pleasure, which I desire or hate" ("J.-J. Rousseau et le problème de la connaissance de soi").
5. Stupidity (*bêtise*) is taken in the sense of *cant*, Podsnappery, as in Baudelaire, Flaubert, Barthes, and in that of *nonsense* (*ineptie*) as in Montaigne (I, VIII).
6. Even in the case of *Roland Barthes by Roland Barthes*, as we shall see.
7. Roger Laporte, *Fugue*, and its continuation both under diverse titles and with a number of publishers collected under the general title *Une Vie, biographie.* Jean Thibaudeau, "Le Roman comme autobiographie."
8. Jacques Borel, *Le Retour;* "Narcisse écrit-il?"; *Un Voyage ordinaire, caprice.*
9. Although the checkered reputation of the novel was, of course, bound up with imputations of futility or worse.
10. However, it must be understood that, by becoming Antichrist, Antisocrates, or Dionysus, Nietzsche does not elude the model of the *Imitatio*

Christi, of the spiritual exercise and religious meditation, where the subject is supposed to put himself, by means of imagination, in the place of Christ Crucified.

11. Alexander Piatigorsky, the Indianist-semiotician, suggests that the conditions for the possibility of this substitution—as in the formula "If I were you, I . . ."—are cultural: they imply a nonconscious distinction between one *person* and another person (the *person* concept, per se, being culturally determined) and between one *situation* and another situation. Data inseparable from theology, at least form an implicit theology. Those conditions, according to Piatogorsky, are not encountered, for example, in the Buddhist culture, which is dominated by the notion of *karma* (Alexander Piatigorsky, "If I Were You: A Few Remarks about Cultural Understanding").

12. A seminal analysis of "the spatial form in modern literature" is found in Joseph Frank's *The Widening Gyre*, 3–62. Discussions of space in literature can be traced back to Lessing's *Laocöon*.

13. The pictorial metaphor is taken up again, at the beginning of I, 28, 135, "Of Friendship," to designate the text of the *Essays* as "grotesque and monstrous bodies, pieced together of divers members, without definite shape, having no order, sequence, or proportion other than accidental," framing a void, the absence of "rich, polished pictures, formed according to art," a gap in which the text of the Other, by turns *Contr'un* (*Against-One*) and "29 Sonnets by Etienne de la Boétie," texts cast according to rhetorical finalities and/or the art which the *Essays* transgress, would become embedded.

14. This essay by Sollers is a variant of Michel Foucault's study on Blanchot: "La Pensée du dehors," a text where Foucault opposed the *cogito* of "I think" to that of "I speak," the latter leading to an outside where the speaking subject disappears (525).

15. Therefore the cited article by Foucault, despite its remarkable intuitions, seems built on sand, for Foucault, while challenging philosophic discourse from inside philosophy, ignores rhetoric in its positivity and the latter's serious grievance against philosophy.

16. During that "classic" period, self-portrayal gives way either to religious meditation (that of Malebranche for example) or to the "scientific" project (that of La Bruyère) of describing "characters" in the manner of Theophrastus. In both cases, the *method* itself is not contested. But, as concerns Descartes and his *cogito*, Jean-Luc Nancy's analyses tend to show that the chosen method of presentation (*Discourse, Meditation,* and—one would add—*Treatise on Passions*) pulls the philosophical approach towards the self-portrait.

17. About which Leiris says he knows nothing, and which Lejeune discusses in *L'Autobiographie en France*, only to dismiss them from his corpus.

18. Jules Vuillemin, *Le Miroir de Venise;* Jean Roudaut, *Trois Villes orientées*.

19. Thus, in *Roland Barthes by Roland Barthes*, the description of the childhood house and gardens:

> The worldly, the domestic, the wild: is this not the very tripartition of social desire? It is anything but surprising that I turn from this Bayonnaise garden to the fictive, utopian solaces of Jules Verne and Fourier.

That mythology is (of necessity) followed by this remark:

> (The house is gone now, swept away by the housing projects of Bayonne.) (8)

And, in Jacques Borel, whose *Le Retour* is a vast self-portrait constructed and contested by means of an itemized inventory of the childhood house, of the *dwelling-place:* "that other house over there, which no longer existed" (20).

20. In Barthes, again, this typical observation:

> The text can recount nothing; it takes my body elsewhere, far from my imaginary person, toward a kind of memoryless speech which is already the speech of the People, of the non-subjective mass (or of the generalized subject), even if I am still separated from it by my way of writing. (4)

And, with Malraux, who has no childhood or autobiography, in the meditation that is central to *Lazare:*

> Images do not make up a life story; nor do events. It is the narrative illusion, the biographical work, that creates the life story. (74)

> Images, not events, unless I search for them. A consciousness without memory. (76)

> An "I" without a self; a life without an identity. The madman assumes one. (84)

21. Barthes writes: "And to speak about oneself by saying 'he' can mean: *I am speaking about myself as though I were more or less dead*" (*Roland Barthes by Roland Barthes*). And, identifying himself obliquely with language, by means of that same "he"—"He sees language in the figure of an exhausted old woman . . . who sighs for a certain *retirement*" (177)—Barthes also imagines "a fiction based on the notion of an urban Robinson Crusoe" (173).

22. See, for example, Jacques Borel's *Le Retour* (348–54): "taking it all in all, panic meditation will have become your specialty, as have, for others, the detective novel, archaeology or linguistics" (359). One may note that the self-portrait combines all those specialties . . .

1. Self-Portrait and Encyclopedia

1. Regardless of the semiotic code (be it humoral, astrological, physiognomic, characterological, psychoanalytical, etc.) implemented in the

description. Clearly, such a portrait can be inserted in a biography, but then it is subordinated to the dominant narrative.

2. Montaigne had already said, "Ce sont icy mes fantaisies; par lesquelles je me tasche point à donner à connoistre les choses, mais moy: elles me seront à l'aventure connuez un jour, ou l'ont autresfois esté, selon que la fortune m'a peu porter sur les lieux où elles estoient esclaircies. Mais il ne m'en souvient plus" (*Essais*, II, X, 387). ("These are my fancies, by which I try to give knowledge not of things, but of myself. The things will perhaps be known to me some day, or have been once, according as fortune may have brought me to the places where they were made clear. But I no longer remember them" [*Essays*, 296].)

3. In an essay on imagination in the post-Romantic period, Jean Starobinski arrived, via a different route, at a similar conclusion. Except that, for the self-portraitist and particularly for Leiris, the retreat into the inner microcosmic space is not separate from a desire to inscribe therein the "great magical realism" of the macrocosm. Whence the ambiguity of the narcissicism at work in self-portrayal:

> For want of being able to open up to imagination the space of the universe, for want of being able to sustain the ambition of a great magical realism, one falls back on internal space, one translates cosmic dreams into intimate dreams, and engulfs oneself in idealistic secession. To imagine is to no longer participate in the world; it is to haunt one's own image under the infinitely variable appearances it can assume. To symbolism, the imaginary is bound up with the Narcissus myth. It is not by accident that the beginning of this century witnessed the definition of the term introversion: *die Rückbiegung der Libido auf die Phantasie* (C. G. Jung, *Psychologische Typen*, Zurich, 1921). ("Jalons pour une histoire du concept d'imagination," 188–89)

4. See Sister Ritamary Bradley, "Backgrounds of the Title *Speculum* in Medieval Literature."

5. Regarding the opposition between *speculum* and allegorical narrative, see James I. Wimsatt, *Allegory and Mirror: Tradition and Structure in Middle English Literature*.

6. Angus Fletcher singles out two major types of allegorical narratives: "psychomachy" and "progress." Both of these types are teleological, "battles for, and journeys toward, the final liberation of the hero" (*Allegory*, 22).

7. Regarding the structure of the *specula*, see Maurice de Gandillac et al., *La Pensée encyclopédique au Moyen Age*. See especially, J. Gründel's study on "L'Oeuvre encyclopédique de Raoul Ardent: *Le Speculum universale*." This mirror is essentially ethical and "psychological."

8. From antiquity on, the divisions of virtues and vices are intrinsically bound to rhetorical invention. One can go back to Aristotle's *Rhetoric* and *Ethics* for the definition of virtues such as munificence-magnificence (*Rhet.*, 1.9). Cicero's *De Inventione* is the *locus classicus* for the definition of cardinal virtues such as Fortitude, which comprises *Mag-*

nificentia, Fidentia, Patientia, and *Perseverantia (De Inventione,* II, LIII, 160–LIV, 165). On the relations of ethics to psychology, in medieval treatises, see Dom O. Lottin's *Psychologie et morale aux XIIe et XIIIe siècles;* the divisions of virtues and vices, with instances of their overlap in medieval treatises, are the subject of a masterly study in chapter 2, "Allegories of Vices and Virtues," of Rosemond Tuve's *Allegorical Imagery.* See, likewise, the list of virtues and their subdivisions in Cicero, Macrobius, Guillaume de Conches, and Alain de Lille, as drawn up in an appendix to Tuve's book, which demonstrates that the tradition of vices and virtues, whose taxonomy is central to medieval thought, was not forgotten as late as the sixteenth century.

9. The analysis followed here in that of Wimsatt *(Allegory and Mirror,* 137–39). One should note that John Gower is also the author of a thirty-thousand-line French poem entitled *Speculum Meditantis* or *Mirour de l'omme,* describing the seven virtues and vices in their struggle to possess man and ending with a paraphrase of the Gospel narrative. *Man* and *meditant* have interchangeable roles in this work, where the *mirror* and the *meditation* on Jesus Christ's terrestrial life remain intrinsically mixed up. Still the book deals with mankind in general and the divine plan rather than with an empirical individual.

10. On can imagine the latter presented in a *Miroir de l'amour* of which we are given some idea through André le Chapelain's *De Arte Honeste Amandi,* even if this celebrated work is a practical handbook and presents itself as a series of dialogues the topics of which are furnished, by the social inequalities between the lover and the woman to whom he pays court, rather than by *generic concepts.*

11. See Morton W. Bloomfield, *The Seven Deadly Sins.*

12. E. R. Curtius, then, did not miss the mark in his study of "the mirror metaphor", when he placed it in the chapter devoted to "the book as symbol" (ch. 16) in *European Literature and the Latin Middle Ages.*

13. Emile Mâle, *L'Art religieux du XIIIe siècle en France.* Mâle adopted the divisions of Vincent de Beauvais' *Speculum Maius* to describe and interpret the iconography of Gothic cathedrals. On this subject, one may also read Adolf Katzenellenbogen's *Allegories of Virtues and Vices in Medieval Art* and *The Sculptural Programs of Chartres Cathedral.*

14. The mirror's ambiguity is inscribed on certain cases fashioned during the Renaissance: *Inspice, cautus eris* (see H. Schwarz, "The Mirror in Art"). One should stress how inseparably rhetorical tradition is bound up with the mirror's allegorical function in Renaissance painting: virtues (Prudence, for example) and vices (like Luxuria and, as represented in Bosch's *The Seven Capital Sins* at the Escorial, Superbia, beholds herself in a mirror held by the devil) are privileged places of Invention. It should also be noted that Prudence, the virtue whose allegorical representation comports a mirror, is itself subdivided into three parts—memory, intelligence, and foresight—and these appear,

each with the face of a man of a different age, in Titian's celebrated allegory. But Memory—at least, as *art*—is one of the parts of rhetoric, one of whose major devices, as we shall see later, is allegorization. So, it seems that, in their rhetorical context, all three—mirror, allegory, and virtues—belong to a vast semiotic system whose host of cross-references, substitutions, and developments are available, and have been passed on, to the modern self-portrait as rhetorical mirror.

15. See Montaigne: "N'est-ce pas une sotte humeur de disconvenir avec un millier à qui ma fortune me joint, de qui je ne me puis passer, pour me tenir à un ou deux (La Boétie, Socrate . . .), qui sont hors de mon commerce, ou plustot à un désir fantastique de chose que je ne puis recouvrer" (*Essais*, III, III, 798). ("Is it not a stupid humor of mine to be out of tune with a thousand to whom I am joined by fortune, whom I cannot do without, only to cling to one or two (La Boétie, Socrate . . .), who are not associated with me, or rather to a fantastic desire for something I cannot recapture?" [*Essays*, 622].)

16. As with Montaigne, this can be reversed into the paradox of a "person without a memory."

17. On the same page, Malraux writes: "And what is a past that is not a biography? An awareness deeper than consciousness that one exists, and that I do not consider knowledge?" And also: "It is not life's balance sheet any more than the dizzying memories of drowning that I encounter."

18. But the self-portraitist seems the more tempted to pose a final transcendental word as he is anxious to escape from the snares of totalizations: Barthes' self-portrait ends with the word *totality*, supposedly written, for that matter, the very day the book was begun . . . This irony—for it is obviously a question of irony—cuts both ways, since it marks the limits of the wild polygraphy and the antistructure invoked in other connections. Yet it is a double irony: for, whereas the word *totality* is the final word in the book entitled *Roland Barthes by Roland Barthes*, it neither is, as already indicated earlier, nor can it be the last word of Roland Barthes's self-portrait, which continues beyond the book. Montaigne, for his part, commits himself to dispersion: "A qui n'a dressé en gros sa vie à une certaine fin, il est impossible de disposer les actions particulières. Il est impossible de renger les pièces, à qui n'a une forme du total en sa teste. A quoy faire la provision des couleurs, à qui ne sçait ce qu'il a à peindre? Aucun ne fait certain dessain de sa vie, et n'en deliberons qu'a parcelles" (*Essais*, II, I, "De l'inconstance de nos actions, 320). ("A man who has not directed his life as a whole toward a definite goal cannot possibly set his particular actions in order. A man who does not have a picture of the whole in his head cannot possibly arrange the pieces. What good does it do a man to lay in a supply of paints if he does not know what he is to paint? No one makes

a definite plan of his life; we think about it only piecemeal" [*Essais*, II, I, 243].)

19. The *in figura* portrait represents the subject with attributes of a personage (deity, saint, mythical or historical hero) to which he is likened. During the Renaissance, the pictorial portrait obliquely transgresses the interdiction that weighs on self-representation: one of the procedures implemented for this purpose is the *in-figura* self-portrait of a painter applying his own traits to a personage—usually one of the apostles—in a religious scene. Most frequently it is the *figura* of Saint Luke, patron of painters and, according to legend, the Virgin's portrayer. This mode of representation takes an odd turn, one that might appear as sacrilegious, as in Dürer's portrait of himself as Christ Mocked; it pushes to the limit the *imitatio Christi* and its efforts to imagine, and empathize with, the suffering of the Passion, an effort likewise made by the meditator in the diverse Renaissance meditation systems leading up to Loyola's *Exercises*. In his "Dürer and Luther as the Man of Sorrows," Roland Bainton reminds us of the Lutheran milieu's fondness for picturing itself as participating in a perpetual Passion play where everyone could assume the role of Jesus Christ: it is in such an *in figura* representation system that the deictic ambiguity of ostension in the *Ecce Homo* formula—which Nietzsche took up in his self-portrait—is played out to the full.

2. The Evolution of Meditation

1. Gusdorf holds up Maurice de Guérin and Leo Tolstoy as examples.
2. This analysis seems confirmed, from another viewpoint, by Kenneth Burke's commentary on Book X of the *Confessions*. Thus: "the contrast between the first nine books and the last four is clear, and clearly involves the distinction between 'rectilinear' and 'circular' terminology . . . The turn from a *narrative of memories* to the *principles of Memory* is itself a technical or 'logological' equivalent of a turn from 'time' to 'eternity' " (*The Rhetoric of Religion: Studies in Logology*, 124).
3. See Pierre Blanchard, "L'Espace intérieur chez saint Augustin d'après le livre X des *Confessions*," where the author compares Augustinian description to mystical psychology's descriptions.
4. In X, V, Augustine formulates a correlation between the obscureness of his knowledge of God and the lacunae of his self-knowledge "*at present I am looking at a confused reflection in a mirror*, not yet *face to face*" (I Cor. 13:12). As long as Augustine is on earth (citing II Cor. 5:6), God cannot be as *present* unto him as he is unto himself, nor is Augustine entirely present unto himself. Even so, faith already bestows on Augustine a better *knowledge* of God than of himself.
5. This refers to the structure of Book X and its relation to the rest of the

work, rather than to the topical influence of the narrative part of the *Confessions* on other confessions and autobiographies, which was studied by Pierre Courcelle in *Les Confessions de saint Augustin dans la tradition littéraire.*

6. See Geneviève Lewis, "Saint Augustin et l'inconscient," *Le Problème de l'inconscient et le Cartésianisme*, (24–33):

> Saint Augustine knows too well the complexity of his own soul to reduce it to the successive series of states of consciousness that parade past the inner gaze. In order to resolve the delicate point of the soul's ability to be to a certain extent outside its field of vision but yet not outside itself, which would be contradictory to its own inwardness, he causes the *memoria sui* to intervene. After all those precautions, the "mysterious retreats" or "secret sinuosities of memory's hidden palaces" . . . must not be interpreted as hypostasizing an inaccessible unconscious: the philosopher uses a language of vivid imagery to translate the permanence of a living reality, to whose underlying presence 'an efficacious action testifies' (E. Gilson): the gushing flow reveals the spring, even if its babble is barely audible.

Etienne Gilson, in his *Introduction à l'étude de saint Augustin*, asserts that the "unconscious" or the "subconscious," terms that translate *memoria*, ought to be capable of stretching to mean "the metaphysical presence unto the soul of a reality that would be distinct from it and transcendent, such as God."

7. Joseph Trabucco's French translation of the *Confessions* lists the numerous passages of Augustine's works that deal with memory (369, n. 596), in particular *De Trinitate*, Books IV and X. For Aristotle's pervasive conception of memory see Richard Sorabji, *Aristotle on Memory*.
8. See Harry Caplan, "Memoria: Treasure-House of Eloquence."
9. In turn, this metaphor, as Harry Caplan points out in "Memoria: Treasure-House of Eloquence," is inscribed in a paradigm of images that all share *container* as a sememe.

> Most common is the metaphor best phrased by Quintilian—memory, treasure-house (*thesaurus*) of eloquence—storehouse of the ideas supplied by invention, or chest, mine, magazine, vessel, cask. Thomas Fuller's comparison of memory to a purse belongs in this class. St. Augustine, St. Ambrose, and others in the Middle Ages call memory *venter animi* (or *mentis*, "belly of the mind"). (215–16).

In a footnote, Caplan also cites Montaigne: I, 9, "Des menteurs": "magasin" (Of Liars: Store); II, 17, "De la présomption": "Réceptacle et l'estuy de la science" (Of Presumption: Receptacle and Case of Science). It should be noted that *venter animi* (or *mentis*) designates the belly as a container and the spirit or soul as a receptacle for the stomach, which, in turn, becomes the contents. Christian *meditation* chews on Scripture as a spiritual food: "To meditate is but to masticate . . . One must take the meat that nourishes the soul, one must chew it, that is to say, meditate upon it so that, in a short while, one may swallow it and convert it into oneself." (*Oeuvres complètes de saint François de Sales*, Annecy Edition, 9:359).

10. Francis Bacon, *Advancement of Learning*: "The invention of speech or argument is not properly an invention, for to *invent* is to discover that we know not, and not to recover or resummon that which we already know: and the use of this invention is no other but out of the knowledge whereof our mind is already possessed to draw forth or call before us that which may be pertinent to the purpose which we take into our consideration. So as to speak truly, it is no invention, but a remembrance or suggestion, with an application" (127).

11. Yet Ricoeur, placing himself in Descartes' posterity, does not take sufficiently into account the fact that an unconscious structuring of the *ego's* discourse according to rhetorical topics can produce the objects, works and acts that are grasped by the *ego* in *reflection:* so, the mirror in question has to be conceived as an encyclopedic *speculum.* Reflection, to the extent that it is a discourse, must pass through commonplaces. Even with Descartes.

12. See Pierre Courcelle's exhaustive book, *Les Confessions de saint Augustin dans la tradition littéraire: Antécédents and postérité.*

13. "This is made especially clear," writes Louis L. Martz, "in one of the great prototypes of the central method of meditation practiced during our period: the *Scala meditationis* of Wessel Gansfort . . .; Gansfort's long treatise, dating from the latter part of the fifteenth century, is filled with references to the logical and rhetorical methods of Aristotle, Cicero, Raymond Lully, Rudolph Agricola, and others; his *Scala* adapts and transforms the methods of these writers for the purposes of interior 'oratory' and debate. And this is true of all meditative treatises: all the ways of speaking and writing that a man has learned will inevitably help to form the thoughts of the 'whole soul' " (*The Poetry of Meditation*, 38–39).

Those interested in a study of the *Exercises*, their background and context, should see H. Watrigant, "La Genèse des *Exercices* de saint Ignace de Loyola"; and also H. Pourrat, *La Spiritualité chrétienne*, 3:19–74. Both these studies pay little attention to the rhetorical matrix.

14. Aristotle, *De Memoria et Reminiscentia*. See R. Sorabji *Aristotle on Memory*, 38–46, 54–57, 93–108.

15. *Zardino de oration* (Venice, 1494), x. II V. X. III R. (cap. XVI, Chome meditare la vita de Christo . . .). Cited by Baxandall, *Painting and Experience in Fifteenth-Century Italy*, 46.

16. For more on the subject, see chapter 3, "Rhetorical Memory."

17. Roland Barthes, suggesting some connections between the *Spiritual Exercises* and rhetoric, also mentioned *topography*, a subdivision of the *energeia* "figure." Leaving out local memory as a part of rhetoric Barthes evoked one aspect of the Aristotelian memory theory: "stating that in

order to remember things one must recognize where they are" (*Sade, Fourier, Loyola*, 61).

18. This is the method also recommended in a spiritual manual, such as the *Zardino de oration*.

19. See also Halbwach's *La Topographie légendaire des Evangiles en Terre sainte*.

20. Fantasy is "an imaginary scenario in which the subject is present and which embodies . . . the fulfillment of a desire" (Laplanche et Pontalis, *Dictionnaire de psychanalyse*, cited by Barthes, *Sade, Fourier, Loyola*, 63, n. 1).

21. A model for this choice can be found in Cicero's *Topica*, XXII, 84–86. This reform, or conversion, is another variant of the death/resurrection or initiatory death topos. Its importance to the self-portrait's economy is traceable as far back as Saint Augustine. The meditation on the house and government of the family is linked to the ethical topics of the *libri locorum* or, even, to the political topics in Bacon's *Essays*, provided that the meditator is an important personage or even a sovereign whose "House" and "Family" are a nation: ethics, "economics," and politics are analogically correlated.

22. On the imagination's status during the Renaissance, see, for example, William Rossky, "Imagination in the English Renaissance: Psychology and Poetics," and Jean Starobinski, "Jalons pour une histoire du concept d'imagination," which provides additional bibliography. See also Graham Castor, *Pléiade Poetics*; I.D. McFarlane, "Montaigne and the concept of the Imagination"; and, for the following period, Elémire Zolla, *Storia del fantasticare*, especially the essay entitled "Il Magistero di Surin et la fantasia francese," 111–36. Imagination, to become an auxiliary of salvation during the Renaissance, was supposed to renounce all that, in general, establishes its worth in the eyes of the moderns, from Romanticism to Sartre's and Lacan's critiques of the imaginary, both of whom reassert the old Christian criticism of imagination from an ontological point of view.

23. See Roland H. Bainton, "Dürer and Luther as the Man of Sorrows."

24. Louis L. Martz has been the first to make this observation in *The Poetry of Meditation*. See also Thomas O. Sloan, "Rhetoric and Meditation: Three Case Studies"; likewise, Jean Rousset, "Monologue et soliloque (1650–1700)."

25. Thomas Wright, *The Passions of the Minde in Generall*, 2nd ed. (London, 1604), 193. Cited by Sloan, "Rhetoric and Meditation," 51.

26. This situation comports *theatrical* elements (see *Hamlet*, for example); it should, however, be considered primarily in the context of the printed book, which is read by a public made up of anonymous, unknown, and scattered individuals.

27. This essay appears in Raymond's *J. -J. Rousseau: La Quête de soi et le rêverie*, 157–85.

28. The relation between this episode of loss of identity through dislocation and the Proustian "awakenings"—particularly the one that opens *A la recherche du temps perdu*—have been noted time and again. Yet, disorientation, loss of identity, and temporary amnesia—an ensemble that Proust calls *metempsychosis*—should be stressed here. The passage in question has also been compared to another, in the *Essays* ("De l'exercitation," "Of Practice," II, VI), where Montaigne describes his coming to, after having fallen off a horse. In this connection, Pierre Grosclaude points out that "patients recovering consciousness after electroshock therapy say that they have felt similar impressions" ("Le moi, l'instant présent et le sentiment de l'existence"). In *Lazare*, Malraux resorts to an analogous *topos* to link places and images to his pseudo death: "When one loses consciousness after an accident, does one really see one's life again?" (113). The death that this text euphemizes as "awareness of my suspended life" (131) is a literary device around which local meditation and remembrance are structured. Lhermitte relates cases displaying symptoms of "labyrinthine vertigo" analogous to those reported by Malraux: "In these critical moments, for five or six steps at the very most, I continue to feel everything, but nothing is anywhere any more; nor am I anywhere any longer" (41). "Where am I?" is inseparable from "Who am I?" or, rather, from "What is a life?" (130). In all such cases, *who am I?* and *where am I?* are modalities of one and the same question: he who returns to life will attempt to answer it by visiting *places*. As if, to relive his humanity, the risen Christ should repeat the stations of the Cross.

29. Still, in the *Examen* (Examination of the Three Ideological Novels) of *Sous l'oeil des babares* (1888), *Un Homme libre* (1889), *Le Jardin de Bérénice* (1891) that make up *The Cult of the Ego*, Barrès also calls his novels *treatises, monographs, spiritual memoirs* (interrupted by "ejaculations"), and *impassioned ideology*. This terminological vacillation is typical of the self-portraitist's generic hesitation when faced with his own, in his opinion unprecedented, text. One feels tempted to say that *Un Homme libre* is a meditative self-portrait transcoded in the register of a "psychological novel" written in the form of a diary. The Plon-Livre de Poche edition of *Le Culte du moi* (Paris, 1966), contains the *Examen* in an appendix and the 1904 preface to *Un Homme libre*.

30. This question is related to the problem treated by Philippe Lejeune in *Le Pacte autobiographique*. But the two are not identical. In fact, in this much more delicate case, a "pact of the imaginary," which no paralegal formula will ratify, is needed.

31. For example, François Mauriac, who wrote in his introduction to *Commencements d'une vie*, in *Ecrits intimes* (11–14; cited by Lejeune, *L'Autobiographie en France*):

> I remember my amazement at the age of sixteen, when I discovered this staggering statement in Barrès's *Free Man: to feel as much as possible by analyzing

oneself as much as possible. This I did from the age of reason on. A child pretended that he was lonely and misunderstood; this is the most exciting game . . . Perhaps some instinct warns him that this entails much more than a game: it is a preparation, an exercise, for becoming a man of letters.

32. See my "Exemplary Pornography: Barrès, Loyola, and the Novel."
33. A formula ("culture du moi" or "culte du moi") borrowed from the German philosophic and literary tradition. See W. H. Bruford, *The German Tradition of Self-Cultivation: "Bildung" from Humboldt to Thomas Mann.*
34. Although Ernest Lavisse, as a typical secular and republican school-master, was a natural enemy for the young Barrès, these two "masters of exercises" would join forces when the time came to prepare French youth for the revenge against Germany. They believed that Gallic individualism was as dangerous as cosmopolitanism, whether aristo-cratic or "rootless."
35. One may infer from this that there is a relation of complementarity between *Un Homme libre,* Huysmans's *A Rebours* and Flaubert's *Bouvard et Pécuchet,* two novels published only a short time before Barrès's work.
36. In this connection, see my "The Venetian Mirror."
37. In *Miroir de Venise,* Jules Vuillemin writes: "Narcissus contemplates himself in the funereal water" (16).

3. Rhetorical Memory

1. Jean Paulhan, *Les Fleurs de Tarbes ou la Terreur dans les Lettres;* see also my "Jean Paulhan et la Terreur."
2. Yet, in his excellent article "L'Entrepôt biologique et le démon comparateur," published after the writing of this chapter, Massimo Piatelli-Palmarini studies the "specificity of psychological memory and the complex relations connecting models of memory to models of Mind." Unlike other biologists and psychologists, Piatelli-Palmarini rejects the models of computer science and cybernetics (information storage and retrieval) and goes back to the ancient mnemonic model. He in fact asserts that "memory and imagination are indissociable . . . new data are retained and organized through an *overabundance* of data" (107). Piatelli-Palmarini does not, however, have enough knowledge of rhetoric to grasp its paradoxes. Thus, he attributes to Locke the metaphor of memory storage as a storehouse which, according to him, still burdens our research. But his metaphor (memory = treasury of invention, etc.) is probably as ancient as rhetorical mnemonics. In fact, local mnemonics perhaps foreshadowed the notion of the mnemic trace as a *trajectory* or a visit through places. It should be added that rhetorical mnemonics combines the ideas of storage and *trajectory:* for this rea-

son, theoretical writings and rhetorical practice keep on producing fruitful confusions between *invention* and *memory*. The rhetorical model still holds discoveries in store for psychologists.

3. Walter J. Ong, that bold historian of rhetoric, who, with William J. Ivins, Jr., was an important influence on Marshall McLuhan, shares these views.

4. See Elizabeth Einstein, *The Printing Press as an Agent of Change*, 66–71.

5. One should remember the central importance in medieval culture of the encyclopedic *specula* and of Lully's *Great Art*, which Leroi-Gourhan disregards.

6. See, for example, *Ad Herennium*, III, XV, 28. The art of mnemonics is presented in chapters XVI-XXIV of Book III.

7. I am thinking, for example, of Bergsonism and of what we might call the "affective memory dispute," which raged at the beginning of this century, the trace of which can be found in Frédéric Paulhan's book, *La Fonction de la mémoire et le Souvenir affectif*. This dispute is echoed and extended in Georges Gusdorf's *Mémoire et personne*, where the opposition between abstract memory and concrete memory plays an essential role. "Abstract" or deliberately organized memory is an agency that "represses" concrete memory, the sole faculty capable of providing "true" remembrance. The thematics of presence is manifest in Gusdorf's text:

> The remembered world is the same world in which I ordinarily live. I am in, and I am consumed by, the world of my memory, and this world is real. It is not a simple parade of objective images, but a universe where I exist, where I can suffer and rejoice, a place of multiple meanings.

8. Yet, one should note that artificial memory is fully aware of affect and the passions.

9. The principal studies are 1. on classical rhetoric: Harry Caplan, "Memoria: Treasure House of Eloquence" and, also, his preface to *Ad Herennium*, both collected in *Of Eloquence*; 2. on the Middle Ages and Renaissance: Paolo Rossi, *Clavis Universalis*; 3. particularly on the Renaissance and in the perspective of "neo-Platonism" and Hermetic philosophy: Frances A. Yates, *The Art of Memory*. The two classical rhetorics giving the most complete picture of *Memoria* are *Ad Herennium* and Quintilian's *De Institutione Oratoria*.

10. Modern commentaries on these texts can be found in Rossi, *Clavis Universalis*, 8–9; Yates, *Art of Memory*, 31–36; Caplan, *Of Eloquence*, 202–4; and, especially, in the introduction to Richard Sorabji's translation of *De Memoria et Reminiscentia*, in *Aristotle on Memory*.

11. See Cicero, *De oratore*, II, LXXXVI, 351–LXXXVIII, 360; *Ad Herennium* III, XVI, 29–XXIII, 38; Quintilian, *Institutio Oratoria* XV, II, 17–26, 32–33.

12. According to Quintilian, one can also resort to a series of "images" so that the series of "backgrounds" will be an album, a museum, a set of slides etc.

13. See Caplan: "That the scheme is an extension of the topical theory of invention is clear to all who are conversant with ancient rhetoric. The *topos* is a place in the mind, a vein, a mine, where arguments, general and special, are to be found" (*Of Eloquence*, 230). Yet, one wonders whether this is a matter of an extension from one such place to another or, rather, of a spatial structure that is common to both these parts of rhetoric and that, likewise, seems to govern the theory of *disposition*.

14. A portrait of the artist before he became a writer, before he "found" (or lost) himself in writing, as suggested by the paradigm of titles that Butor's portrayal evokes: *Portrait of the Artist as a Young Man* (Joyce), *Portrait of the Artist as a Young Dog* (Dylan Thomas). These titles, of course, imply a pictorial metaphor.

15. See G. L. Hersey, *Pythagorean Palaces: Magic and Architecture in the Italian Renaissance*.

16. This is also Octavio Paz's aim in *The Monkey Grammarian*, where the text turns back upon itself, becomes a double helix, a "spiral of repetitions and reiterations resulting in a negation of writing as a path," and a "system of mirrors that gradually reveals another text" recentered on Hanuman, the monkey grammarian of the Ramayana.

17. This inevitably reminds one of the description of Montaigne's tower and library (*Essais*, XVII, 493, a, III, III, 628–29, b-c), where the same patterns appear, circularity and asymmetry between off-center and center positions ("this is my seat"); inscriptions ("sentences") and wall paintings ("grotesques"); and finally, the fantasy of being a builder which Montaigne realizes in his book but not in stone. With respect to such towers, one thinks of G. Bachelard's remark: "The tower is the work of another century. Without a past, it is nothing. The sheer mockery of a new tower!" (*The Poetics of Space*, 41). For the opposite, one will conjure up the Tower of Babel, at once eternally innovative, incomplete, and very old. The tower Jung built to embody his reveries of the past and dreams of nobility becomes ironically anchored in revolutionary history when the foundations yield up the skeleton of a soldier from the Year VII of the French Revolution. The new tower, then, as long as it is properly dreamt and invented according to the descriptive system for such structures, can acquire almost all the value of an ancient tower.

18. See A. R. Luria, *The Mind of a Mnemonist (A Little Book About a Vast Memory)*.

19. A well-documented summary of the notions of correspondence, analogy, and mystical unity, as elaborated in Romantic circles on the basis

of the phenomenon of synesthesia can be found in Antoine Adam's note to Baudelaire's sonnet, "Correspondences."

20. I am merely alluding to this very complex question, on which the reader should consult two essential and complementary works. The first places greater stress on the connections between rhetorical memory and the universal characteristic: James Knowlson, *Universal Language Schemes in England and France 1600–1800*; the second underscores the relations between "mimological" theories of language and poetics: Gérard Genette, *Mimologiques*, chs. 4, 7, and 8 are especially pertinent here.

21. Paolo Rossi, "La Construzione delli immagini nei trattati di memoria artificiale des Rinascimento"; *Clavis Universalis: Arti Mnemoniche e Logica Combinatoria da Lullo a Leibnitz; Frances A. Yates, The Art of Memory;* Benjamin De Mott, "Comenius and the Real Character in England," "Science versus Mnemonics: Notes on John Ray and on John Wilkins' *Essays towards a Real Character and a Philosophical Language,*" "The Source and Development of John Wilkins' Philosophical Language."

22. Cited by Knowlson, *Universal Language Schemes*, p. 80. It is well known that Urquhart also wrote an admirable English translation of Rabelais.

23. This similarity was noticed by Richard Sorabji, *Aristotle on History*, 23–26, 31–34.

24. Shereshevsky's account treats all four of the above lines, but one is enough for our purpose. See A. R. Luria, *Mind*, 45–48.

25. See I.-J. Gelb, *A Study of Writing*, 24–50

26. It should be noted here that Du Bellay was an orphan at the age of ten. Barthes, like Borel, lost his father in early childhood.

27. This enumeration connects the mnemonic systems of the lost house and the dead Eternal City, as Borel suggests here: "Gazing at these ruins, at these grim, poignant figures of collapse and dissolution, the poet looked less for an imperial vision of a triumphant Rome than, removing them for the vision of the naked earth whence the walls, the palaces, the monuments the city had arisen before becoming earth again: images of origin and permanence" ("Du Bellay," 627). Daniel Russell, in "Du Bellay's Emblematic Vision of Rome," sees in the fifteen obscure "Dream" sonnets a series of *emblems*. A series of emblems also constitutes a mnemonic system designed to fix (and, sometimes, to conceal) a topical system such as the virtues and vices, that is, a *speculum*.

28. Halbwachs views the memory operation as "rediscovering, through reflection, an entire systematic ensemble of linked memories, when one of these surfaces." This is an independent reformulation of Aristotle's associationist thesis. Furthermore, the system for the ensemble is furnished by "social frameworks": language, social institutions (family,

social class, religion), and also by space as it is structured in a given culture. The individual can only remember what his culture allows him to perceive and express, what is unconsciously inscribed in institutions: memory always mediates between the individual and his group. One dreams alone, but one remembers in a social framework: the latter combines what we call "encyclopedia," the topic of invention, and local memory, in the rhetorical sense (*La Mémoire collective*, 166–67).

29. There have been, subsequently, some curious examples to the contrary: in eighteenth-century Spain, Torres Villarroel (see Guy Mercadier, *Diego de Torres Villarroel: Masques et miroirs*), and more recently, in France, Roger Laporte, published their self-portraits as a series of pamphlets.

4. Intratextual Memory

1. Among critics who have studied the status of memory in the *Essays*, are Hugo Friedrich, *Montaigne*, 351; S. John Holyoake, "Montaigne's Attitude Toward Memory"; and Alfred Glauser, *Montaigne paradoxal*, 98–99. To these should be added Michel Charles's "Bibliothèques," a fine essay that overlaps certain observations made here.

2. This judgment can be found in a note on Montaigne's memory, which is a commentary on II, XVII, "Of Presumption."

3. But Roger Laporte's *Fugue* deliberately foregrounds it.

4. For a complementary point of view on *genres* during the Renaissance, see Rosalie Colie's admirable little book: *The Resources of Kind: Genre-Theory in the Renaissance*, especially the third chapter, entitled "Inclusionism: Uncanonical Forms, Mixed Kinds, and *Nova Reperta*."

5. Consequently, Montaigne opposes his "grotesques" to the "picture that is rich, polished and cast with art," such as his friend La Boétie's treatise *Voluntary Bondage* (*Essays*, I, XXVIII).

6. Jacques Derrida reached analogous conclusions with respect to Edmond Jabès's *Book of Questions* and Freud's "magic writing pad." Derrida's analysis spins out the "people of the book" periphrasis glossed by Jabès: "You [the Jew] are the one who writes and is written." The Jew is a *bookman*. With some minor modifications, Derrida's commentary on the *Livre des questions* could apply to Montaigne's *Essays* and to the self-portrait in general:

> The poet is thus indeed the *subject* of the book, its substance and its master, its servant and its theme. And the book is indeed the subject of the poet, the speaking and knowing being who *in* the book writes *on* the book. This movement through which the book, *articulated* by the voice of the poet, is folded and bound to itself, the movement through which the book becomes a subject in itself and for itself, is not critical or speculative reflection, but is first of all, poetry and history. [For in its representation of itself the subject is shattered and opened; this sentence is not in the English translation.] Writing is itself written,

but also ruined, made into an abyss, in its own representation. (*Writing and Difference*, 65)

7. Merleau-Ponty's reading of the *Essays* induces him to use rhetorical metaphors that are quite foreign to his phenomenological approach.

8. Cited by Maurice Nadeau, *Michel Leiris et la quadrature du cercle*, 123–24. For a detailed account of Leiris's procedure in *La Règle du jeu*, see Catherine Maubon, *Michel Leiris au travail*, which reproduces some of the index cards used in the writing of *Fourbis*.

9. In fact, when it comes to "linking up" complex statements, to disseminating signifiers and symbolizing signifieds *in absentia*, there occurs a qualitative leap in the elaboration of the text.

10. *Tableau* can also be interpreted in a *taxonomical* or in a *theatrical* sense.

11. See Jean-Yves Pouilloux, *Lire les Essais de Montaigne*, 13. Pouilloux gets so carried away by his ideological condemnation of "humanism" that he fails to recognize how the latter is indissociable, except for the purposes of analysis, from intratextual memory and the "navel reading" process. This seems to me confirmed by the fact that *Fugue*, which reduces the humanist content to its simplest expression, can still induce a "navel reading," provided the reader is himself, to some degree, a writer. The elimination of humanist *contents* is not sufficient to expel humanism from such a project, where one indeed sees it perpetuating itself, if only negatively and through certain effects of intertextuality.

5. Archaic Memory

1. See Jean-Pierre Vernant, "Aspects mythiques de la mémoire et du temps."

2. With the important reservation expressed (in c) on the last page of the *Essays:* "and nothing is so hard for me to stomach in the life of Socrates as his ecstasies and possessions by his daemon, nothing is so human in Plato as the qualities for which they say he is called divine" (III, XIII, 856).

3. See Margaret Mann Philipps, *The "Adages" of Erasmus: A Study with Translations*, 269–96.

4. Montaigne's Socrates should be compared to the Socrates whom Nietzsche condemns and whose theories on the soul and afterlife are rejected in Malraux's *Lazare*. It should likewise be borne in mind that there is, in the self-portrait, a co-occurrence and opposition between the human Socrates and Jesus the man-God. Cardano is *especially* interested in Socrates' demon, which becomes a figure of his own inspiration. Finally, it is evident that Montaigne achieves poetic enthusiasm only in remembering his friendship with La Boétie, another model of human perfection, and the bearer of the *image* of his friend.

5. This is confirmed by Roland Barthes, who extended his self-portrait with *A Lover's Discourse: Fragments*.

6. On the relations between Plato's eroticized anamnesis and Freudian psychoanalysis, see the careful analyses of Yvon Brès, in *La Psychologie de Platon*, 153–77.

7. One sees why the figure of Socrates is inseparable from inscription of the death of the writer's own body and from its immortalization as a *corpus* in the self-portrait.

8. See Gilbert Lascault, "L'Egypte des égarements."

9. An analogous itinerary is laid out in Jean Roudaut's *Trois villes orientées* (Byzantium, Thessalonica, Venice). Venice (into whose mirror and memory the Mediterranean sinks) becomes, as could be expected, the system of places from which the writer's self-portrait begins to take shape.

10. See Jean Starobinski, "Je hais comme les portes d'Hadès."

11. Aristotle, *Topica*, 142 b, 31.

12. Cited by Derrida in "The Pit and the Pyramid," in *Margins of Philosophy*, 99.

13. The passage from Hegel that follows this commentary adopts the tradition in which Thoth is the Egyptian Hermes, with the reminder that according to Jamblicus: "Since most ancient times, the Egyptian priests have placed their inventions under the name of Hermes."

14. *Phaedrus* 275. Derrida does not, of course, miss this aspect of the question. He makes reference to it in his critique of Freud: "Freud and the Scene of Writing," in *Writing and Difference*, 221. For a full commentary on this passage from the *Phaedrus* and the Greek conception of memory when script was displacing orality, despite philosophy's continued attachment to the oral mode, see: J. A. Notopoulos, "Mnemosyne in Oral Literature" and W. C. Greene, "The Spoken and the Written Word," where a positive view of the Greek response to the presence of the living word balances Derrida's negative interpretation.

15. This is particularly noticeable in *Roland Barthes by Roland Barthes*, where the photographs from the family album show *man*, standing on his four, two, and three feet, as well as the figures of Laius and Jocasta. But these hieroglyphs appear at the beginning of the book, and the writing, soon taking over, corrodes them, puts them into words.

6. *The Places of the Return*

1. "Venice is not only a city and a spectacle. It is the privileged place which, by arousing a world of never experienced sensations and impressions, urges the visitor to collect his thoughts in silence, to see himself such as existence has made him," we are told in the back cover blurb of the book.

2. "Confession, essay, poem where one's sometimes aphoristic thought takes over from remembrance or sensation . . .": Vuillemin's generic

hesitation continues throughout the jacket blurb. The same holds true for Borel, who calls *Un Voyage ordinaire* a "caprice"; this is the volume in which, pursuing his undertaking in *Le Retour*, the author designates himself as the *author*, while preserving the pseudonymic system first set up in *Adoration*.

3. Chapter headings are as follows: 1. The Return; 2. The Façade; 3. The Vestibule; 4. Second Floor Vestibule; 5. The Library, I; 6. The Library, II; 7. The Kitchen; 8. Grandmother Lancennes' Room; 9. The Dining Room; 10. The Lavatory; 11. My Grandmother's Room; 12. The Living Room; 13. The Gallery.

4. The game of cards also suggests other meanings: that of "play" and, more specifically, of an incomplete patience (a card is always missing). And since the kings and queens in the French deck have names taken from the Bible (Judith), history, medieval lore, playing cards also permit integrating into a system the "fascinating" image of Botticelli's *Judith*, evoked among other paintings, several pages further on (14) by Borel, who shares this fascination with Leiris (in whose case—cf. *Manhood*—it concerns Cranach's *Judith*). Playing cards immediately introduce in the self-portrait a series of cultural signs that are readily combined with other symbolic sequences (alchemistic operations, myth episodes, the Zodiac, etc.). One can note here that the rough draft of Rousseau's *Rêveries* was written piecemeal on the backs of twenty-seven playing cards. The playing card (with its imaged face and anonymous back, the face being shown and covered, turned and turned about; the thousand uses that can be made of them, such as revealing secret desires and coding them in intelligible terms) is the richest metaphor of the mnemonic *image* used in the self-portrait.

5. While *Le Retour* unfolds in the Paris-province direction, *Un Voyage ordinaire* organizes its meditation-reverie along the opposite route.

6. Mysteriously, the French call a sordid, messy room *un capharnaüm*. This biblical term, used by Borel here, might be kept in mind.

7. This distance can be made manifest in various ways: either according to the Baudelairian model ("Le Cygne"), by modifications that destroy familiar landmarks, to which the relative stability of the human "heart" is opposed, or, on the contrary, by a stability that scoffs at the brevity of human lives (Vuillemin's Venice, Malraux's museum).

8. Montaigne builds this "promenoir" into the *Essays*. While it signifies his abulia, contrasted with his father's active nature, it also designates the writing in which he surpasses his father while ensuring that he would be known to posterity.

9. For those who read French, it would be advantageous to substitute Jacques Borel's excellent introduction to the *Rêveries*, published in *Commentaires*, for the following pages on Rousseau.

10. But Borel, in *Un Voyage ordinaire*, would write:

Then again, I also tell myself sadly that if, in my study, in my attic, I were to try and renew the experience of this writing-voyage, and no matter what title ever fascinated me as much as this one, *Voyage Around My Room*, in all probability I would be reduced to this simple recourse: to describe. That is in fact what they do, those writers who have "nothing to say" (I should talk: Despite what, now and then, slips out!): they describe. (201)

11. Barthes joins photographic pictures to the description of the now demolished childhood house. Montaigne, Jung, and Vuillemin make important use of the house, but for them it is not the sole system of places. With Borel himself, train travel increasingly replaces the house as his withdrawal into the self becomes more precarious, the writing less Ciceronian, and the self-portraitist's anxiety more acute: with all self-portraitists the *places* of the fragmented text tend to substitute for the referential and imaginary unity of the lost house.

12. Note that Borel quotes Roudaut on Butor to approach the question of Self and Book.

13. The modern encyclopedic versions in C. G. Jung and Gilbert Durand claim to be sciences of the collective unconscious and imagination.

14. Borel's preface to Du Bellay's *Regrets*, a sonnet sequence where the failure to reappropriate the Roman past and the nostalgia for the childhood house prompted by exile mark a limit for the humanist venture which, in Du Bellay, is at odds with a subjectivity exacerbated and anguished by a fleeting present.

15. Montaigne wrote his book only to paint himself and represent his moods and inclinations. He himself confesses to this in the foreword to all the editions:

I paint myself, he says, I am myself the subjectmatter of my book. So it appears when one reads it; for there are very few chapters in which he does not digress to talk about himself, and in some whole chapters he talks about nothing but himself. But, despite having composed his book to paint himself, he had it printed so it would be read. He did, then, want men to look at him and pay attention to him, notwithstanding his saying that it is not reasonable to devote one's leisure to a subject so frivolous and vain. All these words do is condemn him; for, had he believed there was no reason to spend one's time reading his book, he would have been acting against common sense by printing it. Thus, one is obliged to believe that he did not say what he was thinking, or that he did not do what he said. (Malebranche, *Recherche de la vérité, Oeuvres*, vol. 3)

16. Jacques Borel, "Narcisse écrit-il?"; this text was later inserted within the context of *Un voyage ordinaire* and its train trip soliloquy: it has now become part of the anxious metadiscourse of Borel's self-portrait, dislocated into several books.

17. For Michel Leiris there are also two phases to narcissism, that of youth and that of old age:

shutting oneself up in a no longer superficial narcissism (which acts as if in front of a mirror) but in that of Narcissus drowned in his visceral depths (anxious about the internal functioning of his organs and with hardly any vision left for the outside). (*Fourbis*, 235)

18. See my essay "The Venetian Mirror."
19. Alas, the French text puns on *devoir* (*devoir de français*, a French composition; *devoir tour court*, simply a duty). Translation, nemesis of the punning shibboleth, stands guard by the dull canal of common sense.
20. See Pierre Hadot, "Le Mythe de Narcisse et son interprétation par Plotin"; see also Hubert Damisch's "D'un Narcisse l'autre."
21. This chapter covers *Biffures*, 72–127. Narcissus appears on 98–99.
22. After Barrès, Jean Roudaut also suggests this in *Trois villes orientées*, whose section on Venice turns into a self-portrait:

> Other memories, extending beyond those of his life, are active in him [the writer]; he himself becomes his own echo. If he is conscious of the series of repetitions and variations that make up his existence in the world, he knows that this series of event is in itself but the repetition of a vaster series stretching out beyond his life. Therefore, suddenly he is alive to what was experienced eight centuries ago and now runs through him. (139)

23. See Aniela Jaffé's introduction. (But does not the same hold true for an inestimable part of Montaigne's oeuvre?)
24. Jean Roudaut confirms this in relation to Venice, a mirror-and-text city:

> He [the writer] paces through the labyrinth of an impersonal memory. Like a long fragmented poem, whose moments are separated by passages (a poem he must put down to understand the words addressed to whom other than himself?), the streets deploy their stanzas, monuments to a graphism other than words, as mysterious as the archaic inscriptions on the temple pediments, the broken sentences on scattered stones, the whorled words above the heads of patriarchs (the memory is also a discourse to himself . . . He can only circulate in spirals through the town. And what he does in one town is what he does from town to town, whirling unceasingly in the maelstrom of his life, without discovering anything at all worthy of settling down for. (*Trois villes orientées*, 187)

25. Here Vuillemin effects a metonymic shift founded on the metaphorical structure of his own body and house within a paradigm of *containers* of the Self. One will also note that Vuillemin uses a system of places (Lorraine, Venice, Paris) which is Barrès's in *Un Homme libre*: Lorraine, a void and ancestral place, is contrasted with Venice, as the opposition between the Church Militant and the Church Triumphant, whereas Paris is the place for the profane activity of barbarians. But the values are reversed: the *cult* becomes a contempt for the Self.
26. See Jules Vuillemin, *Essai sur la signification de la mort*.

7. Compilations and the Essay during the Renaissance

1. Cited by Gusdorf, *La Découverte de soi*, 53–54.
2. Roland Barthes, cited by Claude Jannoud, from an interview taken when Barthes was completing *Roland Barthes by Roland Barthes*. *Le Figaro*, 27 July 1974, reproduced in Roland Barthes, *Le Grain de la voix: Entretiens*, 183.
3. For further information see, by the same author, *Les Sources et l'Evolution des Essais de Montaigne*.
4. The conflict between Wisdom and Eloquence (or between Philosophy and Rhetoric) and humanism's preference for eloquence are studied by Jerrold E. Seigel in *Rhetoric and Philosophy in Renaissance Humanism*, Eugenio Garin has analyzed the relations between rhetoric and politics in Renaissance Italy, in "Réflexions sur la rhétorique" in *Moyen Age et Renaissance*, 101–19; and also in *Italian Humanism: Philosophy and Civic Life in the Renaissance*. On education in general during the Renaissance, see by the same author *L'Education de l'homme moderne*, 157–69, which covers education in France, particularly at the Collège de Guyenne. One can also consult Paul Porteau's book, *Montaigne et la vie pédagogique de son temps*. The relations between rhetorical invention and the imagination of the sixteenth century is treated in detail in Graham Castor's *Pléiade Poetics*, with numerous references to Montaigne's *Essays*. The most knowledgeable work on the essential question of the *commonplaces* of invention is Joan Marie Lechner's *Renaissance Concepts of the Commonplaces*, from which we have borrowed many elements of our argument. A dense but clear presentation of the dialectic of invention, as related to the "method" of Pierre de la Ramée and that of Francis Bacon, is Lisa Jardine's *Francis Bacon: Discovery and the Art of the Discourse*. Finally, there is always much to be gained by consulting Walter J. Ong's *Ramus, Method, and the Decay of Dialogue*.
5. This remark has been amply confirmed by Terence Cave's *Cornucopian Text*, which contains an excellent chapter on the *Essays*.
6. See Aristotle, *Topica*; Cicero, *De Inventione*; *Topica*.
7. Rosemond Tuve's *Elizabethan and Metaphysical Imagery* shows that, in English Renaissance poetry, the mode of production of images (particularly comparisons and metaphors) still follows *logical* steps, in the technical sense of the term; the dialectic places utilized for the production of images are easily locatable for a trained mind (see the second part of the Tuve's work, "The Logical Function of Imagery"). See also Sister Miriam Joseph's *Rhetoric in Shakespeare's Time* for many examples of Elizabethan practices.
8. In this same article ("Romantic Difference and Technology"), Ong holds that the Renaissance's rhetorical culture is a vestige, perhaps even a final resurgence, of oral culture on the threshold of the typo-

graphical era—whence its contradictions and the importance assumed by the collections of "cumulative commonplaces": the recapitulation, as it was becoming obsolete, of a knowledge that had been standardized with a view to retaining and transmitting it within an oral, and subsequently scribal, culture. Printing, by facilitating the indexing of book contents, caused compilations to proliferate; and the typographical book, by replacing memory, provoked first the explosion of rhetoric and then its ruin. The fragments of the rhetorical edifice, caught up in new discursive configurations, will become autonomous disciplines or will become "literature," in the modern sense, although fundamentally modified according to purpose and context.

9. Agricola's logic represents, early in the sixteenth century, the modern —humanist and antischolastic—tendency that very soon prevailed in university teaching in Paris. Around 1530, Agricola's logic replaces Peter of Spain's *Summulae Logicales*, as well as the works of Buridan, Walter Burleigh, Ralph Strode, and Ockham. The moderns win out, though this has no profound effect on the practice of rhetorical invention. Agricola's success is mainly due to his return to the ancient sources. *De Inventione Dialectica* seemed more authentic than the Scholastic treatises, just as humanist neo-Latinism appeared more authentic than scholastic Latin, because one sensed in it a dialogue with antiquity, still alive in the present. See Walter J. Ong, *Ramus, Method, and the Decay of Dialogue*, 100.

10. See Perry Miller, *The New England Mind: The Seventeenth Century*. This major study of the history of ideas illuminates Ramism's influence on all aspects of Puritan thought.

11. Cited by Lechner, *Commonplaces*, 167.

12. Cited by Bolgar, *The Classical Heritage*, 432. Likewise cited by Paul Porteau, *Montaigne et la vie pédagogique de son temps*, 180.

13. Cited by Porteau, *Montaigne et la vie pédagogique de son temps*, 178–89.

14. Cited by Bolgar, *The Classical Heritage*, 273.

15. Cited by Porteau, *Montaigne et la vie pédagogique de son temps*, 185.

16. See Lechner, *Commonplaces*, ch. 4, "Virtue and Vice in the Commonplace Tradition," 201–25.

17. See Bolgar, *The Classical Heritage*, 274. These are preoccupations that we come across again in Roland Barthes, who nudges his text along "by figures and operations"—(especially, *contraries*) used "quite simply to *say something* (*Roland Barthes by Roland Barthes*, 96). A fragment entitled "Dialectics" describes Barthes' procedures of invention. They appear as a degraded version of the Renaissance school dialectic and bear little relation to the Hegelian-Marxist dialectic which Barthes seems to have in mind:

Everything seems to suggest that his discourse proceeds according to the two-term dialectic: popular opinion and its contrary, *Doxa* and its paradox, the stereotype and the novation, fatigue and freshness, relish and disgust: *I like/I don't like.* This binary dialectic is the dialectic of meaning itself (*marked/not marked*) and of the Freudian game the child plays (*Fort/da*): the dialectic of value.

> Yet is this quite true? In him, another dialectic appears, trying to find expression: the contradiction of the terms yields in his eyes to the discovery of a third term, which is not a synthesis but a *translation:* everything comes back, but it comes back as Fiction, i.e., at another turn of the spiral. (68–69)

This *translation,* or displacement, is the quasidialectical move that, since Montaigne, engenders the self-portrait as it swerves away from rhetorical invention without abolishing it. It is one of the main devices of essayistic invention in general.

18. In a study of Malagasy proverbs that obliquely clarifies certain problems addressed here, Jean Paulhan writes: "Ordinarily it is not, with them, [the proverbs] the *phrasing* which catches our attention, but, quite to the contrary, the subject: fable, morality, law of nature. There has been a frequent tendency to see, in the proverbs of a people, the sum total of their knowledge and something approximating their system of the world: as for expressing in detail this system and its applications, that is the business of language . . . Thus, one readily classifies proverbs, not by their phrasing, but by their meaning: proverbs about the family, society, the king" ("L'Expérience de proverbe," *Oeuvres complètes,* 2:11–65)

19. See the study by Margaret Mann Phillips, *The "Adages" of Erasmus.* This type of commented compilation reaches its apogee, in the seventeenth century, with Robert Burton's *Anatomy of Melancholy,* where the portrait of the melancholic is created through an accumulation of everything that people have said and written about melancholy, and quite a few other topics.

20. Cited by Walter J. Ong, *Rhetoric, Romance, and Technology,* 49.

21. Cited by Lechner, *Commonplaces,* 217–18.

22. Cited by Wallace, *Bacon on Communication and Rhetoric,* 16 and 117. Nietzsche, an admirer of Bacon, will remember this passage in *Ecce Homo.*

8. The Rhetorical Matrix during the Renaissance

1. From the rhetorical point of view, the most relevant critical works on Bacon are: Lisa Jardine, *Francis Bacon: Discovery and the Art of Discourse;* Paolo Rossi, *Francis Bacon: From Magic to Science;* Neal W. Gilbert, *Renaissance Concepts of Method;* William S. Howell, *Logic and Rhetoric in England, 1500–1700;* Carl R. Wallace, *Francis Bacon on Communication and Rhetoric.*

2. See, for example, Jacob Zeitlin, "The Development of Bacon's Essays

and Montaigne," regarding the first tendency. For the second, see Hugo Friedrich, *Montaigne*, 358.

3. See Richard H. Popkin, *The History of Scepticism from Erasmus to Descartes*, 44–46; Craig B. Brush, *Montaigne and Bayle*, 62–136; and Hugo Friedrich, *Montaigne*, 105–55.

4. Cited by Stanley Fish, *Self-Consuming Artifacts*, 78.

5. Conversely, Lisa Jardine sees in the *Essays* a new method for presenting and transmitting learning compatible with the Baconian intent of reforming the teaching of ethics. Jardine views the *Essays* as resorting to an "imaginative" or "insinuative" reason that captivates the reader with such nonrational ploys as an accumulation of examples. It is a matter of inducing the reader to adopt spontaneously a certain procedure in each given situation, without revealing to him how the author reached his ethical and political judgments. Reason is bracketed (248). Fish's reading (debunking dialectics) and Jardine's (nonrational propaganda) are antithetical. But both underscore that the *Essays* initiate a transvaluation. Whether he is shaken out of his torpor or insidiously allured, the reader must rid himself of his prejudices and adhere to a new model for the man of action. However, these two readings cannot be reduced to one another, and they point to an ambiguity in Bacon's *Essays*. It is well known that Montaigne's *Essays* have also given rise to contradictory readings.

6. In the preface to his second edition, Bacon asserts that essays (Montaigne's in the first place, it seems) are "scattered meditations." But, according to many contemporaries, essays rank with such *discourses* as Machiavelli's (words to that effect appear in the subtitle to the 1595 posthumous edition of Montaigne's *Essays: . . . Treasury of Several Fine and Notable Discourses*. Here a dual reference to rhetoric can be read: in *treasury* (memory, treasurehouse of invention, etc.) and in *discourse*. See Friedrich, *Montaigne*, 357.

7. The Baconian revolution eventually led to an epistemological dead end, as had the revolution proclaimed a little earlier by Pierre de La Ramée, to whom Bacon was highly indebted, though he denied it. One can find a brief presentation of the Ramus-Bacon nexus in R. Hooykaas, "Pierre de La Ramée et l'empirisme scientifique au XVIe siècle." Neither Ramus's nor Bacon's name appears in the index to *Logique et connaissance scientifique* (under the direction of J. Piaget), *Encyclopédie de la Pleiade*, vol. 17. This book is not a history of epistemology, but it does frequently refer to Descartes.

8. That is, if one accepts Foucault's hypothesis that "The essential problem of classical thought lay in the relations between *name* and *order*: how to discover a *nomenclature* that would be a *taxonomy* or, again, how to establish a system of signs that would be transparent to the continuity of being" (*Les Mots et les choses*, 220; *The Order of Things*,

208). One may also refer to the table on p. 201 of the English version of that work. Here, we encounter again the question of the universal characteristic and real languages, which was already evoked in the context of memory.

9. Among others, I am thinking of the explorations of coenaesthetic perception that outline, with Henri Michaux, a topography of the "space within"; or of the attempted encyclopedia of sensation as interestingly exemplified (because it adumbrates certain commonplaces constituting the self-portrait, like the "middle of life," death, and resurrection) in Jacques Brosse's *L'Inventaire des sens*.

10. See Jean Piaget, "Les Deux problèmes principaux de l'épistémologie des sciences de l'homme," in *Logique et Connaissance scientifique*, 1114–46.

11. Furthermore, Durand cites Halbwachs's *Topographie légendaire des évangiles en Terre Sainte* in order to show that the imaginary is always inscribed in a referential or fictional "geography." But Halbwachs himself, without realizing it, carried on the "composition of places" that structured Renaissance religious meditation. This reveals, at least indirectly, that "archaeology" is descriptive, encyclopedic, and *topical*, in every sense of the term. Barthes subtly suggests this when he writes: "Description, a Western genre, had its spiritual equivalent in contemplation, the methodical inventory of the attributive forms of the divinity or of the episodes of evangelical narrative (in Ignatius Loyola, the exercise of contemplation is essentially descriptive)" (*Empire of Signs*, 78). So we go round in circles among the variants of the same structure: but these variants occur diachronically, which continuously calls into question the priority of this or that variant.

12. The tarot, which appeared in Italy at the outset of the Renaissance, comprises twelve Houses modeled on the zodiacal system. Its Houses and arcana can be used accordingly to evoke both the macrocosm and, according to astrological analogies, circumstances of an individual's life. Roger Caillois writes of the tarot that "there is no conjectural science nor esoteric doctrine (astrology, arithmosophy, alchemy, etc.) that has not been called upon to clear up (or rather to thicken) its mystery; "Les Cartes," in *Jeux et sports, Encyclopédie de la Pléiade*, 23:961. Caillois's discussion of the tarot and its divinatory uses is in itself a small encyclopedia of Renaissance esoteric semiotic systems.

13. Douglas Radcliff-Umstead, "Giulio Camillo's Emblem of Memory."

14. Tuve maintains that poetic images are produced according to the procedures of the Aristotelian or Ramist dialectic.

9. Self-Portrait and Metamorphoses of Invention

1. *The inventory of mythological self* in fact amounts to its *invention* in the rhetorical sense.

2. There is no question *here* of an absolution, in the strict sense; it is obvious, nonetheless, that the figures themselves obliquely insert this discourse into an Augustinian context, by way of the *confession*, the book, and rhetoric.

3. For example, the "fact" that Moses was Egyptian, if one believes the Freudian analysis of the Bible.

4. For classical antiquity, see Robert Weiss, *The Renaissance Discovery of Classical Antiquity*. The philological and historical research of the Renaissance is bound up with its rhetorical theory and practice. See Nancy S, Struever, *The Language of History in the Renaissance: Rhetorical and Historical Consciousness in Florentine Humanism*. It should be added here that *etymology* ranks high among the most efficient (if fallacious) topics of rhetorical invention.

5. For a glimpse at Calvin's hesitations on the subject, see Jean Delumeau, *Naissance et affirmation de la Réforme*, 130–33, and his bibliography.

6. In Jensen's narrative we know that the antique and the modern converge in the Pompeian *topos*.

7. I am alluding here to the protracted analogical illusion lovingly deconstructed by Gérard Genette in *Mimologiques, Voyage en Cratylie*.

8. See Sigmund Freud, *The Interpretation of Dreams*, ch. 6, "The Dream Work," section C, "The Means of Representation."

9. Freud, we know, finds a crucial confirmation of his hypothesis in a now obsolete study by K. Abel on *The Antithetical Meaning of Primal Words* (1884). But Abel borrowed his principal erroneous examples from the ancient Egyptian, encoded in hieroglyph (*Interpretation of Dreams*, 353, n.3).

10. The dialectic of dreams (especially in implementing analogy), or that of their interpretation, is obviously more complex then we have indicated here. But it is always a question of distributing according to logical categories (under dialectic *topics*) a content that stubbornly ignores, or scrambles, the latter.

11. We all know this allegorical narrative by Francesco Colonna is also reputed to be an alchemistic breviary, See Albert-Marie Schmidt's preface to the facsimile re-edition of the French translation of this work. The original edition was published in Venice in 1499.

12. Edgar Wind notes the late date of the main iconographic sources to which Renaissance Platonists referred: they deciphered the voluptuary myths on Roman sarcophagi rather than on fifth century Greek vases, these being unknown to them for the most part: "As the myths appeared to them in a sepulchral setting, it was only natural, and perhaps legitimate, to impute to them a secret meaning, and to read them not as simple tales but as allusions to the mysteries of death and the afterlife, conceived in neoplatonic terms" (*Pagan Mysteries in the Renaissance*, 152).

13. See Paolo Rossi, *Clavis Universalis*, 272, n. 60.

14. In the text of 1938 Leiris transcodes "childhood memories" in the ethnographic register, which allows him to distance himself from them. See my "Michel Leiris: Ethnography or Self-Portrayal?" James Clifford, "Tell about Your Trip, Michel Leiris," in *The Predicament of Culture*, 165–174, and Denis Hollie, ed., *The College of Sociology*.

15. The opposition between culture and savagery, with the writer presenting himself as torn between the two, is adumbrated—for the self-portrait at least—as early as in the notice "To the Reader" of Montaigne's *Essays*. "Des cannibales" (I, XXXI) turns the topos around: "I think there is nothing barbarous and savage in that nation, from what I have been told, except that each man calls barbarism whatever is not his own practice." We should note that savagery can also be our own origin, or that from which each of us must always emerge. Moreover, in Ernest Lavisse's *L'Histoire de France*, the Gaul's cabin is described under the topos of savagery: "These houses had only one door and no windows. The smoke came out through the roof because there was no chimney."

16. This thesis is persuasively argued by John Holland Rowe in "The Renaissance Foundations of Anthropology." Rowe refers to Walter Schroeder's thesis: *De Ethnographiae Antiquae Locis Quibusdam Communis Observationes*. One should also read Margaret T. Hodgen's *Early Anthropology in the Sixteenth and Seventeenth Centuries*.

17. "I was less and less capable of seeing these [Ethiopian] peasants, simply sordid in their avarice, as magi and Atridae" (*L'Afrique Fantôme*, 446–47).

18. The chapter narrating the Khaddidja episode is headed "Look! The Angel Already . . .," a title borrowed from the duo of Radames and Aida "in their funeral vault . . . enshrouded in the darkness where love illuminates them" (239). Note that the court (or face) cards in the French deck bear names mysteriously borrowed from various sectors of Western culture.

19. This is confirmed by reading *A Lover's Discourse: Fragments*, where the erotization of rhetoric and self-portrayal becomes manifest.

20. Barthes's hyperbolic refusal of the rhetorical attitude smacks of denial. In his brilliant *Roland Barthes, Roman*, 165–69, Philippe Roger argued strongly against this last assertion, pointing out that Barthes was, on the face of it, a promoter of rhetoric and not exactly a self-portraitist. This disagreement rests, I believe, on a disagreement as to the meaning of the word *rhetoric* and to the relationship between rhetoric and self-portrayal in general.

21. Since this analysis concerns only the first volume of what subsequently became a series of three books (*Fugue*, 1970, *Fugue/Supplément*, 1973; *Fuge 3*, 1975) and some fragments published in installments as *Suite* (1977–1978), it does not claim to do justice to the whole of Roger Laporte's "biographic" undertaking. It intends only to elucidate the

traits that *Fugue* (1970) shares with other self-portraits, one of the most characteristic features being incompletion, the need for further additions which can appear in various ways: a collective title, or remaining concealed under heterogeneous and temporary titles, as occurs, for example, with Malraux. Laporte's "biography" is therefore just as "incomplete" as all other self-portraits. Currently, Laporte's "biography" is available in one volume, entitled *Une Vie*.

22. For example, the formula borrowed from Breton's first *Manifesto:* "to bring to light the way thought really works"; or the singular expression, also gained from Breton (*Arcane 17*): "enté d'ajours" (with holes grafted on) (24). The denial of the possibility of building a dwelling, a hearth, through writing may also suggest a covert polemic with Bachelard or even Heidegger: it modulates Borel's and Vuillemin's assertions on the impossibility of a *return*. Laporte's text, especially in its main articulations, is a tissue of textual echoes, of sometimes ironic borrowing from Rimbaud, Mallarmé, Bataille. This intertextuality engenders *Fugue*'s individuality, thus justifying Lotman's paradox: the impression of individuality results from the overlap of several semiotic systems at a given structural point (Iouri Lotman, *La Structure du texte artistique*, 120–21). One may also recall that the singularity of the Augustinian meditation in the *Confessions* rests on intertextuality with holy Writ.

23. See Pierre Courcelle, *Les Confessions de saint Augustin dans la tradition littéraire: Antécédents et postérité*, part 1.

24. Where, however, we hear echoes of Rimbaud's *Illuminations*, which precede echoes of Mallarmé.

25. In conjunction with Villon's "Testament," E. B. Vitz offers the following definition of this genre: "A will is the inventory of the furnishings and inhabitants of the testator's world, arranged and associated according to his wishes. As such, it constitutes a representation of the world, more or less complete, and more or less modified by the author's vision and purposes" (*The Crossroads of Intentions*, 111). Such a "representation of the world," if modified by additional formal constraints, might turn into a self-portrait. On the history of the testament as literary genre, se W. H. Rice's *The European Ancestry of Villon's Satirical Testaments*. On the testament as an avowal of faith and evidence of the "inner life," see Michel Vovelle's *Piété baroque et Déchristianisation en Provence au XVIIIe siècle: Les Attitudes devant la mort d'après les clauses des testaments*. See also, *The Apologia of Robert Keayne: The Self-Portrait of a Puritan Merchant*, where the mania for bookkeeping subverts the testamentary dispositions to the point of etching the lineaments of an individual torn between anxieties about divine grace, the practice of usury, and the accumulation of debts. This text is not a self-portrait in our sense of the term, since it is formally confined within the legal pattern of a will and lacks any self-theorization.

26. This preoccupation is inscribed at the start of Montaigne's *Essays*, in "Nos affections s'emportent au-delà de nous" (Our feelings reach out beyond us) (I, III), which deals with testamentary dispositions showing the testator's excessive concern with his corpse or his funeral. But, conversely: "I should find it more sprightly to imitate those who undertake, while alive and breathing, to enjoy the arrangement and honor of their obsequies, and who take pleasure in seeing their dead countenance in marble. Happy are those who can delight and gratify their senses by insensibility, and live by their death" (12). We see how the *Essays* transpose the wish to "live by [one's] death."

27. Gabriel Josipovici (*The World and the Book*, 307–9) observes that "the labyrinth is the dwelling of demonic analogy." With Eliot, Proust, Joyce, Beckett, Borges, Robbe-Grillet, the labyrinth becomes "the privileged image of modern literature." Josipovici also notes that Freud saw in the labyrinth a metaphor for the intestines. This image of the labyrinth mediates between the textual corpus, the fantasy of a fragmented-reassembled body, and Montaigne's excremental metaphor for his own self-portrait.

28. Here Laporte repeats in his own words what Beckett's *Innommable* had said in an exemplary meditation:

> C'est peut-être ça que je sens, qu'il y a un dehors et un dedans et moi au milieu, c'est peut être ça que je suis, la chose qui divise le monde en deux, d'une part le dehors, de l'autre le dedans, c'est peut être mince comme une lance, je ne suis ni d'un côté ni de l'autre, je suis au milieu, je suis la cloison, j'ai deux faces et pas d'épaisseur, c'est peut-être ça que je sens, je me sens qui vibre, je suis le tympan, d'un côté c'est le crâne, de l'autre le monde, je ne suis ni l'un ni l'autre. (160)

—where the notion of the subject as interface is glimpsed. This should be compared to the meditation on membranes in the "Persephone" chapter in Leiris's *Biffures*. See in this connection Jeffrey Mehlman's commentary, *A Structural Study of Autobiography*, 114–50, as well as the subsequent (and contrary) commentary in Derrida's introduction to his own *Marges de la Philosophie*.

[Translator's note: This passage was not translated by Beckett in *The Unnamable* (Grove Press, 1958); instead, two blank pages appear, here as elsewhere in the book, before the English text again corresponds with Beckett's own French original. For the purposes of the above context, the passage might be rendered as follows:

> Perhaps that's what I feel, that there is a without and a within, with me in the middle, perhaps that's what I am, the thing that divides the world in two, the outside on one hand and the inside on the other, it can be as thin as a spear, I'm neither on one side nor the other, I'm in the middle, I'm the partition, I've two sides and no thickness, perhaps that's what I feel, I feel my vibration, I'm the ear drum, the skull on one side, the world on the other, I am neither one.]

29. One thinks not only of Gide, Valéry, and the surrealists but also of lesser known authors and works such as Gabriel Dromard, *Essai sur la sincérité;* Jacques Rivière, *De la sincérité envers soi-même;* Léon Brunschvicg, *De la connaissance de soi;* Louis Lavelle, *La Conscience de soi;* as well as, more recently, Yvon Belaval, *La Souci de sincérité;* and Georges Gusdorf, *La Découverte de soi.* All these writers were involved in a debate on introspection, sincerity, and authenticity that was characteristic of the philosophy of immediacy in the "French style" inherited from Henri Bergson (*Essai sur les données immédiates de la conscience,* 1889).

30. Jacques Rivière echoes here in a minor mode what Bergson says in *Le Rire* about dreamers, the dying, disinterested, "visionary" artists: "They communicate immediately with things and with themselves." Were we to become like them, "we would hear, singing deep in our souls, something like music that is sometimes gay, more often plaintive, always original, the uninterrupted melody of our inner life" (*Le Rire,* 154, cited by G. Poulet, *L'Espace proustien,* 163). Poulet shows what are the links among dreams, unselfishness, and "pure duration:" "Utterly pure duration is the form adopted by the succession of our states of consciousness when our self lets itself live" (*Essai sur les données immédiates de la conscience,* 76). An ontological abyss separates this self that "let's itself live" from Rivière's ethical exertion and the melodic "presence unto itself" of "sincerity." We also see how alien all these are to post-Freudian and post-Heideggerian deconstructions of the "subject."

31. See Jean Rousset, "Les Difficultés de l'autoportrait," which deals in particular with La Rochefoucauld and Pierre Nicole and their conception of vanity as an insurmountable obstacle to the writing of a truthful self-portrait (republished in *Narcisse romancier*).

32. For a critique of Horney and a study of the relations between confessional literature and self-analysis, see Didier Anzieu, *L'Auto-analyse.*

33. Cited by Henri Gouhier, *Maine de Biran par lui-même.*

34. Jean Prévost considered Freudianism to be an outdated fashion in 1927.

35. It is probably no accident if this name is mentioned here to mark the impossibility of the type of "introspective" writing that might engender self-portrayal, though vanity is not contested here as it was in La Rochefoucauld's writings.

36. The French Bible, besides Esaü, contains such names as Moïse and Capharnaüm. The diaeresis is rare in French and thus causes problems for young readers.

37. In an interview with Raymond Bellour after the publication of *Fibrilles,* Leiris compared the composition of *Manhood* to that of *La Règle du jeu:* "In the three books [of the latter] there is a deliberate evolution of the composition—*Biffures* is made up of several chapters but is no longer a mosaic. In *Fourbis,* there are just three chapters. *Fibrilles* is divided into four chapters for the sake of convenience, but is one

continuous text deployed in the entire volume." But this "progress" (which seems to aim at an imitation of autobiography so as to produce magically the conditions of an impossible totalization which narration immediately, if virtually, confers upon the autobiographical narrative) cannot be sustained without transgressing and destroying self-portrayal. And the last volume of La Règle du jeu (Frêle bruit) returns to the fragmentary topics of a commonplace book, which makes it more akin to Manhood than to La Règle du jeu.

38. The first are names of equivocal childhood deities. The second set, of course, is the writing on the wall.

39. This is the Astérix and Obélix (Gallic, Greek, Egyptian, as it were) side of French self-portrayal.

40. Tetable, as in the ill-understood aria from Manon: "Adieu, notre petite table."

41. The dramatic metaphor is the keystone of Kenneth Burke's neorhetorical thinking. Richard Lanham concludes his Motives of Eloquence with the following words:

The new social construction of reality which, for literary critics, at least, Burke began with the dramatic master metaphor, has led to a revolutionary stylistic position now set forth as structuralist dogma: form without content, or rather, form as content; style as thought; the self-conscious personification rather than sincerity; surface rather than depth; conscious, deliberate unreality; the writer as declared poseur. You will remember these not as a creed of a fashionable dernier cri, but as the catalog of charges traditionally made against rhetorical man and his opaque styles. Not altogether without reason did Barthes call the sophist forbear. By whatever aperiodic ambages, the passion for formal rhetoric seems to have returned. (222–23)

42. One recognizes here a transformation (regression—going beyond) comparable to that produced by Montaigne's Essays and foregrounded in the book, especially in connection with such a perfect classroom exercise as the Discourse on Voluntary Bondage of La Boétie, which was introduced and then eliminated in "Of Friendship" (I, XXVIII), as Montaigne moves towards the "antirhetorical" (pre- and postrhetorical) writing of "fantasies." On this point see also Michel Butor's Essais sur les Essais.

43. We meet here again, although so distorted that we may doubt its pertinence, the opposition between discourse and history proposed by Benveniste. The autobiographer is in fact a historian, even if he frequently says I. But he does not have to say you, or here, or now. These deictic devices belong rather to the discourse of the self-portrait. Autobiography, despite Benveniste's assertions, is a historical narrative: paradoxical, contradictory if one wishes, but no more so, after all, than a chronicle or memoirs. The discourse/history opposition has no doubt greater heuristic value for a study of the novel than for autobiography

and the self-portrait. See E. Benveniste, *Problèmes de linguistique générale*, 239.

44. *Glossaire: J'y serre mes gloses* was originally published in 1925 in *La Révolution Surréaliste*. It is a collection of quasidefinitions. Lydia Davis proposes to translate the title item as: "Glossary: My Glosses' Ossuary" (*Sulfur* 15, 3 [1986]:26].

45. We know that the game of goose, a type of sequence that can provide backgrounds and images for invention as well as spatialize the hazards of one's life, appears twice in the "Mors" chapter of *Fourbis*. The first time, Luna Park furnishes the context where the series unfolds: Labyrinth—Game of Goose—Tower of Babel—Hostelry. The second time (74), the labyrinth engenders the game of goose "said to have come down from the earliest Greek antiquity." It is easy to grasp here its symbolic and etymological connotations for Leiris.

46. The lexeme *méli-mélo* (hodge-podge) reappears in *Frêle bruit*, 335, in the context of examples of the *wondrous* "picked almost at random and thrown into the pot as a hodgepodge for a pot-luck dinner."

47. This state of oceanic ipseity is the one whose lost/recovered happiness is evoked by Rousseau, as the lonesome Dreamer of the Fifth Reverie.

48. We know that one of the main *places* (together with the childhood house) of Borel's works is the dismal room where he spent his adolescence, which he always calls the "capharnaüm."

49. Leiris is fully aware of the "French History Textbook" matrix shaping his self-portrait: "My memory being such that it works like a history textbook, those elements that are a bit theatrical remain fixed in it, those which—to the detriment of more discreet, though perhaps highly important elements—are noteworthy mostly by the fact that they admit of illustration." (*Fourbis*, 20–21).

50. Therefore, we see that Leiris's ethnographic work on the secret language of the Dogons, spirit possession in Ethiopia, and acculturation in the Antilles reveals the same fundamental preoccupation and seeks an exotic equivalent for it in order to confirm its generality and exemplary worth. See my "Leiris: Poétique et ethnopoétique."

51. Montaigne, though quite a stranger to esotericism, nevertheless writes: "This great world . . . is the mirror in which we must look at ourselves to recognize ourselves from the proper angle" (I, XXVI).

52. See *Biffures*, 51, where *OE* evokes the antique (whose erotic connotation has already been mentioned in *Manhood*) and especially the name of *Oedipus*.

53. Hiram Haydn called it *The Counter-Renaissance* in the title of his book. It is akin to the Neoplatonic and magical renaissance invented by scholars at the Warburg Institute in London. See also Moses Hadas, *Hellenistic Culture*.

54. The French wordplay, in the manner of Leiris's *Glossary*, is somewhat more satisfactory: "Cratyle, il crache son style."

55. One recalls that in *La Langue secrète des Dogons de Sanga*, Leiris would develop the complementary opposition between a bush Cratylus, whose inspired language is "more closely related than ordinary language to certain elements in the environment" (23), and a village Hermogenes, the guardian of civil society's language.

56. *Fibrilles* produced another variant on this encounter, in the context of a long metadiscursive passage defining self-portrayal and contrasting its duration with the span of a life:

> There is nothing in common between the outcome prepared by these approaches [dialectic invention working with index cards] and the eternal noon or midnight decreed by poetic creation. And if I shake in my dice box the rubble of my past, living clots of the present, and the seeds of a future in embryo, instead of fostering the throw of the dice thanks to which the motion round the clock and the horizons would be finally mastered, I am struggling through a spell which, if it were a question of the weather, might be called unsettled. (224)

57. In *Fibrilles*, Leiris recalls that he proposed *frenzy* "as the right term to designate what should be regarded as the source of the surrealist spirit" (262). One has to assume that he got the word (*fureur, furor, mania*) from his dipping into Renaissance Neoplatonism.

58. Montaigne had already written: "One man . . . produces essays, who cannot produce results" (III, IX), playing on the words *essays* and *effects*.

59. The original alludes here to the verbal virtuosity of the so-called Grands Rhetoriqers of the fifteenth century.

60. Leiris compares himself unfavorably to Aimé Césaire, the complete poet and orator, a Black Orpheus, and an Osiris who lacks nothing.

61. Leiris continuously deplores the idiosyncrasy of his opinions, so inferior in his view to philosophy's universal truths:

> All my blunders, hesitations, faltering words, all the erasures or overloading that are accumulated in each of my sentences . . . in fact translate indecision in my thinking and flaws in my character . . . A tendency to slip away which is paradoxically fulfilled by the very consistent use I make of the first person . . . for it greatly diminishes the scope of my assertions thus to display in the open their subjective nature, reducing them to being but the singularities I admit or the opinions I form, I propose, not as general truths but in strictly personal capacity. (*Biffures*, 267)

62. This abbreviation (*bifur*), used in railway signaling, had served as the title for a literary magazine close to surrealism.

63. As he meditates on the "marvelous"—much further on in *la Règle du jeu*—Leiris confirms: "Facing an overblown marvelous linked to exploded limits, as if from excessive fullness, could there be an undersized wonder where everything would occur as if a lacuna, a gap, or bad joint, betraying vague limits, the confines rather than the frontiers of reality and the imagery were offered up as an appeal to our imagina-

tion?" (*Frêle bruit*, 348). But this deficient wonder is made manifest only through dialectical invention, for it is not a gift of poetic frenzy.

64. Moreover, Cicero provides a comparison pertinent to self-portrayal: "In an enumeration [*partitio*] there are parts, so to speak, just as a body has a head, shoulders, hands, sides, legs, feet, etc."; this suggests the *corpus* metaphor Leiris introduces a little further on in *Biffures* (261).

65. Montaigne plays with this place to deal with friendship ("On Friendship," I, XXVIII) and in other chapters.

66. Leiris is *also* perfectly aware of this situation, which he cannot accept. A little further on he evokes "the enchanted circle inside which reasoning reason, discoursing discourse, and writing writing have shut me up."

67. This place appears briefly at the end of the book as a "consolation prize card" on which it is indicated that in Hebrew Michael (as in Michel Leiris) means "the one who is comparable to God" (278). In other words, the demiurge.

68. Philippe Lejeune, who considers this procedure (*Lire Leiris*, 160–63) to be "related to rhyme," used it himself in the embryonic self-portrait (181–85) that concludes his book.

69. The stock adverbial phrase "*sans tambours ni trompetes*" (quietly, without fuss) provides the linguistic background for this metaphoric oddity.

70. This assertion has been vigorously challenged by Philippe Roger (*Roland Barthes, roman*, 160–69) on the grounds that Barthes was one of the most persistent advocates of rhetoric in contemporary France. No doubt. But if his understanding of tropes and figures served him well in his struggle against the dominant conception of literature as "self-expression," Barthes was nonetheless repelled by rhetoric's inherent collusion with *doxa*, commonplaces, *bêtise*. Barthes wished to be more clever than rhetoric.

71. Pursued in his *Fragments d'un discours amoureux* (*A Lover's Discourse*, 1977) and *La Chambre claire* (*Camera Lucida*, 1980).

72. This is to be compared to what Guez de Balzac had already said in the seventeenth century about Montaigne: "We agree that the Author who wants to imitate Seneca begins everywhere and ends everywhere. His discourse is not a whole body: it is a body in pieces, with its parts cut off; and although the latter are close to one another, they are nonetheless separate. Not only are they not joined by nerves; there are not even cords or aiguilettes to tie them together: so hostile is this Author to all kinds of liaisons, whether of Nature or Art" ("De Montaigne et ses écrits," *Oeuvres*, 2:402–3).

73. In his "Aide-mémoire sur l'ancienne rhétorique," Barthes favored a "good" rhetoric, an eroticized rhetoric, a "dialogue of love" which he found in Plato (177).

74. This is an old story, one that in certain respects repeats that of the

Renaissance, as Perelman and Olbrechts-Tyteca suggest: "Renaissance humanism could have prepared a renewal of rhetoric in the broad sense of the word. But the criterion of evidence, whether it was Protestant personal evidence, Cartesian rational evidence, or the sense evidence of the empiricists, could only disqualify 'rhetoric' " ("Logique et rhétorique").

75. As a logician who knows the score, Jules Vuillemin lucidly says: "There is something arbitrary about these schemes, but I only seek to know what I am: if they help me to achieve this, they will do" (*Le Miroir de Venise*, 32).

10. The "Book," the Opus, and Their Theater

1. Of course, the myth of (God's, Nature's, Man's) Book did not originate with Mallarmé, who simply proposed a modern version of it.

2. The "Book" in question is beyond doubt the volume entitled *Le Livre de Mallarmé* edited by Jacques Schérer from Mallarmé's *Nachlass*.

3. In an interview he granted to Raymond Bellour after the publication of *Fibrilles*, Leiris said furthermore: "What strikes me as extraordinary about the 'Book' is how few jottings deal with its contents. Almost everything concerns the way in which it should be read: one has the feeling that either the contents would be inferrable from the protocol or that Mallarmé already had sufficient knowledge of what the contents would be. How to organize it was his only problem. . . . The 'Book,' because it was absolute, had to be autonomous."

4. One remembers that Rabelais had already somewhat abused this cabalistic cliché in the prologue to *Pantagruel*.

5. Unless the disciple plainly regresses as Claudel did toward the other Bible; unless he transcodes Mallarmé in the register of the Midrash, as Derrida would, whether by direct commentary of the Mallarméan undertaking, or indirectly, by way of Freud's or Edmond Jabès's Jewishness. The Mallarméan sun can also be replaced by Nietzsche's, or one may interpose between the two a play of mirrors, calling this operation *modernity* in a specifically French sense.

6. According to Maurice Blanchot's formula, this is indeed a "Book of the Future." In his study of Mallarmé (*Le Livre à venir*), Blanchot conceives the Book as an unreal *power* that snatches the writer's writing away from him and forces him to write and publish, a power that "confirms the impersonal character of his works. The writer has no rights over them; he is abolished to begin with" (338, n. 1). Blanchot entitled the first part of his study *Ecce Liber*, thus paraphrasing Nietzsche, who himself . . . Therefore the impersonal Book replaces Christ Crucified and even Nietzsche's Antichrist. In the register of impersonality and powerlessness Blanchot exploits a commonplace that haunts the self-portrait: the self-portraitist always is an *Other* to begin with, "dead

as such a one" ("un tel"), "omission of oneself" according to the Mallarméan formulas. One might also write "dead like so-and-so" ("untel"), absent from the text, just as the body of Christ risen is absent from the sepulcher. *Ecce liber* = empty-sepulcher-Book. Blanchot says so in pseudobiblical diction: "he who speaks poetically is liable to meet with this sort of death, which is, of necessity, at work in the true word" (334).

7. See the chapter entitled "Les Tablettes sportives," in *Fourbis*, 75–180.

8. See François Secret, *Les Kabbalistes chrétiens de la Renaissance* and the works of Paolo Rossi and Frances Yates, as well as Douglas Radcliff-Umstead's "Giulio Camillo's Emblems of Memory."

9. Letters from Viglius Zuichemus to Erasmus, in the latter's *Epistolae*, edited by P. S. Allen et al., 9:479, cited by Yates, *Art of Memory*, 131.

10. See Ou-Li-Po, *La Littérature potentielle*. This dream was picked up by science fiction, mainly in Stanislaw Lem's *Cyberiada* (Cracow, 1967)

11. We recognize here, in a modern and simplified form, the great undertaking through which Saint Augustine tried to place pagan rhetoric in the service of Christian revelation.

12. Regarding this allusion, see D. P. Walker, "Le Chant orphique de Marsile Ficin."

13. Letter to Cazalis, dated 14 May 1867: "I am impersonal now, no longer the Stéphane you knew—but the spiritual Universe's ability to see itself and develop through what I once was" (*Correspondance*, 2:345; cited by Schérer, *Le "livre" de Mallarmé*, 22).

14. This *type* (this essence of genre or *mythos*) is one that has been reinvented independently by Mikhail Bakhtin in his *Problems of Dostoevsky's Poetics*, 112–22 and 133–47, and Northop Frye, in his *Anatomy of Criticism*, 308–21. These two authors are, quite strikingly, of the same mind in their approach. While Bakhtin stresses mostly an interaction with the carnivalesque mode, he also deserves credit for having mentioned the link between demonstrative eloquence and the Menippean satire. Frye is clearest in his discussion of the links between *anatomy* (a designation borrowed from Robert Burton's *Anatomy of Melancholy*), Utopia, and the encyclopedia as farce. They both contend that the Menippean form is the intellectual genre that challenges philosophy and theology, ridicules their seriousness, and drags them into the mire. The Menippean form typifies a refusal to draw conclusions.

15. See the synoptic chart of *Foi de fol*, 382–83.

16. There is no theoretical obstacle to a multiplication of self-portraits in any given period. But it is easy enough to imagine what, in practice (within the literary institution), does inhibit the proliferation of such books as those written by Montaigne or Leiris. The chief obstacle is one that Philippe Lejeune ignored in his *Lire Leiris*, where he proposed to "read oneself into Leiris" —a temptation; but Lejeune's own self-reading reads like a pastiche of Leiris. A post-Leirisian self-portrayal would

have to blank out Leiris, just as Leiris blanked out Montaigne. At least this would seem to be the case for French writers.

17. Cited by Schérer, Le "Livre" de Mallarmé, 40).

18. Shakespearean criticism has speculated whether in the "To be or not to be" soliloquy Hamlet invents as he goes along or if he reads aloud from the book in his hand, while the King and Polonius covertly watch his reactions to Ophelia's presence. Thus, Hamlet's existential question is posed in an infinitely ambiguous dramatic and rhetorical context. In a way, every self-portrait repeats this situation and stages its own equivocalness. See Richard Lanham, The Motives of Eloquence, 136.

19. It is curious to note that, in his desire to close Mallarmé's "Book," Jacques Schérer imagines (136) that the snake mentioned on page 25 (A) bites its own tail and forms an ouroboros: no doubt the snake must form a circle in an alchemical context. See C. G. Jung, Psychologie et alchimie, 377.

20. This passage precedes a paragraph where Jung evokes the Lapis-Christus analogy in Raymond Lully.

21. "I've often thought about the techniques of meditation—I believe they can be found in Ignatius of Loyola—to reconstruct, by means of imagination, the Crucifixion scene. I haven't applied these methods, though I thought something in that order should be done for memory. This is rather close to Proust" (interview with Madeleine Gobeil). We know that Georges Bataille, who was on familiar terms with Leiris, had adopted the method of Loyola's Exercises for his own purpose. Leiris's intuition of a relationship between the Exercises and Memory is remarkable, given his apparent lack of historical information.

22. One will note how much more ground the stroll covers under a Maoist influence.

23. In the psychoanalytic register, Leiris distinguishes a negative rhetoric of the lack: that of the inoperative and castrated self-portrait; and a full rhetoric, which reaches its audience, rouses the crowd and incites to revolution: for example, Aimé Césaire's or Fidel Castro's political eloquence.

24. Republished in Brisées, 279–85.

25. "Places about which the question would be whether, once the honors have been done to each one that I've been lucky enough to locate, I would or would not grasp the hieroglyph perhaps inscribed—goodness knows on what ground!—along the itinerary marked by all of them, as the stations of a kind of initiatory journey" (Fourbis, 20).

26. Leiris wrote a long review (republished in Brisées, 199–209) to praise Tristes tropiques, Claude Lévi-Strauss's intellectual autobiography. Interestingly, the latter said about his own work: "I had the feeling, as I was writing it, that I was composing an opera; its passages from autobiography to ethnology correspond with the opposition between recitatives and arias; the leap from South America to Asia with the alter-

nances between vocal parts and orchestral interludes" (interview with
J.-L. de Rambures). Whereas Leiris seizes upon the spatial and paradigmatic metaphor in opera, the autobiographer emphasizes its syntagmatic alternances: this may provide a clue to the differences between
self-portrayal and autobiography.

27. See *Frêle bruit*.
28. "A painter who was with me on my first trip here told me before my
departure: 'There's something theatrical about all Italian art. Look at
Piero himself, he pitches stage sets.' I can't stop thinking about this—
it affects me" (*Le Miroir de Venise*, 86). On the theatricality of Montaigne's *Essays*, see Imbrie Buffum, *Studies in the Baroque: Montaigne
to Rotrou*, 29–43.
29. See E. R. Curtius, *European Literature and the Latin Middle Ages*, 138–
45 and 302–48.

11. Invention as Antimemory

1. One should, however, note that Malraux also envisages anthropology
in a comparatist perspective that rather recalls Montaigne's attitude
towards cannibals and Leiris's point of view as an ethnographer:

> The passion which Asia, vanished civilizations, and ethnography have long
> inspired in me arose from an essential wonderment at the forms which man has
> been able to assume, but also from the light which every strange civilization
> threw on my own, that quality of the unusual or the arbitrary which it revealed
> in one or the other of its aspects. (247)

2. The general title for the self-portrait of Malraux, whose first section is
the *Antimemoirs*. Actually, though with no essential change, compli-
cations arose when *The Cord and the Mice*, which became the second
section, was published. *Lazarus* closes the group. The decomposition-
recomposition is in itself characteristic of self-portrayal.
3. Lotman's remark is germane in this connection: "The more norms
overlap at a given structural point, the more sense will be given to that
element, the more individual, the more extrasystematic it will seem"
(*La Structure du texte artistique*, 121).

12. The Body, Locus of Enunciation

1. In Sartre's writing on the imaginary, there is an absence, which though
not surprising, is nevertheless worthy of attention and significant: the
absence of his own body. It results from a systematic critique of the
foundations of the Bergsonian thesis of *Matter and Memory*, where it is
said that: "All seems to take place as if, in this aggregate of images
which I call the universe, nothing really new could happen except
through the medium of certain particular images, the type of which is

furnished me by my body" (3). But one should nevertheless mention the important pages devoted to the body in *Being and Nothingness*, where it is shown that one lives one's own body rather than knowing it. It is worth noting that the last section of Roland Barthes's self-portrait, *Camera Lucida*, claims to be a homage to Sartre's *Imaginary*.

2. In *Etudes sémiologiques*, 221–31.
3. Cf., for example, Montaigne, Rousseau, Malraux, Laporte. Marin's reflection ties in with an old theological and semiotic tradition that arose in connection with the Eucharist, real presence, etc. Elsewhere ("La Parole mangée," in *Etudes sémiologiques*, 285–92), Marin discusses another aspect of this semiotheology, with respect to *The Logic of Port-Royal*
4. In the pictorial self-portrait as well, see Dürer's *Ecce Homo*. Marin lucidly states what the study of literary self-portrayal keeps suggesting: our reading of the evangelical texts and the resurrection narratives place us within a set of relations whose combinations make up— radically, fundamentally—our present discourse as well as yesterday's or tomorrow's Western discourse" (918).
5. Michel Butor's comment on the structure of Book I of the *Essays*, in his *Essais sur les Essais*, would tend to confirm this analysis.

13. Body and Corpus

1. Note the pictorial metaphor in this passage.
2. This method, as we can now see, anticipates Leiris's reinvention of the procedures of artificial memory.
3. Chapter 11 is a short essay on prudence, where Cardano differentiates between this harpocratic gift and intuition, the latter being subdivided into *euboulia, phronesis*, and *humana prudentia*, all of which he knows he lacks. *Prudentia* is the practical aspect of wisdom and humanism's key virtue. See E. F. Rice, *The Renaissance Idea of Wisdom*.
4. Chapter 46 contains a symmetrical meditation, in which the aspiration to eternal life, in the Christian sense, outweighs the hope of exceptional longevity.
5. See Françoise Joukovsky, *La Gloire dans la poésie française et néo-latine du XVIe siècle*.
6. See Rudolf and Margot Wittkower, *Born under Saturn: The Character and Conduct of Artists*, 287.
7. See Richard Samuel, "Friedrich Nietzsche's *Ecce Homo:* An Autobiography?" 210.
8. See "On Luther the German," 320.
9. These remnants include a few French books, such as Montaigne's *Essays*, the works of the moralists of the seventeenth century, Voltaire, Stendhal, etc.—skeptical and caustic texts, which are, in great part, aphoristic fragments.

10. If one accepts the line of argument presented by Michel Foucault in *La Volonté de savoir*, then Nietzsche turns out to be the philosopher of the rising bourgeoisie: "It is right, then, to relate the valorization of the body to the growth and triumph of bourgeois hegemony," achieved by means of hygiene, eugenics and "racism" (165–66).

11. This section was written in expectation of a "continuation" of which *La Chambre claire* (1980) was, alas, the last fragment published before Barthes's untimely death.

12. There are many, and sometimes surprising, comments about speech and voice in Barthes's essays and interviews. See, for example, "De la parole à l'écriture," *La Quinzaine Littérature*, 1–15 March 1974, collected in *Le Grain de la voix* 9–13.

13. Cardano's prolonged impotence may be symbolic of this "neglect" of the body.

14. On this point see my "Phonograms and Delivery: The Poetics of Voice."

15. See, as an example in this connection, Leslie John Beck's analysis in *The Metaphysics of Descartes: A Study of the Meditations*:

> To philosophize is to commit oneself: to commit oneself to a policy of systematic doubt is fundamentally an act of humility. The purpose of the *First Meditation* is similar to that of the meditations of the first week of the *Spiritual Exercises* on *peccata*, to make the meditator realize the fragility and instability of his ordinary state of mind.

Still, the position of Descartes with respect to self-portrayal should be examined more carefully. Independently, in a collection of analyses appearing under the title *Ego Sum*, Jean-Luc Nancy set out to do just that. In fact, in his study of the *Discourse on Method*, he claims that the book, first published anonymously, implements a pictorial model (to represent one's life as in a painting) and masks the writing subject (*larvatus*), placed in the position of God (*pro Deo*), on a stage which converts theory into a trompe l'oeil, a fable or a work of fiction. Nancy's observations agree with what has been said elsewhere in this book concerning the *imitatio Christi* and the role of theatrical metaphors in self-portrayal. I would however stress the need to reappraise the relations between the major Cartesian texts and rhetoric, both in the light of self-portrayal and through the operations of *method, meditation*, and the *passions*. Evidently, this reappraisal should not overlook Descartes' patently ontological and epistemological intent, nor the narrative or topical structure of the texts in question. On this point see my "Speculum, Method, and Self-Portrayal: Some Epistemological Problems."

16. In her book, entitled *Le Problème de l'inconscient et le cartésianisme*, Geneviève Lewis draws a close comparison between the Cartesian approach and that of Saint Augustine, particularly in Book X of the latter's *Confessions*, with special emphasis on the importance of *me-*

moria sui. The indications provided by the comparisons might be further developed either in the perspective of self-portrayal or according to the topics of psychoanalysis.

17. Bachelard has devised an arresting formula to reinforce such a view: "The unconscious dwells" (*La Poétique de l'espace*, 28). Bachelard, in his own covenant with poetry, conferred a positive value on the imaginary denounced by Sartre:

> In order to evaluate our being within the hierarchy of ontology, and to psychoanalyze our unconscious burrowing among primitive dwellings, we must, outside a standard psychoanalysis, *desocialize* our major memories and reach the plane of the reveries we conducted throughout the *spaces of our solitudes.* (28)

True, this desocialization is only a moment of the process in question; for the spaces of our solitudes are variations on descriptive systems, on topics drawn from the general treasury of a specific culture. But there certainly is a first step, one that has to live through the experience of the desert, through the illusion of the unsaid.

Conclusion

1. See Renzo Vitali, *Gorgia: Rhetoria e filosofia.*
2. See, for instance, Donald M. Frame, *Montaigne, a Biography.*

Bibliography

Adorno, T. W. "Der Essay als Form." *Noten zur Literatur,* 9–49. Frankfurt: Suhrkampf, Verlag, 1963.

Agricola, R. *De inventione dialectica libri tres.* 1515.

———. *De formando studio epistola.* Cologne, 1532.

Anzieu, D. *L'Auto-analyse.* Paris: PUF, 1959.

Apuleius. *The Golden Ass.*

Aristotle. *Aristotle's Poetics.* Translated by S. H. Butcher. Introduction by Francis Ferguson. New York: Hill and Wang, 1961.

———. *De Memoria et Reminiscentia.* Translated by R. Sorabji. London: Duckworth, 1972.

Arnauld, A., and P. Nicole. *La Logique ou l'art de penser* (1660–1683). Introduction by Louis Marin. Paris: Flammarion, 1978.

Artaud, A. "Correspondance avec Jaques Rivière." *Oeuvres complèter,* vol. I, Paris: Gallimard, 1956.

Atkinson, G. "La Forme de l'essai avant Montaigne." *Bibliothèque d'Humanisme et de Renaissance* 8 (1946): 129–36.

Bachelard, G. *La Poétique de l'espace.* Paris: PUF, 1957. *The Poetics of Space.* Translated by Maria Jolas. New York: Orion Press, 1964.

Backès-Clément, C. "Continuité mythique et construction historique." *L'Arc* 34 (1968):77–86.

Bacon, F. *The Essays of Bacon.* World's Classics edition. Oxford: Oxford University Press, 1937.

———. *De Sapienta Veterum.* London, 1609. *The Advancement of Learning.* Edited by G. W. Kitchen. Everyman's Library edition. London: J. M. Dent, 1960.

Bainton, R. H. "Dürer and Luther as the Man of Sorrows." *Art Bulletin* (1947):269ff.

Baker, S. R. "La Rochefoucauld and the Art of the Self-Portrait." *Romanic Review* 65, 1 (1974):13–30.

Bakhtin, M. *Problems of Dostoevsky's Poetics.* Edited and translated by Caryl Emerson. Minnesota: University of Minnesota Press, 1984.

Ballard, E. G. *Socratic Ignorance: An Essay on Platonic Self-Knowledge.* The Hague: Martinus Nijhoff, 1965.

Balzac, J.-L. Guez de. *Oeuvres.* Paris: L. Moreau, 1854.

Barrès, M. *Le Culte du moi (Sous l'oeil des barbares, Un Homme libre, Le Jardin de Bérénice, Examen).* Paris: Plon-Livre de Poche, 1966.

Barthes, R. *Mythologies.* Paris: Editions du Seuil, 1957.

————."Drame, poème, roman." In *Tel Quel, Théorie d'ensemble.* Paris: Editions du Seuil, 1968.

————."L'Ancienne rhétorique: Aide mémoire." *Communications* 16 (1970):172–223.

————. *L'Empire des signes.* "Les Sentiers de la Création" series. Geneva: Skira, 1970. *Empire of Signs.* Translated by Richard Howard. New York: Hill and Wang, 1982.

————. *Sade, Fourier, Loyola.* Paris: Editions du Seuil, 1971. *Sade, Fourier, Loyola.* Translated by Richard Miller. New York: Hill and Wang, 1976.

————. "Interview recueillie par Claude Jannoud." *Le Figaro*, 27 July 1974.

————. *Roland Barthes par Roland Barthes.* "Les Écrivains de Toujours" series. Paris: Editions du Seuil, 1975. *Roland Barthes by Roland Barthes.* Translated by Richard Howard. New York: Hill and Wang, 1977.

————. *Fragments d'un discours amoureux.* Paris: Editions du Seuil, 1977. *A Lover's Discourse: Fragments.* Translated by Richard Howard. New York: Hill and Wang, 1978.

————. *La Chambre claire: Note sur la photographie.* Paris: Cahiers du Cinéma, Gallimard, and Le Seuil, 1980.

————. *Le Grain de la voix.* Paris: Editions du Seuil, 1981.

Bateson, G. *Steps to an Ecology of Mind.* Frogmore, St. Albans: Paladin, 1973.

Baudelaire, C. *Oeuvres complètes.* "Bibliothèque de la Pleiade" series. Paris: Gallimard, 1954.

————. *Les Fleurs du mal.* Edited by A. Adam. Paris: Garnier, 1959.

Baxandall, M. *Painting and Experience in Fifteenth-Century Italy.* London, Oxford, and New York: Oxford University Press, 1972.

Beaujour, M. "The Venetian Mirror." *Georgia Review* 29, 3 (1975): 627–47.

————. "Jean Paulhan et la Terreur." In Jacques Bersani, ed., *Paulhan le souterrain: Colloque de Cerisy*, 118–38. Paris: Union Générale d'Edition, 1976.

————. "Des miroirs ambigus: L'Autoportrait pictural et l'autoportrait littéraire dans leurs rapports à l'imitation." *Michigan Romance Studies* 1 (1980):1–17.

————. "Exemplary Pornography: Barrès, Loyola, and the Novel." In Susan R. Suleiman and Inge Crosman, eds., *The Reader in the Text: Essays on*

Audience and Interpretation, 325–49. Princeton: Princeton University Press, 1980.

———. "Genus Universum." *Glyph* 7 (1980):15–31.

———. "Speculum, Method, and Self-Portrayal: Some Epistemological Problems." In John D. Lyons and Stephen G. Nichols, eds., *Mimesis: From Mirror to Method, Augustine to Descartes*, 188–96. Hanover and London: University Press of New England, 1982.

———. "Théorie et pratique de l'autoportrait contemporain: Edgar Morin et Roland Barthes." *Revue de l'Institut de Sociologie de Université de Bruxelles*, fasc. 1–2, 1982.

———. "Une Mémoire sans sujet: *Memoria* à la Renaissance." *Corps Écrit* 11 (1984):103–10.

———. "Les Equivoques du sacré: Michel Leiris et *L'Afrique fantôme*." In S. Teroni, ed., *L'Occhio del Viaggiatore: Scrittori francesi degli anni trenta*, 165–76. Florence: Leo S. Olschki Editore, 1986.

———. "Phonograms and Delivery: The Poetics of Voice." In N. F. Cantor and N. King, eds., *Notebooks in Cultural Analysis* 3 (1986):266–79.

———. "Rhétorique et littérature." In Michel Meyer, ed., *De la métaphysique à la rhétorique*, 157–74. Faculté de Philosophie et Lettres XCIX, "Philosophie et Histoire des Idées" series. Brussels: Editions de l'Université de Bruxelles, 1986.

———. "Michel Leiris: Ethnography or Self-Portrayal?" *Cultural Anthropology* 2, 4 (November 1987):470–80.

———. "Leiris: Poétique et ethnopoétique." *Modern Language Notes*, 105 (1990):646–55.

Beck, L. J. *The Method of Descartes: A Study of the "Regulae."* Oxford: Clarendon Press, 1964.

———. *The Metaphysics of Descartes: A Study of the "Meditations."* Oxford: Clarendon Press, 1965.

Beckett, S. *L'Innommable*. Paris: Editions de Minuit, 1953.

Belaval, Y. *Le Souci de sincérité*. Paris: Gallimard, 1944.

Bellour, R. "Entretien avec Michel Leiris." *Les Lettres Françaises*, 29 September 1966, 3–4.

Bémol, M. "Le Représentation de l'esprit et l'expression de l'inexprimable." *Revue d'Esthétique* 15 (1962):139–65.

Benveniste, E. *Problèmes de linguistique générale*. Paris: Gallimard, 1966.

Bergson, H. *Essai sur les données immédiates de la conscience*. Paris: Alcan, 1889.

———. *Matière et mémoire*. Paris: Alcan, 1896. *Matter and Memory*. Translated by Nancy Margaret Paul and W. Scott Palmer. New York: Macmillan, 1912.

Besançon, A. *Histoire et expérience du moi*. Paris: Flammarion, 1971.

Blanchard, P. "L'Espace intérieur chez Saint Augustin d'après le livre dix des *Confessions*." *Congrès International Augustinien*, Paris, 21–22 September 1954. Paris: Etudes Augustiniennes, s.d., 535–42.

Blanchot, M. *L'Espace littéraire*. Paris: Gallimard, 1955.
———. "La Parole vaine." In *L'Amitié*. Paris: Gallimard, 1971 (postface to *Le Bavard* of Louis-René des Forêts, "10/18" series, Paris: Union Générale d'Editions, 1963).
———. *Le Livre à venir*. "Idées" series. Paris: Gallimard, 1959.
Blin, G. *Stendhal et les problèmes de la personnalité*. Vol. 1. Paris: José Corti, 1958.
Bloomfield, M. *The Seven Deadly Sins: An Introduction to the History of a Religious Concept, with Special Reference to Medieval English Literature*. East Lansing: Michigan State University Press, 1967.
Blunt, A. "Self-Portraits." *Burlington Magazine* (1947):219ff.
Bodin, J. *Methodus ad Facilem Historiarum Cognitionem*. Paris, 1572. *Method for the Comprehension of History*. Translated, with notes, by B. Reynolds. New York: Columbia University Press, 1945.
Bolgar, R. R. *The Classical Heritage and Its Beneficiaries: From the Carolingian Age to the Renaissance*. New York: Harper Torchbooks, 1964 (Cambridge University Press, 1954).
Boon, J.-P. *Montaigne: Gentilhomme et essayiste*. Paris, Editions Universitaires, 1971.
Borel, J. "Du Bellay: Poète du retour." *Critique* 242 (July 1967): 619–30.
———. "Narcisse écrit-il?" *La Nouvelle Revue Française* 257 (May 1974):22–30.
———. "Problèmes de l'autobiographie." In Michel Mansuy, ed., *Positions et oppositions sur le roman contemporain: Actes du colloque de Strasbourg*. Paris: Klincksieck, 1971 (republished in *Commentaires*. "Les Essais" series. Paris: Gallimard, 1974).
———. *Le Retour*. Paris: Gallimard, 1970.
———. *Commentaires*. "Les Essais" series, no. 188. Paris: Gallimard, 1974.
———. *Un Voyage ordinaire, caprice*. Paris: Editions de la Table Ronde, 1975.
Borges, J. L. *El Aleph*. Buenos Aires: Emecé, 1957.
Bornscheuer, L. *Topik: Zur Struktur der gesellschaftlichen Einbildungskraft*. Frankfurt: Suhrkampf Verlag, 1977.
Boyce, B. *The Theophrastan Character in England to 1642*. Cambridge, 1947.
Boyd, J. D. *The Function of Mimesis and Its Decline*. Cambridge: Harvard University Press, 1968.
Bradley, Sister R. "Backgrounds of the Title *Speculum* in Medieval Literature." *Speculum* 29 (1954):110–15.
Bréchon, R. *L'Age d'homme de Michel Leiris*. "Poche Critique" series. Paris: Hachette, 1973.
Brée, G. "Michel Leiris: Mazemaker." In James Olney, ed., *Autobiography: Essays Theoretical and Critical*, 194–206. Princeton: Princeton University Press, 1980.
Brès, Y. *La Psychologie de Platon*. Paris, PUF, 1968.

Brosse, J. *Inventaire des sens*. Paris: Grasset, 1965.

Bruaire, C. *Philosophie du corps*. Paris: Editions du Seuil, 1968.

Bruford, W. H. *The German Tradition of Self Cultivation: "Bildung" from Humboldt to Thomas Mann*. Cambridge: Cambridge University Press, 1975.

Brunschvicg, L. *De la connaissance de soi*. Paris: Alcan, 1931.

———. *Descartes et Pascal leteurs de Montaigne*. Neuchâtel, à La Baconnière, 1945.

Brush, C. B. *Montaigne and Bayle: Variations on the Theme of Skepticism*. The Hague: Martinus Nijhoff, 1966.

Bruss, E. W. "L'Autobiographie considérée comme un acte littéraire." *Poétique* 17 (1974):14–26.

———. *Autobiographical Acts: The Changing Situation of a Literary Genre*. Baltimore: Johns Hopkins University Press, 1976.

Buffum, I. *Studies in the Baroque: Montaigne to Rotrou*. New Haven: Yale University Press, 1957.

Burgelin, P. *La Philosophie de l'existence de Jean-Jacques Rousseau*. Paris: PUF, 1952.

Burke, K. *A Rhetoric of Motives*. New York: Prentice-Hall, 1950.

———. *The Rhetoric of Religion: Studies in Logology*. Berkeley and Los Angeles: University of California Press, 1970.

Burton, R. *The Anatomy of Melancholy* (1621–1640). Edited by A. R. Shilleto. 3 vols. London: 1927.

Bush, D. *English Literature in the Earlier Seventeenth Century, 1600–1660*. Oxford: Clarendon Press, 1945.

Butor, M. "Une Autobiographie dialectique." *Critique* (December 1955). Republished in *Répertoire*, Paris: Editions de Minuit, 1960, and in *Essais sur les modernes*, 361–76. "Idées" series, Paris: Galliard, 1964).

———. *Le Génie du lieu*. Paris: Grasset, 1958.

———. "L'Usage des pronoms personnels dans le roman." In *Répertoire II*, 61–72. Paris: Editions de Minuit, 1964.

———. *L'Emploi du temps*. Preface by Georges Raillard. Paris: Union Générale d'Edition, 1966.

———. *Portrait de l'artiste en jeune singe*. Paris: Gallimard, 1967.

———. *Essais sur les Essais*. "Les Essais" series, no. 133. Paris: Gallimard, 1968.

Caillois, R. "Les Cartes." *Encyclopédie de la Pléiade*. Vol. 23, *Jeux et sports*, 951–69. Paris: Gallimard, 1967.

Capellanus, A. [André le Chapelain.] *De arte honeste amandi*.

Caplan, H. "Memoria: Treasure-House of Eloquence." *Of Eloquence: Studies in Ancient and Medieval Rhetoric*. Ithaca and London: Cornell University Press, 1970.

Cardano, G. *De Vita Propria Liber*. Paris, 1643. *The Book of My Life*. Translated by J. Stoner. New York: E. P. Dutton, 1930. Republished by Dover, 1963.

Caramaschi, E. "Maurice Barrès et Venise." In *Maurice Barrès: Actes du colloque organisé par la Faculté des Lettres et des Sciences Humaines de l'Université de Nancy (22–25 October 1962)*. Paper no. 24. Nancy: Annales de l'Est, 1963.

Carre, J. H. "André Malraux and His *Antimémoires:* The Metamorphosis of Autobiography." *Genre* 6, 2 (June 1973):233–49.

Cassirer, E. *The Individual and the Cosmos in Renaissance Philosophy.* Translated by Domandi. New York: Harper Torchbooks, 1963.

Castor, G. *Pléiade Poetics: A Study in Sixteenth-Century Thought and Terminology.* Cambridge: Cambridge University Press, 1964.

Cave, T. *The Cornucopian Text: Problems of Writing in the French Renaissance.* Oxford: Oxford University Press, 1979.

Charles, M. "Bibliothèques." *Poétique* 33 (1978):1–27.

Chastel, A. "L'Autoportrait à la Renaissance." Text of unpublished course. Collège de France, 1970–1971.

Cicero. *Topica, De Oratore, De Inventione.*

———. (pseudo Cicero) *Rhetorica ad Herennium.* Introduced and translated by H. Caplan. Cambridge, Mass., and London: Loeb Classical Library, 1964.

Cilleruelo, L. "La 'Memoria Dei,' segun san Agustin." *Augustinus Magister: Congrès international augustinien.* Vol. 1, pp. 499–509. Paris: Etudes Augustiniennes, 1954.

Clark, C. E. "Un Dictionnaire des idées reçues au XVIe siècle: Les 'Epithètes' de Maurice de la Porte." *Revue des Sciences Humaines* (1970): 187.

Clifford, J., ed. *Sulfur* 15 (1986), featuring new translations of Michel Leiris.

———. *The Predicament of Culture: Twentieth-Century Ethnography, Literature, and Art.* Cambridge: Harvard University Press, 1988.

Colie, R. L. *The Resources of Kind: Genre Theory in the Renaissance.* Berkeley: University of California Press, 1973.

Colonna, F. *Le Songe de Poliphile.* Facsimile republication with a preface by A.-M. Schmidt. Paris: Club des Libraires de France, 1963.

Courcelle, P. *Les Confessions de Saint Augustin dans la tradition littéraire: Antécédents et postérité.* Paris: Etudes Augustiniennes, 1963.

Curtius, E. R. *Europäische Literatur und lateinisches Mittelalter.* Bern: Francke, 1948. *European Literature and the Latin Middle Ages.* New York: Harper Torchbooks, 1963.

Damisch, H. "D'un Narcisse l'autre." *Nouvelle Revue de Psychanalyse* 13 (1976):109–46.

David, M. V. *Le Débat sur les écritures et hiéroglyphes aux XVIIe et XVIIIe.* Paris: SEVPEN, 1965.

Dawson, E. *The Practical Methode of Meditation,* 1614. In L. L. Martz, ed., *The Meditative Poem,* 3–23. Garden City, N.Y.: Doubleday, 1963.

Delumeau, J. *Naissance et affirmation de la Réforme*. Paris: PUF, 1965.

De Mott, B. "Comenius and the Real Character in England." *PMLA* 70 (1955):1068–81.

———. "Science versus Mnemonics: Notes on John Ray and on John Wilkins' *Essay* Towards a Real Character and a Philosophical Language." *ISIS* 48 (1957):3–12.

———. "The Source and Development of John Wilkins' Philosophical Language." *Journal of English and Germanic Philology* 57 (1958):1–13.

Derrida, J. *De la grammatologie*. Paris: Editions de Minuit, 1967. *Of Grammatology*. Translated by Gayatri Spivak. Baltimore: Johns Hopkins University Press, 1974.

———. *L'Ecriture et la différence*. Paris: Editions du Seuil, 1967. *Writing and Difference*. Translated by Alan Bass. Chicago: University of Chicago Press, 1978.

———. *Marges de la philosophie*. Paris: Editions de Minuit, 1972. *Margins of Philosophy*. Translated by Alan Bass. Chicago: University of Chicago Press, 1982.

Descartes, R. *Discours de la méthode*.

———. *Méditations métaphysiques*.

———. *Regulae*.

———. *The Philosophical Writings of Descartes*. Cambridge: Cambridge University Press, 1985.

Dieckmann, L. *Hieroglyphics: The History of a Literary Symbol*. St. Louis: Washington University Press, 1970.

Dromard, G. *Essai sur la sincérité*. Paris: Alcan, 1910.

Dubois, C.-G. *La Conception de l'histoire en France au XVIe siècle: 1560–1610*. Paris: Nizet, 1977.

Durand, G. *Les structures anthropologiques de l'imaginaire*. 2nd ed. Paris: PUF, 1963.

Eco, U. *La Structure absente*. Paris: Mercure de France, 1972.

Eggs, E. *Moglichkeiten und Grenzen einer wissenschaftlichen Semantik, Dargestellt an den Zeichen "temps," "espace," und "mémoire" in Marcel Proust "A la recherche du temps perdu."* Europäische Hochschulschiften, Reihe XIII, vol. 12. Bern-Frankfurt: Herbert and Peter Lang, 1971.

Ehrmann, J. "Le Dedans et le dehors." *Poétique* 9 (1972):31–40.

Eisenstein, E. L. *The Printing Press as an Agent of Change*. 2 vols. Cambridge: Cambridge University Press, 1979.

Ellenberger, H. F. *The Discovery of the Unconscious*. New York: Basic Books, n.d.

Else, G. F. *Aristotle's Poetics: The Argument*. Cambridge: Harvard University Press, 1957.

Finkielkraut, A. "L'Autobiographie et ses jeux." *Communications* 19 (1972):155–69.

———. "Desire in Autobiography." *Genre* 6, 2 (June 1973):220–32.

Fish, S. *Self-Consuming Artifacts: The Experience of Seventeenth-Century Literature*. Berkeley: University of California Press, 1972.

Flahault, F. *L'Extrême existence: Essai sur les représentations mythiques de l'intériorité*. Paris: François Maspéro, 1972.

Flaubert, G. *Bouvard et Pécuchet*. Paris: Garnier, 1965.

Fletcher, A. *Allegory: The Theory of a Symbolic Mode*. Ithaca: Cornell University Press, 1964.

Foucault, M. "La Pensée du dehors." *Critique* 229 (June 1960):523–46.

———. *Les Mots et les choses: Une Archéologie des sciences humaines*. Paris: Gallimard, 1966. *The Order of Things: An Archeology of the Human Sciences*. New York: Vintage, 1973.

———. *L'Archéologie du savoir*. Paris: Gallimard, 1969.

———. *La Volonté de savoir*. Paris: Gallimard, 1976.

Frame, D. *Montaigne: A Biography*. New York: Harcourt Brace and World, 1965.

———. *Montaigne's "Essais": A Study*. Englewood Cliffs, N. J.: Prentice Hall, 1969.

Francastel, P. *La Figure et le lieu*. Paris: Gallimard, 1967.

Frank, J. "Spatial Form in Modern Literature." *The Widening Gyre: Crisis and Mastery in Modern Literature*. New Brunswick, N. J.: Rutgers University Press, 1963. Republished by Midland Books, Indiana University Press, 1968.

Frappier, J. "Variations sur le thème du miroir de Bernard de Ventadour à Maurice Scève." *Cahiers de l'Association Internationale des Etudes Françaises* 2 (1959):134–58.

Freud, S. "Pour introduire le narcissisme." 1914.

———. *Essais de psychanalyse appliquée*. Paris: Nouvelle Revue Française, 1933.

———. *The Interpretation of Dreams*. Translated by J. Strachey. New York: Avon, 1965.

———. *Dora: Analysis of a Case of Hysteria*. New York: Collier, 1967.

Friedrich, H. *Montaigne*. French translation by R. Rovini. Paris: Gallimard, 1968.

Frye, N. *Anatomy of Criticism*. New York: Atheneum, 1967.

Galay, J.-L. *Philosophie et invention textuelle*. Paris: Klincksieck, 1977.

Gandillac, M. de., J. Fontaine, J. Châtillon, M. Lemoine, J. Gründel, and P. Michaud-Quantin. *La Pensée encyclopédique au Moyen Age*. Neuchâtel: UNESCO-Baconnière, 1966.

Gantheret, F. "Remarques sur la place et le statut du corps en psychanalyse." *Nouvelle Revue de Psychanalyse* 3 (1971):137–46.

Garin, E. "Alcune osservazioni sul *libro* come simbolo." In Enrico Castelli, ed., *Umanesimo e simbolismo*, 91–102. Padua: CEDAM, 1958.

———. *Italian Humanism: Philosophy and Civic Life in the Renaissance*. New York: Harper and Row, 1965.

————. *L'Education de l'homme moderne*. French translation. Paris: Fayard, 1968.

————. *Medioevo e Rinascimento*. Bari: Laterza, 1961. *Moyen Age et Renaissance*. Paris: Gallimard, 1969.

Gasser, M. *Das Selbstbildnis*. Zurich: Kindler, 1961. *Self-Portraits: From the Fifteenth Century to the Present Day*. New York: Appleton Century, 1963.

Gelb, I. J. *A Study of Writing*. Rev. ed. Chicago and London: University of Chicago Press, 1963.

Genette, G. *Figures*. Paris: Editions du Seuil, 1966.

————. *Figures II*. Paris: Editions du Seuil, 1969.

————. *Mimologiques: Voyage en Cratylie*. Paris: Editions du Seuil, 1976.

Girard, A. *Le Journal intime et la notion de personne*. Paris: PUF, 1963.

Glauser, A. *Montaigne paradoxal*. Paris: Nizet, 1972.

Gobeil, M. "Entretien avec Michel Leiris." *Sub-stance* 11–12 (1975).

Gouhier, H. *Maine de Biran par lui-même*. "Les Écrivains de Toujours" series. Paris: Editions du Seuil, 1970.

Gower, J. *Confessio Amantis*. 1390.

————. *Speculum Meditantis*, or *Miroir de l'Omme*. End of the fourteenth century.

Granger, G.-G. *Essai d'une philosophie du style*. Paris: Armand Colin, 1968.

Greene, T. "The Flexibility of the Self in Renaissance Literature." In Demetz, Greene, and Nelson, eds., *The Disciplines of Criticism*, 241–64. New Haven: Yale University Press, 1968.

Greene, W. C. "The Spoken and the Written Word." *Harvard Studies in Classical Philology* 60 (1951):23–59.

Gregg, V. *Human Memory*. London: Methuen, 1975.

Grenier, J. Introduction to J.-J. Rousseau, *Les Rêveries du promeneur solitaire*. No. 1516. Paris: Livre de Poche, 1965.

Grosclaude, P. "Le Moi: L'Instant présent et le sentiment de l'existence chez J.-J. Rousseau." *Europe* 391–92 (1961):52–56.

Gusdorf, G. *La Découverte de soi*. Paris: PUF, 1948.

————. *Mémoire et personne*. 2 vols. (vol. 1: *La mémoire concrète*; vol. 2: *Dialectique de la mémoire*). Paris: PUF, 1951.

————. "Conditions et limites de l'autobiographie." In G. Reichenkron and E. Haase, eds., *Formen der Selbstdarstellung: Festgabe für Fritz Neubert*, 105–23. Berlin: Duncker und Humblot, 1956.

Haas, G. *Essay*. Stuttgart: Netzlersche Verlagsbuchhandlung, 1959.

Hadas, M. *Hellenistic Culture: Fusion and Diffusion*. New York: Norton, 1972.

Hadot, P. "Le Mythe de Narcisse et son interprétation par Plotin." *Nouvelle Revue de Psychanalyse* 13 (1976):81–108.

Halbwachs, M. *Les Cadres sociaux de la mémoire*. Paris: Alcan, 1925.

————. *La Topographie légendaire des évangiles en terre sainte*. Paris: PUF, 1941.

————. *La Mémoire collective*. 2nd ed., enlarged and revised. Paris: PUF, 1968.

Hamlin, C. "The Poetics of Self-Consciousness in European Romanticism: Hölderlin's *Hyperion* and Wordsworth's *Prelude*." *Genre* 6, 2 (June, 1973):142–77.

Hart, F. R. "Notes for an Anatomy of Modern Autobiography." In R. Cohen, ed., *New Directions in Literary History*. Baltimore: Johns Hopkins University Press, 1974.

Hartlaub, G. F. *Zauber des Spiegels: Geschichte und Bedeutung des Spiegels in der Kunst*. Munich, 1951.

————. "Das Selbstbildnerische in der Kunstgeschichte." *Zeitschrift für Kunstwissenschaft* 9 (1955):97–124.

Haydn, H. *The Counter-Renaissance*. New York: Scribners, 1950. Republished by Harcourt, Brace and World, n. d.

Heissenbüttel, H. "Anmerkungen zu einer Literatur der Selbstentblösser (M. Leiris, Breton, Michaux)." *Merkur* 20 (1966).

Hegel, G. W. F. *Aesthetics*. Translated by T. M. Know. Oxford: Oxford University Press, 1974.

Henry, M. *Philosophie et phénoménologie du corps: Essai sur l'ontologie biranniene*. Paris: PUF, 1965.

Hersey, G. L. *Pythagorean Palaces: Magic and Architecture in the Italian Renaissance*. Ithaca and London: Cornell University Press, 1976.

Hodgen, M. T. *Early Anthropology in the Sixteenth and Seventeenth Centuries*. Philadelphia: University of Pennsylvania Press, 1964.

Hollier, Denis. *The College of Sociology, 1937–39*. Translated by Betsy Wing. Minneapolis: University of Minnesota Press, 1988.

Holyoake, S. J. "Montaigne's Attitude Toward Memory." *French Studies* 25, 3 (July 1971):257–70.

Hooykaas, R. "Pierre de le Ramée et l'empirisme scientifique au XVIe siècle." From "La Science au XVIe Siècle," Colloque International de Royaumont, 1957. *Histoire de la pensée*, 2: 299–313. Paris: Hermann, 1957.

Horney, K. *Self-Analysis*. New York: Norton, 1942, 1968.

Howell, W. S. *Logic and Rhetoric in England, 1500–1700*. Princeton: Princeton University Press, 1956.

Hunter, I. M. L. *Memory*. Harmondsworth, Middlesex: Penguin, 1964.

Huysmans, J. K. *A rebours*. Paris, 1884.

Hytier, J. "Le Roman de l'individu et la biographie." *Cahiers de l'Association Internationale des Etudes Françaises* (1967):87–100.

Ivins, W. M., Jr. *Prints and Visual Communication*. Cambridge: MIT Press, 1953.

Jaeger, W. *Paideia: The Ideals of Greek Culture*. 3 vols. Translated by G. Highet. Oxford, 1938–1945.

Jakobson, R. "Concluding Statement: Linguistics and Poetics." In T. A. Seboek, ed., *Style in Language*. Cambridge: MIT Press, 1960.

————. *Questions de poétique.* Paris: Editions du Seuil, 1973.

————. *Main Trends in the Science of Language.* New York: Harper Torchbooks, 1974.

Jardine, L. *Francis Bacon: Discovery and the Art of Discourse.* Cambridge: Cambridge University Press, 1974.

Jones. R. F. "On the Dialogic Impulse in the Genesis of Montaigne's *Essais.*" *Renaissance Quarterly* 30, 2 (1977):172–80.

Joseph, Sister M. *Rhetoric in Shakespeare's Time.* New York: Harcourt, Brace and World, 1962.

Josipovici, G. *The World and the Book: A Study of Modern Fiction.* Stanford: Stanford University Press, 1971.

Joukovsky, F. *La Gloire dans la poésie française et néo-latine du XVIe siècle.* Geneva: Droz, 1969.

Jung, C. G. *Memories, Dreams, Reflections.* Compiled and edited by A. Jaffe. Translated by R. and C. Winston. New York: Vintage, 1961.

————. *The Collected Works of C. G. Jung,* vol. 12. Translated by R. F. C. Hull. Princeton: Princeton University Press, 1968.

————. *Psychologie et alchimie.* Translated by Pernet and Cahen. Paris: Buchet-Chastel, 1970.

Katzenellenbogen, A. *Allegories of the Virtues and Vices in Medieval Art.* London: Warburg Institute, 1939. New edition, New York: Norton, 1964.

————. *The Sculptural Programs of Chartres Cathedral.* New York: Norton, n. d.

Keayne, R. *The Apologia of Robert Keayne: The Self-Portrait of a Puritan Merchant.* Edited by B. Bailyn. New York: Harper Torchbooks, 1965.

Knowlson, J. *Universal Language Schemes in England and France, 1600–1800.* Toronto: University of Toronto Press, 1975.

Labarrière, P.-J. "Le discours du corps." *Esprit* 423 (April 1973):901–12.

Lacan, J. *Ecrits.* Paris: Editions du Seuil, 1966. *Ecrits: A Selection.* Translated by Alan Sheridan. New York: Norton, 1982.

Laferrière, D. "The Subject and Discrepant Use of the Category of Person." *Versus Quaderni di Studi Semiotici* 14 (1976):93–104.

Lafond, J. D. "Les Techniques du portrait dans le *Recueil des portraits et éloges* de 1659." *Cahiers de l'Association Internationale des Etudes Françaises* 18 (1966):139–48. See also discussion, 270–79.

Lamy, Dom. Fr. *De la connaissance de soi-même.* Paris, 1699.

Lanham, R. A. *A Handlist of Rhetorical Terms.* Berkeley: University of California Press, 1969.

————. *The Motives of Eloquence: Literary Rhetoric in the Renaissance.* New Haven: Yale University Press, 1976.

Lapassade, G. *L'Entrée dans la vie: Essai sur l'inachèvement de l'homme.* Paris: Editions de Minuit, 1963. 3rd ed., 1969.

Laplanche, J., and J.-B. Pontalis. *Dictionnaire de psychanalyse.* Paris: PUF, 1967.

Laporte, R. *La Veille*. Paris: Gallimard, 1963.

———. "Le Oui, le non, le neutre." *Critique* 229 (1966):579–90. Published in *Quinze variations sur un thème biographique*. Paris: Flammarion, 1975.

———. *Fugue*. Paris: Gallimard, 1970.

———. *Supplément*. Paris: Gallimard, 1973.

———. *Fugue 3*. Paris: Flammarion, 1975.

———. *Suite*. Paris: Hachette, 1979.

———. "Moriendo" (English translation). *Origin*, 5th series, no. 2 (Winter 1983).

———. *Une Vie (La Veille, Une Voix de fin silence, Pourquoi?, Fugue, Supplément, Fugue 3, Codicille, Suite, Moriendo) biographie*. Paris: P. O. L., 1986.

La Rochefoucauld, F. de. *Maximes*. Edited by J. Truchet. Paris: Garnier, 1967.

Lascault, G. "L'Egypte des égarements." *Critique* 260 (January 1969):54–74.

Lausberg, H. *Handbuch der literarischen Rhetorik*. 2 vols. Munich, 1961.

Lavelle, L. *La Conscience de soi*. Paris: Grasset, 1933.

Lechner, Sister J. M. *Renaissance Concepts of the Commonplaces*. New York: Pageant Press, 1962.

Leclaire, S. *Psychoanalyser: Essai sur l'ordre de l'inconscient et la pratique de la lettre*. Paris: Editions du Seuil, 1968.

Lecointre, S., and J. Le Galliot. "Essai sur la structure d'un mythe personnel dans les *Rêveries du promeneur solitaire*." *Semiotica* 4, 4 (1971):339–364.

Lee, R. W. *Ut Pictura Poesis: The Humanistic Theory of Painting*. New York: Norton, 1967. First published in *Art Bulletin*, 1940.

Leiner, W. "Du portrait dans les épitres liminaires." *Cahiers de l'Association Internationale des Etudes Françaises* 18 (1966):149–58.

Leiris, M. *L'Afrique fantôme*. Paris: Gallimard, 1934.

———. "Le Sacré dans la vie quotidienne." *La Nouvelle Revue Française* 51, 298 (1938):22–34.

———. *L'Age d'homme*. Paris: Gallimard, 1939. *Manhood*. Translated by Richard Howard. New York: Grossman Publishers, 1963.

———. ". . . reusement!" *Domaine Français*, 235–39. Geneva and Paris: Editions des Trois Collines, 1943.

———. *Aurora*. Paris: Gallimard, 1946.

———. *La Langue secrète des Dogons de Sanga*. Paris: Institut d'Ethnologie, 1948.

———. *La Règle du jeu, Biffures*. Paris: Gallimard, 1948.

———. *Fourbis*. Paris: Gallimard, 1955.

———. *Fibrilles*. Paris: Gallimard, 1966.

———. *Frêle bruit*. Paris: Gallimard, 1976.

———. *Brisées*. Paris: Le Mercure de France, 1964.

————. *Mots sans mémoire*. Paris: Gallimard, 1969. Includes *Simulacre* (1925) and *Glossaire j'y serre mes gloses* (1939).

Lejeune, P. *L'Autobiographie en France*. "U 2" series. Paris: Armand Collin, 1971.

————. "Ecriture et sexualité." *Europe* (February-March 1971):113–43.

————. *Lire Leiris: Autobiographie et langage*. Paris: Klincksieck, 1975.

————. *Le Pacte autobiographique*. Paris: Editions du Seuil, 1975.

Le Men, J. *L'Espace figuratif et les structures de la personnalité*. Paris: PUF, 1966.

————. "Le Moi, l'autre, et la symbolique spatiale." *Les Etudes Philosophiques* 3 (1971):335–42.

Leporeus Avallonensis, G. *Ars Memorativa*. Paris, 1520.

Leroi-Gourhan, A. *Le Geste et la parole*. 2 vols. Paris: Albin Michel, 1965.

Lewis, G. *Le Problème de l'inconscient et le cartésianisme*. Paris: PUF, 1950.

Lhermitte, J. *L'Image de notre corps*. Paris: Nouvelle Revue Critique, 1939.

"Lieux du corps." *Nouvelle Revue de Psychanalyse* 3 (1971).

Lotman, I. *La Structure du texte artistique*. French translation. Paris: Gallimard, 1973.

Lottin, Dom. O. *Psychologie et morale aux XIIe et XIIIe siècles*. 6 vols. Paris, 1942–1960.

Loyola, San I. de. *Ejercicios espirituales*. *Obras completas*, 153–238. Madrid: Biblioteca de Autores Cristianos, 1952. *The Spiritual Exercises of St. Ignatius*. Translated by Louis J. Puhl, S. J. Chicago: Loyola University Press, 1951.

Luria, A. R. "Memory and the Structure of Mental Processes." *Problems of Psychology* 1 (1960).

————. *The Mind of a Mnemonist (A Little Book about a Vast Memory)*. Translated by L. Solataroff. New York and London: Basic Books, 1968. *Une Prodigieuse mémoire*. Neuchatel: Delachaux et Niestlé, 1972.

Lyons, B. G. *Voices of Melancholy: Studies in Literary Treatments of Melancholy in Renaissance England*. New York: Norton, 1975.

Maine de Biran, M. F. P. *Oeuvres de Maine de Biran accompagnées de notes et d'appendices*. 14 vols. Published by T. Tisserand. Paris: Alcan, 1920; Paris: PUF, 1940.

McCarthy, M. *Venice Observed*. New York: Harcourt Brace and World, 1963.

McFarlane, I. D. "Montaigne and the Concept of Imagination." In *The French Renaissance and Its Heritage: Essays Presented to Alan M. Boase*. London, 1968.

Mâle, E. *L'Art religieux du XIIIe siècle en France*. Paris, 1989. New edition, 2 vols. Paris: Le Livre de Poche, 1968.

Malebranche, N. de. *Recherche de la vérité*. *OEuvres*, vol. 3. Paris: Charpentier, n. d.

Malraux, A. *Anti-Memoirs*. Translated by Terence Kilmartin. New York: Bantam, 1968.

————. *Le Miroir des limbes—Lazare*. Paris: Gallimard, 1974.

————. *Le Miroir des limbes*. Vol. 1: *Antimémoires;* vol. 2: *La corde et le souris*. Paris: Gallimard, 1976.

————. *Lazarus*. Translated by Terence Kilmartin. New York: Holt, Rinehart, and Winston, 1977.

Mandel, B. J. "The Autobiographer's Art." *Journal of Aesthetics and Art Criticism* 27 (1968):215–26.

Mannoni, O. "L'Analyse originelle." *Les Temps Modernes* 22, 253 (1967):3136–52.

Mansuy, J., ed. *Actes du colloque de Strasbourg*. Paris: Klincksieck, 1971.

Marcel, G. *Journal métaphysique*. Paris: NRF, 1937.

Marin, L. "Du corps au texte: Propositions métaphysiques sur l'origine du récit." *Esprit* 423 (1973):913–28.

————. *Etudes sémiologiques*. Paris: Klincksieck, 1971.

————. *Utopiques: Jeux d'espaces*. Paris: Editions de Minuit, 1973.

Marrou, H. I., *Saint Augustin et la fin de la culture antique*. Paris: E. de Boccard, 1937.

Martz, L. L. *The Poetry of Meditation*. New Haven: Yale University Press, 1954.

————, ed. *The Meditative Poem*. Garden City, N.Y.: Doubleday-Anchor, 1963.

Maubon, C. *Michel Leiris au travail: Analyse et transcription d'un fragment de Fourbis*. Pisa: Pubblicazioni della Società Universitaria per gli Studia di Lingua e Letteratura Francese, Pacine Editore, 1987.

Mauriac, F. *Ecrits intimes*. Geneva and Paris: La Palatine, 1953.

Mehlman, J. "Towards Leiris: On Literature and Bullfights." *Genre* 6, 2 (1973):204–19.

————. *A Structural Study of Autobiography*. Ithaca: Cornell University Press, 1974.

Melanchthon, P. *Elementorum rhetorices*. Paris, 1532.

"Mémoires." *Nouvelle Revue de Psychanalyse* 15 (1977).

Mercadier, G. *Diego de Torres Villarroel: Masques et miroirs*. Paris: Editions Hispaniques, 1980.

Merleau-Ponty, M. *Phénoménologie de la perception*. Paris: Gallimard, 1945.

————. *L'Unité de l'âme et du corps chez Malebranche, Biran, et Bergson*. Published by J. Deprun. Paris: Vrin, 1968.

————. *Signes*. Paris: Gallimard. *Signs*. Northwestern University Press, 1964.

Michaux, H. *L'Espace du dedans*. Paris: Gallimard, 1966.

Middleton, A. E. *Memory Systems, Old and New*. 3rd ed. New York, 1888.

Miller, P. *The New England Mind: The Seventeenth Century*. Vol. 1. Boston: Beacon Press, 1961.

Montaigne, M. de. *The Complete Essays of Montaigne*. Translated by Donald Frame. Stanford: Stanford University Press, 1958.

————. *Essais*. "Bibliothèque de la Pléiade" series. Paris: Gallimard, 1962.

Morand, P. *Venises*. Paris: Gallimard, 1971.

Morris, J. N. *Versions of the Self: Studies in English Autobiography from John Bunyan to John Stuart Mill*. New York and London: Basic Books, 1966.

Munteano, B. "Des 'Constantes' en littérature: Principes et structures rhétoriques." *RLC* 31 (1957):388–420.

———. "Humanisme et rhétorique: La survie littéraire des rhéteurs anciens." *RHL* 58 (1959):145–56.

Murchisson, C., ed. *A History of Psychology in Autobiography*. 3 vols. Worcester, Mass.: Clark University Press, 1930.

Murphy, J. J. *Rhetoric in the Middle Ages: A History of Rhetorical Theory from Saint Augustine to the Renaissance*. Berkeley: University of California Press, 1974.

Nadeau, M. *Michel Leiris et la quadrature du cercle*. Paris: Julliard-Lettres Nouvelles, 1963.

Nahm, M. C., ed. *Selections from Early Greek Philosophy*. New York: Appleton Century Crofts, 1934.

Nancy, J.-L. "Larvatus pro deo." *Glyph* 2 (1978):14–36.

———. "Mundus est fabula." *Modern Language Notes* 93 (1978):635–53.

———. *Ego-sum*. Paris: Aubier-Flammarion, 1979.

Nicole, P. *Essais de morale* (1671–1714). 6 vols. Texts chosen and commented on by Emile Thouverez. Paris: Gabalda, 1926.

Nietzsche, F. *On the Genealogy of Morals* and *Ecce Homo*. Edited and translted by W. Kaufman. New York: Vintage, 1969.

North, H. *Sophrosyne: Self-Knowledge and Self-Restraint in Greek Literature*. Ithaca: Cornell University Press, 1966.

Notopoulos, J. A. "Mnemosyne in Oral Literature." *Transactions of the American Philological Association* 69 (1938):465–93.

O'Connor, Sister M. C. *The Art of Dying Well: The Development of the Ars Morendi*. New York: Columbia University Press, 1942.

Olney, J. *Metaphors of Self: The Meaning of Autobiography*. Princeton: Princeton University Press, 1972.

———, ed. *Autobiography: Essays Theoretical and Critical*. Princeton: Princeton University Press, 1980.

Ong, W. J. *Ramus, Method, and the Decay of Dialogue*. Cambridge: Harvard University Press, 1958.

———. "From Allegory to the Diagram in the Renaissance." *JAAC* 17 (1959):423–40.

———. *The Presence of the Word: Some Prolegomena for Cultural and Religious History*. New Haven: Yale University Press, 1967. New edition, New York: Simon and Schuster, 1970.

———. *Rhetoric, Romance, and Technology*. Ithaca: Cornell University Press, 1971.

Ou. Li. Po. *La Littérature potentielle*. "Idées" series. Paris: Gallimard, 1973.

Panofsky, E. *Early Netherlandish Painting*. 2 vols. "Icon Editions" series.

New York: Harper and Row, 1971. First published Cambridge: Harvard University Press, 1953.

———. *Studies in Iconology.* "Icon Editions" series. New York: Harper and Row, 1972.

Pascal, R. "Autobiography as an Art Form." In F. Böckmann, ed., *Stil und Formprobleme in der Literatur.* Verträge des VII Kongresses Internationalen Vereinigung für Moderne Sprachen und Literaturen in Heidelberg. Heidelberg, 1959.

———. *Design and Truth in Autobiography.* London: Routledge and Kegan Paul, 1960.

Paulhan, F. *La Fonction de la mémoire et le souvenir affectif.* Paris: Alcan, 1904.

Paulhan, J. *Oeuvres complètes.* Paris: Cercle du Livre Précieux, 1966.

Paz, O. *Le Singe grammairien.* "Les Sentiers de la Création" series. Geneva: Skira, 1972. *The Monkey Grammarian.* Translated by Helen Lane. Seaver Books, 1981.

Pellegrini, C., ed. *Venezia nelle letterature moderne.* Venice and Rome: Istituto per la Collaborazione Culturale, 1961.

Pellegrino, M. *Les "Confessions" de Saint Augustin: Guide de lecture.* Paris: Alsatia, 1960.

Perelman, C., and L. Olbrechts-Tyteca. "Logique et rhétorique." *Revue Philosophique de la France et de l'Etranger* 140 (1950):33.

———. *Traité de l'argumentation: La nouvelle rhétorique.* 2 vols. Paris: PUF, 1958.

———. *L'Empire rhétorique.* Paris: J. Vrin, 1977.

Perkins, J. A. *The Concept of Self in the French Enlightenment.* Geneva: Droz, 1969.

Petronius. *Satyricon.*

Peyre, H. *Literature and Sincerity.* New Haven: Yale University Press, 1963.

Phillips, M. M. *The "Adages" of Erasmus: A Study with Translations.* Cambridge: Cambridge University Press, 1964.

Piaget, J., ed. *Logique et connaissance scientifique.* In *Encyclopédie de la Pléiade,* vol. 22. Paris: Gallimard, 1967.

Piatigorsky, A. " 'If I Were You' (A Few Remarks about Cultural Understanding." *Russian Literature* 5, 1 (January 1977):37–40.

Piattelli-Palmarini, M. "L'Entrepôt biologique et le démon comparateur." *Nouvelle Revue de Psychanalyse* 15 (1977):105–25.

Poirion, D. *Le Roman de la rose.* "Connaissance des Lettres" series. Paris: Hatier, 1973.

Pontalis, J.-B. *Après Freud.* Paris: Julliard, 1965.

Pope, M. *The Story of Decipherment from Egyptian Hieroglyphics to Linear B.* London: Thames and Hudson, 1975.

Popkin, R. A. *The History of Scepticism from Erasmus to Descartes.* Rev. ed. New York: Harper Torchbooks, 1964.

Porteau, P. *Montaigne et la vie pédagogique de son temps.* Paris: Droz, 1935.

Pouilloux, J.-Y. *Lire les Essais de Montaigne.* Paris: Maspéro, 1969.

Poulet, G. *L'Espace proustien.* Paris: Gallimard, 1963.

——. *Entre moi et moi.* Paris: José Corti, 1977.

Pourrat, P. *La spiritualité chrétienne.* 3 vols. (Vol. 3: *Les temps modernes).* Paris: J. Gabalda, 1927.

Praz, M. *Mnemosyne: The Parallel Between Literature and the Visual Arts.* Bollingen Series, vol. 35, no. 16. Princeton: Princeton University Press, 1970.

Prévost, J. *Essai sur l'introspection.* Paris: Au Sans Pareil, 1927.

Proust, M. *A la recherche du temps perdu.* 3 vols. "Bibliothèque de la Pléiade" series. Paris: Gallimard, 1955.

Prudence. *Psychomachia, Patrol.* Vol. 60, series 19 sq.

Quintillian,. *Institutio Oratoria.* 4 vols. London and Cambridge: Loeb Classical Library, 1969.

Radcliff-Umstead, D. "Giulio Camillo's Emblems of Memory." *Yale French Studies* 47:47–56.

Raillard, G. Postface to *L'Emploi du temps* by M. Butor. "10/18" series. Paris: UGE, 1966.

Rambures, J.-L. de. "Entretien avec Claude Lévi-Strauss." *Le Monde,* 21 June 1974, 26. Republished in *Comment travaillent les écrivains,* 178. Paris: Flammarion, 1978.

Ramnoux, C. "Nouvelle réhabilitation des Sophistes." *RHM* 73 (1968):1–15.

Ramus, P. [Pierre de La Ramée]. *Dialectique* (1555). Edited by M. Dassonville. Geneva: Droz, 1964.

Raymond, M. "J.-J. Rousseau et le problème de la connaissance de soi." *Studi Francesi* 18 (September-December 1962):457–72.

——. *J.-J. Rousseau: La Quête de soi et la rêverie.* Paris: José Corti, 1962 (3rd printing 1970).

Reichenkron, G., and E. Haase, eds. *Formen der Selbstdarstellung: Festgabe für Fritz Neubert.* Berlin: Dunker und Humboldt, 1956.

Rice, E. F. *The Renaissance Idea of Wisdom.* Cambridge: Harvard University Press, 1958.

Rice, W. H. *The European Ancestry of Villon's Satirical Testaments.* New York: Syracuse University Monographs, 1941.

Ricoeur, P. *De l'interprétation.* Paris: Editions du Seuil, 1965. *Freud and Philosophy: An Essay on Interpretation.* Translated by Denis Savage. New Haven: Yale University Press, 1970.

Rider, F. *The Dialectic of Selfhood in Montaigne.* Stanford: Stanford University Press, 1973.

Riffaterre, M. "Les *Antimémoires* d'André Malraux." *Essais de stylistique structurale,* 286–306. Paris: Flammarion, 1971.

Rimbaud, A. *Une Saison en enfer.*

Rivière, J. *De la sincérité envers soi-même* (1912). Paris: Gallimard, 1943.

"Roger Laporte." *Digraphe* 18–19 (April 1979).

Roger, P. *Roland Barthes: Roman.* Paris: Grasset, 1986.

Ronat, M. "Le Passé composé." *Action poétique* 45, 4 (1970):37–45.

Rosolato, G. "Recension du corps." *Nouvelle Revue de Psychanalyse* 3, "Lieux du corps" (Spring 1971):5–28.

Rossi, P. "Immagini e memoria locale nei secoli XIV et XV." *Revista critica di storia della filosofia* 2 (1958):149–91.

———. "La Costruzione delle immagini nei trattati di memoria artificiale del Rinascimento." In Enrico Castelli, ed., *Umanesimo e simbolismo,* 161–78. Padua: CEDAM, 1958.

———. *Clavis universalis: Arti mnemoniche e logica combinatoria da Lullo a Leibniz.* Milan and Naples: Ricciardi, 1960.

———. *Francis Bacon: From Magic to Science.* English translation. Chicago: University of Chicago Press, 1968. First ed. Bari: Editori Laterza, 1957.

Rossky, W. "Imagination in the English Renaissance: Psychology and Poetics." *Studies in the Renaissance* 5 (1958):48–73.

Roudaut, J. *Michel Butor ou le livre futur.* Paris: Gallimard, 1964.

———. *Trois villes orientées.* Paris: Gallimard, 1967.

Rousseau, J.-J. *Reveries of the Solitary Walker.* Translated by Peter France. Harmondsworth, Middlesex: Penguin, 1979.

Rousset, J. "Monologue et soliloque (1650–1700)." *Ideen und formen: Festschrift für Hugo Friedrich,* 203–13. Frankfurt: Vittorio Klostermann, 1965.

———. "La Première personne chez Chasles et Marivaux." *Cahiers de l'Association Internationale des Etudes Françaises* 19 (March 1967):101–14.

———. "Les Difficultés de l'autoportrait." *Revue d'Histoire Littéraire de la France* 69, 3–4 (May-August 1969):540–50.

———. *Narcisse romancier.* Paris: José Corti, 1973.

Routh, H. V. "Origins of the Essay in French and English Literatures." *Modern Language Review* 15 (1920):28–40, 143–51.

Rowe, J. H. "The Renaissance Foundations of Anthropology." *American Anthropologist* 67, 1 (February 1965):1–20.

Russell, D. "Du Bellay's Emblematic Vision of Rome." *Yale French Studies* 47, "Image and Symbol in the Renaissance" (1972):98–109.

Sabbadini, R. *Il metodo degli umanisti.* Florence, 1920.

Saint Augustine. *Les Confessions.* Introduction, translation, and notes by J. Trabucco. Paris: Garnier-Flammarion, 1964. *Confessions.* Translated by R. S. Pine-Coffin. Baltimore: Penguin, 1964.

Samuel, R. "Friedrich Nietzche's *Ecce Homo:* An Autobiography?" In Schludermann, Brigitte, et al., eds., *Deutung und Bedeutung: Studies in*

German Literature Presented to Karl-Werner Maurer. "De Propietatibus Litterarum," Series Major, 25. The Hague: Mouton, 1973.

Sartre, J.-P. *L'Imagination.* Paris: Alcan, 1936. New edition, Paris: PUF, 1949.

——. *L'Etre et le néant.* Paris: Gallimard, 1943.

——. *L'Imaginaire* (1940). "Idées" series. Paris: Gallimard, 1966.

Sayce, R. A. *The Essays of Montaigne: A Critical Exploration.* London: Weidenfeld and Nicolson, 1973.

Schefer, J.-L. *L'Invention du corps chrétien: Saint Augustin, le dictionnaire, la mémoire.* Paris: Galilée, 1975.

Schérer, J. *Le "Livre" de Mallarmé.* Paris: Gallimard, 1957.

Schilder, P. *The Image and Appearance of the Human Body.* London: Psyche Monograph no. 4, 1935.

Schön, P. M. *Vorformen des Essays in Antike und Humanismus.* Wiesbaden: Mainzer Romanistische Arbeiten, Franz Steiner, 1954.

Schroeder, W. "De Ethnographiae Antiquae Locis Quibusdam Communis Observationes." Thesis. Halle, 1921.

Schwartz, H. "The Mirror in Art." *Art Quarterly* 15, 2 (Summer 1952):96–118.

Sebeok, T., ed. *Style in Language.* Cambridge: MIT Press, 1960.

Secret, F. *Les Kabbalistes chrétiens de la Renaissance.* Paris, 1964.

Seigel, J. E. *Rhetoric and Philosophy in Renaissance Humanism.* Princeton: Princeton University Press, 1968.

Servier, J. *Histoire de l'utopie.* "Idées" series. Paris: Gallimard, 1967.

Sharatt, P., ed. *French Renaissance Studies, 1540–1570: Humanism and the Encyclopedia.* Edinburgh: Edinburgh University Press, 1976.

Shumaker, W. *English Autobiography: Its Emergence, Materials, and Form.* Berkeley: University of California Press, 1954.

Simon, R. *Robert Burton (1577–1640) et L'Anatomie de la mélancolie.* Paris, 1964.

Simon, R. H. *Orphée médusé: Autobiographies de Michel Leiris.* Lausanne: L'Age de l'Homme, 1984.

Sloan, T. O. "Rhetoric and Meditation: Three Case Studies." *Journal of Medieval and Renaissance Studies* 1 (1971):45–48.

Sollers, P. "Littérature et totalité." *L'Ecriture et l'expérience des limites.* Paris: Editions du Seuil, 1970.

Sonnino, L. A. *A Handbook to Sixteenth-Century Rhetoric.* London: Routledge and Kegan Paul, 1968.

Sorabji, R. *Aristotle on Memory.* Providence: Brown University Press, 1972.

Spicker, S. F., ed. *The Philosophy of the Body.* Chicago: Quadrangle Books, 1970.

Starobinski, J. "Jean-Jacques Rousseau: Reflet, réflexion, projection." *Cahiers de l'Association Internationale des Etudes Françaises* 11 (May 1959).

——. "Hamlet et Freud." *Les Temps Modernes* 22, 253 (June 1967):2113–35.

————. "Montaigne et la dénonciation du mensonge." *Dialectica* 22, 2 (1968):120–31.

————. "Jalons pour une histoire du concept d'imagination." *La Relation critique*, 173–95. Paris: Gallimard, 1970.

————. "Le Style de l'autobiographie." *Poétique* 3 (1970):257–65. Republished in *La Relation critique*, 83–98. Paris: Gallimard, 1970.

————. "Je hais comme les portes d'Hadès." *Nouvelle Revue de Psychanalyse* 9 (Spring 1974).

————. *Montaigne en mouvement*. Paris: Gallimard, 1982.

Struever, N. S. *The Language of History in the Renaissance: Rhetorical and Historical Consciousness in Florentine Humanism*. Princeton: Princeton University Press, 1970.

Tabourot des Accords, E. *Bigarrures*. Paris, 1662.

Teyssèdre, B. *Foi de fol: Récit drolatique enchevêtré de plagiats et d'exemples*. Paris: Gallimard, 1968.

Théorie d'ensemble. Tel Quel. Paris: Editions du Seuil, 1968.

Thibaudeau, J. "Le Roman comme autobiographie." *Tel Quel* 34 (Summer 1968):67–74. Republished in *Théorie d'ensemble*, Tel Quel, 212–20. Paris: Editions du Seuil, 1968.

Thibaudet, A. *Montaigne*. Edited by F. Gray. Paris: Gallimard, 1963.

Thomas, J. J., ed. Michel Leiris issue of *Sub-stance* 11–12 (1975).

Todorov, T. "Esthétique et sémiotique au XVIIIe siècle." *Critique* 308 (January 1973):26–39.

————. *Poétique*. "Points" series. Paris: Editions du Seuil, 1973.

————. *Théories du symbole*. Paris: Editions du Seuil, 1977.

Tuve, R. *Elizabethan and Metaphysical Imagery*. Chicago: University of Chicago Press, 1947.

————.*Allegorical Imagery: Some Mediaeval Books and Their Posterity*. Princeton: Princeton University Press, 1966.

Untersteiner, M. *The Sophists*. Translated by K. Freeman. Oxford: Oxford University Press, 1954.

Vance, E. "Augustine's *Confessions* and the Grammar of Selfhood." *Genre* 6, 1 (March 1973):1–28.

————. "Le Moi comme langage: Saint Augustin et l'autobiographie." *Poétique* 14 (1973):163–77.

Vannier, B. *L'Inscription du corps: Pour une sémiologie du corps balzacien*. Paris: Klincksieck, 1972.

Vasoli, C. *La Dialettica e la retorica dell'Umanesimo: "Invenzione" e "methode" nella cultura del XV e XVI secolo*. Milan, 1968.

Vernant, J.-P. "Aspects mythiques de la mémoire et du temps." *Mythe et pensée chez les Grecs*, 1:80–124. Paris: François Maspéro, 1971. *Myth and Thought among the Greeks*. London and Boston: Routledge and Kegan Paul, 1979.

Vico, G. *The Autobiography of Giambattista Vico*. Translated by M. H. Fisch and T. Bergin. Ithaca: Cornell University Press, 1964.

————. *The New Science of Giambattista Vico.* 3rd ed. Translated by T. Bergin and M. H. Fisch. Ithaca and London: Cornell University Press, 1970.

Vilain, J. "L'Auto-portrait caché dans la peinture flamande du XVe siècle." *Revue de l'Art* 8 (June 1970):53–55.

Villey, P. *Les Sources et l'évolution des "essais" de Montaigne.* 2 vols. Paris, 1908.

————. *Les Essais de Montaigne.* Paris: Nizet, 1946.

Vincent de Beauvais. *Speculum Maius.* 4 vols. Douai, 1624.

Vinge, L. *The Narcissus Theme in Western European Literature up to the Early Nineteenth Century.* Lund: Gleerups, 1967.

Vitali, R. *Gorgia: Retorica e filosofia.* Urbino: Argalia: 1971.

Vitz, E. B. *The Crossroad of Intentions: A Study of Symbolic Expression in the Poetry of François Villon.* The Hague and Paris: Mouton, 1974.

Vives, J. L. *Introductio ad Sapientiam . . .* Parisiis: Apud Simonem Colinaeum, 1527.

Vovelle, M. *Piété baroque et déchristianisation en Provence au XVIIIe siècle: Les Attitudes devant la mort d'après les clauses des testaments.* Paris: Plon, 1973.

Vuillemin, J. *Essai sur la signification de la mort.* Paris: PUF, 1948.

————. *Le Miroir de Venise.* "Dossiers des Lettres Nouvelles" series. Paris: Julliard, 1965.

Walker, D. P. "Le Chant orphique de Marsile Ficin." *Musique et poésie au XVIe siècle,* 17–33. Paris: CNRS, 1954.

Wallace, K. *Francis Bacon on Communication and Rhetoric.* Chapel Hill: University of North Carolina Press, 1943.

Walsh, J., Jr. *Portrait of the Artist.* Catalogue of an exhibition at the Metropolitan Museum of Art, New York, 18 January-7 March 1972.

Watrigant, H. "La Genèse des *Exercices* de Saint Ignace de Loyola." *Etudes* 71 (1897):506–29; 72:195–216; 73:199–228.

Webber, J. *The Eloquent "I": Style and Self in Seventeenth-Century Prose.* Madison: University of Wisconsin Press, 1968.

Weinberg, B. "Montaigne's Readings for 'Des cannibales.' " *Studies in Honor of William Leon Wiley,* 261–79.

Weintraub, K. J. *The Value of the Individual: Self and Circumstance in Autobiography.* Chicago: University of Chicago Press, 1978.

Weiss, R. *The Renaissance Discovery of Classical Antiquity.* New York: Humanities Press, 1973.

Wenzel, S. "The Seven Deadly Sins: Some Problems of Research." *Speculum* 43 (1968).

Whyte, L. L. *The Unconscious before Freud.* New York: Basic Books, 1960. New edition, London: Social Science Paperbacks, 1970.

Wilden, A. "Par divers moyens on arrive à pareille fin: A Reading of Montaigne." *Modern Language Notes* 83, 3 (May 1968):577–97.

————. "Montaigne's *Essays* in the Context of Communication." *Modern Language Notes* 85 (1970):454–78.

Williamson, G. *The Senecan Amble: Prose from Bacon to Collier* (1951). Chicago: University of Chicago Press, 1966.

Wimsatt, J. I. *Allegory and Mirror: Tradition and Structure in Middle English Literature*. New York: Pegasus, Western Publishing, 1970.

Wind, E. *Pagan Mysteries in the Renaissance*. Revised and enlarged ed. New York: Norton, 1968.

Wittkower, R. and M. *Born under Saturn: The Character and Conduct of Artists*. New York: Norton, 1969.

Wright, T. *The Passions of the Minde in Generall*. London, 1621.

Yates, F. A. *The Art of Memory*. Chicago: University of Chicago Press, 1966. French translation: *L'Art de la mémoire*. Paris: Gallimard, 1975.

———. *Theatre of the World*. Chicago: University of Chicago Press, 1969.

———. *Zardino de oration*. Venice, 1494.

Zeitlin, J. "The Development of Bacon's Essays, with Special Reference to the Influence of Montaigne upon Them." *Journal of English and Germanic Philology* 27 (October 1928):469–519.

Zolla, E. *Storia del fantasticare*. Milan: Bompiani, 1964.

Name Index

Agricola, Rudolph, 169–70, 171 173, 174
Alciati, Andrea, 135
Alcibiades, 128, 265, 311
Aphthonius, 172
Apuleus, 46, 274
Ardent, Raoul, 28, 169, 171
Aristotle, 52, 111, 170, 172, 192, 262, 328
Artaud, Antonin, 4
Augustine, St., 3–4, 7, 9, 10, 13, 19, 34,
  35, 36, 37–71, 84, 144, 221, 222, 274,
  290, 319, 321, 329, 330, 337, 345
Aulu-Gellius, 167
Avallonensis, Guglielmus Leporeus, 211

Bachelard, Gaston, 100, 102–3, 190
Backès-Clément, Catherine, 203
Bacon, Francis, 1
Bacon, Lord Francis, 13, 20, 60, 73, 89,
  120, 127, 134, 138, 176–78, 179–90,
  194, 195, 246, 247, 262, 316, 339
Barrès, Maurice, 16, 19, 64–71, 229
Barthes, Roland, 7, 8, 9, 14–16, 17, 31–
  33, 34, 50, 52–53, 64, 98, 99, 100, 101–
  2, 165–66, 193, 194, 195, 215, 216, 238,
  258–63, 283, 317–27, 343, 345
Bataille, Georges, 8, 222, 226
Baudelaire, Charles, 17, 67, 88, 150
Baxandall, Michael, 48
Beckett, Samuel, 5, 11
Biran, Maine de, 230, 287, 297

Blanchot, Maurice, 8, 11–12, 221, 340,
  344
Boccaccio, Giovanni, 134
Bodin, Jean, 174
Bolgar, R. R., 171
Bolzani, Giovanni, 135
Borel, Jacques, 6–7, 15, 17, 96, 98, 100,
  101, 102, 131, 133, 139–56, 193, 217,
  319, 321, 343
Borges, Jorge Luis, 73, 269
Bouaystuau, Pierre de, 167
Breton, André, 90, 223
Brosse, Jacques, 230
Bruaire, Claude, 327–33
Burke, Kenneth, 75, 197
Burton, Robert, 272
Butor, Michel, 82–84, 86, 124, 125, 131–
  34

Camillo Delminio, Giulio, 191, 267–68,
  269
Caplan, Harry, 92
Cardano, Girolamo, 2, 88, 90, 250, 262,
  307–11, 317, 318, 322–23, 343
Champollion, Jean-François, 88, 206,
  208
Chateaubriand, François René, Vicomte
  de, 19
Chaucer, Geoffrey, 29
Choul, Guillaume du, 134

Subject Index

About the Author

MICHEL BEAUJOUR is professor of French at New York University. He is the author of *La France contemporaine* with Jacques Ehrmann of *Le Jeu de Rabelais,* and of many articles. He has also been an editor of the *Cahiers de l'Herne*.